The Autobiography of
WILLIAM SANDERS SCARBOROUGH

AFRICAN AMERICAN LIFE SERIES

A complete listing of the books in this series
can be found online at http://wsupress.wayne.edu

SERIES EDITORS

MELBA JOYCE BOYD
Department of Africana Studies
Wayne State University

RONALD BROWN
Department of Political Science
Wayne State University

The Autobiography of

WILLIAM SANDERS SCARBOROUGH

An American Journey from Slavery to Scholarship

Edited with an Introduction by
MICHELE VALERIE RONNICK

Foreword by
HENRY LOUIS GATES, JR.

WAYNE STATE UNIVERSITY PRESS   DETROIT

Library of Congress Cataloging-in-Publication Data

Scarborough, W. S. (William Sanders), 1852–1926.

The autobiography of William Sanders Scarborough : an American journey from slavery to scholarship / edited and with an introduction by Michele Valerie Ronnick ; foreword by Henry Louis Gates, Jr.

p. cm. — (African American life series)

Includes bibliographical references and index.

ISBN 0-8143-3224-2 (hardcover : alk. paper)

1. Scarborough, W. S. (William Sanders), 1852–1926.   2. African Americans—Biography.
3. African American scholars—Biography.   4. African American college presidents—Biography.
5. Classicists—United States—Biography.   6. Wilberforce University—Biography.   7. Slaves—
Georgia—Macon—Biography.   8. African Americans—Intellectual life—19th century.
9. African Americans—Intellectual life—20th century.   10. Classical philology—Study and
teaching—United States.   I. Ronnick, Michele V.   II. Title.   III. Series.

E185.97.S28A3 2005

973'.0496073'0092—dc22   2004011624

∞ The paper used in this publication meets the minimum requirements

of the American National Standard for Information Sciences—

Permanence of Paper for Printed Library Materials, ANSI Z39.48–1984.

For my mother, Elizabeth Ann Ronnick,
and my father, Albert Jacob Ronnick

(1903–1995)

Ad astra per aspera

Contents

Contents

ACKNOWLEDGMENTS

I have accumulated numerous debts of gratitude to people, stateside and abroad, for their contributions to my effort to bring William Sanders Scarborough "back to life." I have been assisted as well by casual conversations with strangers whose names I never learned while chatting in used book stores or standing over copy machines in libraries.

For materials in archives and elsewhere, I am much obliged to Candace Pryor and Latoyra Weston at the Interlibrary Loan Department and Mike Hawthorne, senior clerk, of Purdy-Kresge Library at Wayne State University; Brenda B. Square at the Amistad Research Center, Tulane University; Scott Sanders at Antioch College; Cathy Lynn Mundale and Karen Jefferson at the Atlanta University Center, Robert W. Woodruff Library, Atlanta; Steven Tomlinson at the Bodleian Library, Oxford; Sheila Darrow at the Hallie Quinn Brown Library, Central State University, Wilberforce, Ohio; Sarah Hartwell at the Rayner Special Collections Library, Dartmouth College; Leonard Ballou (1926–2004) at Elizabeth City State University, North Carolina; Joseph Greer at the Green County Public Library, Xenia, Ohio; an unknown hero at the William R. and Norma B. Harvey Library, Hampton University, Virginia; Andrea B. Goldstein and Susan Halpert at the Houghton Library and the Harvard University Archives; Ida Jones, Joellen El Bashir, and Clifford L. Muse, Jr., at the Moorland-Spingarn Research Center, Howard University; John Hodgson at the John Rylands Library, Manchester, England; Diane Shaw at the David Bishop Skillman Library, Lafayette College, Easton, Pennsylvania; Muriel McDowell Jackson at the Genealogical and Historical Room, Middle Georgia Regional Library, Macon; Sue Parker and Floyd Thomas at the National Afro-American Museum and Cultural Center, Wilberforce, Ohio; Walter B. Hill at the National Archives and Records Administration, Washington, D.C.; John Aubrey of the Newberry Library, Chicago; Roland M. Baumann and Ken Grossi of the Mudd Center Library, Oberlin College; Eva M. Greenberg at the Oberlin Pubic Library, Ohio; Elizabeth L. Plummer, Thomas J. Rieder, and Mathew Benz at the Ohio Historical

Society, Columbus; Terri Nelson at the Princeton Public Library; Diana Lachatanere at the Schomburg Center for Research in Black Culture, New York Public Library; Kitty Oliver and Chris Howard at the Sidney Lanier Cottage, Macon, Georgia; Cynthia Wilson of the Tuskegee University Archives; Michael McCormick and Anne Sindelar at the Western Reserve Historical Society, Cleveland; and Jean Mulhern, Jacqueline Brown, and Linda Hasting of the Rembert E. Stokes Library, Wilberforce University.

For scholarly support and technical advice, I am indebted to the following at Wayne State University: Norma and Bernard Goldman; Walter F. Edwards, director of the Humanities Center; Alfred Cobbs; Guy Stern; Robert Sedler of the School of Law; Todd Duncan, Pariedeau Mars; Murray Jackson (1926–2002); and Sarah Miller. My thanks also to Jane Hoehner, Kathryn Wildfong, and Adela Garcia of Wayne State University Press and to Melba Joyce Boyd and Ron Brown, editors of the African American Life Series. I also thank Dr. Irvin D. Reid, president of Wayne State University, who suggested that I bring this manuscript to Wayne State University Press. Many thanks also to Nancy Skowronski, Peter Gulewich, and Conrad Welsing of the Detroit Public Library for support of this work.

I am also grateful to Craig Bertolet and Robin Sabino of Auburn University; Meyer Reinhold (1909–2002) and Herb Golder of Boston University; Joan Bryant of Brandeis University; Joseph D. Lewis of Central State University; James Tatum of Dartmouth College; David Bright, Randall K. Burkett, and Mark Sanders of Emory University; Titus Brown of Florida A & M University; Jim O'Donnell of Georgetown University; Henry Louis Gates, Jr., Richard Newman (1930–2003), Zeph Stewart, and Richard Thomas of Harvard University; John Quinn of Hope College; Carrie Cowherd of Howard University; John Curran of Marquette University; Vincent Caretta and Judith Hallet of the University of Maryland; Kevin Gaines, James Jackson, Elizabeth James, Richard Janko, Jim Porter, Sarah Rappe, and John Woodford of the University of Michigan; Dolan Hubbard of Morgan State University; William Dominik of the University of Otago, New Zealand; Andrew Feldherr, Nell Painter, Valerie Smith, and Cornel West of Princeton University; Patrice Rankine of Purdue University; Ward W. Briggs, Jr., and Michael Mounter of the University of South Carolina; Margaret Wade-Lewis of State University of New York at New Paltz; Charles Blockson of the Blockson Collection, Temple University; Mark Farmer of Valparaiso University; Lucious Edwards of Virginia State University; and Muriel Brailey of Wilberforce University.

To my friends who have encouraged me along the way, I say "I couldn't have done it without you!" These are Timothy Taffe; Kevin G. Piotrowski and family; Steve Erickson; Melvin McCray; Bruce Roffi; Marilynn Rashid; Mrs. Lewis T. Bennett and family; Howard Finley; Christine Allen-Bruno and family; Sara and Reggie Wilcox; Truman Kella Gibson, Jr.; Joseph and Marina Palmeri and family; John Russ; Rhonda Collier; Dennis Dickerson; William Robinson, Jr.; George Davis, II; Cully Sommers; Gene R. Stephenson; Suesetta Talbert McCree; Sheila Gregory Thomas; Ralph Luker; Mary Ann Rodriquez; Lisa Ruch; Donna Jones; Adelaide Cromwell; Ruth Wright Hayre; Delores Wright; Leni Sorensen; and Sarah A. Grant, great-granddaughter of Mrs. Scarborough. I am also very grateful to students at Wayne State University who have responded with warmth and enthusiasm to my work.

For putting the manuscript on computer disk, I must acknowledge the contributions of Natalie Carter and Charles Alexander; and for help in getting the manuscript in shape, Jennifer Backer, an incomparable copyeditor, and Dorothy Hadfield, a wonder-working indexer. I am especially grateful to Joe D. Kieleszewski, the College of Liberal Arts, and the Department of Classics, Greek, and Latin at Wayne State University for providing funds to produce the index.

Finally I thank the members of my family circle: my mother, Elizabeth Ronnick; my brothers, Michael William Ronnick and David Louis Ronnick; my sister-in-law Holly Hoodenpyle Ronnick; my niece, Anna Klein Michaeli, and her husband, Eitan; Kevin L. Perry; and Henrietta Coon and her children, Nathan, Caroline, and Gregory.

FOREWORD

Recently, I told a colleague that Phillis Wheatley is "hot." An African-born slave in Revolutionary America, Wheatley wrote dozens of poems that betrayed a learned understanding of the classics—so learned that her authorship was called into question by Boston's intellectual elite (let's forget for a moment, if we can, the question of how she learned to read and write). Wheatley submitted to a grueling examination by late-eighteenth-century Boston's literary lights, who were ultimately satisfied that this black teenage girl had indeed written the poems she claimed to have written. Wheatley's authorship was legitimated and her intellect authenticated. Still, she died around age thirty, free but in poverty. My colleagues and I have worked for years to restore her to a place in the African American canon, and indeed, to the American literary canon.

It is a measure of our success in doing so that not only are films being proposed about Wheatley but that people are coming out of the woodwork now, family genealogies in hand, claiming Wheatley as their own. To do so means, of course, that these same people—generally northerners who are not used to thinking of themselves as descended from slaveholders—must come to terms with their slaveholding ancestry. But come to terms they will if it means they can claim Wheatley as a part of their own family—an enslaved part, but a part nonetheless.

William Sanders Scarborough is long overdue for an act of similar restoration. The first-time publication of his autobiography, shepherded for years by Michele Valerie Ronnick, Associate Professor of Classics, Greek, and Latin at Wayne State University in Detroit, is the first step in this restoration. Born a slave on February 16, 1852, in Macon, Georgia, Scarborough had become the nation's preeminent black classicist by the time of his death in 1926. A professor, textbook author, and university president, Scarborough was a groundbreaking figure whose career, in Ronnick's words, "marks the advent of the professional African American intellectual willing and able to make a lifetime commitment to the academy."

This may seem like rarefied stuff. Although active in public life as well (he served on the General Committee of the NAACP in its early years, was a member of the American Negro Academy, and was a spokesman for African American Republicans in Ohio, for instance), Scarborough must be remembered primarily as the third man of African descent to become a member of the American Philological Association, in 1882, and its first lifetime black member, as well as the first to join the newly formed Modern Language Association, in 1884. He attended philological conferences, published papers, and taught Greek and Latin at a university; in other words, he did the work that a professional academic does. But if the study of the classics seems marginalized today, it must be remembered that in the late nineteenth century this field was the measure of erudition and the quality of one's education. The emphasis on the classics in the American curriculum was a legacy of Europe, and to have a black man succeed in this field of study meant that another legacy was upended: the Western idea that blacks did not possess the intellectual capacity to learn. Scarborough, the member of many scholarly societies, was a learned man who effectively rebuked prevalent theories of African intellectual inferiority and cultural primitivism, as Phillis Wheatley had done one hundred years earlier with her poems.

Scarborough lived, studied, and taught during a period when theories of college education were shifting from a classical "learnedness" to a modern practicality, from a celebration of scholarship to an emphasis on vocation. His adherence to the value of the classics as a scholarly foundation for the discipline, hard work, and industry necessary for success in the American economy put him in stark opposition to one of the most dominant black figures of his day, Booker T. Washington, whose program for practical education—skip the classics and go straight to the discipline, hard work, and industry—came to overshadow Scarborough's in the early decades of the twentieth century. Ronnick tells us that by the early 1920s the classics were virtually eliminated from educational training for blacks (a trend seen also, but to a lesser degree, among whites). When Scarborough died in 1926, the classics lost their best-known and most eloquent African American defender.

If a *New York Times* obituary is a good measure of fame, or at least public importance, Scarborough did not die in obscurity. The *Times* noted the uniqueness of his contribution, referring to him as the "first member of his race to prepare a Greek textbook suitable for university use." But just as the classics passed out of general American awareness, so, too, did Scarborough, who has long been an invisible player in an arena dominated by the formidable figures of Washington and W.E.B. DuBois.

With the rise of black studies in the 1960s and the establishment of departments of African American studies in the decades following, a conservative figure such as Scarborough could get lost, or mistaken for a scholarly Uncle Tom who immersed himself as much as possible in the world of white academia. Starched collars and Greek grammars, after all, would seem to have little relevance to the study of African American contributions to the life of the nation. However, what we forget by forgetting Scarborough is his radical act of self-fashioning: a former slave became a professor through force of will, through a determination to use his intellect rather than his brute strength as a means of defining his position in American life. Were it not for Scarborough, the first professional black classicist, it is conceivable that the departments that have spent many years ignoring him would not exist: he provides a model for African Americans' formal entry into and full participation in the academy. If his story is highly individualized and even atypical, it is also a larger story of the authentication and recognition of the African American as an intellectual being.

Ronnick's brilliant achievement in rejoining Scarborough with his public is, happily, not isolated. The past several years have seen a number of scholars, including myself, going back into the eighteenth and nineteenth centuries and finding copious evidence of African American intellectual activity and contribution. But it is, nonetheless, a stunning act of recovery. With *The Autobiography of William Sanders Scarborough,* Ronnick invites us to engage with the radical thinker and activist who has too long been thought of—if he has been thought of at all—as a fusty Victorian gentleman who "acted white." Although not the norm, Scarborough was in fact a standard.

Finally, it is worth noting that, in 2001, the Modern Language Association instituted the William Sanders Scarborough Prize, awarded to an outstanding scholarly study of black American literature or culture. Although it is unlikely that a grammar in his beloved Greek or Latin could take this prize, Scarborough would take comfort in knowing that the organization in which he was a groundbreaking member now offers him a distinction that few of its other members can claim. It is also worth noting that this volume and Ronnick's herculean labors to bring her fellow classicist "back to life" will enrich us for years to come.

Henry Louis Gates, Jr.

INTRODUCTION

This is a study in transgression and transcendence. It is the self-portrait of a black man born in slavery who broke through a nexus of biased cultural assumption to reach the self-actuated state of full personhood. It is the story of a man who experienced his "first" liberation through the cultivation of his own intellect at a time when education for members of his race was interdicted by law. And finally, it is a blow-by-blow account of his heroic struggle to rise above seemingly insurmountable obstacles in order to stand upright in the formal dress of civilized life with his humanity authenticated.

Accident of birth placed William Sanders Scarborough in a place, in a time, and in a bodily form that regarded him as a warm-blooded machine to be bought and sold with the livestock and worked like a "two-handed engine," as John Milton might have described it. But his unflagging commitment to self-betterment, his dauntless courage, and his untarnished nobility of purpose—each founded on the bedrock of support of his faith, friends, and family—determined otherwise. The young Scarborough, suffused with an inborn affection for arts and letters, was destined for a different way of life. He had great ambitions for himself and for his race. And his egregious efforts would bring him great acclaim.

Issues of domination, control, and denial vis-à-vis race, gender, and class (and what is currently called "identity politics") were raised to the "second power" in Scarborough's case. He quickly learned in this doubled universe to negotiate together and apart the stratifications in black society and in white society, first in the South and then in the North, and later in Europe. Throughout it all his unquenchable thirst for learning remained atypical "Negro" behavior. In the eyes of the general public a learned black man was a walking oxymoron, a contradiction in terms, both preposterous and frightening. "Learned" in that time meant having a command of the classical languages—Greek and Latin. This was part and parcel of the university experience. Black people rarely received such training, and when they did they were rarely accepted. Their presence was unsettling to others—both black and white—and they were marginalized. Their claims to learning, when not wholly disregarded or pronounced fraudulent, were overly scrutinized. Grotesque caricatures such as Mark Twain's "mulatter" college professor and James Corrothers's "Black Cat Club" demagogues were examples of such ridicule. The roots of this belittlement go back to the eighteenth century. Then, David Hume likened the Latinity of the free black Jamaican Francis Williams (ca. 1700–ca. 1770) to a parrot's ability to imitate human speech in his essay *Of National Character* (1754). In Boston, the slave Phillis Wheatley (1753–1784) was compelled to prove her command of literature and her knowledge of classical poetry in live demonstrations. Williams and Wheatley survived their ordeals, but they were dismissed as exotic oddities, freakish untouchables, and then forgotten.[1] Their senior years were spent in obscurity. And there the matter lay, dormant for decades.

But the perplexing and threatening idea of a learned person of African descent who could read Greek and Latin did not disappear. It came back with renewed energy a century later as post–Civil War America dealt with the challenge of educating thousands of newly freed slaves. This was a situation without precedent, one that affected every aspect of American life and precipitated a national identity crisis. Who should (or would, for that matter) teach these people? Many of them were full-grown adults. What system or timetable could be set to effect this? Who would pay for this? Where could the work be done? And finally—the most important question of all—what should these people study? The humane literature of classical antiquity, or practical things such as technical skills and methods of farming? The decisions made during those years concerning the appropriate curriculum for these new citizens, the African American freedmen, had tremendous consequences. The solution to some of today's problems, paramount among them the conundrum presented by the black "egghead," who is ridiculed for his studious habits and branded as a sellout acting "white," lies in an understanding of what happened in this period.

Historical Background

For centuries in Europe a classical education was the requisite training for any person who wished to participate or move forward in the enterprises of the Western world. But with the Age of Enlightenment came elements of doubt. Eighteenth-century American educators and intellectuals, products of the earlier tradition, were influenced by new trends of skepticism, and they keenly argued over the reasons for and against the study of Greek and Latin. Francis Bacon's idea that knowledge must be pursued for its utility and social support held sway among them. Much energy was spent trying to figure out whether any manner of what they called "useful knowledge" could come from the study of ancient languages.[2] In 1768 William Livingston, the first governor of New Jersey, scoffed at the idea that training in the classics would be any help in clearing the wilderness for farming. With him were other anti-classicists such as Thomas Paine, Francis Hopkinson, Benjamin Franklin, and Benjamin Rush, who concluded that there was no place for dead languages in the new republic. On the other side was a large group that included such men as Rush's friend John Adams, James Logan, and James Madison, who were keenly interested in the study of classical antiquity and ancient languages, and Thomas Jefferson, who felt that the classical languages provided a firm foundation if not an ornament to most types of study.[3]

The debate among this group of elite white men was never resolved, and the problem was compounded when the question of the classical curriculum was asked in regard to real outsiders such as women, Jews, and blacks. In the latter case questions of racial inferiority and accusations of inherited mental inadequacy dating back to earlier times rose to the surface.[4] With isolated exceptions such as Williams, Wheatley, and later Alexander Crummell (1819–1898), who studied Greek from 1846 to 1853 at Cambridge University, the opportunity for African Americans in significant numbers to obtain traditional liberal arts training in classics really began at the end of the Civil War, reaching its peak at the turn of the century. While many black Americans made it their life ambition to achieve economic independence and material gain—principles that have been so closely associated with the name Booker T. Washington, as to seem not only synonymous but exclusively his own today—other black Americans hungrily devoured the "bread of Knowledge," as Frederick Douglass put it. These people, the advance guard of what DuBois would later call the "Talented Tenth," wanted to learn everything and eagerly embraced all aspects of the classical curriculum, which had been the universal standard for white people.

Two camps formed—or seemed to. This division was affirmed to the white mind when men such as the Massachusetts reformer Samuel J. Barrows in 1891 declared in the pages of the *Atlantic Monthly* that "two aristocracies are appearing in the colored race—the aristocracy of culture and the aristocracy of wealth."[5] This artificial—not to mention illogical— dichotomy was anti-intellectual and anti-communitarian. And although

Barrows thought he saw "culture and prosperity" coming together among the younger generation, the two ideas took separate courses. Promulgated by the popular press and placed in the collective consciousness, the split caught on. It said in short that a black person had one of two paths to follow: the thoughtful, cultured, and ultimately impractical path of the classically based liberal arts curriculum or the utilitarian path of technical and manual training. This separatist theory was soon put into practice across the country, and the two programs were treated as if they were mutually exclusive.

Students, civic leaders, politicians, educators, and philanthropists were "forced" to choose. The philanthropists were by no means united, and because the philanthropic endeavors were supported by three different groups (faith-based missionaries, Northern industrialists, and the black community), conflicts arose over many issues. As time passed the polyphony of voices participating in the debate receded from memory and a few figures came to the fore as the "spokesmen" for the two camps. Contributions of men like Scarborough were forgotten while Booker T. Washington, the pragmatist, and DuBois, the theoretician, took center stage and have held it ever since. By the 1920s the progressive educational program that sought to eliminate the useless, ancient languages from the curriculum had taken hold, and the historically black colleges and universities, which at their outset offered many opportunities for training in the classics, changed direction entirely.[6] Classical departments were eliminated, and the sole surviving department is housed at Howard University.[7]

The study of this phenomenon—the examination of what caused it, what destroyed it, and what impact it has had on the present intellectual, economic, social, and racial life of this country—has rarely attracted the attention of scholars from either classics or African American studies.[8] The intellectual community has either been satisfied with the work of classical scholars such as Frank Snowden or Lloyd Thompson, who have focused their studies on evidence found in the ancient civilizations of Europe, Africa, and the Near East, or they have been engrossed in the fiery debate between the Sinologist Martin Bernal and the Hellenist Mary Lefkowitz, which has sunk into a quagmire of tribalism and personalized argument immersed in a struggle for cultural hegemony.[9]

William Sanders Scarborough's life (1852–1926) forces us to look beyond these perspectives and examine things from a different and, in fact, mutually beneficial angle. He commands us to consider the development of black classicism, a concept I termed "Classica Africana" in 1996.[10] The name is patterned after the book *Classica Americana* (1984) by Meyer

Reinhold, who studied the impact of the classics on eighteenth- and early nineteenth-century America. This new subfield of the classical tradition, Classica Africana, explores an area overlooked by Reinhold and examines the undeniable impact, both positive and negative, that the Graeco-Roman heritage has had on people of African descent in their creative and professional endeavors. Nineteenth-century African American rhetoric, for example, is suffused with classical topoi and it abounds with intertextual references to the thoughts of both pagan and Christian writers. No modern scholar can gain a full understanding of its meaning, design, or cultural and intellectual impact without taking the classical tradition and its pedagogical transmission into account.

If one considers a small but exemplary sample, made manifest by the following careers, a pattern quickly emerges. In Europe there were men of African descent, such as Juan Latino (1516–c. 1601), Latin scholar in Granada, and Anthony William Amo (1703–c. 1760), who wrote a dissertation on a legal topic in Latin in Amsterdam and later became a lecturer at the University of Wittenberg. In the New World, there were those with roots in the Caribbean besides Francis Williams such as Edward Wilmot Blyden (1832–1912), who taught Greek at Liberia College and corresponded with Gladstone about Homer, or Derek Walcott (1931–) and his well-known work, *Omeros.* Among nineteenth-century Americans we have Sarah Jane Woodson (1825–1907), preceptress of English and Latin at Wilberforce University, and one of the first (if not the first) black women on a college faculty; John Wesley Gilbert (c. 1865–1923), who was the first black to attend the American School in Athens; Wiley Lane (1852–1885), who was the first black professor of Greek at Howard University; William Henry Crogman (1841–1931), who taught Greek for forty years at Clark Atlanta University; John Hope (1868–1936), who taught Greek and Latin at Atlanta University and Morehouse College, both of which he later served as president; and Jessie Redmon Fauset (1885–1961), who studied classical languages at Cornell University.[11] During the twentieth century, writer Langston Hughes (1902–1967) was inspired to study classics by his high school Latin teacher, Miss Helen Chesnutt, the daughter of writer Charles Chesnutt. The Harlem Renaissance poet Countee Cullen (1903–1946) translated Euripides's *Medea;* Robert Hayden (1913–1980) wrote poetry about the Greek hero Perseus, and Rita Dove (1952–) envisioned Demeter and her daughter Persephone in Paris. Toni Morrison (1931–), who minored in classics at Howard University, has infused her novels with classical motifs. The experimental novelist Percival Everett (1956–) employed the myths of Dionysus and Medea to construct plots for two of his books, *Frenzy* (1997) and *For Her Dark Skin* (1990). Examples such as these proliferate throughout African American literature.[12]

Outstanding among these cultural figures was William Sanders Scarborough, who was the first professional scholar of African American heritage in the field of classical studies.[13] For more than three decades he was looked upon as one of the most learned men of his race. This first edition of his autobiography gives us the basis upon which to make a long overdue and well-merited reassessment of his life.

The Man

Scarborough was born with the status of a slave in Macon, Georgia, on February 16, 1852, to Frances Gwynn Scarborough, a woman owned by Colonel William K. DeGraffenreid. For reasons unknown, DeGraffenreid allowed her to marry and live with her husband, Jeremiah, in their own home. As a boy, the precocious Scarborough was encouraged to study—albeit surreptitiously because the education of blacks was illegal and punishable by law in many parts of the South. The young Scarborough said that he "daily went out ostensibly to play with my book concealed." In this manner he reported that he "continued to evade the law and study."

He was not the only black youngster of his generation hiding his books and gaining his education through stealth. Frederick Douglass was taught to read in secret by his owner's wife. So too was Susie King Taylor, who was born a slave in 1848 in Savannah, Georgia. She and her brother learned to read and write secretly at the house of her grandmother's friend, Mrs. Woodhouse. She described this process in her memoir *Reminiscences of My Life in Camp* (1902): "We went everyday about nine o'clock with our books wrapped in paper to prevent the police or white peoples from seeing them. We went in one at a time, through the gate, into the yard to the kitchen, which was the schoolroom. . . . After school we left the same way we entered, one by one, when we would go to a square about a block from the school and wait for each other."[14]

After the Civil War things changed abruptly. The young Scarborough enrolled in the Macon schools, where he excelled. He was no longer a secret scholar. Several years later after studying at Atlanta University, Scarborough earned both his B.A. and M.A. degrees in classics from Oberlin College and began to teach at Wilberforce University soon after. Over the course of the next several years, he rose to national distinction by publishing *First Lessons in Greek,* a text that according to his obituary in the *New York Times* made him "the first member of his race to prepare a Greek textbook suitable for university use." With this book came fame as he simultaneously demonstrated his own intellectual capacity and that of his entire race. The mindless prejudices of men, who maintained ingrained ideas of "negro inferiority," were directly challenged. In particular, John C. Calhoun, who was reported to have said to Samuel E. Sewall and David Lee Child, two Boston attorneys, that "if he could find a Negro who knew the Greek syntax, he would then believe that the Negro was a human being and should be treated as a man," was undone—at least for the moment.[15]

During his career Scarborough contributed over twenty scholarly pieces to the official publication of the American Philological Association (APA), *Transactions and Proceedings of the American Philological Association* (TAPA).[16] These were written summaries of papers he had presented orally at the annual APA meetings where he engaged other scholars. In his era, anyone with an interest in philology, ancient or modern, affiliated with the APA, which was founded in 1869. Later, the "modernists" founded the Modern Language Association (MLA) in 1883. Scarborough was not the only member of African descent in the APA. During the latter half of the nineteenth century, a number of men of African descent joined the organization. Of these, Scarborough was the first to successfully pursue a lifetime career in the classics, according to the standards recognized today, including affiliation with professional organizations on the national and international levels, attendance and activity at meetings, and an active publication record. Other African American classicists also joined the APA and/or taught courses in the classics at the college and university level during this period.[17]

In January 1907 he was among those members of the joint session of the APA and the Archaeological Institute of America who were received by President Theodore Roosevelt in the Blue Room of the White House when the annual meeting was held in Washington, D.C. In 1921, five years before his death at age sixty-nine, he represented the APA as an international delegate to a session of the Classical Association held at Cambridge University.

In addition to philology, Scarborough maintained throughout his life two other especial interests: pedagogy and politics. The three were often combined in his work. He was keenly interested in fostering professional and scholarly progress in languages in general, and in classics in particular.

Toward the end of his life he was saddened to observe that "now as the controversy grows concerning the classics, [there are] no young colored men of the immediate present who are even meditating on special classical study. It is a great mistake, as the race will find out to leave this field to others with the breadth and culture obtainable in it. This is to say nothing of the opportunity to serve the race especially in the field of African linguistics."

When Scarborough joined the APA in 1882 at the age of thirty, he became the third man of African descent to do so, after Richard T. Greener, who joined in 1875, and Edward Wilmot Blyden, who became a member in 1880.[18] In 1884 he became the first black member of the MLA.[19] In the wider community of scholars, he took his place by joining a number of other learned societies, such as the American Social Science Association, the American Academy of Political and Social Science, the American Negro Academy, the Archaeological Institute of America, the Egyptian Exploration Fund, and the Japan Society. Under Professor Francis Andrew March at Lafayette College, he was part of the unofficial team of readers working on the North American Reading Program (NARP) for the *Oxford English Dictionary*. He was also on the General Committee of the NAACP in its formative years.

He found time for religious service as well. Following his father's practice, he was actively involved in the African Methodist Episcopal Church. In 1892 he began what turned out to be lifelong service as an editor of the *A.M.E. Sunday School Union*. He was a delegate in 1901 and in 1921 to the International Ecumenical Methodist Conferences held in London. Classical education was valued by churches of every denomination, and very much by the A.M.E. Church. Generations of students, many of whom became pastors, ministers, reverends, and bishops, were taught by men like Scarborough, and what began as classical and secular learning was transformed on the pulpit into non-secular and evangelical preaching.

His own writings are testimony of the wide range of his intellectual pursuits, for he published essays on topics beyond classical philology concerning the careers of Henry Tanner, Paul Laurence Dunbar, Alexander Pushkin, and Goethe.[20] Broader themes addressed European travelogues, considered national politics, explained military training at Wilberforce University, critiqued the convict lease system, and explained Creole folktales. These works appeared in both journals and newspapers. From 1888 to 1889, he contributed four pieces to *Education*, the first on Caesar's Gallic Wars; the second on the accent and meaning of the Latin word for the wild strawberry tree (*arbutus*); the third on Vergil's fourth eclogue; and the fourth on Iphigenia in Euripides, Racine, and Goethe. In addition to essays on classical topics for the schoolroom, he explained and interpreted issues of interest to both African Americans and Americans of European descent in a wide range of publications. These works appeared in numerous journals and newspapers including the *Christian Recorder, Christian Register, Journal of Education, American Negro Academy, Southern Workman, Voice of the Negro, Indianapolis Freeman, Frank Leslie's Weekly, New York Times, A.M.E. Church Review, Forum, Arena, African Times and Orient Review, Current History, The Independent,* and several Ohio newspapers. His last published paper was a U.S. Government Document, number 1404, titled "Tenancy and Ownership among Negro Farmers in Southampton, Virginia."

For several decades, Scarborough was a leading spokesperson for the African American constituency in the Republican Party in Ohio. His activities brought him in contact with national leaders such as Warren G. Harding, John Sherman, Andrew Carnegie, James G. Blaine, and John F. Slater. Scarborough used these connections to champion the cause of civil rights and liberal arts education for African Americans. From his point of view, true freedom resided not only in equal protection of the law, but also through equal and full access to culture and education.

He openly opposed the narrowness of Booker T. Washington's mandate for technical training. He felt that Washington served as a much-needed leader, but in the face of Washington's widespread popularity, Scarborough remained the staunch defender of higher learning for African Americans. He stated in a 1902 essay, "The Negro and Higher Learning," that "without in the least undervaluing the sphere and influence of industrial training, we may affirm that higher education is, after all, to be the most powerful lever in the Negro's development and in the ultimate perfection of humanity at large."[21] Later in a commencement address, "The Negro Graduate—His Mission," delivered in 1908 at Atlanta University, Scarborough cautioned the new graduates that "the Negro who has . . . advantages of culture must be alert to see that higher aspirations toward learning are not laughed down; scorned, ignored, crushed."[22]

Scarborough was always opposed to unilateral programs of industrial education. In fact in 1892 Scarborough was driven from his professorship at Wilberforce University in a political struggle to privilege the utilitarian training over liberal arts. At great financial cost to himself, he found employment at Payne Theological Seminary, where he was supposed to raise his own salary. During this period, he relied on his wife's income and what he could earn from his writings. In 1897, after a five-year hiatus, he was reappointed to Wilberforce and named vice president. During part of this traumatic exile (1894–1896), W.E.B. DuBois filled Scarborough's position as professor and department chair of classics. From 1908 to 1920, Scarborough served as president, doing "more to make Wilberforce nationally and internationally known than any other person save Bishop Daniel Payne," the school's founder.[23] Suffice it to say Scarborough's experience as a college president was taxing. Nevertheless, he accepted the challenge and did his duty.

In 1886 Scarborough expressed his concerns about the negative effect that the elective system was having on college studies in an article, "The New College Fetich," which appeared in the *A.M.E. Church Review.*[24] This was his subtle answer to Charles Francis Adams's controversial lecture, "The College Fetich," delivered to the members of the Harvard University chapter of Phi Beta Kappa in June 1883. In this presentation, Adams contradicted two generations of the Adams family and denounced the classical curriculum. Using his own career as evidence, he declared its product "superficial learning." And although he did not object to a college Latin requirement, he felt that the study of ancient Greek "was a positive educational wrong." Furthermore, he concluded that in a "utilitarian and scientific age, the living will not forever be sacrificed to the dead."[25] Scarborough, whose scholarly attainments were mainly in ancient Greek, the bane of Adams's college days, was not reactionary. However, in that 1886 essay Scarborough predicted that the romance languages would become part of college admission standards.[26] Nevertheless, he was concerned that the elective system in general would destroy genuine scholarship and prevent students of all colors from gaining a wide command of culture.

In an article published in *Forum* in 1898, shortly after his return to Wilberforce, he assumed the rhetorical posture of an anonymous, adversarial interlocutor, and in regard to higher education for African Americans asked: "Why waste higher education thus? Why not give the Negro industrial training exclusively? Why not give him a pick instead of Greek and Latin?" To which he responded that higher education "is not wasted on the race no matter what facts are found as to his condition . . . it is no more wasted on the race than it would be on white boys and girls, some of whom . . . follow pursuits more or less menial in character . . . it is not wasted because . . . there is hope of a future for other boys and girls—a future with better conditions."[27]

In 1903, for an essay published by the American Negro Academy, he wrote that "industrial training is needed, too, to teach how to earn a living, but ...something else—the higher education—must be counted upon to teach [pupils] how to live better lives, how to get the most and the best out of life."[28] W.E.B. DuBois would later gain an international audience for voicing a program using similar ideas. But on this particular topic Scarborough had anticipated many of the ideas now associated with DuBois. One thinks immediately, for example, of Scarborough when reading this statement published by DuBois in 1918:"Anyone who suggests by sneering at books and 'literary courses' that the great heritage of human thought ought to be displaced simply for the reason of teaching the technique of modern industry is pitifully wrong and, if the comparison must be made, more wrong than the man who would sacrifice modern technique to the heritage of ancient thought."[29]

Mode and Method

While reading Scarborough's narrative, the reader must heed C. S. Lewis's warning to avoid "chronological snobbery," which is the feeling that one's own era is the best and brightest. For it will seem to some readers that Scarborough got it all wrong, that he wasted his vital years in attainments of no consequence such as the study of the dead languages, and conclude quite illogically that because he is not now recognized among the "brand names" of a few figures that we regularly venerate today, he was a failure. Detractors will revile him as "Uncle Tom Scarborough," a second-rate talent whose career was based on ideas that were naively moralistic and unoriginal. With a frown others will see him as a pathetic dupe of the Republican Party and offer up Warren G. Harding, whom Scarborough counted as a friend, as proof. These conclusions spring from a shallow perception and low motives including selfishness. The small-minded reader is unhappy when Scarborough doesn't behave and things do not occur the way the reader thinks that they should. But let these criticisms come forth. The condition of the forgotten or the disenfranchised cannot be altered without opening it up to public analysis.

Let it also be said that Scarborough is no literary master, but he is a competent narrator and far and away the best witness to his own life. An autobiography by definition is an account of a life told by the one who lived it. Unlike heterobiography, a life story given by another person, the author of an autobiography cannot describe his last moments on earth or learn posterity's verdict. Here in this edition definitive elements of autobiography and heterobiography are combined. In twenty-eight chapters,

Scarborough brings the reader from his childhood in Georgia to his retirement in Ohio. The final chapter is a portrait of his decline and death written by his wife. I, as editor, have corrected the textual infelicities in the narrative and supplemented Scarborough's words with numerous explanatory notes and documentary evidence.

The first three chapters describe Scarborough's life during slavery and are, in effect, a slave narrative. Taken as a whole, however, his cradle-to-grave account offers valuable new evidence concerning the theory and practice of black autobiographical writing. His experience also reveals the critical role that the A.M.E. Church has played in stimulating and sustaining the intellect of its members—the key to mental health—amid intra-denominational cohesion and conflict.

Scarborough's account is especially valuable to historians of this period. He was, like a veritable Forrest Gump, an eyewitness to many events. He saw Jefferson Davis led away as a prisoner of war. He heard Richard Wright call out, "Tell them we are rising!" He sat at the table with John Sherman at the first Lincoln Day Banquet held in Ohio. He saw Frederick Douglass cut a pigeon wing at Cedar Hall shortly before Douglass died, and he attended the funeral of Booker T. Washington. Scarborough had no script to follow in describing his unorthodox life, and in the public presentation of himself he was compelled to find his own design. At times his testimony seems to get bogged down in myriad names and dates, which are presented in a relentless chronological sequence. But as the reader becomes aware of Scarborough's need to authenticate himself in the world, this mass of details is realized as Scarborough's own proof that he actually did what he said he did.

His autobiographical record is in fact a priceless repository for us. It stands as a primary source to a key period in American history. Because it is a black perspective and because it is an account that was not previously available to scholars and the reading public, it assumes even more importance. Furthermore, without this detailed record, his path-breaking career would have been utterly lost to history. He lived in a time of great racial divide, and many of the white people with whom he interacted, however cordial they might have been to him in person, did not mention him in their own writings. He was visibly invisible.

His fellow classicists, for example, did not mention him in their published writings. But like a proverbial raisin in milk, he could not have been missed in meetings that usually had fewer than fifty attendees. Scarborough, for his part, mentioned by name the classicists he admired and those who treated him respectfully. He often quoted from their letters to him. On the other hand, he left out the names of those who were snide or abusive to him. One wonders if he knew of—and surely he did—the older generation of classicists who had supported the African American struggle to gain freedom and civil rights. This group of abolitionists and neo-abolitionists includes men such as Charles Beck (1798–1866), professor of Latin at Harvard University, who assisted travelers on the Underground Railroad; Andrew Sledd (1870–1939), professor of Latin at Emory, whose article against lynching published in the *Atlantic Monthly* in 1902 cost him his job; Alpheus Crosby (1810–1874), professor of Greek at Dartmouth, who edited a series of textbooks for freedmen; and Charles Dexter Cleveland (1802–1874), who as a youth joined with his fellow classmate at Dartmouth College, Salmon P. Chase, to give anti-slavery lectures in 1844 and 1845.[30]

To the reader's irritation, Scarborough is never as candid as the reader would like. But scandal, tale telling, and backstage drama did not interest him. He selected his words with care, and he always came down on the side of caution. His immediate audience was a heterogeneous group of friends, foes, and former students, black and white, in the United States and abroad, and from all walks of life. He wrote his narrative in the last four years of his life, a time when he was overextended in the service of Wilberforce University. For twelve arduous years, Scarborough put away his scholarly work. This period was followed by two lonely years in Washington, D.C., without his wife while working for the Harding administration. By the early 1920s, Scarborough was fully retired and living quietly with his wife in Wilberforce, but without the financial support and vocational prestige of a Carnegie teacher's pension. The couple had undoubtedly seen it all. Together they had given almost ninety years of unbroken service to the Wilberforce community and to the world at large.

The tone of his words is consistently one of uplift and optimism, which is a quality found in many other African American writers of the nineteenth and early twentieth centuries, from Frances E. W. Harper and William H. Crogman to William Pickens.[31] He was never less than dignified, and he falls silent in portions of his narrative when the reader expects a litany of complaint, self-pity, or rage. Instead, he maintains a forward gaze, thereby encouraging the reader to look to the future and to rejoice in new patterns of progress and achievement. He led by example and repeatedly shows his reading audience how he turned pain into artful action, anger into spiritual enlightenment, and frustration into faithful commitment to God, the all-provident.

This is the foundation of Scarborough's will to act despite daunting or impossible tasks. In the classical sense, such courage marks him a hero, for it is the essence of heroism to take up a quest against all odds with little more than life and limb, and through a transcendent act reach a higher standard of achievement. It is in that moment, according to the classical paradigm, when frail mortals attempt to do something great, that they rival the immortals. But the hero's success does not ensure lasting acclaim. Instead, he may find that he is misunderstood, reviled, and even ostracized. This dialectic was also a part of Scarborough's experience.

It is no surprise that his prose is—as Cornel West has noted—"touched with Victorian conceit."[32] A proper gentleman of natural reserve, he could wax sentimental and was capable of manly weeping, as was evidenced during a reception held at his home for a group of shell-shocked African American World War I veterans. Photographs from every period of his life present him as the portrait of propriety. He always appears in a finely tailored suit, white shirt, and tie. Precise and patrician in deportment, he was also handsome, vital, and charismatic, conveying a contradictory image. This restraint was similarly expressed in his conservative, personal life. In his own words he never danced, and he kept his wineglass turned down at dinner parties. He amused himself with checkers and croquet, and refreshed himself with music. And yet underneath the polished demeanor of this Victorian man of letters was the soul of a revolutionary and the spirit of a subversive whose words and deeds were quietly breaking down conventions of prejudice. The era required such constraint and camouflage. He intentionally concealed much of his private life and his private thoughts out of a sense of propriety and in self-defense. From an early age Scarborough realized the eyes of the world were upon him. In his youth he was a model student, and in his maturity he was a race exemplar. As one of the earliest advocates for African American academic endeavor, he became an intellectual icon for a people who were continually accused of not having an intellectual tradition.

Not only was his life regarded as exemplary, so too was his home. The Scarboroughs called their house in Wilberforce Tretton Place, derived from Tretton Park, the setting in Anthony Trollope's novel *Mr. Scarborough's Family* (1883). This witty, literary allusion reiterated the bookish Scarboroughs' reverence for literature and their sense of humor. They lovingly engraved the name on their personal stationery, and the house was a pleasant setting over the years for many gatherings of students, friends, and family.

In 1900 Tretton Place acquired celebrity when a photograph of it titled "Professor Scarborough's Home" was showcased as one of six "Negro Homes" at the Universal Exhibition in Paris.[33] Subsequently, Tretton Place became the residence of Wilberforce's next several presidents. In 1973 the house was placed on the National Register of Historic Places by the National Park Service of the U.S. Department of the Interior. On April 3, 1974, Mrs. Scarborough's birthday, the house, which was then occupied by Lionel H. Newsom, president of Central State University,[34] was destroyed by a tornado.[35] Today the site of Tretton Place lies underneath a parking lot for students at Central State University.

Interracial Marriage

Other aspects of Scarborough's personal world were no less extraordinary. He embraced Gandhi's admonishment "to be the change you wish to see in the world." In his autobiography he reveals little about his wife, who was a white divorcée. The two met in Macon in the mid-1870s when he was on the faculty of Lewis High School and she was Sarah Cordelia Bierce, the school's principal. Born in Danby, New York, on April 3, 1851, to Phoebe Cordelia Bierce (1820–1896) and George Washington Bierce (1819–1907), she arrived in Macon with the American Missionary Association (AMA) after completing the classical course at the famed Oswego Institute in upstate New York in 1875. This was a new start in life for her. In 1865, when she was only fourteen years of age, Sarah married Solomon Roper Grant (1843–1923). Their marriage quickly dissolved. Grant did not support her, and she said that her very life was threatened. In 1870 her parents persuaded her to separate. One of their sons, Harry Irwin Grant, died at the age of eight months and eight days in Minnesota, and the other, Francis Granger Grant (1866–1910), was left in the care of her parents. Much can be surmised here, because neither Scarborough's nor his wife's papers reveal details about his wife's first marriage.

In 1876, after arsonists destroyed Lewis High School, the two colleagues separated in order to find work.[36] For a short period Scarborough taught in South Carolina and then returned to higher education at Oberlin College. It is not clear what Sarah Bierce did, but there is some suggestion that she suffered a nervous breakdown. Perhaps something more than fate brought them together again as faculty members at Wilberforce University under President Benjamin Lee. On August 2, 1881, A.M.E. Bishop William F. Dickerson married the two kindred spirits in New York City. What this

INTRODUCTION

alliance meant to them and what they experienced together in life can only be imagined, for almost nothing of their personal memorabilia survives, not even a wedding portrait. Their interracial marriage, however, must have been "notorious." It preceded Frederick Douglass's marriage to Helen Pitts by three years and lasted for forty-five years. Once again Scarborough and his wife were daring iconoclasts, and their marriage was long remembered in the area.

Helen Hooven Santmyer (1895–1989), the author of the best-selling novel *And the Ladies of the Club,* also published a set of vignettes about life in and around Xenia, Ohio. These appeared in a book titled *Ohio Town* (1962), including a cautionary tale that appears to be a profile of Sarah Scarborough:

> One old tale about the university used to overwhelm me when I was young, with a smothering sensation of compassion and horror, and when I was grown could still move me to wish for an American Balzac to write it down. Balzac, because the story needs to be treated in the manner of *Eugenie Grandet:* daily life described in such minute detail in the beginning that the readers can feel it going on and on in the same fashion, year in, year out, while nothing ever happens except that time passes, and in the end you have a life wasted, nobility of purpose come to futility. But perhaps this life was neither wasted nor futile; I suppose that no one really knows: once upon a time, long ago, in Boston before the Civil War, when abolition was fought for passionately by those who believed in it, three young girls—innocent, hoop-skirted, naive Victorians—solemnly pledged themselves to prove their belief in the equality of the races by marrying Negroes. One of them fulfilled her vow. All the remaining decades of the nineteenth century and into the twentieth she lived out at the university, while her husband, who was not without distinction among his own people, rose from teacher to professor to dean to college president. In a community and a time when the color line was rigidly drawn by other races, she saw only the guests he brought to the house. She survived him for a long, long, while. All those years when I was growing up she lived there in the same house, utterly alone, cut off from humanity. Year after year, when you went past it you could see how by degrees, the place took on a haunted air behind its gloomy screen of hemlocks—how increasingly it came even more than its neighbors, to have the look that Negro houses then had: shutters a little awry, steps a little broken, foundations yellow with rain-splattered clay.[37]

Despite the absence of names and that many of the "facts" seem to be inventions for a folktale, this anti-miscegenation story ridicules the Scarboroughs' lifestyle and politics, and reflects the racist, morbid imagination of its author and the public reprehension concerning interracial marriage. Santmyer's view almost assumes public policy; an anti–mixed marriage bill appeared before the state legislature in Columbus, Ohio, in 1913. Passage of this bill could have driven them out of Ohio, and/or outlawed their thirty-two-year marriage. The Reppert Bill, as it was known, failed to pass, but the press showcased the couple as a public predicament. On Thursday, March 13, 1913, the *New York Age* ran a four-tiered headline on its front page: "Intermarriage Bill Would Break Up Homes; Lower House of Ohio Legislature Passes Unjust Reppert Bill; Mixed Families in Peril; President Scarborough of Wilberforce Would Be Among Those Affected If Bill Becomes a Law."[38] Despite the infamy of the moment, the Scarboroughs never commented on the subject or the article in their personal papers.

Meaning

Making headlines was nothing new to Scarborough. In his youth his name appeared in the *Macon Daily Telegraph* at the very start of his educational endeavors.[39] In his adult life, he was constantly in the spotlight as he waged battles for the rights of African American students to pursue an education in classically based liberal arts curriculum. Today the questions Scarborough faced with regard to the needs of African Americans in higher education are still being raised. Moreover, the diminished status of classical studies in higher education for students of any color is a frequent topic of discussion for classicists. For like liberal arts in general, the study of classics in particular has come under heavy fire. But the widespread, yet rudimentary acquaintance among the reading public with certain aspects of the Bernal-Lefkowitz debate suggests that there is a strong and perhaps truly enduring interest in learning about classical antiquity and studying the classical languages among people of African descent. The achievement of William Sanders Scarborough holds pride of place in the history of black classicism in America, and a widespread comprehension of his accomplishments is a key component to future discussions about scholarship.

For more than forty years, Scarborough was an engaged intellectual, public citizen, and a concerned educator. In terms of his classical studies he accomplished as much as some of the better-known figures from this era, and in fact more than many. Scarborough was, in the widest sense of the word, a pioneer. He not only broke through barriers of race and class but stayed the course. His life ran contrary to many currents of his age. As a man of African descent who excelled at Greek and Latin, his attainments challenged all those who maintained ideas about the intellectual deficiencies of his people to reconsider their positions. At the same time, he confounded those who thought that his erudition was merely a thin coat of white-washing.

Scarborough's unfailing efforts to gain membership in numerous learned societies helped blacks gain access to professional organizations. In this way he confronted Jim Crow head-on with his intellect and thereby cleared the pathways for many African American intellectuals. On the political and social front, his dedication to the Republican Party acquainted him with politicians all over Ohio, in many states across the country, and with every seated president. He spoke out on many different issues including the reprehensible treatment of the Hawaiian and Philippine peoples, the inhumanity of the convict lease system in the South, and the mistreatment of black soldiers after World War I.

Furthermore, his prominent public and scholarly profile throughout his extensive university career heralded the start of African American intellectualism within the academy. Scarborough's career marks the advent of the professional African American intellectual willing and able to make a lifetime commitment to the academy. Moreover, Scarborough combated the racial charge of inferiority by becoming fluent in the classical languages. His path-breaking career enabled other people of African descent, especially the younger generation, to more readily set their own course. W.E.B. DuBois explained to his high school principal, Frank Homer, who had firmly supported DuBois's study of Greek and Latin, that "I did not know that Homer was quietly opening college doors to me, for in those days they were barred with ancient tongues."[40] As a high school student in Great Barrington, Massachusetts, DuBois, who was sixteen years younger than Scarborough, could not have known that Scarborough was also opening doors for him.

In a 1909 essay titled "The College as a Source of Culture," Scarborough encouraged educators to remember that

> [t]he automobile and aeroplane experiments, the great tunnel and bridge building, the business and the money getting—all are sending forth a siren call [to students] to hurry out into the world and do something at once, forgetting that there should be time given to culture getting, if the world as a whole, is to find the broad paths to human progress. . . . We are here to see that . . . young people rise above the idea of being mere wage earners. We are to strive to create such an atmosphere for the pupil that everyone will

be eager to reach out, and not be content with anything less than general culture as a foundation of specific work.[41]

With William Sanders Scarborough begins an important chapter in the history of the American mind, both black and white. His philological pursuit of the both classical and modern languages was unprecedented in his time. Today black scholars across the country who work with language in any aspect, from Aramaic, English, and German to Italian, Sanskrit, and Zulu, are in Scarborough's debt. Though childless in life, in death he may count all of these academicians as his descendants, his natural heirs.

Manuscript

Upon his death on September 9, 1926, Scarborough left his unpublished autobiography, a manuscript that his wife and Miss Bernice Sanders, a summa cum laude graduate of Wilberforce University in 1915, began editing in the early 1920s. When Mrs. Scarborough died in Cleveland on July 1, 1933, the manuscript was bequeathed to Miss Sanders.[42] Miss Sanders must have left the manuscript at the university because Arthur Stokes cited the work in the notes of his article "Historical Justification for Scarborough," published in the *A.M.E. Church Review* in 1956, and Francis Weisenburger summarized its contents in a pair of articles he published about Scarborough's career in *Ohio History* in 1962 and 1963. At some point Miss Sanders's employer, Truman Kella Gibson, Sr., president of the Supreme Life Insurance Company of America in Chicago, took an interest in this project and had the pages typed by William F. Savoy, a district manager in the company in Columbus. In 1970 Professor Wilhemena S. Robinson at Central State University in Wilberforce, Ohio, determined to write a biography of Scarborough, and Mollie E. Dunlap, former head of the Hallie Quinn Brown Library at Central State University, referred her to Mr. Gibson, who wrote the following response to Robinson on February 13, 1970:

Dear Mrs. Robinson:

I am pleased to advise you that I am sending by express the autobiographical material of Dr. Scarborough. The original sheets were typed by one of my former associates, Mr. William F. Savoy of 415 North Nelson Road, Columbus, Ohio. Mr. Savoy has done some work in earlier years for the Association for the Study of Negro Life and History and if you have any question concerning the typed material, I am certain he would be very happy to confer with you. After you have finished with them, you are [privileged] to do what ever you wish.

Before Miss Saunders' [sic] death, we sent a few of Dr. Scarborough's books to the Atlanta University Library, but I have no record of just how many or what kind they were. It is possible that the Librarian at Atlanta might be able to give you some information about them assuming that record was kept.

As I said in my brief preface, my interest in Dr. Scarborough has always been great, partly because we were residents of Macon, Georgia, partly because we attended Ballard High School and Atlanta University and lastly because there is a reference in his papers to Gibson, a mechanic of the early days who may have been my grandfather, as he (Gibson) was a skilled printer artisan. But, I have no record of his attachment to Dr. Scarborough. I shall follow your work with great interest and hope you will be able to finish the work in the near future.

My very best wishes,
I am sincerely yours.
T. K. Gibson

P.S. The autobiographical material is being sent to you by Parcel Post.[43]

Dr. Robinson then began to edit the text. She received a fellowship for her project, "William Sanders Scarborough: Scholar and Administrator," for "research and the cost or partial cost of publication" from the Association for the Study of Negro Life granted under the auspices of Dr. Charles Harris Wesley, former president of Central State University.[44] In the first footnote[45] of a preliminary, eighteen-page essay to the larger work, "William Sanders Scarborough: Scholar and Disillusioned Politician, 1852–1926," Robinson recounted the history of the manuscript as it passed from Scarborough to his wife, to Miss Sanders, and ultimately to Robinson.[46] But for reasons unknown, Dr. Robinson failed to publish the book. Moreover, the original version of the manuscript disappeared. It is no longer at Central State University, where Robinson said she left it, victim perhaps to the violent force of the tornadoes that tore through Wilberforce and Xenia in 1973.

I recovered the two typed manuscripts by Savoy and Robinson from the collection of the Ohio History Society, and this edition is based on Savoy's manuscript. I maintained as much of the original as possible, including Scarborough's use of archaic spellings such as "Hayti" instead of "Haiti." I was compelled to shift the voice of the whole text from a confusing pattern of third-person/first-person narrative into the first person for the sake of cohesion. Various forms of Victorian diction color the text, and it is not clear whether Mrs. Scarborough, Miss Sanders, Mr. Savoy, or Mr. Gibson interjected the various corrections in grammar or spelling into the text with brief handwritten notes. I also removed, without notation, a certain number of dashes to improve the flow of the text. In addition, I changed the title of chapter XXIX from "The End" to "Mrs. Scarborough's Record of Professor Scarborough's Last Days." Except for the deletion of the dashes, the insertion of commas, and the stabilization of voice, I placed all other editorial changes or my additions in brackets. Although the manuscript was typed with care, there were no explanatory notes whatsoever, and it has taken me fully eight years to iron out the peculiarities of Scarborough's narrative. I have not been uniformly successful and reconciled that some of them should remain.

Scarborough very likely assumed that his account would be published within a short time of his death. He wrote under the presumption that the reader would be familiar with the events and personalities he discussed, and that little or no explanation would be needed. But the passage of nearly eighty years distances today's reader from such ready recognition. Furthermore, he often left out important details such as a specific day, month, or year of a certain event. And for the sake of confidentiality, he often veiled the identities of some personalities by omitting some names entirely, or by coding names into initials such as "Dr. T," "Mr. R.W.R.," "J.W.H.," "Mr. N.," or "R." This discretion created myriad and exasperating puzzles, some of which may never be resolved. Nevertheless, I endeavored to verify each and every detail to benefit the presentation of William Sanders Scarborough's life, an "American Journey from Slavery to Scholarship."

Scarborough lived the life of a "scholarly Horatio Alger," sidestepping, overleaping, or capitalizing on the limitations fate had placed upon him. Nevertheless, he remained permanently ensnared, as we all are, by race, gender, and human frailties. Amid his many successes there were numerous startling and painful setbacks, which were often displayed for public scrutiny. Scarborough's account of his life is a study of principled behavior sustained by the virtues of humanity, dignity, and fortitude. There is hardly an event of his era that is not refracted in some way through his "lens." Scarborough's autobiography provides a remarkable look into the development of an exemplary black citizen-scholar, who dedicated himself to intellectualism and racial uplift. In the current debates about diversity in the university and its curriculum, his insight is invaluable foresight.

CHAPTER I

Parentage

According to the census of 1850 there were in the state of Georgia [in the decade of my birth] 193 free colored males between the ages of twenty and thirty. My father, Jeremiah Scarborough, was one of this number having been set free some years before by his master who was convinced that slavery was wrong and washed his hands of the stain. The same census gives 287 as the number of free colored females in Georgia between the ages of twenty and thirty.[1] My mother, Frances Gwynn, was not included in this number.

My father was born near Augusta, Georgia about 1822.[2] One of his great grandfathers was said to have been a full-blooded African, the son of an African chief. To this descent he always referred with a feeling of superiority. This infusion coupled with a strain of Anglo-Saxon blood gave to him a carriage of dignity that became him well though he was not a stalwart man. He was rather short of stature and somewhat stocky build, brown skin, rounded pleasant face, with high forehead, and a kindly eye that observed everything.

My mother was of very mixed blood.[3] Her mother was a mulatto with Anglo-Saxon admixture. One of her grandfathers was a Spaniard and another was a full-blooded Indian of the Muskhogean stock, so named from the powerful confederacy of North American Indians among whose tribes were the Mitchhite [Hitchiti] portion of the Seminoles and of the Yamari [Yamasee] and Yamacraws as ethnological history records.[4] The last two named tribes lived on the lower Savannah river. They are known in history as especially friendly to the English colonies there. The name—Yamacraw—was a most familiar word to my childish ears, and I think this tribe must have been the one to which my mother was related. She was born in Savannah, Georgia about 1828—the daughter of Louisa and Henry Gwynn. Her Indian ancestry was very apparent in many ways; in her more than ordinary height, high cheek bones, reddish brown complexion, and in other characteristics especially of disposition. She was a woman of strong personality and determined will.[5] She had strong "likes" and "dislikes" with

23

almost always a good basis for them. Always of a cheerful disposition, wearing usually a smiling countenance, she was a favorite with young people, and partly brought up several children outside of her own family. Some of these served her with an attachment that lasted through her lifetime. One of these, a cousin, Matilda Thomas, came to our home to care for her the last year of her life.

The early life of both [my] parents was spent in Savannah where my father went to live when quite young, and where he early became connected with the Georgia Central Railroad, remaining with it as a trusted employee until his death in Macon, Georgia in 1883.[6] My mother came to Macon, Georgia when she was about twenty years of age and there married my father. His position with the railroad company was a very responsible one. He was given charge of all new men—white or colored—to be instructed as to their duties. At times in later years he was even made conductor of excursion trains and given full authority which was respected by all. Here I may say that when he was freed a sum of money regularly was set aside from his wages by the railroad company for his use should he ever decide to go North. As he was unable to secure my mother's freedom at once he remained with her in the South. In the end he failed to receive any of the money set aside for him.

Both parents, even in those early days, had been able to secure some educational advantages, as the free Negroes in that extreme southern section around Savannah and Charleston had opportunities not allowed in the upper part of the gulf states—Georgia and South Carolina. There were some private schools carried on openly for and by a free people, and there were clandestine schools, the number of which would have startled the South had it known of their numerous existence. Even the schools allowed to exist were closely watched as [seen] in the case of Daniel A. Payne of Charleston, who afterwards became a bishop in his [A.M.E.] church.[7] He was considered too progressive and [was] forced to leave his school and flee to the North. Knowing the worth of education my father gathered all that he could as time went on and learned not only to read and write but how to transact his business. My mother also learned to read and write in these same clandestine schools.

There were many free people of color who gained considerable education in these ways. My mother's half brother, John Hall, was one of this number. I mention him here not only because of his unusual attainments, but because of the influence he had over my life. His face, form, and general appearance are well remembered by me [al]though he died while

I was but a boy. His Indian blood was also very apparent. He had not only acquired a remarkable education in books, far above his fellows generally, but he had also such a knowledge of carpentry as to make him a "boss workman." Very few excelled him and as he was universally trusted and respected, he was kept constantly employed. At that day many men of color were allowed to become master workmen in many industries—a necessary thing where they had to perform the labor for the South in cities and on plantations. This proved to be a fortunate thing for them in later years. This uncle became my boyish ideal while I was very young. He was a great help to me in furthering my book education which my parents had determined I should have. He also purchased for me a kit of tools and instructed me in the use of hammer, saw, and plane. I took to the work very readily and decided then to be a carpenter, busying myself in my boyish way in their use at every opportunity.

My father was a man of intensely positive character, upright and without deceit. Policy [sic] never seemed to enter his mind. He was slow of speech and of a very retiring disposition, avoiding public company, but enjoying the social companionship of a few. With strong moral and religious convictions he took the highest ground in carrying them out, never permitting vice to flaunt itself before him in any shape without rebuke of some kind. As he never swerved an inch from the course he had determined upon as the right one, he made enemies as well as friends, but the latter were many. [They] looked up to him, respected him, and stood by him. His honesty, integrity of purpose, and his love of justice made him honored, revered, and esteemed by all who knew him—white and black. He was a great friend to the young people who sought him for advice and also financial aid which last he gave to many according to his means. He was a member of the Methodist Church in early years, but joined fortunes with the African Methodist Episcopal Church when it became established in Macon at the close of the Civil War.[8] One of the strictest of churchmen, he would rather miss a meal than a church service. Intensely Methodist he stood by his church in every way, grieving to see anything go wrong, but sturdily standing by pastors and brethren. He was quite indulgent to me, much less strict in discipline than was my mother who had her views as to my bringing up and let nothing interfere with them. Both invariably insisted upon obedience, good behavior, and good manners. They were willing I should have playtime, but being very industrious themselves, they did not tolerate idleness in me, and as I early became the only child, my mother found plenty for me to do in the house. I had to help wash dishes and sweep.

Through this I gained the nickname of "Miss Sallie" among the boys and girls who soon learned that they must wait for my company until household duties were done.

Three children had been born to my parents: John Henry, older than I, who died in his fourth year, and Mary Louisa, a sister younger than myself, who died in her second year, leaving me, William Sanders, as an only child upon whom my parents hung their hopes. With such parentage and connection I began life February 16, 1852 in a house on Cotton Avenue, Macon, Georgia, a building long since torn down.[9]

I was born under the slave system, and because of the law I followed the condition of my mother.[10] She, however, fortunately for us all, was only nominally in servitude, as the man who claimed her services allowed her to have her own time to spend as she pleased, for which she was paid a small sum. She was thus virtually her own mistress and at her marriage had her own home and was enabled to give good care to her family. Because of this situation I never felt the harsh, inhuman restrictions of slavery, nor did I as a child encounter many of the embarrassments which beset the large number of my companions. I have never been ashamed of my birth conditions; I have left that to the slaveholders. Neither have I ever felt it a thing to boast of as showing the depths from which I sprung. However, I learned to know as I passed into manhood that I was born into a struggle upward like all of my color. I learned also to realize how blessed I had been from infancy. This I am proud to record to my parents honor and credit in the days of that terrible American institution—human slavery.

My father died in October 1883 from a second stroke of paralysis. He served the railroad company to the last month of his life. He is buried in Macon, Georgia. I then brought my mother to my Northern home where she lived for twenty-nine years a contented, happy life in the loving care we sought to give her for all that had been done for me to help me on to what I had achieved. She passed away in 1912—the night of the great *Titanic* disaster—a patient sufferer from that dread disease—cancer, the poison of which is thought to have come from a snake-bite in her younger years.[11] This had disabled her for a long time and curiously broke out at each recurrent season of the accident.

Throughout all my manhood years it has been my happy thought that both parents lived to see their son attaining a place in the world such as they had coveted for me from my birth, and for which they had worked and sacrificed. Blessed are their memories.

Boyhood Days

As I already said, the services of my mother were only nominally claimed, though she "belonged" to Colonel William DeGraffenreid, a man after whom I thought I was named.[1] I must pay a passing tribute to this man for his kindness to my parents and me. He was an aristocratic, influential Southerner, a fine lawyer and a man of high standing in his church. He held broad views in regard to the Negro and was one Southerner who was thoroughly liked by every colored man and woman who knew him. He had proved himself a friend and did not fear to express this friendship. It was he who not only helped to make it possible that my parents could have a home for themselves in which they could rightly rear their children, but it was he who furnished all my books through my entire college course later on. I owe him a debt of gratitude for long continued interest in me and the many kindnesses shown me.

There were good slaveholders as well as bad ones, and all were slaves together—slaves to a system [that] the good ones could not always see how best to discard for the good of all concerned. One great enemy the Negroes then had was the "Cracker" class of people. These poor whites hated the Negro because the Negro felt above them. He often had more money and always had more protection. My boyhood altercations almost invariably took place with this class. They thought I was "too big." Even to the present day the descendants of this class hold the same enmity to and jealousy of the progress of the race.

There was another man to whom [I as a] boy owed much help, but it was of a different character from that given by Colonel DeGraffenreid. This was a Mr. J. C. Thomas, a man of an entirely different type—a very peculiar man, intensely southern, and as a rule opposed to anything that meant progress to the Negro, yet for some reason he took an interest in me and taught me to read and to write, though my parents first put me in the path of knowledge by teaching me my letters.[2]

It is to be remembered that in those days it was dangerous both to teach and to receive instruction. The penalty for the instructor was fine and imprisonment, and for the instructed one, severe corporal punishment. Notwithstanding this Mr. Thomas gave me daily lessons in private. Whether this was known or even guessed in a general way I cannot positively assert, but I have always had reason to believe that many persons—both white and colored—knew of it. But whether known or not, I was never molested nor was my teacher. Perhaps the reason none of us as a family were subject to many annoyances was because of the influence of Colonel DeGraffenreid, and too, it may have been in part due to my father's connection with the railroad company by which he was well known and trusted, and "Jerry Scarborough's boy" was also well known everywhere in the city. At any rate my education and educational activities went on undisturbed.

I did not parade my efforts, however, as I daily went out ostensibly to play with my book concealed, but really, as time went on, to receive further instruction from free colored friends who helped me on, and living by themselves, my parents had unusual freedom for such opportunities to further my education. This learning was soon put to a practical use.

I was often called upon by friends of the family to write "permits." Without these a colored man would have been punished for the misdemeanor of visiting his family. My conscience has never troubled me for rendering this assistance, though I would not recommend as good ethical training such continued practice by a boy for any length of time. However, all of us then felt justified in it because of the system under which we were forced to live.

My first lesson in responsibility came about in the following way. I must have inherited from my father a love for railroad cars and travel which has remained with me through life. He used often to take me in the cab with him on the excursion trains he was given to run and all the employees were kind to me. It was my delight to be around the cars. When I was about five years old one of my pleasant duties was to carry his dinner to him in the yards—some two miles from our home. I had to cross a deep ravine and climb a high embankment. One day a severe storm of rain and wind overtook me and blew me down the embankment many yards from the main path. [I did not know] which way to go, but some men found me and set me on the right path to my father. Through it all, however, I hung on to the dinner pail and delivered it to him safely.

As I continued to evade the law and study, I mastered before I was eight years old *Webster's Blue-back[ed] Speller,* the main educational book of that day.[3] I was also studying arithmetic, geography, and history under a free family near home. But though books came first, I liked to play as well as any boy, liked to hunt, fish, swim, and roam the fields and woods. I admit to the possession of an inquisitive, adventurous disposition, which often led into dangers as I was let to rove about quite freely, my parents believing that I should learn to take care of myself and trusting my good sense to do so. This led me to have some exciting experiences that remained in memory. [One] instance had to do with snakes with which the southern woods and streams abounded.

Once while swimming I was warned by my companions of snakes in the water. Knowing they did not bite beneath the surface, I dove beneath and swam about seeking for a safe exit above for so long a time that I came near drowning. Another time a big snake chased me furiously through a sugar cane field. I succeeded in escaping it only by frequent turnings and twisting among the tall standing stalks until I found a way out. Again, I climbed a large oak tree in search of a bird's nest. Finding a hole, I thrust in my hand to discover a large snake comfortably coiled within. It is needless to say that I did not stand upon making a swift withdrawal and retreat to the ground.

I liked to play pranks and crack jokes, and I am told to this day that a love of jocularly teasing people has not left me. I used often to urge playmates to action and take the role of an innocent bystander. Like all boys I did things, too, for which I was sorry, though only once of which I speak elsewhere, did I have trouble of any serious sort because of my mischievous doings. As to my playmates, they were mostly Irish boys, living near my home, who treated me well and often defended me against outsiders and larger boys, who sought to plague me. Many of these later rose to eminence in the world.

The shadows of the Civil War were then hovering over the South. My first intimation of it came from these playmates. In our excursions to the pine woods near Macon, we would climb the trees and make seats among the branches, talking for hours in common about many things. In one of these talks a boy called across to me from his own particular limb and told me teasingly that a big war was coming and the outcome was to be very terrible. He said that the Yankees were going to try to set my people free and that many would be killed and many other dire things would happen. He sought to see if he could frighten me. He did succeed in disturbing me very much. I very soon climbed down and ran home to tell my parents what I had heard. Then for the first time, they talked over the situation with me, explaining it as best they could. It is well known what endeavors the South made to keep the Negro people in a state of ignorance and fear. At one time with this effort in view those in East Macon were prevented from going to those on the west side of the Ocmulgee River. But those who could read could not be kept in ignorance and there were many ways of communicating knowledge.

In this, too, I soon became an instrument. After the Civil War had begun, my father decided that aside from my lessons still studied privately, I must have knowledge of some trade. [This was my] first industrial training. Instead of carpentry as I had early hoped, the shoemaker's trade was chosen and I was apprenticed to it in the shop of a friend of my father—Mr. Gibson—a most thorough and skillful workman.[4] Here, every morning, after cleaning up the shop and getting things in readiness for the workmen, it became my duty to read to them the morning paper, so that they might be kept informed quietly and secretly of the progress of the war. Just in sight of the shop was an elevated spot where the Confederate flag was unfurled, if victory was with the South. Each morning I was sent out to observe this and report. It was a day of depression when I found the flag flying aloft, but one of elation when it was dangling idly on its staff.

I continued in the shoemaker's shop for over two years where I learned to make my own shoes and do work for others, but found time however to continue my surreptitious studies and read every book I could lay hands on, for I felt sure there was something in store for me higher than the work of shoemaking. This feeling became more pronounced as the war proceeded and it began to be understood among us that the Union forces would be successful and that then there would be a general change in our condition as people.

Those were days full of privations as well as repressed excitement for all—white and black alike. Prices for everything needful were very high, food was scarce, and fare was scanty. Sugar, tea, and coffee were never seen by most of us during those turbulent times. We used to roast corn for coffee or sweet potatoes sliced and burned to a crisp with sugar cane for sweetening.

My parents had moved several times from the east to the west side of the Ocmulgee River trying always to better their living conditions. They had at last moved back to East Macon where they lived during the war and where they finally built a home on a piece of land given my father by the Mr. Thomas before mentioned.[5] Here I had a chance to put my small knowledge of carpentry into practice. Here [my] family lived the remainder of their lives in Macon.

Other dangerous experiences occurred after this move. On one hot day, while crossing the bridge when going home, a drunken man seized me as I reached midstream and swung me out of the bridge opening, threatening to drop me into the river. Though severely frightened, I kept quiet which perhaps led him to draw me back to safety, when I made haste to scamper home. At another time, the Mr. Thomas mentioned before, who owned a grocery store on the outskirts of the city, was obliged to go away for a few days and left me to care for the opening of the store each day. He left a gun in case of any danger which came when two drunken men came in one morning and found me alone. One made a remark to me that I did not understand. Because I did not reply he threw up his gun at my breast. I was helpless as I could not reach my own gun, but kept quiet. His more sober companion knocked down the weapon and again I was saved. The same man came back later to the premises and killed a man.

Another escape was when I was employed in a store and a man came in demanding where I had taken his laundry. As I knew nothing of it he marched me out before his gun to several places. At last in a crowd of passers-by I darted down a side street and once more I was saved. Negro human life was cheap in those days.

As the war went on, colored boys were always in danger when found on the streets. As a rule they were seized and made to do duty in the hospitals where the Confederate soldiers lay sick and dying. I had several narrow escapes and several times felt sure that I would be captured, when commanded to halt at the muzzle of a gun, but somehow my feet always served me well and I managed to slip away.

None of the dangers of the times seemed to frighten me enough to keep me off the streets in leisure hours. I was curious to see and hear what was going on and often went out to camp, delighting to see the Floyd Rifles' drill.[6] All through life military maneuvers were a delight to me. I admit I must have given my parents many anxious hours though they seemed to have confidence in my ability to keep out of trouble, which I am sure I never sought, though sometimes it found me.

The war days wore on. Months passed and these ran on into years. I was kept busy at home and at my trade, and life passed with alternate periods of elation and depression as news crept to our ears of the victories and defeats of the Union forces. As a people, however, we had to conceal our real feelings, because of our situation and only in stolen meetings or hushed tones were we able to express our hopes and fears. My father was given much latitude of movement because of his connection with the railroad. He thus avoided being pressed into many kinds of services, as he had only to state his employment to be let alone, as all knew too well the value of the transportation service and knew it was not to be tampered with at any point. I still read and studied privately, feeling that I must be prepared whatever might be the outcome. Indeed, our family in the privacy of home nursed the hope that should victory rest with the South in the end, then would come the moment when my father would be in a position to take advantage of the arrangement made years before by the railroad officials should he desire to come north. Then our friends would see that his long services were rewarded by allowing my mother to accompany him. But we could not divest ourselves of all anxiety as to the future as these dark years wore on.

In the spring of 1864 came what is known in history today as the brilliant campaigns of Grant and Sherman when the latter began his "March to the Sea" and the siege of Atlanta took place. History tells of Sherman's endeavor to reach the Macon road over which came the stores and ammunition that alone maintained the Confederate Army in Atlanta. We could distinctly hear the guns only 103 miles away during the whole of that eventful period. They were busy and trying days for my father. He had to keep his post on the railroad and help see to the transportation of troops, upon which the South so much depended at that moment. What an irony in it all—compelled to labor that his own people might not be freed! But it saved his life probably, for further and better work for the race, as no matter what dangerous duty the Macon troops tried to force upon him with others, he always had the unanswerable excuse that he must hurry back to the railroad. As the summer drew on the Confederate soldiers, who were entrenched only a few rods back of our home, were suffering from thirst, and some came with their guns to compel us all to take water to them. We with some friends were eating watermelon for our lunch. Father's excuse which always held good saved him from the disagreeable duty as did that of one of our friends, a baker, who had "to go and bake bread for the army." I remember well that I filled a very dirty pail with no compunction as to cleanliness and followed after the soldiers. I was more anxious to see the troops at closer range than to quench their thirst.

Life took on a more distracted aspect with increasing anxiety on all sides. Frantic prayer meetings were held on the "Macon Green" by the distressed white people [when] it became more certain that victory would be with the Union. As Wilson's forces were known to be nearing the city, my first actual contact with the war came in July of that year when Stoneman's raid took place.[7]

Deep impressions were made upon me as to what the immediate outcome was to be and might mean to my family. It was a depressing sight when the raid failed, [and] I saw General Stoneman with his cavalry staff pass by our house, a prisoner of the Confederate forces. I had sufficient knowledge as a boy of twelve to understand that by this capture the Union Forces had lost much, and tears rolled down my cheeks.

From the first we had known of the Emancipation Proclamation issued by Abraham Lincoln in January of the preceding year, and we felt sure that if the Union forces could not win now our condition as a race would inevitably be worse than before. Our spirits rose again when Atlanta fell in September. The fall and winter months passed with eager watchfulness of every movement we could learn of events. Then we were again thrown into a gulf of despair when in the following April the news of the assassination of Lincoln reached our ears. Throughout the city my people took the tidings with the deepest sorrow and foreboding. What effect would his death have upon the final issue? What would become of the future I had hoped for? We could only grieve and wait in patient silence for the coming march of events.

In a few days Macon faced its second immediate danger as it became known that Wilson's forces were approaching the city. Life now took on a panic stricken aspect with the daily prayer meetings of the white people on "Macon Green," while we looked on breathlessly, secretly praying that victory would rest with the Union Forces in the end.

For some days I had been kept at home though my curiosity was unabated. We were living in East Macon directly in front of the earthworks thrown up by the Confederate soldiers and shells were flying directly over our heads into the city doing much damage. People moved from place to place seeking safety, but we remained in our own house. Everywhere there was a state of turmoil and distress.[8] I had finally been allowed to venture out upon the streets. There I saw Confederate soldiers coming into the city one after another at first at full speed on horses and mules—then in rapidly increasing groups and numbers giving the alarm that the Union Forces were entering the city. Then came several of these shooting in the air [and] showing they were in command. I hurried home to my anxious parents who knew not what might happen at this moment of peril. We slept little that night, uncertain as to whether the constant rumbling meant the flight of the Southern people or the entrance of the Union troops. It was not until later that we learned that the surrender of the city by General Howard Cobb had taken place outside of the city limits.[9] We learned too, that our fine bridge over the Ocmulgee River, separating East Macon from West, was only saved from being burned by the retreating Confederates by the prompt arrival of the vanguard of the Union forces, whom I had seen entering behind the fleeing enemy.

Then in order that the Union soldiers might gain possession of but little of the city stores provided for the Southern troops, the city authorities had broken open some of the storehouses, letting the people take what they would, rather than let them fall to the Northern victors. They had also poured streams of liquor into the streets. Now the Union Forces broke open the rest of the commissariat stores and allowed the Negro people to carry away what was not used by themselves. Many useful and needed things were thus gained by my family. I recall that my own share of the spoils consisted of an abundance of boxes of penpoints, pencils, envelopes, and paper.

Another never to be forgotten scene was fixed in my mind [namely] that of the announcement of freedom to the colored people. Officers had been detailed by General Wilson to announce the new relations now to exist between the white and blacks. The meeting was held in the Presbyterian church.[10] The house was packed. I saw and heard as I sat perched in an open window—a joyful boy who knew now that there was a possibility of his dreams becoming a reality. The effect upon the people cannot be described—only imagined. There was that rejoicing with cries and tears by which only a long enslaved and suffering people could voice their emotions as they realized that the day of freedom, so long prayed for, had at last dawned. The next day nearly every Negro family, who had served a white family, as it seemed to me, moved out regardless of what it might mean to begin a new life under a new regime.

This was such a radical movement that I am forced to believe that it was at that moment that rancor and bitterness sank roots deep into the hearts of the South. One party was exulting in the conditions that struck off its shackles and made it free. The other party was despondent, humiliated, and angry because it had not only been beaten and defeated, but had lost long-accustomed service, and worse than being made dependent, it was forced to do for itself.

The life that I now began to live changed its nature. Soon after General Wilson made his headquarters in Macon I was hired to work in a bookstore owned by Mr. J. Burke. [He was] a strong Methodist, a man intensely Southern in feeling, [al]though naturally broad and sympathetic.[11] Here I had wide opportunity to read as I wished, for he was very indulgent to me. Indeed, he soon accepted the new situation even to the extent of becoming very friendly and helpful to the incoming teachers sent from the North to aid our people. As is well known all books published in the South during the war had but one side to present to the public, which was done with strong partisan expression and great care had been taken, that [no other] should be available to readers. So I could now see what literature the South had fed upon during these years—literature that had been instilling so many warped ideas into the Southern minds.

General Wilson had been in the city a short time when this store was burned. Later Mr. Burke established another one and a few years later, and of him I purchased my set of books for freshman college for which our old friend Colonel DeGraffenreid paid.

I was a busy and industrious boy from the first. My first real "greenback" was made by selling with other boys, both white and black, the *Macon Telegraph*—the leading newspaper of the city.[12] We were permitted to pass the lines for the purpose of selling to the soldiers. Sometime before this I had been selling strawberries from a garden [for] one hundred dollars per quart in Confederate scrip. It had lost its value [after the war] and for the first time I looked upon real money made in Washington by the Federal Government. I made considerable money by selling papers and my father carefully put it away for me in a walnut box beautifully made with lock and key by my carpenter uncle. I have kept it to this day. The Northern soldiers were very kind to me and often questioned me as to what I was going to do. Even then I knew of such colored men as Frederick Douglass and John Langston as ideal men of the race, and had selected the law like the latter as a profession and planned to be an orator like the former.

There was another unforgettable scene I witnessed. It was on a day in May when Jefferson Davis was brought a captive to Macon, under a special guard—the wagon guarded on all sides by soldiers with guns.[13] I had climbed a tree in front of the Carrier House on Mulberry Street and was within a few feet of him as he was taken within. My feelings, I must admit, were largely that of boyish exultation that I had seen him brought to my home city mixed with some disappointment as to his general appearance which seemed to me to hold nothing of what I felt the great Confederate leader should be. I saw him but once again after his liberation from prison when he made a speech in Atlanta.

[A] new order of things came in many ways with freedom. I recall the coming of colored troops to take the place of the white ones in Macon. The former met with much opposition from the Southern white citizens. Some incidents were amusing to onlookers, as many times the white people would go out into the gutters and mud, often to the detriment of their attire, rather than acknowledge defeat and be humiliated by walking beneath the Union flags stretched out over the sidewalks. Still, although everything was under military rule and an ill repressed feeling was ever present, I do not recall any incident of great disorder.

Other changes soon followed which touched my life. When the general rights of my people were fixed, the Freedmen's Bureau was established in Macon, and colored postmasters were made for the city. [They were] Henry McNeal Turner and John G. Mitchell as assistant.[14] These with John Langston were the first distinguished people of my race I had ever met. The former came to attend the First Conference of the African Methodist Church in Macon, and J. M. Langston came to address the people of the city generally.[15] Of the latter I purchased my first great book— *The Life and Services of Abraham Lincoln.*[16] All were strong capable men. [With] John G. Mitchell, an early graduate of Oberlin College, I was destined later to be closely associated in my Northern home and work.

In the Freedmen's Bureau I found employment at odd times as a clerk before I finally left Macon. In it I put my small savings from selling papers and my father also made deposits there, looking forward to my future college expenses. I withdrew mine in time but his book, still in my possession, shows a loss on its pages, when the bureau collapsed. There are many things connected with what is known as the Reconstruction Period of which I speak later.

Macon and Atlanta School Days

T he first great event which was to take place in my young life happened as the Civil War closed. For the first time I was free to read and study and go to a real school in a real schoolhouse, and be taught by a real teacher without any further subterfuge to gain an education.[1]

My first real schoolteacher was Miss Kidd, a white lady from the North who opened a school for the colored children in what was then the "Triangular Block" in a room directly over the one where my life had once been threatened.[2] She had about fifty pupils who paid a small tuition fee. The work was of course largely elementary, though there were a few advanced classes. To these I belonged. Here I had an opportunity to review the subjects studied secretly during the preceding years and to strengthen the weak places, thus fitting me for other work soon to be entered upon.

I did not remain in this school very long, however, as the American Missionary Association opened one in the city at once on the close of the war and I soon enrolled in its classes.[3] These were at first held in any available quarters. Mrs. Sarah Proctor (Ball), one of my teachers, fifteen years later refreshed my memory on this point when she wrote me thus so pleasantly from her Northern home:[4]

> I well remember the chills you used to have when I taught in the old slave quarters connected with our home near Spring Garden; our crowded school in the old stable; the writing of compositions and map drawing in the old Methodist Church; the singing with Miss Cook in what used to be a dwelling house; our prayer meetings in the chapel and the many other things at last in the new building. I always think of you as a large schoolboy with book ever in hand, studious, obedient, and attentive. . . . It does me good to be remembered by my old scholars, especially when they have gone up and beyond me as you have.

This letter [made me reflect upon those days.] I recall cultured, sympathetic, self-sacrificing men and women who left homes of comfort and ease to help a newly freed people to acquire all they could give, yes, more than this—to endure ostracism, insult, and calumny. For the South, not content then with trying to make the colored people feel by statement and action that these friends were of the low classes of the North, even of the scum of society, turned their backs upon them and treated them with every possible indignity. I've often wondered in passing years who among ourselves today would face for the race all that these brave people faced in that trying period. Yet there were a few Southern people who stood by these courageous ones.

The new building referred to in the foregoing [paragraphs] was Lewis High School. It was erected by the American Missionary Association aided by the Freedmen's Bureau, and named in honor of General Lewis, who, as Bureau Officer, rendered active service in promoting its interest.[5] It was burned together with the adjacent chapel and teacher's home in December, 1876 just after the exciting period connected with the contested election of President Hayes, [and was] believed undoubtedly to be the work of incendiaries opposed to the school. It was rebuilt later and renamed the Ballard School.

Mr. John R. Rockwell of Connecticut with others conducted this school at first, and among its teachers was the most estimable lady whom I later married.[6] Both were ever the loyal friends of our people. He was a Yale man of forceful personality, accurate and thorough, an earnest, Christian gentleman loved and honored by his pupils—just the character for us to imitate. Rich and influential, he was giving a full need of self-sacrificing service to a lowly people. He proceeded at once to put his students under regular military drill, and just before I left the school I had been promoted to be an officer in the Cadet Corps he organized. Those Macon school days were far from being monotonous. I passed my time studying hard that I might master my subjects, and was absent from my classes but two days in the three years and over that I spent there. This happened when I was kept at home to help in building our house.

I studied here Latin, algebra, and geometry, but was largely alone in my classes which I found to be a disadvantage. In regard to my studies, I owe much to Mr. Haley, a Dartmouth man, and a splendid type, who had quite the entire charge of my work there.[7] I was not idle out of school, as in vacation periods. I found myself quite in demand to give private lessons to grown men and women who desired to learn to read and write, and one summer was spent in a brickyard where I did my part of the work as well as the best of them. Life went on evenly. I rarely had fusses or fights with boys although often indulging in sham rock battles. Only once did I find myself in serious trouble.

Just who was to blame I do not know to this day but I do know that I was drawn into an altercation and drew blood from my opponent, making a wound of such character that I came near being expelled from school. I was obliged to appear before Mr. Rockwell and other teachers, and explain my part in the affair. My mother, believing I was not the aggressor, walked over two miles to be present. The matter was sifted and settled by Mr. Rockwell's rigid justice, the understanding being reached that a repetition of such a fight would result in both of us being considered no longer members of the school. It taught me a valuable lesson and I avoided all such troubles in the future. "Rock battles" lost interest for me ever after.

At one vacation time I became a contestant for a prize and won it by an essay. It attracted the attention of the Southern papers which saw fit to mention my effort saying that the subject I had taken for the occasion was about as fitting as a "pig in the parlor."[8] But I received some notice at least. The same paper years later in life paid similar attentions to my efforts.[9] [I was] often stopped as I passed a certain hotel where white men congregated who took delight in putting questions to me in geography, history, and especially algebra. One of these was: "What is the difference between a—b and a^2—b^2?" From the expression on their faces [at the correct answer] I am sure that I came out as winner to their astonishment. At least the report was at once circulated around the city that Jerry Scarborough's boy had held his own. Most of these tilts were, however, carried on pleasantly.

In Macon I began to think of preparing to enter Yale College influenced largely in this by a Yale instructor and also by reading a religious tract that fell into my hands in which a Yale student debated the question whether he should become a Christian or not. This tract I read with great interest and was helped by it to form opinions in regard both in spiritual things and to my future college life and work that I am sure would not otherwise have been formed this early in life. By it and by other wise influences about me I was led then to begin a Christian life. I joined my mother's church—the Presbyterian. Later in life my connections and position led me to attach myself to my father's church—the African Methodist Episcopal.[10] After my conversion I took an active part in Sunday School work notwithstanding my youth and also became a member of the church choir, singing a passable tenor.

[Clustered] around [these Macon school days] are most precious and pleasant memories of days spent as a student, and later as a teacher— memories which stir my pulses to this day—memories filled with deep appreciation of and gratitude to those who thus influenced my youth. There are many I would wish to honor here. Though the names of some have gone from recollection, their influence has ever been felt and their friend-ships cherished. Of one I must speak—Mrs. Mary E. C. Smith—a noble woman who served the race faithfully and loyally from the day she landed at Hilton Head, S.C. from the transport that carried the first teachers to the Southland.[11] Later she came to teach in Macon and was associated with me in after years in Lewis High School. She was a lifelong friend of my father's family and of myself, and wife. She was a regular and beloved vis-itor to our Northern home until death claimed her in 1920. Some of these Macon teachers I met [later] in Atlanta and was to again to be under their instruction.

Under Doctors Strieby, Beard, Pike, and the work of the American Missionary Association changed vastly for good in an educational and a moral way the entire Negro people of the South wherever these schools were located and from which to untold lengths influence spread even changing somewhat the sentiment of the people respecting the Negro in the country at large.[12] With us ambitions were aroused, and better citizens were made by this contact at a time when we were especially susceptible to influences making for better or worse. I repeat, we owe to these organ-izations—to these individuals who endured so much for our uplift—a debt of gratitude that should never be forgotten. No one [who] understands this should allow to go unrebuked [the] slighting remarks by colored unthink-ing youth of the present. They know not what was undergone in those days that served to place the race on the upward road in the struggle it has made since freedom.

It is true that I was but a boy at this time, but I had thought much over a condition and a situation not then fully understood. I stored up much as I listened to others, filling my mind with thoughts of use to me in later years. My lot as I have intimated, was widely different from that of [other] Negro boys, but I was in the midst of slavery even if not fully a part of it. I had stood by and had seen slaves sold on the auction block and had watched situations created by change of masters—sometimes made better, more often made worse. It seemed to me just a game of chance. I saw the cruelty and inhumanity of all this terrible slave trade, and as a boy I hated it with a fierce hatred. But it puzzled me to recon-cile many things, so contradictory, to my mind. I could not see how peo-ple who read the Bible and attended the same church that we attended and served the same God, could preach his goodness and yet keep human beings in slavery and treat them as so many were treated. I heard the Bible texts treated with specific reference to obedience to masters. I puzzled much over the situation. It will be remembered that white preachers were over the Negro churches in those days as a rule, and wherever a Negro did at times preach to his people, as in the Presbyterian and Methodist Churches, he officiated always under the direction of some white pastor. It thus became easier for the white people to devise means of instruction to keep the Negro people from too much freedom of thought. Indiscreet utterances were punished in some way.

As I heard much secret talk and much public expression by Southern people to the effect that the war could not have been averted, I often wondered why it was not prevented by the national government [and] why it did not purchase the slaves and free them. I thought the United States had plenty of money and that it would be an easy matter and the right thing to do. The talk that I heard especially from lovers of peace made this thought ring perpetually in my mind.

It is many years now since that day, but not long ago there fell into my hands a leaflet by Dr. Daniel D. Mead, a vigorous advocate of peace methods.[13] It discussed Jean de Bloch's views on war.[14] Dr. Mead said: "From the United States Bloch drew another illustration to a reinforcement that war is usually the costliest as well as the most brutal way of settling people's quarrels. If nations could count the cost beforehand they would seldom go to war. Take for instance the Civil War of the United States of America. According to some calculations it would have cost the United States some eight hundred dollars a head to have bought up all the slaves and emancipated them. The war occasioned the country losses of one kind and another, amounting to $5,000,000,000, to say nothing of all the deaths and misery entailed."

My boyish immature thoughts in the midst of that conflict seem to have been in harmony with Dr. Mead's statement of the Frenchman's views. I had then no full knowledge of the horrors of war nor of the blessings of peace, but I saw war's horrors near enough to look ahead and discern if vaguely the desirability of peace and its blessings. As a man in these later years I have been a member of The League for the Enforcement of Peace, though in the last great conflict—the World War—I could not advocate peace at any price.[15] I felt then as I feel now, and I deem my attitude a consistent one, that America under the circumstances should have entered the World War long before it did, to compel an earlier peace, and save the enormous sacrifice of human life—of my own race as well as of other peoples.

As a growing youth I remained in Lewis High School until 1869 when both parents and instructors decided that it was best for my advancement that I be placed elsewhere. I needed wider opportunities and more contact with others in class work. I was seventeen when I entered Atlanta University in the fall of 1869.[16] At this time I had completed nine books of Legendre's geometry, had two years of Latin, including some prose, and one year of Greek, had studied civil government, advanced arithmetic, history, and algebra along with some English prose and drawing.[17] Thus equipped I went to Atlanta and settled down with a definite plan in life, still looking forward to a professional career in law after school days were over.

I spent two years in Atlanta, disappointed again because I found myself the sole member in most of my classes—alone in advancement.[18] Yet despite this, I agree that these two years were both fortunate and formative ones. I had already formed studious habits. My lessons were always easily learned and always took precedence over all else. A record card [I] preserved, signed by Edmund A. Ware, then president, chronicles my "deportment as 100" and my "standing in Greek, Latin, and mathematics, 98."[19]

In Atlanta I was placed at once under the immediate care and instruction of Prof. Thomas Chase, a Dartmouth man, under whom I continued my Greek studies.[20] He at once became a controlling influence in my life, but it was President Ware, a Yale man, who became my ideal—a man I loved to honor. Under these—something to care for and to live up to.

My Atlanta life was passed in the atmosphere of a Christian home. It was made such, though a dormitory life, by the assiduous care given us by those in charge, from the matron to the president himself. Sunday was never a long day with us. The day's services were made of such deep interest that all students were glad to see the day come. When President Ware did not himself preach to us he would often read a sermon by Henry Ward Beecher or some other celebrated preacher and comment on the subject discussed.[21]

It was not all class work in which I engaged at Atlanta. It will be remembered that this university began its operation under the American Missionary Association only four years after the Civil War closed. The echoes of that conflict had hardly died away. Its effects were everywhere in evidence in the city and especially on the campus. Atlanta University was built where many large breast-works and fortifications had been thrown up by the Confederate forces to keep out the Union troops. It became now a part of the students' work to spend a certain portion of each day—two hours at least—in leveling these reminders of the war so that the grounds might be beautified as a college ground. It was with satisfaction and pleasure that I helped in this work.

Thirty-nine years later I was to stand with redoubled pleasure upon the university platform as an invited guest of its new President, Edmund Ware's son, a true representative of his sainted father, and as Atlanta's first graduate, deliver that son's first commencement address.[22]

At Atlanta aside from my instructors there were students whose later careers have done honor to the race. Three life-long friends have made names for themselves in the world. One is Miss Lucy Laney who by her own energy and efficient work after graduation, built up a school in Augusta, Georgia, known as Haines High School—an honor to herself, to [the] race, to the state and country.[23] Another was Henry O. Flipper, who after I left Atlanta, went to West Point where, though he suffered much from race prejudice, he graduated with distinction.[24] He was assigned as Second Lieutenant to the Tenth Cavalry and went to Mexico. I speak of him in particular as this prejudice followed him, blighting his career in the end as far as the army was concerned. He was the first young man of color to graduate from West Point. Of this Richard T. Greener wrote me some twenty years later a [description of a] conversation he had with a white military officer who admitted as a fact the injustice done young Flipper in Mexico in the trouble that led to his dismissal from the army.[25] But he claimed as one of his friends "it could not be successfully combated because of powerful influence." This same influence I myself met when Flipper's friends years later, were again striving, but unsuccessfully, to gain his reinstatement in the army.

The third friend I speak of is connected with an incident that has become historical. On one Saturday evening all the students were gathered together in one large room to study our lesson at a common study hour, as was the custom. Two or three teachers had charge of the room to give aid when students wished help in some perplexity. While we were at work a representative of the Freedmen's Bureau visiting the school came to the room and said that as he was soon returning North he would like to take back to General Howard some sentiment which would show our aims and purposes in life.[26] We were called upon to write these. I recall writing; "We are coming." The one chosen, however was one written by "Bob Wright" as we called him then: "We are rising." It was written in his good King's English too, [al]though the newspapers insisted on putting it into a dialect form. It was this sentiment that the poet Whittier immortalized in verse and also immortalized "Bob."[27] In after years Bob held the leading place in the education of Negro youth in Georgia, as the president of Georgia State Industrial College. He was also a leading figure in Georgia politics for a long time. Today he is president of a bank for the race in Philadelphia of which I find myself a director.[28] Only recently (1925) he wrote me: "Scarborough, who would have thought of all this in our Atlanta days?" Truly the boy is father of the man.

While I was at Atlanta the state legislative committee visited the school and attended the examinations being held there. As I was largely alone in my classes, some of these made the examination exclusively a personal affair—wholly my own. Calhoun had publicly made the assertion that no Negro could learn Greek.[29] The outcome I quote from a clipping taken a few years later from a New York letter to the Boston *Congregationalist,* where in a report of the meeting of the Congregational Club, this item is found in reference to the oft repeated Southern claim of the inability of the Negro to receive higher education: "Rev. Dr. Strieby cited the experience of the Southern schools of the American Missionary Association, as a sufficient reply to the charge of Negro inferiority and reminded the club of this Atlanta examination in Latin, Greek, Geometry, Algebra, etc., which drew from ex-Governor Brown of Georgia and his legislative committee the frank avowal of their conversion to the faith that the Negro can be educated in the higher branches as well as the whites."[30] Many years later I was guest of this Congregational Club and was introduced as the "author of a Greek grammar, who had thus early refuted Calhoun's statement."

My vacation periods at Atlanta were spent largely at home in Macon giving private lessons to old men and women as a help toward expenses. One vacation was passed in teaching in Cuthbert, Georgia where I began to build up an educational work that has become permanent. This was the time of the Franco-Prussian War. Every afternoon after school was closed I would go to a friend's grocery store and spend an hour or more reading to those who congregated to listen to the news of this war, as I had done a few years before during the Civil War to the parties in the shoe shop in Macon. This school at Cuthbert was my last effort at teaching in the South for the time being.

At the close of two years I had obtained all that Atlanta University was giving its students.[31] I graduated but with no graduating experiences. There were no essays, no addresses, no music, no diploma, no bouquets—only the knowledge of work satisfactory accomplished which would help me on and up. It was just as well. After all it is the work done that alone counts. The South was not then prepared for any commencement demonstration in a school for Negroes. To allow it to exist was all that could be expected in those days.

My two years in Atlanta University were happy ones and full of inspiration. I had gained much useful knowledge, and had experienced that contact with cultural people which was of inestimable worth to me. I have always felt grateful for all that Atlanta gave me in many ways and I am proud to know my name heads the list of Atlanta's graduates, as both President Ware and Myron Adams have written me: "You are really our first graduate and must always consider yourself such. We place your name at the head of our alumni list."[32]

But even a first graduate, no matter what position he may reach in after life, often fails of merited recognition by his Alma Mater, especially if cautious fear suggests that it may be considered as an endorsement of social equality.[33] I was no exception.

Four Years in Oberlin College

As soon as I had finished my course in Atlanta I began preparations to enter a Northern college. I had really fitted myself for Yale having completed all that was necessary to this end. There were influences at work, however, that caused a change in my plans and instead I entered Oberlin College in Ohio.[1] [Al]though I had given up going to Yale, I had not given up the early dream of being a lawyer. But Providence had a career in store for me other than that of the law, and going to Oberlin was the first step in that direction. I have always looked upon this as a providential one.

I was now to leave the South for the first time and leave my home which I was not to see again for four long years. But the joy of achieving my ambitions, the cordial welcome that met me in the North, and the novelty of the new life, all helped to assuage the sorrow I felt at a parting that meant so much to my father, my mother, and myself. They were brave and I hid my own grief, though the succeeding years saw many a moment of homesickness and longing. However, I had work to do and so did they, for were not all our early hopes now about to be realized? Years before, a foremost man of the race, Henry McNeal Turner, had said to them while I was a mere lad: "Educate that boy if you have to work your fingers off." Had they not obeyed and were they not now to continue to the end?

So there was a brave parting with them and other friends and a journey northward to a new land, a new school, and a new home, with two episodes which I found very exciting in my first experience out in the world as a youth. Before reaching Nashville a man of my own race attempted to rob me of the money which was to pay my expenses for the first year at Oberlin. Learning I was on my way to school and supposing I had money, he slipped his hand into my pocket. I caught it, and hastened to another seat. He slipped out of the car at the first stop. This made me wary of my fellows. Again when on my way to Louisville, a drunken man rushed through the car, waving a knife in his hand, creating a panic. I saw him coming and made my escape to the platform where I remained until the conductor had quieted him and restored calm among the passengers. But my seat was near a door henceforth.

On reaching Oberlin, through friends I was most fortunately placed at once to live in the family of one of the former professors—Prof. Henry E. Peck, then dead, but known throughout the country for the part he had taken with John M. Langston in the "Oberlin Rescue."[2] He had been jailed with others because of activities in connection with the "Underground Railroad" founded in 1833 to rescue slaves who passed through Oberlin to Canada on their way to freedom. The history of Oberlin's broad stand in that early day under its first President—Asa Mahan—is well known and most interesting.[3] It had been for years and was still to be for years to come the one great school where the Negro was as welcome as the white student.

Professor Peck had once represented this country to Hayti.[4] In this family, so broad in its sympathies, I found and made my home for four years. I shall never forget their kindness. Here I had access to his large library, and rare association with the family and their friends. Here stopped many of the great men who visited Oberlin. Here I was to meet as honored guests of the family: Dr. Richard Storrs, the eminent Congregationalist preacher, Dr. John Hall, and Dr. Leonard Bacon of New Haven, for Oberlin was a Congregationalist school.[5] Here, too, the revered ex-President Charles Finney often came.[6] All of this was a help to me in my work there, preparing me to make what I have made of my life as a whole in the world of letters.

There was also a splendid community of colored families there living in Oberlin. Chief among these was that [of] John Langston whose home was opposite Professor Peck's. With this family I formed an early and close connection through the son, Arthur, who was also in college.[7] Judge Gibbs' family was another one of the prominent ones settled there.[8]

The next thing after finding a home was to report to the proper college authorities for examination for entrance. Because of my preparation I was able to pass successfully and enter the Freshman Class with no conditions. My happiness may be easily judged. As I was a raw colored boy from below the "Mason and Dixon" line, there was much curiosity as well as interest in the outcome. It did not take long for my success to become known by the boys of the class and by interested citizens as well. My stock at once went up and I had smooth sledding from that time on. I had come up from the far South a green, unsophisticated lad and had entered into an entirely new environment—a life very different from the one I had before lived. Yet such was the spirit of the college that I found myself helped at every turn and soon adjusted nicely to my new conditions. It was a proud and happy day when I too wore the Freshman cap with a blue visor holding "O.C." and a star in the center. I was indeed one of them.

One thing surprised me—to find so few colored students in the college as the opportunities then offered by that institution were such that most any young man who desired a college course could do so. Expenses were low and several funds available for poor students. One could then go through Oberlin comfortably on $250 to $300 a year, and keep up society and class dues, attend concerts, and dress respectably. What a difference now!

Following my day, the number for years has seemed to grow less. At that time I found there Arthur Langston ('77), Robert Bagley ('74), who became a lawyer of high standing. Matthew Anderson ('74), who later graduated at Princeton Seminary, took work at Yale, and later in life established a school in Philadelphia under Presbyterian auspices that has given him prominence and standing in industrial educational lines.[9] There were also White of '71 and Mary Church of '77, who afterwards became the wife of Judge Terrell. Helen Parker of '73, and others whose names memory fail to recall.[10] One, Miss Anna Jones, alone was a member of my class of '75, graduating from the Ladies' Literary Course.[11] All were brilliant students as I recollect their progress. Then there was George Smith, who did not graduate but with whom I formed a friendship that was renewed a half century later in Washington.

In this new field of endeavor and activity and in a class of students representing the best in American life with a heredity behind them that I did not have and could not possess because of circumstances over which I had no control, I realized keenly from the start that I must make good, and to this end must apply myself with determination.

I at once plunged deeply into my work. I soon found that I could also be of aid to others who frequently came to me to help them out in some tangled expression in Latin or Greek or some problem in mathematics. I had formed some systematic habits of study in Atlanta and I now tried to have system in all that I did. I made it a rule immediately after dinner to spend an hour on the playground and then a little later, an hour in the reading room, then go to my room to go over my lessons or possibly do a little physical labor. At night I went over my lessons again even though I might have to attend some society meeting or lecture. It was "lessons first!" Again the next morning I would review these to test my memory of the work. When time for recitation came I usually found myself prepared.

Sometimes our recitations began at eight in the morning continuing until eleven or twelve, with occasional recitations in the afternoon.

The library was my chief resort at every spare moment. Every week I would take out two or three books which I would read carefully. I had learned Bacon's maxim: "Reading maketh a full man." I delighted in history and biography and spent my spare moments in reading from Prescott's works.[12] It was an incentive. If a blind man could accomplish what he did, I certainly with two eyes should do something worth while. I pored over Emerson and De Quincey and of course with everybody else in that day enjoyed *Tom Brown at Oxford*.[13] Those hours with De Quincey were to be most vividly recalled a quarter century later on my first visit to England when in Manchester. I was taken by my host, Dr. Axon, to see the De Quincey collection in Greenheys.[14] Old-fashioned as these authors may be deemed today, they certainly have been able to afford many men and women that strong cultural food necessary to inspire to high endeavor. I know that those hours were a great help to me then and later on. I also took up the study of Spanish with some Spanish students, who entered the college, and made some progress in the language.

In most respects life at Oberlin was about the same as found in other colleges as I was told. Athletics did not then play such a part as they now do. I think we had more real hard mental work then than students have in these later days. We were expected to get our lessons, and excuses were not easily accepted. Not that we did not have some "slackers"; but the faculty saw to it that they went the way that slackers should go in the end. We had our monthly "Rhetorical" and our Thursday "Literacy" where all must be present, when we were addressed by prominent visitors and members of the faculty. Then there was the Musical Union—an organization designed to promote interest in both vocal and instrumental music. One could hear there the masters of the musical world and this influence became a part of my life [al]though I regret to say I did not then take advantage of musical opportunities as I later felt that I should have done. Yet I had inculcated in me more fully an appreciation of good music born in me and fostered by childhood experiences when I often heard the young people render selections from "Il Trovatore" on their picnic excursions in the woods near my Macon home. They were my favorites and I have heard them rendered many times since, always recalling pleasant memories, but never with such poignant effect as when in 1911 they floated to my ears in Coblentz from a moonlight excursion party on the Rhine.[15] I had traveled a long distance since my boyhood days.

I was also a member of one of the three college literacy societies with Greek names. Mine was Alpha Zeta. No fraternities and in fact no secret societies were allowed at Oberlin. In this literary society [I had] the honor of trying my forensic skill at different times with young men who have today reached prominence, among them Theodore Burton, a distinguished member of Congress.[16] I consider it as such especially with him for he was a brilliant debater and taxed his opponents to the utmost. I am especially proud of a friendship that has lasted through the years. Ernest Ingersoll, who became a well known naturalist, was in college at the same time as myself, but in a class ahead of me.[17] He then gave every evidence of future success in the lines of his choice, natural history and physical sciences.

Social life played a comparatively unimportant part in those days as far as I can remember. It was largely a matter of class socials, to which I was ever welcomed and never made to feel neglected, ostracized, or lonely. There were other social gatherings, however, and we were allowed to attend theaters and amusements in adjacent cities that relieved the routine of study. Our mission was to study and most of us kept it steadily before us, though there were many good times. I forgot I was a colored boy in the lack of prejudice and the genial atmosphere that surrounded me and enjoyed such life and amusements with others as these presented themselves to us. I have always been glad I did not go to Yale in the first place and that, when some of our class left in the junior year for that college urging me to accompany them, I remained in Oberlin.

We had our fun as well, though I recall no disorder such as seen in colleges of later day[s]. Perhaps our most serious bit of fun was our burial of Thucydides when we had finished that Greek author. We had a Greek funeral and his books were gathered, boxed, and solemnly burned with appropriate ceremonies. I made a good mourner for I had a fondness for Thucydides which my philological friends of later years had reason to know. One [would] jokingly call that authority my *magnum opus* because of several papers [I later] presented relating to his works.

Though my parents regularly sent me a stated sum, I thought that I should do what I could to help pay expenses and in my spare time I sawed nineteen cords of wood for Professor Peck's family, getting both exercise and money. There were long vacation periods in the winter months affording opportunity for poorer students to obtain work—either manual labor or teaching in country districts. Two of these I spent in the latter manner. I had two letters of recommendation. These, yellowed with time, I treasured throughout my life. They bear the dates of November 26, 1872 and the names of W. H. Ryder, professor of Greek, and G. W. Shurtleff, professor of Latin.[18] The former stated, "Mr. W. S. Scarborough is a member of our Sophomore Class. He is a good scholar, an earnest Christian, and a young man of talent and sense. I take pleasure in recommending him as in my opinion qualified to teach school successfully." The latter declared, "He is member of the Sophomore Class and is a good scholar and a faithful Christian. He is gentlemanly in bearing and possesses all the qualities required in a successful teacher."

I obtained my first position at Enterprise Academy, Athens County, Ohio.[19] This school had gained a considerable prestige under a certain Reverend Dr. Boles. The studies were largely elementary and the students came largely from West Virginia. Among these I distinctly recall a Miss Olivia Davidson who became in after years the first wife of Booker T. Washington.[20] Mr. E. C. Berry, a leading man of color in Athens, was the one who met me and took me to the school where I was to spend these months.[21] He proved himself most helpful to me and this acquaintance grew into a close friendship. His career in itself shows what a young man of color could accomplish even in those days. He was not only a man of splendid character, but was business-like and thrifty. Beginning with a livery, he later went into the restaurant business. Out of this came a gem of a hotel which he managed in Athens for years with such ability and success that all traveling men always sought it and made it well known to all who wished first class entertainment. There was no color prejudice exhibited. He built a small Baptist church for his people, and retired a few years ago to a well earned rest. Years after my meeting with him, I was instrumental in gaining his appointment to a trusteeship in the university of which I had then become vice president. I am pleased to recollect that this first Northern effort at teaching was a success. I soon had doubled the attendance and when I left I was assured that I had done a good work.

In my junior year the winter vacation was spent in a similar country place at Brook Place, not far from Bloomingsburg, Ohio, and near Washington Court House. Here I was some ten miles from a post office to which I rode a borrowed horse each Saturday for mail-home letters and the papers taken for reading matter for leisure hours. In these two experiences I cleared some $200.00 which I put away carefully to help out on expenses and lift a part of the burden from those who were straining every nerve to keep me well cared for at Oberlin.

I was often asked what impressed me most in those early days at Oberlin. I have always felt that it was the strong religious spirit that characterized the institution coupled with the personality of the strong individual characters I met there. I was fortunate to be a student there while ex-President Finney was still living. He was a most remarkable man and his influence was everywhere manifest. All revered him for his great piety and his interest in humanity. It was an inspiration to sit and listen to him, as I have many times as he often visited at the home of Mrs. Peck. To hear his account of his early life, his struggles, and the influences brought to bear to make him the man he had become [was enlightening]. He was then not engaged in the college work, but was the pastor of the First Congregational Church. He was a power in Oberlin, loved and respected by all, [al]though all did not agree with him in every way. It is true that the student body found it hard to remain sometimes for his sermons which often occupied two and three hours with prayers of great length, and legitimate excuses were often sought. Such is youth! But there was no mistaking his fervid sincerity in all that he said and did. The spirit of Finney was the spirit of Oberlin.

President Fairchild was another grand man in my day who wore Mr. Finney's mantle as Elisha did that of Elijah.[22] He was not only a Christian and a gentleman, but a scholar as well, ranking with the heads of other great institutions. He impressed himself indelibly upon the generation of his time. He knew how to treat his students and was loved and honored by them. He made all feel that he was their friend. Especially did the poor, needy student, boy or girl, find in him a friend indeed. He and Mrs. Fairchild took pleasure in having the students in their home, and different classes would frequently be invited there for an evening of enjoyment. To these he took delight in showing the pictures and souvenirs gathered from his travels abroad. Many such an evening was I with my class a most welcome guest at his home and learned how valuable to a student's life is such contact with teachers. [This was] a lesson never to be forgotten when I became instructor and president. My house and home were ever open to the student body, many of whom tell me to this day of the influence such contact has had over their lives. Oberlin College thrived under his presidency as it had under Asa Mahan and Charles Finney. These three names alone inspired every ambitious student to make the most of himself in life.

There were others—members of the faculty whose religious life, character, and instruction had much to do with the influencing of youth in those days. I could give a long list, but speak here of the few—of that all round man, a man who was said to know something of everything, Professor Churchill, one of the best mathematicians of his time, of Professor

Shurtleff, the brilliant Latin teacher, and of Professor Ryder, the learned instructor in Greek.[23] These with others were all equally admired, all equally fitted for their work, all men with the power of impressing themselves upon the students.

There was another—not a professor, but a woman of rare gifts and power, who cannot be passed by as I recall her life and work. Mrs. A. F. Johnson will ever be remembered by the girl students who were fortunate enough to be under her care.[24] Though strict in discipline every girl knew that she sought only to make of each a useful woman and loved her and esteemed her accordingly. The Oberlin of that day cannot be separated from this woman who indelibly impressed herself upon Oberlin life.

Surrounded by the influence of such noble men and women, it would be a stolid student indeed who would not be impressed and I was not the only one who felt their influence. I am sure that every member of my own class as well as of other classes recognizes this influence as a molding one in their lives. I have always rejoiced that I was led to Oberlin rather than Yale.

And then there was MY CLASS—the Class of '75.[25] Of course it was a famous class and is today because of the eminence reached by so many of its members. In its relation to Oberlin it has been spoken of as has the class of '55 in relation to Yale. It has been called also a class of rich men, though not all achieved wealth. Some have done so and have enriched their Alma Mater by their good fortune. It contained nearly seventy-five members at first though but fifty-two graduated. It has supplied its Alma Mater with six trustees. One became head of the American Missionary Association. Hart is with the Sage Foundation, giving help to the unfortunate ones of the world; another, Starr, is a brilliant lawyer in Chicago; another is regarded as one of the most eminent surgeons of the country; another, who in his junior year left Oberlin and graduated from Yale, was Andrew Carnegie's lawyer; another, the youngest member, made a remarkable invention in connection with aluminum and amassed a fortune. He died early, enriching Oberlin by a magnificent bequest. Another, a brilliant lawyer, did not forget his school mother and a splendid Art Museum stands on the campus as a monument to his affection for her. One is a leading lawyer in Pennsylvania, another is engaged profitably in mining stocks; another owns a large bank and controls the finances of his section; another is a Supreme Court Judge in one of the Western States; another was Speaker of the House of Representatives at one time in Iowa. Another, whose people had gone as missionaries to Siam, was born there but educated in Oberlin and returned to that country to take up important work with the Siamese Government. There are others prominent in literature and other lines. Four became college presidents.

My college course was finished in 1875. [And] the 42nd Annual Commencement which took place August 5, 1875 was a great occasion when the thirty-six graduates from the Classical Course took their places and in turn proceeded to enlighten the world upon thirty-six erudite subjects. I was the only colored member in that course, and, slightly changing the words of a classmate uttered at a reunion fifty years later, I stood on the platform at the First Church telling the world about, "The Sphere and Influence of Genius," and received my sheepskin. It was my license to begin a life time of hard work. The sixteen members of the Class from the Literary Course had graduated the previous day. Miss Anna Jones, with whom I was a few years later to be associated at Wilberforce University in Ohio, was the only colored member from that course. Ex-President Finney sat on the platform on that memorable day. It was his last public appearance. He died a few days later.

Seeking a Path

A s a young man from Georgia, I graduated from the course of Liberal Arts with the degree of A. B. at the age of twenty three. [I felt my] school days at an end and [I faced] my future with serious intent. It was a matter of great concern to me as to what I might find to do. It is not easy for the world to realize my situation and what these four years meant to me. I was a poor, colored young man carrying away with me memories of my Alma Mater. (Its friendships, its care, its protection, its opportunities, and above all its unprejudiced atmosphere) and how I was about to enter new spheres, to meet prejudice and opposition and to battle a way upward. Perhaps I took the matter too seriously, for I was but one of a growing number of colored students coming out from the schools at that time. But my environment and training had served to make me feel that I had a duty to perform in regard to the race problem confronting us as a people. It was expected of me, as of every other Negro graduate, to devote my best endeavors to the elevation of my race and to changing public sentiment in regard to it.

As I prepared to leave the school and friends so endeared to me, my first thought was of home and the parents from whom I had been separated for four long years. I decided that I would make the homeward trip by way of New York and thence by steamer to Savannah. I wished to look around a bit. On leaving Oberlin for Cleveland I met my first opportunity for service when two Catholic priests approached me with the proposition that I "go to Rome and enter the college of the Propaganda [sic] fitting myself for the priesthood."

I do not know whether they had been present at my graduation or were impressed by my appearance. They were quite persuasive and intimated that, should I accept, the way would be opened for me. I was left to think it over. I had a high respect for this church as I had some warm Catholic friends at home. Later, when I reached home I was urged by these to take this course that I might return and take charge of a Negro Catholic Church in this country, for which work there were then no young men of color fitted. Though anxious to serve my race, I still felt sure that I was not intended for the priesthood. Then, too, I had been too long trained in Presbyterianism and Congregationalism to entertain such an offer.

On my way to New York I stopped at Princeton to visit my friend, Matthew Anderson, who had previously graduated from Oberlin. There were two other colored youths studying at Princeton Seminary, Francis J. Grimké from Lincoln University and [D.W.] Culp from Biddle.[1] My arrival created some anxiety as well as curiosity on the part of Princeton officials. No Negro had ever entered the college proper, though some were in the seminary. Naturally my advent created some uneasiness. It was at once rumored that I had come to take post-graduate work in the college. I have often wondered what would have happened had I made the rumored attempt, but I was only reconnoitering.

In New York another opportunity presented itself. Friends offered to obtain a scholarship for me in the Harvard Divinity School, if I would devote myself to theological preparation for entrance into Unitarian Church service, but to this offer, too, I felt no inner response. I [wondered] why so many should have thought that my work must lie in theological paths. I can interpret [this] only on the theory that those interested knew better than I how few were the openings for a Negro graduate in those days except in this field and that of teaching, both of which were still limited. Even the schools established in the South by Northern philanthropy held little opportunity for even their own graduates as I was soon to find out. How changed [it is] in fifty years! Today we have made our way into all walks of life. We have our own colleges and universities conducted by our own people, the institution and support of which make one of the most remarkable records in education in the history of the Negro's progress in over sixty years from slavery.

I had spent four years in an exceptional environment, tending to engender trustfulness and a sense of freedom of movement. Two incidents on this journey southward however showed me that it was another world that I was now entering. In fact travel for a Negro there was a hazardous undertaking. My journey came near being delayed for a time by my confidence in people. Just before sailing I went into a Jewish store near the pier to buy a cap for twenty-five cents. I had no change so I gave the man a five dollar bill. I waited for the change for some time as I was told he had to send a man out to get it. It looked as though I would not sail with the ship if I waited and I had extra money. But after considerable parleying and some rather daringly warm words on my part the proprietor decided it best to get the change for me. I stepped aboard just before the gang plank was withdrawn. It taught me one lesson, and I was soon to have another.

On reaching Savannah after a trip in which I showed myself not the best of sailors, I went to take the omnibus transfer to the railroad station. I entered the vehicle without thinking I was in the South and that there would be any objection. But there was. The driver attempted to force me out as I refused to go. Warm words followed and quite an excitement was raised. It ended in my deciding that discretion was the better part and I took a seat by the driver. I was in the South again and brought face to face with the fact that a Negro in that section had still little freedom and must meet discrimination and intimidation at every step.

I found myself at last in Macon among familiar, and yet unfamiliar scenes, for changes had taken place in these four years. My heart was gladdened by the sight of my parents, of their joy at seeing me again and of their pride in the son for whom they had spent these years of sacrifice, toil, and anxious hours. I was also both glad and thankful that I could return to them bearing high testimonials of my work and life for those four years.

One of these I kept through the years.[2] It bears date of August 10, 1875 and reads:

> The bearer, Mr. Wm. S. Scarborough, has just completed the full course of study in this college. He is a young man of high character, good scholarship, and successful experience as a teacher. He is commended to the confidence of any from whom he may seek employment.
>
> James H. Fairchild
> President of Oberlin College

Then as now I considered it my passport into a world of usefulness. I was cordially received by my old friends and it was determined that I should remain in Macon and engage in teaching. At first I had made an effort to find a place in Atlanta University.[3] I had addressed my old friend and instructor, E. A. Ware, to that effect. His reply showed that the time was not then ripe for a Negro teacher in that school, a fact that the broad-minded man deplored in the letter he sent. He said: "I do not know how you heard of a vacancy here. I should like much to have you with us, but I am truly sorry to say that there are trustees still in our school who do not see things as I do and who do not consent to employing colored people to teach here."[4] The time had not come for this and I agreed to remain in Macon where the citizens called a meeting and resolved to raise a certain small sum to pay my salary. With this understanding I began work in a private school for a brief period. Then the American Missionary Association appointed me an assistant in Lewis High School where I had received my early education.[5]

With me were first associated two ladies from the North, who almost immediately gave place to two others sent down by the A.M.A. One, my old friend and veteran teacher, Mrs. Smith, mentioned previously, the other, a graduate from a famous Northern normal school who, too was seeking a path for service. She had been called by the A.M.A. to Macon after a brief stay in similar work in Raleigh, N. C. There could have been no more fortunate selection for the work. These two ladies, educated, cultured, and utterly devoid of prejudice were in every way fitted to forward a work that had seemed to languish for a while. It now flourished under the new management and closed a successful year.

In the summer I went North again, visited the Centennial Exhibition in Philadelphia, and went to visit my friend [Matthew] Anderson in New York. Here I was earnestly besought by the Rev. Dr. Pike, one of the secretaries of the association, to go to Africa for service in the A.M.A. work. I was to devote myself to the study of languages and dialects with the reference to future translation of the Bible into these. My friend was still engaged with the A.M.A. assisting in the classifying for publication its records and papers relating to the Mendi Mission in Africa.[6] But I had not become particularly drawn as yet to special linguistic studies, liking all equally well. Feeling myself quite assured of employment at home, I decided that my duty called me to remain near my parents. [Thus] I did not consider it favorably, and [I] returned to my work in Macon.

I have often much regretted that some young man of the race did not enter early this field of usefulness and of study to throw more light upon Africa's past history. It is a wonderful field. The ground was hardly touched even by white scholars. It should offer an inducement to the ambitious Negro scholar that should not be ignored. More and more I see the need of our youth holding to classical and philological study in order that some one may rise up to enter upon such work with the interest we alone possess.

It was about this time that I made my first "dip into politics." I was made a delegate to the Republican State Convention held in Atlanta, Georgia. It was desired that I let my name be considered to represent Georgia in the Cincinnati Convention where President Hayes was nominated. This I refused as I had then no desire to enter politics, though intensely interested in the outcome. I followed the events in the ensuing exciting months. They were especially exciting for the South. On election day every effort was made to intimidate the race at the polls, and it was thought best to close the school in Macon for the day at least. Then as the Tilden-Hayes contest for the presidency began, the Negro became a special target on which to vent hatred and animosities. Schools for the race everywhere—especially those taught by Northern teachers—were in danger. In December the blow fell on the Lewis High School, when one night the school, church, and teachers' homes were destroyed by fire.[7] Happily there was no loss of life, though but little aside from personal possessions was saved from the flames. To accomplish even this to their credit it must be recorded [that] a few staunch Southern friends lent every aid to and saved the teachers.

It had been a strenuous autumn, and aside from political dangers, the yellow fever then sweeping through the South brought its peril to all [and demanded] combative and preventive measures. It brought both work and responsibility upon the teachers who had returned from the North despite this to take up their work again for the year. The situation after the fire now became a most discouraging one. The two lady teachers refused to be daunted by it though their own personal safety was threatened. They pluckily resolved to stay and fight it out even if they had to set up a private school. Professors from Atlanta University were sent down by the A.M.A. to confer with them and look over possibilities. They were to decide whether or not to abandon the Macon work. The result was to permit these ladies to continue it as best they could. The best they obtained of was cramped quarters for the school in the basement of the colored Presbyterian Church, where the regular descent of the long [staircase] spanning its length afforded not only daily physical exercise, but that of Christian patience and forbearance as well. As for living quarters they had secured but one small room, warmed by Yankee ingenuity which sent a stovepipe out through the opening made by removing a pane of glass. This condition was at last mitigated by the unselfishness of Mrs. John R. Rockwell, who with her family was again spending a winter in the South after many years, who occupied the large home across the street. For over a decade it had been the "Teachers' Home," but [it was] given over this year [to] the two teachers who had occupied a smaller house till now made homeless.

But A.M.A. teachers were inured to dangers and hardships and they kept at work ending the year. They returned North while the A.M.A.

debated the question of the continuance of Macon work or of transfer of these teachers to Fisk University at Nashville, Tennessee. The former was decided upon, but the privations and overwork of these months had so told upon their health that physicians advised both to remain in a northern climate for a time. Mrs. Smith returned to southern work again in a couple of years. The other teacher's path was marked out for her elsewhere as will be seen later.[8] For me, however, the disaster had necessitated a change. The decision to close the school was a disaster to me for I had to find employment elsewhere.

This was at once provided by two friends in my father's church, Bishop R. Cain and Rev. J. M. Brown who later became a bishop.[9] The former was probably one of the strongest men of color in the adjoining state of South Carolina. He had been a member of Congress and was a leader in his state in all matters of public interest that served his people during Reconstruction Days. The A.M.E. Church had established a school for the race at Cokesbury, known as Payne Institute. This school (of which I was now called to take charge) was in time moved to Columbia. It has since developed into a flourishing college [called] Allen University.[10] Entirely managed by the race, it is an honor to its founder and the Church of Allen. It shows the growth that has come from the early seeds planted in the South, [growth that was] sturdily fostered through the days of tribulation [during] the Reconstruction Period.

This offer I accepted and at once entered hopefully upon my new duties. The conditions in the South during that period were especially unfavorable to us as a people; in South Carolina very especially so for a teacher of colored youth. Briefly stated the situation in South Carolina in what was the Reconstruction Period was this at the moment: the "carpet baggers" and ex-Governor Moses had become notorious in the administration of the state.[11] Wade Hampton and Governor Chamberlain were contending for the supremacy.[12] There was dual government for a time. The state was rent by the contending factions in the struggle for leadership. These conditions made it unsafe for a man of color to take a prominent part in anything. One whom the South was pleased to call an "educated nigger" was especially an object of suspicion.

It is to be noted as a matter of the history of those days, that one Negro, Professor Richard T. Greener, from Harvard College, the first one to graduate from Harvard, was then teaching in the University of South Carolina, instructing both white and colored students. He was equipped for any position, a scholar and a gentleman whom I was to know well in after years. He had come from the North with the purpose of aiding the Northern and some Southern men to carry on the work of Reconstruction, hoping to help his race in that perilous time. After the control of the states in the South had been surrendered to the Southern white people, as one result of the presidential election finally seating Hayes, the people, white and black, in this section who had made his election possible, were ignored. With the South in the saddle again many politicians, who had professed great love for the race and had made use of the Negro for their personal aggrandizement in riches and power, turned against the race. It took place among those who laid so much blame on the race for the abuses occurring during this period. They claimed that all the troubles of the period were due to the placing of the ballot into the hands of the Negro.

All of this [returned] to my mind afresh by reading Dr. Washington Gladden's book where he claimed this act to have been a great error.[13] Dr. Gladden was not in the midst of affairs in the South at this time. I was. [A]nd I must say that granted there were mistakes and much corruption, it is equally certain that this was due to the Negro being made the tool of designing men. It is my firm belief that without the ballot the race would have remained for an indefinitely extended period a submerged, if not practically re-enslaved, people. Its present progress would have been deferred far into the future. It was then and still is his one strong weapon for use in defense of his rights. A weapon the South has ever been seeking to wrest from him where it has suited its interests. A weapon the deprivation of which he will ever resist, as long as he has breath. For this he had fought and died, not only to make the wide world safe for democracy but to make safe our rights as a part of the American body politic.

As one result of the trouble at this time, Professor Greener was finally forced to give up his Southern professorship and return North where he was connected with Howard University for a time. Later still he was appointed as Consul to Vladivostok, Russia.[14] One incident [shows] the state of affairs when I took up my work as a teacher in Cokesbury. As a teacher in Cokesbury, every Saturday afternoon I could see men in red shirts practicing military drill near my schoolhouse. It was no secret that this drilling was for the purpose of intimidating the race generally and especially suppressing anyone who played too prominent a part in any line of work for it. I succeeded in arousing no direct antagonism to myself as I attended to my business teaching, and helping my pupils.

In view of all these things, coupled with rumors of the rapidly growing Ku Klux outrages being committed, I shortly decided it neither necessary nor safe for me to continue labors in Cokesbury. I left the South and spent the following months in Oberlin Theological Seminary in the study of Oriental languages, thinking that after all the ministry might have to be the final choice of a profession. It proved to be a fortunate preparation as the years passed by. The late summer found me again in New York with my friend [Matthew] Anderson who was still with the A.M.A.

My interest in Africa was now aroused by my Southern experiences, my recent studies, and the Negro emigration movement then stirring our people.[15] We discussed the offer made [previously] by Secretary Pike which was now renewed. What might have been that result, I have often wondered. But at this juncture I received a letter, remailed from my southern home, asking my plans for the future and desiring further correspondence. Coming as it did from a school in Ohio of which I had often heard but had never visited [although I was] quite near it at times in my vacation teaching, I was indeed curious, and sent an immediate reply. While waiting for further particulars I went over to Philadelphia.

The Path Found

In Philadelphia I met almost immediately Bishop Daniel A. Payne of the African Methodist Episcopal Church. He was a slightly built man of color who had in his youth been forced to flee from Charleston, S.C. in 1834. [He had left] his work of teaching free colored people because of his progressive ideas, or as a Southern on-looker said because "he was raising hell in Charleston." He went to Pennsylvania and continued his studies at Gettysburg Seminary. In 1844 he had stirred the race by a series of essays relating to education. Through his interest in the subject and his indefatigable efforts he had become the promoter of Negro education. He was the leading founder of the school whose president had just written me, and as I soon learned, had preceded him in its presidency.[1]

Bishop Payne was a man of small stature, but with such a superior mind and ability that he was a recognized leader in Negro education. He was a man also of disconcerting frankness as I immediately learned [when he informed me] that I had been elected to the chair of Latin and Greek in Wilberforce University located in Greene County, Ohio. He followed up his announcement as he looked me over with the blunt statement that he thought me too young for the place. It was not a very pleasing introduction, but after knowing him better, I learned not to take his plain speech too much to heart and to interpret the twinkling eye and twitching lip that accompanied his utterances. I replied to his statement with the assurance that I would do my best to fill the place and would grow older with time. The answer seemed to please him. The outcome was that he made no further objection and became my staunch friend and supporter in the trying years that followed until his death.

Though I never learned positively who presented my name for this position I have always thought it to have been the Dr. John Mitchell of whom I have spoken as serving in my native city as postmaster at the close of the Civil War.[2] He was also a graduate of Oberlin and had always been interested in my career. At this time he was making his home at this school to which he had given service in some of its earliest years. He, too, was to be a loyal friend for life.

At this point it seems in place for various reasons, general, historical, and personal, to give a brief sketch of the rise of the school to which Providence had led my footsteps, a young man of twenty-five, and where I was to find my life work. It forms a most interesting chapter in Negro education especially in Ohio. The facts condensed are these gathered from my many addresses in later years when I had frequent occasion to relate the history of Wilberforce University while pleading its causes. I compiled them from a paper prepared by Governor Donahey when Auditor of the State of Ohio to show the progress of Negro education in the state, from Bishop Payne's diaries, and from the records of the conferences held in the early days by both the white Methodist Church and the African Methodist Episcopal Church.[3]

By all of the early laws of Ohio, Negro children were not expected to enter the public schools when these were established in 1821. In fact a statute of 1829 forbade their entrance. In 1849 provision was made by law for the establishment of separate public schools for colored children "where twenty or more might reside," but no white person was to be taxed for their support. If there were less than twenty children the law permitted them to attend a white school, but only on condition "that no white man objected."

Ohio kept this law on its statute books (with some improvements in 1853) until 1887, when its "Black Laws" were repealed. But long before this repeal the colored population of the state, reaching near 30,000 was determined to take steps to educate the youth of the race. The sentiment aroused between the passage of the Fugitive Slave bill and the breaking out of the Civil War was seeking expression. The demon of slavery had reached the zenith of its power and was preparing for its deadly struggle with the genius of liberty.

The African Methodist Episcopal Church was first aroused to action by Bishop Payne's stand on education in 1833. These sentiments were endorsed in the four small conferences in this church in 1833. In 1844 the Ohio Conference took steps to select a location for a seminary of learning on the "Manual Labor Plan" which should also prepare [students] for the ministry. Property to this end was purchased twelve miles from Columbus, Ohio, and a school chartered as Union Seminary which began its existence in 1847. It continued until 1863 under two members of the race who were to attain eminence in later years, Rev. John M. Brown, as bishop and Frances Ellen Watkins Harper, as poetess.[4]

In the meantime the white Methodist Episcopal Church was also stirred to action on the subject. In 1853 it took steps which concluded in the purchase of property known as "Tawawa Springs" near Xenia, Ohio for a school of high grade for the entire colored race. In August 1856 every necessary legal step was taken to constitute it a body corporate under the name of Wilberforce University, after the noted English Abolitionist, William Wilberforce.[5] Its Indian name, Tawawa, means "Sweet Water." Here had been the happy hunting grounds of the Shawnee Indians. Tecumseh himself was born at Oldtown only a few miles distant. At that time it was the summer resort of many of the Negro elite of Cincinnati and surrounding towns.

The work thus begun was continued with a white Methodist minister, Dr. Richard Rust, as president from 1858 until 1863.[6] Then it was forced to close because most of the pupils were the children of Southern white planters who could no longer support them there after the Civil War began. Bishop Payne, who had been associated with the enterprise from its inception, bought the property for $10,000 in behalf of the A.M.E. Church, having nothing wherewith to pay save faith in God and friends of the race which faith was justified.

The school was then newly chartered and organized as the property of the entire church. Union Seminary was then abandoned and the two schools were merged into one as Wilberforce University, a school under the control of the Negro himself in the year of universal emancipation. These facts make it unquestionably the oldest Negro school in the country, as well as the first organized effort of the race to help itself.[7]

The property was nearly paid for when on the day President Lincoln was assassinated the school was burned to the ground. The work did not cease. A new building was erected and Bishop Payne became its president and leading spirit until 1870 when Rev. B. F. Lee, just graduated from its theological department, was named as his successor. It was President Lee who had first addressed me for the job at Wilberforce. I received a post card saying:[8]

I am very glad you have decided to cast your lot in with us at Wilberforce University. Let this settle the case and conclude the engagement. We shall expect you on the 4th of September.

Very truly yours,
B. F. Lee

I spent the remainder of the summer in New York and Philadelphia, reading in the libraries and gathering up all possible information that would be of service to me as a teacher of the classics. I reached Wilberforce University on the date set.

A driver of a little carry-all drawn by a white horse met me at the station and conveyed me to the institution three and a half miles distant.[9] [It consisted] of one large brick building of three stories and basement, the upper story still unfinished. This one building was used for chapel, recitation, dining room, and dormitory quarters for its students and some teachers. My room was assigned me and I learned that my duties included overseeing the boys in this left wing.

The campus was a pleasant one, shaded by many old trees. A row of cottages stood on either side stretching to the highway in front which was reached by footpaths and two primitive stiles. In one of these cottages the president lived [on a footpath that] the boys had dubbed "Smoky Row." In the center was a well of never-failing water with its old pump, and in the nearby ravines were the springs whose medical qualities of iron and sulfur had once made the place famous as Tawawa Springs. They were then useless for conveying water as the lead pipes once laid had been torn up and melted into bullets at the beginning of the Civil War.

My young professor's imagination was at once captured by the situation as well as by its history which I soon learned here. I saw magnificent possibilities which should have been utilized to the utmost making it the "Mecca" of Negro education. The school catalogued four organized departments with a faculty of eight teachers, four being products of the university, with two white teachers in the law department, resident in the nearby city [Xenia], and two white ladies resident at the school. The student body was small, scarce 100, some well advanced in age, but with a goodly proportion of splendid young minds whose possessors have made a fine record since that day.

In its past career some strong men and women—both white and colored—had served it, coming from England and Scotland, from Oberlin and Mount Holyoke. From this last noted institution I found Mrs. Alice Adams, a most beautiful character, beloved by all as "Mother Adams." Her son, Myron, in later years became president of Atlanta University, and her stepson, Prof. William Adams, had already given some years of service to the school.[10] It was to his chair that I had been appointed. She grew to be ever a loyal friend to me and mine. The other lady called to take charge that same year of the normal work was a classical graduate of the famous

Oswego Normal School, New York, then presided over by that great educator, Dr. E. A. Sheldon.[11] It was she who had been a co-worker with me
in the South, when our school was burned in Macon, Georgia.[12] It was a
curious coincidence, too, that while negotiations were going on with the
president for my services, Bishop Payne was also negotiating through Dr.
Sheldon for hers. Her arrival at Wilberforce was almost simultaneous with
mine. Like myself her work had been interrupted by the burning of the
Macon School and she, too, had found up to the present no satisfactory situation elsewhere.

There had been in the past many strong, loyal white helpers, who
had encouraged and fostered the school. Among them were Chief Justice
Chase, then Governor of Ohio, and Gerrit Smith, the noted abolitionist.[13]
There were many colored men who deserve mention and who would
receive it [here], did not space forbid. But this record cannot in any sense
of the word be considered a full history of the school, much less that of the
church to which it belongs. I must say, however, that by its charter
Wilberforce University had "forbidden from the first any distinction as to
color or race among trustees, students, or faculty."

When I came to this work there were no white trustees left on its
board, and only two white members on its faculty outside of the law department. For some years after, there continued to be a few white students.
Today, nearly half a century later (1924) it has no representative of the white
race, either in its faculty, its trustee boards, or its student body. For weal or
woe, the Negro colleges and universities of today are being rapidly manned
and managed entirely by the Negro himself. In desiring and assuming this
great educational responsibility those chosen for the task must be well
equipped, broad and cultured, strong, wise and tactful. The race must put
aside selfish aims, jealousies and animosities if the experiment is to become
an ultimate success.

Widening Fields—
Working, Learning, Growing

I came to Wilberforce University full of enthusiasm and determined to do my share to help on a school with such a history and such prospects. I was proud to be connected with it, but I saw much to be done, however, coming as I did with Oberlin memories and ideals. I soon saw three things to be learned. The first was that my "chair" was a "settee" as a philological friend years later facetiously termed it. As time passed I learned it was capable of indefinite extension with all sorts of additions.

We began the day with prayers at 8 a.m. and were engaged in continuous recitation till noon. We resumed work at 1 p.m. keeping it up until 4 or 5 p.m., ending with prayer period again often by lamplight. The teachers residing in the dormitory were also expected to board there and superintend the manners of the students as well. As need demanded and an unoccupied period occurred, I had to add at times mathematics, chemistry, philosophy, and rhetoric to my Greek and Latin schedule. Monday was the only day that one might possibly claim for [one's] self. The Oberlin fashion obtained here as it allowed the theologues to lose no classes when they went out weekly to preach to small charges in nearby towns and return on Monday. It was a good arrangement as it obviated the temptation to spend Saturday as a holiday in recreation alone, leaving preparation of lessons for Sunday hours.

Sunday, too, held its work for teachers. The only chapel served as community church as well, with service twice a day which we were expected to attend, sometimes hearing a sermon from a faculty member or a distinguished visitor, and often from the "preps" in the Seminary whose wells of knowledge were far from deep. The members of the faculty were also called upon to teach in the Sunday School and serve at times as superintendent. A weekly prayer meeting and a missionary society called for weekly service.

Duties did not cease with class work and church work. I found myself from the first made Secretary of the Faculty which was a job of itself as it was my duty to gather and send out monthly report cards to parents.[1] Then there was another position which I had to take this term. The mail for the school was brought daily from Xenia by a trustworthy student. It was then distributed from the chapel rostrum at noon by some teacher. This was enlivened occasionally as when after reading a name and putting down several letters addressed to the same party [by] saying, "ditto," there was heard in a perplexed undertone: "Who is Ditto?"

This distribution grew irksome and took much time, but I unwittingly added another job to my list when I applied to Hon. J. Warren Keifer, the Representative in Congress for the district, asking his aid in establishing a Post Office at Wilberforce.[2] General Keifer replied assuring me of his support adding: "It has seemed to me strange that there has not been a post office at Wilberforce long ago." [The post office] became a reality at once and with it came my commission as postmaster. There is a tradition that one had once before been established there, but I was never able to trace it to the Government, nor to learn, if so, why it was dropped.[3]

This added labor did not last long however as I was soon required to give over the position and tiny salary to the Secretary of the school [J. P. Maxwell]. [This was a] thing I did not regret for a moment. Only I did miss the salary. The second thing I had to learn which was sufficient to produce uneasiness, and was absolutely detrimental to the morale in any field of labor, and especially so in that of education, [was the want of funds].

My salary, though but eighty dollars monthly, was not an assured thing, not even at the end of the year. Then the deficit was paid by notes and arrangements [which] had to be made in the city whereby these notes could be sold. This was a direct way to encourage the incurring of debts [because], we had to meet these debts individually though the school might fail to meet the notes when due. We all ran into debt. It was necessary to live and I felt that I must also grow. It not only discouraged thrift, but hampered some of us greatly. Beginning thus I edited without ceasing the school paper for over forty years. Personally it became at length a blessing in disguise for as time went on it forced two pens to turn to profitable channels to meet needs and aims.

The third thing I learned I [called] "an intangible something." The vital bearing it had on progress causes me to speak of it at length. I came soon to perceive that in my desire for growth I was being viewed as a source of alarm. I knew the school had traditions and I had no intention of disrespecting them nor disregarding them, nor of trying to wrench rudely the staid institution out of its beaten track. But I believed in progress and was ambitious to broaden the work, to strengthen it in many lines and develop its great possibilities. Progress seemed to call for some changes. These it seemed impossible to accomplish readily, as there seemed lacking the necessary breadth of comprehension and clearness of vision. [This] I think [was] due to the fact that the majority of my colleagues had experienced but little of outside contact with educational work. [They] were limited to that afforded by Wilberforce courses and thus could not appreciate fully needs [nor] accept willingly innovations proposed by one who was not an alumnus [and who] had to be considered an "outsider." To illustrate, when I proposed bringing Peloubet's *Lessons* into Sunday School work as help to teachers, it was frowned on by some as a dangerous if not unnecessary innovation in a Methodist School.[4] I could not then understand why opposition could be made to any ideas that helped on the school and the race. But the years were to teach me many more things.

I learned in a short time that revolution was not possible and wisely contented myself with slow evolution, as did the teacher [Sarah C. Bierce] who had taught with me in the South and had similar ambitions and desires for bringing about progress. My helpful colleague and I decided to begin with small things. As the library then held but few works of value, we set about establishing reading rooms for both sexes. To these many papers and periodicals were contributed by our friends in the east. Within the first year we thus had two reading rooms quite well supplied, and a literary society had been established for the girls. The boys already had one. As soon as possible we turned over the management to the students, helping by counsel and direction when needed. My colleague did more as will be seen. We were always sure of encouragement and cheer by Bishop Payne. He delighted in any movement looking to progress. He also had the discernment to realize when it was being made and the breadth to praise and cheer on the worker.

[Bishop Payne] really had three hobbies in education, if we may speak of them as such—Normal work, French in which he was an excellent scholar, and Natural Science, the progressive work undertaken years before and which led to his exile from the South. He could appreciate also and deprecate the inertia that hampers as well as does vigorous opposition, and he was even now to share in a repetition of old educational experiences when my colleague [Sarah C. Bierce] undertook the movement leading to the establishment of Payne Museum. She like myself occupied a "settee" and taught Natural Sciences and French also, when necessary. She had only her own small collection of minerals with which to work. Endeavoring to advance her work she had at once addressed Prof. H. A.

Ward of Rochester, N.Y., who made a business of supplying museums to colleges throughout the country.[5]

He came to Wilberforce accompanied by Prof. Franklin Hill, then curator of Princeton Museum, one who knew well our school and its struggles because of previous connection with Horace Mann's college—Antioch [College] at Yellow Springs, Ohio, a few miles distant.[6] The result was a letter to Bishop Payne and a proposition from which these extracts are taken:

> A fortnight ago, I made a short visit to Wilberforce University, driving out from Xenia. I have for several years been much interested in this institution, ever since my good friend, Prof. F. C. Hill, now of Princeton, took me over there in 1874, and showed me how much the students were interested in our department of Natural Science in which he lectured, yet how poorly off they were in illustrative material. Since then I have made some effort to raise funds for a Cabinet in this department. I had nearly succeeded in his with my valued friend, Mr. Gerrit Smith, of Peterboro, N.Y., when he suddenly died, and I failed there, as I have failed in like efforts since.
>
> Wilberforce University is really at this moment without anything in this department except an earnest teacher, whom I found to be most earnest and enthusiastic in her work, yet expressing herself as well nigh disheartened by reason of the absolute lack of all material with which to illustrate her teaching. I promised to send her, partly as a temporary loan, partly as a gift, a small series of specimens in one department. And I further promised her that I would write to you the letter which I am now doing [and offer you a plan].
>
> For such a museum I should charge ordinarily $2000 or $2200. But I am especially interested in the success of your university, and would greatly like to see the study of Natural Science fairly undertaken by the students who attend there. We would call the cost of $2000 and my donation to it $600.[7] Will you be able to raise from friends of education the lacking $1400, and shall you wish to undertake the effort?

Bishop Payne at once accepted the offer and set about raising the required amount. The local board did build the cases and, "allowed the installment if at no expense to itself," as he records in his *Recollections*. The instructor [Bierce] went to Rochester and with Professor Ward selected the museum. She afterwards returned to Wilberforce and spent the summer in placing it with Professor Hill's assistance in the upper story of the one hall then in existence.

Thus Wilberforce University obtained its museum. This encouraged the forward [thinking] ones to go on. The ladies from a Philadelphia church fitted out a much needed music room, and Bishop Payne secured from Mr. Ware of Boston a small, fine collection for the beginning of an art room.[8]

But I realized I must go slowly and steer safely between the Scylla of increasing work and the Charybdis of inert opposition.[9] I felt keenly the danger of succumbing to the inertia especially about me and feared falling into the ruts so fatal to all progress. To avoid this I sought at once some outlets. I found that for my own growth and happiness as well I must gain more contact with the outside world. The school by situation was provincial in many respects. The nearest town was over three miles distant. There were no diversions save those created within the school itself, as the community was then very small.

We had, however, the usual advantages of a small college in the early period of its history. There was the close contact of teacher and student that is of untold help in the formation of character and in culture. I tried always to keep in mind what in my own teachers had influenced me most in my own teaching and associations. There was little to distract students from the real purpose of the school. The educational, social, and religious life closely mingled. But such advantages were largely on the student's side. The instructors suffered from lack of that outside association that broadens views and stimulates endeavor.

The one outer contact available came from Antioch College, the Unitarian school, which for some years had provided us with excellent weekly lectures by members of its faculty—Professors Weston, Claypole, Gilman, and others.[10] They also brought to us their visitors, prominent men and women, whom I now met for the first time. Doctors Bellows and Edward Everett Hale were among these.[11] The latter had been a trustee of our school in its first years and became my friend and helper in later life. My correspondence for aid through periodicals was already bearing fruit, as men like Doctor Winship of the *New England Journal of Education* visited us to see our work and needs.[12] I did not then think I should become in time a frequent and welcome contributor to his journal.

These contacts stimulated me to find other outside channels where I might be of service and broaden my outlook and acquaintance. One was that of the lecture field which I made use of shortly. This field was suggested by meeting Wendell Phillips on a never to be forgotten evening when he lectured in Xenia and warmly greeted the Wilberforce teachers with assurance of a never failing interest in the welfare of the race.[13] I recall an amusing incident connected with these first efforts in this direction:

I had prepared my first lecture, "Outlooks on the Practical," and tried it upon every audience I could find. These were then almost wholly [scheduled] in some A.M.E. Church. There was one in Richmond, Indiana, that opened its doors to me. To it I had sent cards advertising [the lecture] which were freely distributed. As I proceeded with my lecture I had occasion to notice many mystified looks. It was not until I was ready to leave that I learned the reason. I hinted my observation to one of the elders. He said rather diffidently, "I reckon, Professor, they didn't quite get what you meant, and I must say, I don't quite see its connection with your subject," he added, as he handed me one of the printed cards. To my chagrin it read: "Outlooks on the Protocol." Well, I saw if he did not. My handwriting has never been of the clearest and it must have been very poor when I wrote the copy for that card. Since then I have tried at least to make my A's so they would not be mistaken for O's. The elder laughed heartily when I explained the error, but I have never been able to discover whether my audience ever saw any relationship between the printed title and my lecture.

After my initial bow on the lecture platform I continued to speak among my people. I also began to write short articles for the few Negro papers then in existence. Such work I have continued throughout my life. There is scarcely a Negro publication for which I have not written more or less at some time or other. I have considered it a help not only to such, for these were not able to pay except in rare instances, but I deemed it one way to help onward the race as well as give myself desired outlets. Many of these publications have had but a brief existence, but a few have survived the years.

Shortly I discovered another channel for expression and participation—that of public life and its affairs. I rapidly made acquaintances with public men. Beginning with the city nearby I found its public men easy to approach and they kindly took me in as a representative of the race who might be helpful in public life. With my courteous manner, a winning geniality, my education and culture, I soon found myself well received throughout my political district, and was soon sought to address political gatherings, and kept in touch with the leading men in the state. From that day to this I have been in close touch with these men and have helped to forward all movements I deemed for the good of the race, state, and country at large, using influence by voice and pen to this end.

I enjoyed the sense of growth I discovered in myself and the increase in achievement [that] came with being forced onward into the various fields of endeavor. I felt, too, that whatever success was made by me was not only personal, but success for the race. We cannot rise as a mass. It must be done through individual efforts here and there increasing constantly that number that can lift us up, creating a power strong enough to command recognition and respect and overcome prejudice. The handicap is mass ignorance by which we are even now so unjustly judged. I meant to do my part in the uplift and influence by example and precept my students to be of that number that came out from the schools [that] would lead in dispelling this ignorance.

When years later a classmate wrote me at the zenith of my work. "I have noted always that you have ever been consistent in unfailing work for the uplift of your race" [the classmate remarked]. I considered those words to be a real benediction. To this end I labored. Despite all outside activities I never neglected my class work and steadily kept myself to my Oberlin habit of preparation by study and reading. From the first I began to build up a library. My first purchase was a set of Prescott's works which I had found so interesting and stimulating in Oberlin days in Professor Peck's library.

From the first [the students and I] worked together most harmoniously. A few were much older than I, but I had the good will, respect, and confidence of all. They came to me for advice and sympathy and I am glad to say I can recall few instances where needed reproof was taken unkindly. This was true throughout my life. I was always beloved by my student body. I was known to all as the student's friend. Their eagerness [to make] progress stimulated me to study for improvement in methods of teaching. This in turn led me soon to determine upon a step that was to bring me prominently before the educational world. I had to decide the particular channel in which my intellectual ability was to be exercised in coming years.

Authorship—Greek Book—Marriage

During the years [after] college I had been doing general work, getting my bearings, finding myself. This was especially true of the first four years spent at Wilberforce University. As I entered upon the 80's I gradually began to concentrate. This was due to a growing dissatisfaction with my class work as mentioned in last chapter. Many things now began to happen rapidly.

In order to make my class work more efficient I began to cast about for devices that might assist in making the ancient tongues living languages and for the best texts for the same purpose. I designed cards for parsing and verb work in Latin grammar, and found them very helpful. In searching for text books in Latin I found one that seemed to bring best results. But seeking one that would most fully meet my class wants in Greek, I at once conceived the daring idea: Why not write such a book myself?

The few close friends to whom I confided this ambition enthusiastically encouraged me to "go ahead." Among these was Prof. Richard T. Greener, before mentioned in connection with his South Carolina experience. I had recently made acquaintance with him through letters and was now carrying on an interesting and inspiring correspondence. The older man who was a most excellent and enthusiastic classical scholar had already written: "I have long known you by reputation and have caught glimpses in your writings of a spirit kindred to my own———I am expecting great things from you." Now he urgently insisted: "Finish your book by all means." "Your work, in my humble judgment, will be the most important undertaking by any colored man. None has ever written a Greek book. If you do the work well, you will do your race the best service yet rendered us in the domain of pure scholarship."[1]

The book was finished—*First Lessons in Greek*—after earnest careful effort and was issued from the press in the early summer of 1881. It was the day before typewritten manuscripts and it was Greek. Every word had to be carefully and painstakingly written out by hand. This was done for me by the one most interested in my success, who wrote a clear, fine hand,

and who bound me to the task by incessant and inexorable calls for "copy, copy."[2] I found no difficulty in securing a publisher in A. S. Barnes and Company, who accepted the work without knowing my color, agreeing to print it at my expense, 1,000 copies for $1000. Though it was a daring financial venture for a poorly paid professor, I was justified in the end as the sales at least met the expense.[3] When the astonished firm learned my color, it became especially desirous of making it a success.

The book was widely and well advertised by circulars bearing strong commendations and cogent reasons for its adoption. The head of the firm, a trustee of the Adelphi Academy in Brooklyn, N.Y., a white school of over a thousand pupils, led the way by at once securing its adoption there.[4] It was thereafter used in many other white schools. It brought me many commendatory letters and congratulations from both educators and friends.[5] I presume to present a few.

From Northwestern University it is no small praise to say that "Professor Scarborough had done just what he undertook." "Amid the books of this class there is none better. The model is an excellent one and the author had admirably executed his task," says the professor of Greek at Adelphi. Others added their appreciation. Oberlin College [sent] praise and congratulations from President Fairchild, Professor Frost, and others all showing pride in my achievement.[6] Close friends were particularly jubilant.

But of all the valued words none touched me as deeply as did the expressions from Professor Greener and Bishop H. M. Turner. The latter was especially "hilarious" in an article published in the *Christian Recorder*—the organ of this church.[7] Quizzically voicing his pleasure on the receipt of the book in a long article in this leading church paper, Bishop Turner wrote:

> Is he that little fat baby boy I first saw in Macon, Ga., when holding a great revival there? Is he the son of Jerry Scarborough whom I installed as one of the trustees of the A.M.E. Church in Macon in January, 1866? Is he that little Billy Scarborough who was so constantly at Sabbath School, and who used to look at me so intently when I addressed the school? Is he the little fellow whose father I told years ago, "Give that boy a collegiate education, if you have to work your fingers off to do it?" Is he that wrinkled browed lad I afterwards saw in Atlanta University analyzing Homeric sentences before a crowded hall of spectators, among whom were many who had said a thousand times that "the Negro can't be educated"? Is he the young man I read about a few years since, graduating from Oberlin College with commendable honors? And now is it this baby, the Sabbath School urchin, the

university lad, the college graduate, that has the impertinence, the rudeness, the blushlessness [*sic*] to send me his text book in Greek? From whence came this audacity to sit up late and rise early to harvest his precious moments till they have culminated in giving a text book to the world, which goes to challenge the critics of the age, and laugh to scorn its would be contenders?

Professor Scarborough deserves the gratitude of our people everywhere for this book which by virtue of its merits must be a success. He will rank in the future as the pioneer in original authorship. A work of literary merit like this will do more to lift our status to respect and exaltation than a thousand flaming speeches, or all the grumbling we could do about our prescribed condition in a thousand years. We have been on the talk for generations, now is the time to be on the do. May God raise up another W. S. Scarborough.

Professor Greener expressed his appreciation in a more scholarly, but no less appreciative vein. From a long article he published on the subject of the new book a few paragraphs are taken:[8]

This Greek book is the first venture of one of our race in the classic field—
——How would our hearts have burned within us in those (Oberlin) days could the prophet have told us then while the Emancipation Proclamation was ringing in our ears, that an infant, or one, not long loose from leading strings would write *Greek Lessons* for our boys to learn. "What has he done?" says Emerson, "is the divine question which searches men and transpires every false reputation. Pretension may sit still, but cannot act."[9] "What have we done?" is the question for the race. Professor Scarborough in this modest volume of 147 pages, has done something, and merits the applause of the race.

Professor Greener closed this article with the following paragraph which though written nearly a half century later, is so large a measure true today that I present it as my own insistent claim for continued study of the classics leading the youth of the present generation to take the words seriously to heart, for by our deeds we shall rise.

Greece has been excelled by no land in the matter of perfection or form of her unrivaled language. The tendency of modern education is away from the classics, and in this money-making utilitarian age, he is considered a mild sort of lunatic who follows a study or pursuit for its own end. The money-makers are the mass of any race. The race developers are the few silent workers, the far-seeing, wide planners, who, unnoticed, or at best only slightly known by their contemporaries, become the famous men with posterity. We have a coterie of young men, the product of the educational impetus of the last twenty years (1860–80) who are ambitious, well fitted, earnest, and active. If they can ever break through the crust of the ignorant fossils who sit like an incubus upon the race or ride it as the old man of the sea rode poor Sinbad, in the way of selfish schemes, petty crochets, ridiculous pedantry, and absurd idiosyncrasies, we may accomplish something.[10] Professor Scarborough deserves the thanks of the young men, for the encouragement he has given us. *Macte virtute.*[11]

Many similar letters were received as time went on, notably from such men as John F. Slater, who wrote that "if what I had tried to do for the promulgation of education among your race should result in any more such worthy publications, I should feel that my efforts had been amply rewarded."[12]

Of this "maiden effort," I regret that some errors crept into the work, particularly in the printing as I was at great distance from the publisher which made proof reading of Greek a difficult task. But I have been repeatedly assured by worthwhile critics that I had no reason to be ashamed of the work. In spite of errors I knew I had helped the race further in refuting for the second time Calhoun's infamous aspersion of my race.[13]

The favorable reception of this work was the needed stimulus to carry, me, the young author through the trials and discouragements of my school situation. As for my students, their delight and pride were unbounded as they took up for study their own professor's book. It brought me recognition in many ways and helped to fix me as an authority in classical education, leading me at once to admittance to the great scholarly organizations. With this Greek book I really entered upon my philological career.

Almost co-incident with the issue of my Greek book one other event took place, my marriage. Destiny or Providence as one may choose to determine it, had shaped and directed the life of another as well as [my own]. As mentioned in [the sixth] chapter, Bishop Payne had secured the service of a teacher as Normal Principal. At the same time the authorities were seeking my services, my co-worker in Macon, Ga., Miss Sarah Bierce, who had experienced a similar closing of doors leading to other paths, came to Wilberforce. We two had now labored together in Wilberforce University for four years. In August [of] 1881 we cast our lots together for life and with like ideals, tastes, hopes, interests, and ambitions joined hearts and hands to the same end as we entered upon a lifetime of labor and self sacrifice for the race.[14]

Whole-souled congratulations with gifts now came to us, but none were more valued for significance than the one sent by Misses Sarah and Lucy Chase, Eastern ladies who had traveled widely, and long known to us as they were often at Antioch College and frequent visitors to Wilberforce University.[15] It was a pearl spar acorn necklace with a card bearing, "From Greece, the isle where burning Sappho loved and sung. God bless you both."[16] So we have ever been blessed with loyal friends[!]

Thereafter, I ever had a faithful, loyal, untiring comrade and helper whose hand has ever been ready to lighten my labors and forward our mutual interests.[17] With the acquisition of loyal friends representing both races I was henceforth to be continually stimulated and urged to continue achievements as the years passed. Her usefulness was to be extended.

In this connection I note a fact showing our friends' interest in us and their desire for our assistance in progressive movements. In December 1882 the Sunday School Union of the A.M.E. Church was established with Bishop Payne as president and Rev. C. S. Smith as secretary.[18] Immediately the latter wrote Mrs. Scarborough: "It is with more than ordinary pleasure that I inform you of your election as a Honorary Member of the Board of Managers of the Sunday School Union of the A.M.E. Church. We shall be pleased to learn of your acceptance, and to have an expression of your views as to the utility of the movement, which we desire for publication in the first published report of the Union to be issued about the first of January, 1883." This is significant as with this movement I was [soon to have] close connection with the S.S. Union, editing its literature, which connection was continued through [my] life.

In the same year I entered into a partnership with a member of my Oberlin Class of '75, Isaak Walton Fitch, as co-editor in publishing the *Authors' Review and Scrapbook,* which was used in white public schools. This work continued for a couple of years, when because of his distance from the place of publication (Pittsburgh) and its accruing financial obligations, [he was forced] to abandon the venture. "Poor Fitch[!]" He and I had purposed so many things in Oberlin—literary life and a large library—but his visions were cut short by his death in Bonaca, Honduras in 1892, while searching for health—the first of our class of '75 to pass away.[19]

My pen was now becoming busy in general work—for Negro papers, in beginning philological study, and dabbling into politics into which I was now being rapidly drawn. The next decade was to be crammed with activities of various kinds, but with literary work always taking precedence.

Indeed through the coming years I was to waver often in a choice of a final field of work. Should I leave Wilberforce for other fields? Give up teaching and go into journalism, as some urged, or go abroad to devote myself to philology, or turn to politics? In the end, and to the end of life, I continually worked in all of these fields. "It is safe to say," writes one who knew me well, "that no Negro held the place [Scarborough] did, for he gained lasting recognition in all these," and, as another said [about me,] "[he] worked untiringly using every inch of his strength and life."

Philology and Politics

With the success of my book other recognition began to flow in upon me, the young teacher. My Alma Mater bestowed upon me the degree of M.A. and Liberia College gave me that of LL.D.[1] This last I appreciated as coming spontaneously from my own race. Then in July 1882 came the first great honor. At the meeting at Harvard University of the American Philological Association which elected me to membership in that body of scholars.[2]

Professor [Richard T.] Greener at once wrote me, "It was unanimous[————]I see that the newspapers are noticing it. It is a well merited compliment. You and Blyden are in on merit.[3] The rest of us are 'honoraries.' Let us be discreet."

This honor was the signal for me to begin research work that I might prepare a worthy paper to present before this body. Circumstances conspired to delay this presentation for two years. The illness and death of my father [from June to October 1883] took me twice to the South bringing me added obligations as well as consuming my time and causing me much concern. There was also the lack of material for research. The University Library afforded none, and I was distant from large libraries. I learned that some of the works desired were not even available in this country.

Fortunately, I had in 1880 made the acquaintance of an English man of letters, Mr. W.E.A. Axon of Manchester, England.[4] He was a man of rare ability and of distinction as an antiquarian and a classicist, who was also one of the editors of the *Manchester Guardian*. This acquaintance had come through two English ladies, the Misses Impey of Surrey, who were then editing the *Anti-Caste* leaflets, which were devoted to the interests of the colored races.[5] They had visited the United States, and had learned of the Greek book and other works and they had told Mr. Axon of it. He at once introduced himself to me, the author, by letter which led not only to correspondence growing out of mutual love for the classics, a correspondence both interesting and valuable, but to a life long friendship. [Axon] never flagged in interest and helpfulness for one whom he seemed to consider a protégé as well as a friend.

To him I turned for advice and assistance in procuring certain necessary works, especially *Das Verbum* which I deemed most needful.[6] Mr. Axon at once put me in the way of possessing it. This valuable assistance made it possible for me to make satisfactory preparation of my first philological paper on "The Theory and Function of the Thematic Vowel in the Greek Verb."[7]

In the meantime I was elected to membership in the Modern Language Association and to the American Spelling Reform Association.[8] I was also made a member of the American and Foreign Anti-Slavery Society. Thereafter, my philological and literary efforts touched all these fields, as contact aroused my interest, and circumstances brought to my notice points to which I was able and proud to contribute my bits of knowledge.

The research work now undertaken which was to launch me well upon a philological career became most fascinating, as I put forth every effort to make a creditable showing at my first meeting with the Philological Association in July 1884 at Dartmouth College.[9] My finished paper was submitted in advance to Prof. Charles Lanman of Harvard.[10] It brought in reply this most cordial letter: "I am glad to present your paper to the executive committee and glad you will be present to make the personal acquaintance of the members whose interests are one with yours."

It was such a momentous occasion to me. I went to Hanover, N.H. where Dartmouth College is located with a party of [well-known] professors, leaving Cambridge in a special car. Among this number were Professors Goodwin (President of the Association), W. D. Whitney, T. D. Seymour, Tracy Peck, J. H. Wright, Charles Lanman, and R. C. Jebb, the noted Greek scholar from Glasgow University, Scotland, who had just delivered the Commencement address at Harvard.[11] On my arrival I found myself made the guest of Professor Parker at his beautiful home, together with Professors Whitney, Seymour, and Peck. The receipt of my paper was all I could have desired. I was highly congratulated on it, especially by Professor Jebb. Professor E. G. Sihler of Columbia University at a later meeting told me that [Jebb] made [an] enthusiastic mention of it as he recalled the meeting.[12]

All this was very pleasing to me, as were two other incidents connected with this meeting. One of the students called me to his room to see his library. To my surprise and gratification he handed me my own Greek book, saying he had studied it with pleasure and profit at Kimball Union Academy.[13] Two similar incidents came into my life later, which I may as well mention here. Leaving New York one day for Philadelphia as I took the parlor car in Jersey City, a young white man of fine appearance hurried into my car asking if I were Professor Scarborough. He said that while standing in the station he had heard my name mentioned and as he had studied my Greek text book he wished to meet and shake hands with me, and to congratulate me on the preparation of such a book fitted alike for all students, white and black. The other incident took place when I was in a church conference in Wheeling, W. Va., presided over by our Bishop Derrick.[14] A white clergyman of the Presbyterian Church was called upon to address the conference. He made an enthusiastic speech, saying in the courses of his remarks that he had studied a Greek book written by a colored man. His statement brought continued applause as Bishop Derrick with pride called me forward and said, "Here is the author."

The crowning occasion of this Dartmouth meeting was the reception given the Association by Mr. Hiram Hitchcock, part owner of the Fifth Avenue Hotel, New York City, at his magnificent summer home.[15] Professor Parker's daughter, just graduated from Bradford Academy—a most gracious lady who did the honors of his home—constituted herself my escort to this [event] and every care was taken that I should receive every courtesy.[16] The occasion gave me acquaintance of the host who invited me to stop at his hotel whenever in New York. Of this invitation I availed myself ever after when in that city until it was finally closed. I was always warmly received although some Southerners at times showed their objection to my presence. I felt myself and my race honored by being thus made welcome at this historic hotel where leading Republican statesmen [have] so long gathered in the "Amen Corner" to discuss national and international affairs.

This meeting was closed by a trip over Lake Memphremagog in Canada.[17] It had opened to me a new world of thought and endeavor. There I began lasting friendships with men high in university circles, who ever after made me feel that I was one of their number and who gave courteous attention with no hint of prejudice. I profited by their knowledge [and] research, and gained inspiration to take back to my own college for the benefit of my students. I was fired by this contact to delve deeper into the work I desired to accomplish. It was a liberal education in itself to be associated with such men.

At this point it is well to relate [my feelings in regard] to Professor Greener's and my own hopes that Negro youth would not be led to abandon these channels of culture. At the time of my election to the Philological Association, only two other men of color had received its recognition, Dr. E.W. Blyden, known as the African scholar and linguist (1880) and Professor

83

R. T. Greener (1881).[18] Now (1920) I can find but four more of our race group who have become members. They were: Prof. William Bulkley (1895), Prof. L. B. Moore (1896), Prof. John Gilbert (1897), and Professor Crogman (1898).[19] As far as I can ascertain not one, except Doctor Blyden and myself ever presented a paper before the Association.[20]

This is to be regretted. They have missed much in opportunity to bring race recognition. I feel sure that one would in time have done so had he lived. This one was young John Gilbert a graduate of Brown University who had secured opportunity to study in Greece, and had very scholarly ambitions. He wrote me in 1892 expressing a strong desire to meet me saying, "I am trying to walk in your footsteps by making myself, like you, an eminent Greek scholar."[21] He did attend one of the meetings later on.

I see now, as the controversy grows concerning the classics, no young colored men of the immediate present who are even meditating on special classical study. It is a great mistake, as the race will find out, to leave this field to others with the breadth and culture obtainable in it. This is to say nothing of the opportunity to serve the race especially in the field of African linguistics.

About this time I formed connection with a rising newspaper man of the race, Harry C. Smith who had established the *Cleveland Gazette*.[22] He was and still is an uncompromising defender of the race and its rights. For some time I and Mrs. Scarborough wrote editorials for his paper as he was beginning and struggling to gain a firm foothold in the newspaper world. He later became a member of the Ohio Legislature and the author of a strong Civil Rights Bill for the protection of our people.

The next year became an eventful one for me as it decided the question of change for me as well as led me more directly into active political life. I was still considering finding another field of labor, debating the acceptance of the invitation by authorities to take a principalship in the public schools of Brooklyn, N. Y.

[There was] a rapidly growing desire of the A.M.E. Church at this time for greater opportunity for literary expression. One form [that this desire] took was the establishment by the General Conference of the A.M.E. Church in May of a literary magazine, the *A.M.E. Church Review*. Dr. B. T. Tanner, then editor of the *Christian Recorder*, the leading organ of the church, was elected to the editorship.[23] The vacancy thus created was filled by the election of President B. F. Lee of our university to the editorship of the *Recorder*. This in turn created a vacancy in the university presidency. To this the able Dr. John G. Mitchell was at once elected president, but circum-

stances caused him at once to refuse this position. It was filled by the election of his brother, and early graduate of the university—Prof. S.T. Mitchell,
then head of a public school in Springfield, Ohio, and a man of ability and
energy.[24] He was the first layman to receive such an appointment, but he
at once entered the ministerial ranks by ordination, thus preserving what
was then an inviolable tradition.

Urged by friends including the newly created president and the
enthusiastic magazine editor, all of whom were loath to lose my services
to the university to which my rising prominence was giving much prestige, and possibly losing me from the church altogether, I weighed carefully the new situation created by these changes.

I was in a sense somewhat anchored at the school. I had purchased
a few acres of land nearby, erected a barn for horse and carriage, and had
contemplated building a home as soon as financially able. I was closely
attached to my students, and [I was] now entering upon new classes [which]
were a stimulation to my philological studies. There seemed to be promised a new literary outlet with some added financial resources, when Doctor
Tanner [sought] my aid in assisting [the] launch [of] his new periodical
by an article on the Greek in the New Testament.[25] I was to participate in
his opening literary symposium on race problems arising from recent
Democratic victories. It included such prominent men of color as Frederick
Douglass, B. K. Bruce, R. T. Greener, Ex-Governor Pinchback with others.[26] And I was not ungrateful for the church recognition [that my] staunch
friend had secured by making me a delegate to the coming Methodist
Centennial in December.

There was still another very deciding influence. I must confess
[that] the coming political campaign weighed heavily in my reaching a
decision. The restlessness of the entire race incident upon recent Southern
massacres taken together with those recent Democratic victories and the
disturbing supineness in some Republican quarters, were seriously threatening division of the Negro vote. [This was the] concerted endeavor being
made by certain politicians of the race, some of whom were already in the
Democratic camp. This endeavor aimed at abandonment of the Republican
party, alliance with the Democratic party, or the formation of a new independent party. As Foraker says in his book: "The Negro vote was so large
that it was not only an important but an essential factor in [the] Republican
party to carry the state if that vote was arrayed against it."[27] The Negro
press in the state was aggressively opposed to [Foraker's] re-nomination in
1851 because of the many ugly stories circulated.

I had been more or less actively engaged in Ohio politics since 1879 when I took part in forwarding the candidacy of Hon. Alphonso Taft for governor.[28] As an uncompromising Republican I was ready to take part in the conflict for the party's success which I deemed necessary to us as a people. I yielded now to the wishes of my friends and [having decided] to remain in Ohio, [I] was re-nominated in June to my position as head of Classical Department.

I had already stepped into the political arena in the preceding spring. Because of the political situation I had heartily endorsed an inter-state convention of leading colored men to be held in Pittsburgh in April. I believed that times and conditions demanded action on our part. If we should sit and look idly on, while our rights are being trampled under foot, our liberty placed in jeopardy, and our brethren in the South butchered like cattle, we shall prove unworthy of the name of citizens.

Before this convention I delivered an address on "Our Political Status" in which I said: "Justice is trampled under foot, in the face of the stern fact that the National safety lies in National Justice, and that no government is safe that permits such outrages to escape punishment." I spoke of the "heroism of the race at Fort Wagner, Milliken's Bend, Port Hudson, Fort Pillow, and other places when the country's interests were at stake," and declared the race's attitude as follows:[29]

"All the Negro wants, gentlemen, is a chance. It is not that he desires greater favors than other people. It is not that he is never satisfied, and will always be a disturbing element in Church and State. It is not that he does not appreciate blessings already received, and is not grateful to those by whom they were bestowed. It is that he desires to be protected in the enjoyment of natural rights, whether civil or political, which God has given to every citizen, whether black or white."

While I questioned what should be done to change the political status, I cautioned that "we cannot afford to be rash or indiscreet in any conclusions we may come to. It is easier to avoid mistakes than it is to correct them after they are made."

Reviewing the history of both Democratic and Republican parties, I argued that though some were clamoring to ally the race to the Democratic party with a Democratic victory, "the colored citizen had more to lose than any other class of individuals" [and] that it would be as great a folly to support an Independent party, as to stand aloof from the two existing ones which would give advantage to the Democrats. I argued that white men "might divide on all measures, local and national, but colored men for the present at least, were narrowed down to civil and political rights—protection before the law. Until these rights are fully assured, all other questions among us, as it seems to me, must of necessity be subordinate."

I concluded that though there was much to be regretted in the supine attitude of conciliation of the Republican party, the Democratic party should not be supported nor the Republican abandoned. [A]fter all, all that has been done for the Negro has been done by the Republican party.

Furthermore the emancipation act brought upon the party new duties and responsibilities and established new relations between man and man. Therefore it is the duty of this great party with which we have acted so long, to see to it that no unjust distinctions be made in favor of one class at the expense of another.

I called upon the race to present a united front and advised that a petition, full and comprehensive, expressive of our grievances and with our desires explicitly stated as to protection and recognition, be submitted to the Republican Convention [scheduled to meet] in Chicago, June 3rd. I added: "We ask that such laws be enacted as shall secure to every citizen of the country, regardless of race or color, the full enjoyment of every civil and political right accorded to the most favored, and that all statute laws discriminating against us as a people, be repealed."

I scorned the prejudice that could not rise above infamous color-line as a disgrace to the American people. I put myself on record as favoring mixed schools, mixed churches, and mixed everything else that will tend to wipe out these invidious distinctions, and will enable one to live without always thinking about his color, whether he is white or black.

The speech was put in pamphlet form and widely distributed.[30] It was commended by the press as a "ringing logical appeal for the rights of the race" and "a wise counsel at this momentous time, bound to have no inconsiderable influence in the coming election in bringing about a more perfect unity among us and a closer understanding in aiding us to bettering our political status."

Going further into the national contest I must say that it was an exciting convention in Chicago that June. I knew much of its inside workings. The Negro's strength was recognized at once by the making of Hon. John R. Lynch, a colored man of national prominence from Mississippi, temporary chairman over Senator Powell Clayton, white, of Arkansas.[31] This aroused bad feelings, and led to further dissatisfaction in the Republican ranks. But I wish to give here my testimony to Governor

Foraker's loyalty to Sherman then and thereafter.[32] He nominated Sherman in a splendid speech and stood by him as he did in a later contest.

As to the outcome and my own political preference, I stood for John Sherman because he had played such a noble part in seeking to ascertain the causes of the fiendish Southern acts against the race, and I felt with others that he had done enough for the nation to deserve the nomination but I early recognized the opposition when my article favoring his nomination was declined by the *Chicago Tribune* with the following reason: "I consider John Sherman the very man whose nomination would place the Republicans on the defensive and keep them there until the election was over."

This was emphasized in a letter from Whitelaw Reid of the *New York Tribune* who wrote me after the election of Cleveland and who had considered Blaine "our best candidate and had no sort of doubt that he would have been elected by a handsome majority, but for the Burchard Incident.[33] I should have been perfectly satisfied, however, with Sherman as a candidate, but would have expected a harder contest for him in New York than we had with Blaine." With Blaine nominated, I did all that I could to elect him and received a cordial letter of thanks for my "good service" after his defeat.

[The] Republican differences which had resulted in the Democratic success in the state campaign of 1883 had brought Governor Hoadly to the gubernatorial chair of Ohio.[34] I had worked whole heartedly for [J. B.] Foraker's nomination, but if we could not have Foraker for Republican governor no better choice could have been made than that of Governor Hoadly, as he was a strong anti-slavery man, who was noted for his friendship for the colored race.

When the campaign of 1885 was entered upon in the state, our rights as a people, demanding free ballot and fair count, became a leading plank in the Republican platform. The outrages against us, not only in the South, but in the North as well, were preventing our free use of the ballot.[35] [This came up during] the candidacy of [J. B.] Foraker again for governor of Ohio. That June he spoke at our university shortly after nomination.

Foraker made it an occasion to explain clearly and to deny the libelous statements as to his attitude toward the race and to prove his loyalty to its interests. In that speech he also protested against limiting the race to utilitarian studies and claimed, as I have always done, "nothing was so well calculated to strengthen the mind and give one the power of analysis and logical arrangement of thought and argument as a study of the ancient languages." He was elected and took his seat in 1886, a fortunate thing for the race in the events closely following. Still I am sure had Governor Hoadly been in the chair we would have had similar support in what followed.

The Pittsburgh speech had at once made me felt in political circles. I had "come to the front" to be recognized as a press item said, "as a fearless leader of party and race, ready to do battle for either." During the two years following the Pittsburgh speech I had my hands full for there arose matters that called for time, attention, and influence of every friend of the race and of the university. So I donned my armor with other leading men of color in Ohio in the attempt to wipe out the infamous "Black Laws" from its statute books, thereby mixing schools, putting an end to discrimination in educational lines, and "freeing us from other unjust and humiliating distinctions."

Bishop B. W. Arnett, whose home was at Wilberforce, had now been elected to the House of Representatives in the Ohio Legislature.[36] There was now prepared and he put before the legislature what was called the Ely-Arnett Bill to rid Ohio of the "Black Laws." Doctor Arnett was a powerful speaker and worker, himself, and with Senator Ely and the united efforts of the race and white friends everywhere, we labored to create sentiment favorable to its passage. [W]ith the unwavering support of determined friends in the House and Senate, and lastly with the strong influence of Governor Foraker, the severely contested fight went on to a victorious finish.

Ohio had redeemed itself. Its fair name was now relieved of the blot that had so long disgraced it. Though recurring efforts of Ku Kluxism in after years sought several times to re-enact some of these features, these were always promptly and sturdily repudiated.

The night of the 16th of February, 1887 witnessed an immense Jubilee Meeting in the "Wigwam" at Springfield, Ohio in celebration of the event. It was participated in by distinguished speakers of both races. Among these I recall especially Gen. J. Warren Keifer, Senators Ely and Pringle, Hon. B. W. Arnett, Rev. James Poindexter, Mr. C. M. Nichols of the *Springfield Republic*, Gen. Asa S. Bushnell, Mayor Goodwin, T. F. McGrew, Esq., Rev. G. W. Zeigler, Rev. W. H. Warren, J. K. Mower, Esq., James Buford, and my humble self.[37]

I wish I had the power to reproduce the rejoicing enthusiasm, the ringing eloquence, and the deep sincerity of the occasion. Our own Arnett and Poindexter rose to most eloquent heights as they congratulated their fellows upon this triumph at last of "justice long delayed." I shall carry to my grave not only pride in this great achievement but also the memory of that brilliant scene, equaled to me by but one other, that memorable meeting in Macon when a boy, I sat perched in a window and heard given to my people the declaration of our new rights under freedom. We had gone a wonderfully long way upwards in a little more than two decades. Not content with this mass meeting of thanksgiving, I with twenty others signed a call for another equally great celebration which took place March 16th in the City Hall of Columbus, making it a general jubilee over this grand triumph of the principles of freedom.[38]

Philology and Other Literary Work

The abolition of the "Black Laws" was not the only piece of legislation of importance to the race in the state.[1] There was one other having to do with the growth of the university itself. The school had progressed under its new president, but this very progress had increased financial burdens with no adequate increase of resources. These had always been small. Now, looking about for larger means President Mitchell found possibilities in the Morrill Act by which Congress had allotted certain funds to colleges carrying on agricultural work.[2] He prepared a long and strong argument and petition for presentation to the State Legislature, begging a share in this fund. Ohio State University was already doing agricultural work and was desirous of obtaining the fund. The authorities of the two institutions took counsel together and succeeded in effecting a compromise, whereby the [Ohio] State University might receive the fund and the state would establish and sustain a department at Wilberforce, where agricultural and industrial work should be carried on in conjunction with that of teacher training.

Despite the fight over the "Black Laws," this measure creating what was to be known as the Combined Normal and Industrial Department [C. N. & I.] at Wilberforce University was passed by the Legislature with but little serious opposition. Governor Foraker staunchly upheld it and appointed a strong board of trustees on the part of the state seeking from the first as he said, "a mixed board that would work harmoniously to bring about the best results." He made Mr. J. A. Howells, editor of the *Ashtabula Sentinel* and brother of William Dean Howells, the author, together with his close friend and a race helper, Dr. R. McMurdy, its first Republican trustees, and as its first Democratic one, Senator O'Neill who had worked zealously for both race measures in the legislature.[3]

An adjoining farm was at once purchased and the first hall erected was named O'Neill Hall, as a deserving tribute to Senator O'Neill. This new arm of the university opened its work in September 1887 and grew rapidly into a strong one under this new law. This agreement now called for the transfer of the Normal Department of Wilberforce University to

state control and support. It afforded financial relief and assurance of continuance of the growth already made and insured enlarged facilities. This
transfer also included the principal of the department, Mrs. Scarborough,
who was destined to remain with it as such until 1914, at which time its
expansion and added labors led her to resign the principalship for less arduous duties in a professorship of History of Education and of Principles of
Teaching. In this she continued until 1921 when she resigned, after serving in this state educational work for thirty-four years making a total of
service to the university and race of forty-four years.

While these legislative measures were being considered, an opportunity seemed to present itself to me for the change I still felt desirable.
Early in 1885 I was urged by friends to apply for the Professorship of Greek
at Howard University, Washington, D.C., the school for the race supported
by the government. A vacancy had been caused by the death of Professor
Wiley Lane and it was greatly desired that another man of color should
succeed him.[4]

A trustee wrote me: "Can you be named as a candidate? Give all
definite information about yourself for the ear of one or two of the trustees.
I may state frankly that it may require [a considerable effort] to succeed
Professor Lane with another colored man. Of two other possible men, neither is a communicant of any church, a fact which might tell against them
in a contest. But putting these things aside, I have no hesitation whatever
in considering you not only the most available candidate, but the strongest
one for the place. I have no doubt that your old professors at Atlanta and
Oberlin might exert some influence with such of the trustees as are of the
Congregational denomination and likely to be swayed by the American
Missionary Association."[5]

I thought it over and decided to apply. My requests for recommendations brought promptly strong letters from President E. T. Ware of
Atlanta, President J. H. Fairchild of Oberlin, and Professor Judson Smith.[6]
But in the end he was right, it was a fight.[7] Professor Smith "changed his
mind" and President Fairchild felt it necessary to explain by a lengthy letter to me his change of vote in which he said, "You will understand I did
not know when I wrote you that K—— was an applicant." K—— was his
son-in-law.[8]

Professor Greener wrote me how the vote stood, adding, "I think
had T—— been more energetic you might have got the place, but I suppose in truth they naturally don't care to lose you at Wilberforce. I can't
blame them however much I regret our loss."[9]

All this is significant in view of late[r] developments and shows the trend of feeling existing even then as to the manning of Howard University. In fact an earlier letter from another trustee had claimed that Howard had "started wrong and will not fulfill its mission and I do not think the time is so far distant before we capture the institution." Since then the time has been slowly approaching when right, justice, and expediency are being recognized in allowing the race to conduct its own educational experiments, though I deprecate the segregation that seems perforce to attend the movement.

I (for some reason) seemed fated to continue work where I was. I submitted and plunged anew into classical and philological studies while at the same time I continued political work as the previous chapter shows. But as I had often said, I looked upon politics not as my vocation, but as a pleasurable avocation—a change necessary to me. So though these years saw much political activity on my part, I neglected neither literary nor classroom work. Busy as ever I was scarcely done with a bit in one line before [being] employed in another.

With the avenue to Howard closed, I began a new literary venture suggested by my classroom work and busied myself in spare moments with the preparation of a book of *Questions on Latin Grammar*. This proved to be a somewhat superfluous task as I found in sending it to the publisher that a similar work had just been issued by Professor Comstock.[10] He advised that there might be little profit. [B]ecause of this I gave up its publication, not feeling financially able to stand any loss. Still it was not lost time and labor altogether as it helped on philological study. In the meantime I had prepared my paper, "Fatalism in Homer and Virgil" and presented it at Yale University in July (1885).[11]

At Yale I renewed my acquaintance with Dr. William Hayes Ward recently returned from the Wolfe Babylonian Expedition.[12] I little thought then, that I should come to know him well as a valuable friend as years passed, both by becoming a contractor to his paper, the *Independent,* and by entertaining him in my Wilberforce home. As President of Wilberforce University I had invited him to deliver an address to our Literary Societies at a Commencement not long before his death.

Here I also began my acquaintance with Professor Harrison of Washington and Lee University, Virginia.[13] Professor Harrison had just returned from Germany where he had translated into that language the results of his study of provincial speech common in America, and especially of the Negro dialect in North Carolina, analyzing, classifying, and, as far as possible tracing its origins. We were sitting in Sloane Library. I had inadvertently dropped my pencil. He hastened to recover and return it to me courteously. Then as I thanked him, he eagerly asked whether I agreed with the opinions expressed by him and whether he had said anything offensive in reference to the forms of speech attributed to the Negro. I replied to the latter question saying there should be no offense taken at results arrived by research, but as to agreement with these results, I would answer better could I have the opportunity to read the paper carefully.

He replied he would be glad to send me the manuscript (over 100 pages) for perusal and retention. I have it still and consider it a remarkably valuable piece of research, for which I thanked and congratulated him reserving my opinion until I had time to review it. Later I had to point out that parts of the forms of this Southern dialect that he had concluded coming from Negro sources, were not Negro at all, but they had crept into speech through other sources, from Spanish and French, while many had passed through so many mouths that it was impossible to state their origin.

He was pleased to accept the truth of my criticism, and thus began a friendly and helpful correspondence that continued up to his death. He invariably sent me his later efforts asking my opinion. A further perusal of these papers led me to give some close attention to dialect forms, especially after I soon became a member of the American Dialect Society, where I made good use of this study in several papers and magazine articles.[14]

The social function of this Yale meeting was a trip on [Long Island] Sound of which I retained a most kindly remembrance of Professor Whitney's assiduous attention to me, striving as he always did to see that I was not overlooked in anyway.[15]

These seeming small things in a gathering like this have been a great pleasure. They have led me to feel that though color may and does have a power to hamper and bring embarrassments at times, yet with men of letters, men of great learning, whether Americans or not, are men of little or no prejudice. In fact, I received from my entrance into this philological society whole-hearted acceptance shown from the first, honoring me with immediate appointment with Professors Whitney and Richardson on the committee of nomination of officers for '85 and '86.[16] Only a man of my race can understand what all this fellowship and these amenities meant to me.

I recall to mind certain members whom I found especially helpful and delightful associates. Professor Whitney remained ever a true and loyal friend always taking the kindliest interest in all I did and eager to share his interests with me. He sent me his frequent articles, and especially those pertaining to his controversies with Prof. Max Müller whom he criticized with unhesitating severity.[17] He would ask my opinion of the stand taken by himself. There were times when he took me into his confidence relating to the antagonism existing between the German philologist and himself. Both were splendid scholars and I, as in the case of my political friends, greatly regretted [that] their different views had brought about such feeling as existed between them.

Professor March of Lafayette was another fine scholar and good friend.[18] He and Professor Whitney were intensely interested in spelling reform. He was head of publication of the *Murray's Dictionary* in London, I think, and frequently asked me to contribute and to offer suggestion in changes of forms of words.[19] So I may be pardoned if I think I may possibly have had to do with that publication. In fact, these and other broad-minded scholars including Prof. C.P.G. Scott, a pupil of Professor March, always tried to show me that they recognized what I had done and the standing accorded me in the world of philology.[20]

As both Professor Whitney and Professor March were strict advocates of phonetic spelling as was also Dr. William Hayes Ward, they invited me to join the Spelling Reform Association.[21] Later I did so saying, "I did believe that some reforms in our spelling were necessary," but I was not as radical as they. However, I agreed with Doctor Scott and others that an extreme position on the subject would be detrimental to the understanding of the origin of many words that had important etymological relations. I wrote some articles for educational journals expressing my views. Doctor Ward carried out in his paper—the *Independent*—his convictions following certain rules adopted by the Spelling Reform Association.

The Yale meeting inspired me now to greater efforts. I busied myself at leisure moments the following year in preparing for presentation at Cornell University in July, 1886, my most ambitious piece of work up to that time. This was *The Birds of Aristophanes*.[22] This was suggested by papers previously presented on the Greek [Old Comedy].

My aim was to arrive, if possible, at the author's meaning in the *Birds*. There have been various interpretations, but my thought was that it had political significance more than anything else. I so discussed it, [but] to do this required much study and research both as to times and conditions in the preceding age and the one subsequent to its production. The discussion in German on the subject by Süvern was obtained, and my wife and I spent many pleasant hours in its translation for the purpose that I might gather fully his position on it, and I credit to this author some of the views I adopted.[23] The following year I enlarged it and a company in Boston published it as a monograph.[24] This booklet, though not designed for school purposes, was used in some schools and extracts were taken from it by educators in this country and abroad.

Again my effort was heartily received with much commendation. One of the most highly valued was from Dr. A. M. Elliott, Professor of Romance Languages in John[s] Hopkins University, who had proposed me for membership in the Modern Language Association.[25] He wrote me thanking me for a copy, and said it interested him greatly adding, "We need more scholarship of this kind in the United States. You scored a good point it seems to me." Well, that was "praise from Herbert" indeed. Some years later I learned that the *Birds* had been highly spoken of in a German periodical with no reference made to my race connection.

I remember the social features of this Cornell meeting as a banquet and an excursion down Cayuga Lake to the noted college for women— Wells College—where a reception was given.[26] [There] we learned that Mrs. Cleveland was one of its graduates, in which fact the authorities took great pride, showing us her room, but [this] did not appeal to one professor, who observed in contemptuous undertone, "What interest have we in her room?"

It was at this time [that] I was again strongly urged by philological friends to go to Greece and take up work in the School of Classical Studies at Athens.[27] I was told again some means might be obtained to assist me. This had been an early dream. Sadly, again I was forced to give it up as my meager salary and family obligations would not warrant it, so I abandoned the thought and I never went.

About this time Rev. W. J. Simmons called for my aid in preparing biographies for his race book *Men of Mark*.[28] This was soon followed by a call from Dr. Garland Penn who begged assistance in a volume he was producing.[29] To all these I gave a helping hand in preparing the desired work, encouraging as always every such indication in the race of literary progress.

The summer of 1887 found me at the University of Vermont in Burlington where I presented two papers before the Philological Association, one on "Grote's Interpretation of Anelpistoi (VI. 17)," the other on "'Ancipiti' in Caesar (*B.G.* I. 26)," both of which were later enlarged and published in the Boston *Journal of Education*.[30]

I was then thinking seriously of substituting some other work in my Greek class for the *Anabasis,* and chose Andocides, which I further intended to edit for that purpose. There was no American edition as far as I knew, [and] the one I used in my classes was by a European author.[31]

I wrote for the *Journal of Education* notes concerning this proposed change, which drew from my friend, Doctor Barrows of the *Christian Register* a letter suggesting "Cebes Tablet" rather than Andocides, because of "its ease and its moral lesson," adding, "I would think it an excellent thing to revive it in our schools. It is used in Germany, and has been revived in England.———has edited an edition here."[32] I did not expect ready acquiescence of schools to accept either change, and it is mentioned here to show my alertness in watching public opinion so as to improve classical work for my pupils.

By this time Governor Foraker and I had become great friends. [He was] a friend who grew more staunch with the years, one whose friendship I always prized. He showed this at this time in his intent effort to make me a trustee of Ohio State University upon the resignation of Mr. Peter Clark.[33] "I had fully determined upon it," he wrote that same year, "but there were those who contended the best interests of the university can be served by putting in a representative of agriculture, I am compelled to bow to the interests set forth by ex–President Hayes. The controversy is of such importance that every other consideration must give way to public good, and after investigation I find I must agree." To know, however, that he even thought of me, was an honor.

In Politics and Magazines

With the opening of 1888 I was not only to face rapidly increasing work in literary channels, but to find myself at once prominently put to the front in political circles. On February 15th there was held at Columbus, the first Lincoln Day Banquet of the Ohio Republican League. This league had been organized and promoted by James Boyle (later a secretary to Governor McKinley).[1] These banquets helped much to create political enthusiasm in the state. At no time was there the bored apathy so often seen these later days.

This banquet, first of others to follow annually for some years, was a great occasion. To me it was especially memorable as I was invited to be one of the twelve speakers to respond to toasts. The only man of color on the program, I found myself in most distinguished company. The other speakers were Governor Beaver of Pennsylvania, Governor Luce of Michigan, Senator John Sherman of Ohio, Hon. James P. Foster of New York (President of the Republican League of the United States), Hon. Charles Foster (ex-Governor of Ohio); Murat Halstead (editor of the *Cincinnati Commercial Gazette*), Hon. Benjamin Butterworth, M.C., Hon. Wm. H. West of Bellefontaine, Ohio; General Gibson of Tiffin, Ohio; and W. H. Smiley (editor of the *Tribune* of Warren, Ohio).[2] The speakers were entertained first at dinner by Governor and Mrs. Foraker.[3] Here, I was seated between Senator Sherman and Governor Beaver, and rode to the State House with Sherman.

It is little wonder, that seated by the famous brother of General Sherman, the guns of Atlanta resounded again in my ears, as in the days when my future hung in the balance. Here I was joining hands with the equally famous brother to help my race on to further enfranchisement. I may be pardoned if even now my heart throbs with pride, as I recall the scene as we all stood in the receiving line in the State House and later sat together at the banquet table. In turn I was called to respond to the toast: "Why I am a Republican." I received an ovation of applause and was told

I had acquitted myself with honor. The press also spoke of my "able eloquent response" and "my cogent reasons."

This event seemed to fix my status in the political world. I found myself plunged at once into the center of things. In July I went to Chicago to help again to nominate Sherman for the Presidency. Much has been said and written of this convention and the events that led to the nomination of Benjamin Harrison [instead of Sherman]. I have no place or space to repeat these. They may be found in Governor Foraker's work, *Notes of a Busy Life,* a copy of which he sent me at once on its publication in 1916. It gives a full, logical, authentic account of the facts relating to his connection with Sherman's candidacies. But I must add my testimony, because of my knowledge of inner affairs of that convention, to assert unequivocally again that Governor Foraker, despite all assertions, stood by Sherman loyally and faithfully as long as possible, and he turned to Harrison only when the uselessness of continued support of "Ohio's first choice" was plainly evident. I did the same. It was not treachery on his part that caused Sherman's defeat, as some have claimed unjustly, giving the final vote to Harrison.

But in the words of the *Toledo Blade,* speaking of Sherman's selection from the start: "Yet Governor Foraker, obeying instructions of his state, and indulging in the hope of success, held the Ohio delegates solid for Sherman to the last."[4] He did this in the face of circumstances most discouraging in every particular.

Of Sherman as a man I must say that though many have called him cold and unapproachable, unable to win and hold real friendships, I personally cannot agree with them. I always found him approachable and sympathetic. Whether this was due to his interest in my race which he always showed, I cannot tell. I only assert the fact. He was sensitive and ambitious and I can see how in the passing years, as he saw his presidential ambitions defeated again and again and fade away, he became suspicious. I fancied, however, that after this convention, I saw a perceptible coolness in his friendship for me.

The acuteness of the political situation, however, which was developing much friction, alienation, disaffection, even bitter rancor and hostility in Republican ranks, was such that it called for every possible effort to elect Harrison. To this end it was necessary to hold the Negro vote, which because of disaffection and the fact that it held a balance of power, was a source of anxiety to every Negro Republican who agreed with all that I had said in my Pittsburgh address. At first it was thought that a race convention would be the best way to attain this end, but this plan was abandoned for another seeking to reach the greatest number of voters.

It was in September that I received the following letter from Frederick Douglass:[5]

Cedar Hill
Anacostia, D.C.,
September 8, 1888

My dear Scarborough:
I write you upon the instant of receiving the decision of the National Executive Committee in respect of the Convention. It has been decided that it will not be best to attempt it, but instead they propose sending forth an address to the colored citizens of the United States signed by well known colored citizens. I am asked to prepare the address with such assistance as I may require. I have written the committee assuring it that I am willing to undertake the service, but also asking them to telegraph you at once to come to me at the committee's expense. I do hope you will be able to come. I know of no more among us, whose heart is more in the work than yourself. Hence I want your aid, both in the preparation and promulgation of the address. The National Committee will be at home until September 15th and we shall want at least two days to prepare the address. Come therefore as soon as you possibly can.

Very truly yours,
Frederick Douglass

A five column spirited, urgent—yes, I may say eloquent—appeal was prepared by us, signed by Frederick Douglass, myself representing Ohio, and other prominent Negroes: Robert Smalls, South Carolina; Isaac S. Mullens, Massachusetts; W. H. Johnson, New York; P. B. S. Pinchback, Louisiana; F. L. Barnett, Illinois; I. C. Wears, Pennsylvania; J. W. Cromwell, D.C.; J. M. Townsend, Indiana; John R. Lynch, Mississippi; Perry Carson, D.C.[6] It was widely distributed before election and we were assured that it did much to win Republican votes at the polls in November.[7] I did much personal work in this campaign and was pleased to receive a letter from President Harrison after election, sending me "sincere thanks for your congratulations and the part you played in securing the results of the Chicago Convention."

Recognition of my [growing] political status in Ohio came at once in another way, when I again became one of the speakers at the Second Annual Banquet of the Ohio Republican League held in Columbus, February 12, 1889. Hon. John M. Langston had been placed on the program to respond to the toast, "The Colored Man in Politics," but his presence became doubtful, and I was asked to take his place.

There were some slurring attempts to belittle the occasion and my part in it by some colored politicians who claimed it was only by "accident" that I was asked and on the spur of the moment and spoke of it as a "snub" to others. It was neither accident nor snub. The real situation is shown here by the chairman's letter:

My dear Professor Scarborough,
Mr. Langston, we learn, will be hardly able to reach here. Will you not be prepared to take his place?

Yours truly,
D. J. Ryan[8]

I accepted with the full understanding that I would be a speaker in any case and Langston also, if he should arrive. I spoke and when Langston, who had at the last moment been further delayed by a wreck, wired he would speak, if they would wait for [a] time. They voted to do so and at a late hour he found his audience awaiting him and delivered his address.

It is true as one paper said: "The colored contingent of the Republican State League no more met with the snub than the white contingent. Every Republican in Ohio cannot be expected to speak at a banquet lasting a few hours. We feel sure that the colored Republicans were greatly honored by the addresses of Messrs. Langston and Scarborough as any other representative men of the race."

Now I had no desire to monopolize this honor, and, knowing the feeling, when I was in conversation with several leading men I suggested names of other race men. I recall that at the Seventh Annual Banquet Hon. B. W. Arnett spoke, and Hon. H. C. Smith at a later one in Cincinnati.[9] I do not recall other speakers. Still, in May I was on the program of the Lincoln Banquet held in Chillicothe responding to the toast on Lincoln. In October a request came from Hon. Charles Kurtz, asking me again to substitute for John M. Langston, who "is unexpectedly called from [the] Pomeroy and Ripley appointment Oct. 31 and Nov. 1.[10] May we not announce you as substitute?"

At the close of the year 1888 I received a letter from Bishop B.T. Tanner saying: "George Cable has written me desiring me to name the man whom I suppose best qualified to contribute an article on the 'Negro Question' for one of leading magazines of the country.[11] I scanned the whole field of my acquaintance and at last stopped with you. I suppose you have heard from him by this time." I had, and I soon heard from the *Forum*.[12]

Its editor immediately solicited an article on "The Future of the Negro," saying: "I send you this with copies of the *Forum,* containing different articles by the writers on the 'Negro Question.' I desire that the discussion be continued until something like decisive results be obtained. Of course the views of the Negro race must of right be presented and I am anxious to have them set forth by an acknowledged representative of the Afro-American opinion. Will you not consent to prepare for the *Forum* such an article of 3,800 words on the situation and future of the Negro race in this country[?]" In a later letter I was asked to state my race in the article.

This was only the beginning as requests for articles now were pouring in upon me. *Leslie's Weekly,* Harrison's paper, solicited signed articles and for some years thereafter I contributed to its editorial pages such articles both signed and unsigned.[13] Dr. Joseph Cook asked for a contribution to *Our Day* and John A. Sleicher followed with a request for 2,500 words on "The Dangers of Negro Oppression," desiring "your autograph to be appended" and "a cabinet photograph enclosed to be reproduced."[14] The *New York Tribune* also asked me to write on the "Negro Question," stating my views and opinions, following it soon by a request for an article on "The League Movement." In the March *Forum* of 1889 my article on "The Future of the Negro" appeared, and I received my first check as a magazine contributor.[15] It was another proud and happy moment in my life.

Then B. O. Flower of the *Arena* called for an article on the "Race Question" and suggested that I read Senator Hampton's article in the July number, then review Hampton's and Breckenridge's.[16] "Touch on your views of the practicability of establishing colored colonies in Africa and the government enabling all to go who wished and were dissatisfied, not making it compulsory."

At this time industrial education for our people was being strongly advocated. Under the able leadership of Booker T. Washington, Tuskegee

Industrial Institute was rapidly coming to the front with strong financial backing by leading white philanthropists.[17] The American Academy of Political and Social Science had just published an article on the subject by Washington. It now asked me "as an exponent of the Higher Education for the Negro" to review this article for its pages.[18] I did so and it was received as "very able and fair."

I must say that we stood as advocates of education in these two different channels. The trend of opinion had eagerly turned to this comparatively new idea of disposing of the Negro's preparation for the future and I with others saw the dangers of this over emphasis on industrial training to the exclusion of culture and higher training. For some years it seemed necessary to oppose this strenuously and I did so with voice and pen. The two camps became almost a battle ground that this higher education might not be submerged. However, Doctor Washington and I remained good friends, [who] understood and appreciated each other's work when the danger point seemed passed.

In this same year Ohio was more fully sensing its lack of state normal schools and the State Superintendent asked me to speak on this subject before the Ohio Central Teachers' Association. I had also been asked to present a paper at the Nashville meeting of the National Association of Teachers which I did.

The press said: "The papers showed thoroughness of preparation and acquaintance with the history of the Negro schools of the country that was commendable. The grounds taken were rather more radical and out of line with the paper presented by the preceding speaker. The speaker said

> the solution of the Negro question rests with himself. All his past history proves that the Negro youth is as studious, as able and capable as any. The difficulties of ignorance and superstition have not held him back. Wherever he has entered the list he has held his own. The education of the Negro is the true solution of the Negro question. When he becomes strong and polished he will have no difficulty in holding his place in the world. The Blair bill will do much towards bringing him to the point of success and it should be favored by all who desire the true elevation of the Negro.[19] No better disposition could be made of the surplus. No investment would bring better return. Such Southerners as George W. Cable, Professors Baskervill and Smith will help the onward progress of the cause.[20] The Negro should demand as his right that every city, town, and hamlet in the land where the Negro lives should give equal facilities in schools and every other convenience to the Negro that is accorded to the white. The Negro must demand recognition for these things and strive to maintain the vantage ground he now holds.

Soon after this I received a letter from Dr. Selim Peabody of the University of Illinois, who presided over the session and who wrote:"I was much pleased with your paper and the discussion that followed.[21] I earnestly desire the advance and prosperity of your people. I believe the young men of ability and character must be the chief reliance in such movements and I trust that while waiting for the movements which must necessarily only be gradual to be enduring, [that] they may never lose courage and hope." My reception in this part of the South was a cordial one and reporters were kindly disposed, though one nearly caused my identity to be lost by writing of me as "J. H. Scarborough."

My political and magazine articles had launched me before the public as a leading representative of the race, an upholder of its higher education and its rights. It was beginning to become the day of free speech from the Negro, when his rise and influence were foreseen and when wise ones saw the need and the right to give him a hearing.

Immediately after the publication of my *Arena* and *Forum* articles I began to be the target, too, for any one who disagreed with my views and expressions. I expected this from the South which I did not try to placate and was not disappointed. I received many letters, vituperative, abusive, and insulting, because of my utterances. But very few of these were signed. One, especially, which followed a *Frank Leslie* editorial I wrote, was sent to me by the editor, who hotly characterized the author a "brute" because of its foul language and offensive epithets, "too foul to print."[22]

But to offset such, I received many others agreeing with my statements, my views, and strongly sympathizing with the situation and myself personally on account of personal treatment received by me at various times. One such from Mr. Foraker of my own nearby city—Xenia, Ohio— expressed especial indignation that I whom he knew so well "as a gentleman and a scholar" should be subjected to such indignities. This was the more pleasing to me, as from the same city at three different times came anonymous letters nearly as abusive as those from the South. I have always wondered who wrote these, whether one who always glared at me on meeting him on the street, was the cowardly writer. The Northern press gave me much praise from which I quote on my *Arena* article on the "Race Question."[23] The Pittsburgh press said:"The paper is a credit to the author and his race—temperate, logical, able. The *Arena* has admitted a leading thinker of the colored race to reply to the leading Southerners." Another paper called it "a clear and earnest study of the subject" and another [said] "he ably argued the cause of his race."

One mention of the article rather amused me. It came from a paper of my native city, Macon, Georgia, the *Macon Telegraph,* the paper which as a boy I had sold to Union troops at close of Civil War. It was headed, "A Macon Negro's Piece," and proceeded in a tone that showed it torn between the Southern desire to attack a Negro and a bit of civic pride that even "a Macon Negro" had written a piece that gained admittance to a prominent magazine in the North.[24]

I had not been able to attend the Philological meeting at Amherst College in 1888. For which meeting, however, I had prepared a paper in "Observations on the Fourth Eclogue in Virgil" which was read for me by Professor Elwell, professor of Greek and Sanskrit at Amherst, and later it was published in *Education.*[25]

Now in July 1889 I went to Lafayette College at Easton, Pennsylvania, and presented the first of a series of "Notes on Andocides" with the desire of profiting by discussion and suggestion in carrying out the hope of future annotation of work of this author, and adapting the German edition to our American schools and colleges.[26] There was no American edition to my knowledge. The one I used in my class was an English one. These discussions were most fruitful as I gained the opinion of the best minds on this author. I found others with intentions similar to my own, but again, [al]though I nearly completed my own, it was doomed to lie in manuscript because of expense attached to publication, especially of a Greek work. At Easton our excursion was to the beautiful Paxinosa Inn in the Pennsylvania mountains, where we were feasted. Here I met again my friend Professor Whitney who ever alert to look after me, called me to sit at the table with himself, Professors Goodwin and Merriam.[27]

This meeting was followed by my first trip to [the] Hampton Institute in Virginia, that other splendid small industrial school for the race.[28] In the meantime I had seen the man to whom I had become closely attached re-elected as Governor of Ohio for the second time, and for whom I had done all possible to insure it by speaking and writing.

Here I mark an ambition that had grown in the last few years along with the latent desire for change that had possessed me through some years. From the time I had heard Professor Harrison's paper in 1885 this ambition had begun to form in my mind. I desired to study the colored situation in Hayti, its language and folk-lore, a rich field for the philologist, I deemed it. My political connection, too, had now become such that I felt encouraged to make application for the position of Minister to Hayti.[29] In this I was backed by many friends both in political and literary circles.

Governor Foraker espoused my cause most warmly—no stronger plea could have been made, where he said of me to Hon. Benj. Harrison, President-Elect:

The enclosed biographical sketch will advise you that Professor Scarborough is a self-made, highly educated, and cultivated educator and writer. He desires to be appointed Minister to Hayti. I take great pleasure in commending him to your favorable consideration as a gentleman in every way, worthy and well qualified to fittingly represent our government in that office. He was born a slave, got his education through his exertions, and has made for him-self, although yet a young man a national reputation among the scholars of the country as one of the most scholarly of them all. But he is more than a scholar. He is a man of broad comprehension and good practical executive ability. He has been an unswerving and able advocate and defender of Republicanism all his life. I do not know of any one in all the land who can possibly present better claims for this recognition than Professor Scar-borough. His appointment would give great pleasure to the colored people of the nation, and to all our people generally. I earnestly appeal to you to make this appointment if you can possibly find it consistent with your views to do so.

The governor followed this letter with another to the Hon. James G. Blaine, then Secretary of State, saying:[30]

Professor Scarborough is one of the best representatives of his race in point of ability and character that I have ever known. He is the author of several text books that have received the highest commendation. He stands, in short, in the very front rank of educators, whether of his own or our race. I do not know of any one who would more intelligently or worthily represent our government in the mission to which he aspires. His appointment would not only secure a good representative of our government, but also it would be a just recognition of the active, zealous, working and fighting Republicans of our state.

Frederick Douglass had returned from Hayti after having served as minister there for two years. His work had fully deserved the appoint-ment. Now I felt I might have a chance, as I had strong backing from Ohio Representatives and Senators and other men of prominence. There were of course other aspirants. Mr. John Durham of Philadelphia [was] one.[31] I called upon Mr. John Wannamaker to ask his support not knowing the Wannamaker interests were backing Mr. Durham.[32] Mr. Wannamaker greeted me cordially, [and] said [that he] knew me well by reputation, but was surprised to see I was so youthful in looks at least. We talked for some time. He spoke of what I was accomplishing for my people, and suggested that "political preferment of that kind meant but little to one who had the opportunities to educate his people and influence the young for good" that I had. Others advised me along the same line, and as always there were geographical as well as political complications. It ended by Mr. Durham receiving the appointment.

Hon. Charles Foster, who was Secretary of Treasury under President Harrison, had taken an interest in me and by his suggestion I had the offer of the Liberian Mission or the Consul-Generalship at Santo Domingo, but I declined to accept these as they did not offer me the literary inducements that Hayti did.

Bishop Tanner who had strongly upheld my claim in his paper wrote me, "you have some barking at your heels. I am sure you would have obtained it, but the foes were largely of your own household," referring to local aspirants.[33] I expected it and saw my first political ambition fail. Providence evidently had a hand in the whole movement, and I have rejoiced since the failure more than I can express in words because it has given me an opportunity to develop in other lines more congenial to my tastes than anything in a political way could do.

One other friend who advised against it was Mr. Robert C. Ogden, Mr. John Wannamaker's partner, whose interested advice I valued highly.[34] He had urged me for sometime to visit [the] Hampton Institute. I had also received a most cordial invitation from Gen. Samuel Armstrong, its warm, true-hearted principal, in which he said, "I want much for you to come and see us. I feel drawn to you."[35] Thereafter I was to be a frequent and welcome visitor to the summer conferences instituted by him to talk with the people, not to them, and by this I was going to form new literary associations and friends which were to be invaluable to me in many ways.

Thereafter, I was to become a steady contributor to the *Hampton Southern Workman* for a long period.[36] Stirred by the interest in folk-lore and reminded of Professor Harrison's paper, I produced for the Hampton Conference "The Negro in Fiction as Portrayer and Portrayed."[37] In this paper I took issue with the Negro dialect used by books then coming from the press on the Negro and articles in magazines by white writers who were beginning to see the literary possibilities in the portrayals of the Negro life and speech.

My political stand for our rights as a people now brought me in close connection not only with Governor Foraker, but with William

McKinley, then in Congress, Hon. Benjamin Butterworth, Generals Grosvenor, Keifer, Gibson, and Kenney. [Included, too, were] Asa Bushnell, later Governor Bushnell, Charles Kurtz, Judson Harmon, in fact with all the leaders and officials of that time, even of both parties.[38] From each and all with rare exceptions, I have been invariably received and treated with utmost courtesy. With many of them I have had through the years not only close political connections, but with some strong personal friendships and most notably with Governor Foraker, for whom I worked heartily and now saw elected to this office. When he lost the third term nomination in 1889, I in a sense went down with this high-spirited leader of men. It was some time after that before I could regain my former enthusiasm in political work.

1890 had seen a Democratic Governor of Ohio elected, after the campaign in which Governor Foraker had as he expresses it "had gone to the well once too often" in what "was not a good year to run." Governor Foraker retired from office entirely. The bad feeling now growing up in Republican ranks and among those with all of whom I had most friendly relations led me to hold myself a little more aloof from politics at the moment, while I gave more attention to literary work.

The year 1890 had kept me equally busy in my varied lines. The Boston *Journal of Education* carried my article on "New Words and Their Uses." *Our Day* published in July my article on "The Political Necessity of a Federal Election Law."[39] In the *Arena* one on "The Race Problem" saw light in October and one on "Lawlessness vs. Lawlessness" in November.[40] The conference in Hampton attended in July brought out my paper read there on "The Negro's Duty to Himself." In March the *Manchester Guardian* (England) of which my friend Axon was an editor, published my "A Negro's Views of the Negro Question."[41]

In July I was chosen to represent my home county, Greene, at the Republican Judicial Convention of the State. Another invitation came to meet the International Congress of Orientalists at Stockholm in September.[42] This was tempting but a European trip was still out of the question. The editor of the *Bibliography of American Methodist Literature* wrote for my biography, [and] my aid in grouping together the works of Methodist publications.

I went to the National Convention of the Y.M.C.A. in Louisville and delivered lectures there and in Frankfort. There was a paper read before the Classical Conference in Washington in February on "Importance of Classical Studies." As the year drew on I was invited to be the orator on

Emancipation Day in September at Clarksburg, West Virginia. There was an address also given before the American Association of Colored Youth in Atlanta [in 1890].

The combined literary work of myself and wife, who for some time had been contributing short stories to *The Youth's Companion, Golden Days,* and other magazines, had led us to feel justified in building a home after ten years of campus life. I had purchased a short time before a few nearby acres in which the wild beauty we saw possibilities heretofore ignored by all except Bishop Brown, who had once had the same desire, but abandoned it, after unsuccessfully burning a brick kiln. He had held to the property and was delighted to have us do what he had desired to accomplish.

We proceeded slowly with this undertaking amid the criticism of confreres on its size and architecture, quite new to that section. However with a new sense of independence gained from increasing channels of work and knowledge of growing back salary due for years, I overlooked all annoyances and I turned with new zest to my work as my wife and I mutually overlooked the home arising in the midst of magnificent oaks and elms. Christmas vacation of 1890 saw us set up our "Lares et Penates"—our household gods, my "Tretton Place," named from the home of "The Scarborough Family" of Anthony Trollope's novel.[43] Here we continued to work and grow as the years passed on.

At this time I received from Mr. Axon his latest book, *William Lloyd Garrison the Liberator,* the first page of which bore his dedication from which I copy a few sentences:[44]

My Dear Scarborough:
I do not know to whom this brief biography of William Lloyd Garrison could be so appropriately dedicated as to you, who so worthily represent in the younger generation the better instincts and higher aspirations of the Negro race. Your own career if you will allow me to say so, is a proof alike of the mental capacity and of the moral power of the Negro race. Freedom, Justice, and Temperance are still watchwords of a host marching to a victory that cannot be prevented or denied. In testimony of your efforts to hasten that day I venture to inscribe your name at the head of this little book.

December 1890
William E. A. Axon

My friends were delighted at this honor, but my foes . . . ! The early months of 1891 ran on into May, when I suddenly encountered a small cyclone of controversy and of unexpected publicity. It came about by an act of my Oberlin classmate, W. H. Tibbals, then a professor in Park College, Missouri.[45] Unknown to me, my name had been presented for admission to the Western Authors and Artists Club in Kansas City, Missouri. A heated debate followed but I was rejected, a few voting for me, some against, and some non-committal. The press east and west made much of the incident, commenting variously.[46] A few are given here. The *Kansas City Star* covered the matter in giving Professor Tibbals' argument in presenting my name.

Professor Tibbals stated that:

> Professor Scarborough was a regular contributor to the *Harper* periodicals, the *Forum, The North American Review, Frank Leslie's Periodicals,* and the *Century* magazine; that Professor Scarborough was a classmate of his at college, had graduated with the highest honors and today [was] the most brilliant alumnus of the class. He was furthermore a member of the American Philological Society, which contains such men as Professors Whitney and Marsh, Doctor Patton, President of Princeton College, and others, and that these men were not ashamed to sit side by side and grasp the hand of a colored man, who was in point of education and brilliancy every bit their equal.[47] Professor Scarborough was the only man of that class who had ever received the degree of LL.D.[48] But with all these facts the gentleman was rejected.

The editorial page of the same paper carried the following:

> It is drawing it mild to say that the action of the club is a great surprise to the public. It shows a narrow spirit not commonly entertained by men and women of letters. The pursuit of literature is supposed to develop the better and kindlier sentiments of human nature, and to cultivate higher ideals of justice. It ought to broaden rather than contract the mind and heart, and that has been its general influence in all ages.
>
> It is well known to the club that Professor Scarborough is a man of distinction in the world of letters. . . . There was no doubt whatever as to his intellectual claims upon the hospitality of the club. He would have been an honor to the organization, and, on the fair simple basis of qualification, would have been esteemed a valuable and desirable member. To exclude him on account of his color was to set up a false distinction, which, happily, is becoming obsolete in this country, but which is strangely at variance with the progressive spirit of the great West. It was a serious blunder which will reflect upon the liberality of the club, and make it the subject of unenviable comment.

The inability to look beneath the exterior of a man and estimate him for his true worth denotes a serious limitation which should not be found in people who are engaged in the work of instructing the public and giving form to popular sentiment. To rule out a man of acknowledged attainments, high character and correct habits on the score of blood was a manifestation of bigotry on the part of the club which can scarcely fail to cripple its influence. It is apparent that it will require a few more shining lights like the elder Dumas—who was a mulatto—to effectually break down the color line in literature.

The *Kansas City Journal* had this to say: "The broad minded secretary (wife of a leading Democrat) was rebuked at the next session for inserting in the minutes the statement 'that the club showed by its action that it desired to be known not so much as an organization of brains, but to establish a white caste and thereby rejected the applicant'. This obnoxious paragraph was ordered stricken out, the press said, as it was 'highly improper to insert an individual's opinion.'"

Some papers called the incident "a scheme to use a prominent Negro to advertise an unknown organization." It remained for the Democratic *Kansas City Times* in an endeavor to be fair, to reveal the true situation as fear of that bug-bear—social equality—when it said:

When a gathering of any kind is more definitely social and ladies participate the line is distinct. To argue about it as an abstract proposition is worth nothing while every human being knows that the condition exists and will change only very slowly. The literary club in question is largely social and two-thirds probably of its members are ladies. Without any notice whatever it was confronted with the dilemma of rejecting a man of admitted literary qualification or of doing without the presence of a considerable proportion of its members at meetings. The vote was closer than a ballot on Professor Scarborough's name would have been at any ordinary gentleman's club, where the reasons for his admission would be stronger.

The controversy raged for some time and several leading Eastern and Western papers congratulated me for my "escape from such a crowd." Tibbals wrote me he did it "to test the club" and added, "it hasn't hurt you, and has given you a lot of publicity. Let it go. But when will the South learn sense?"

But *tempora mutantur* [times change]. A few years later, the oldest club in London, the Society for the Encouragement of Arts, Manufactures, and Commerce, made me a member.[49] Later still the Missouri Classical

Association begged me to accept a membership in it.[50] Nor did this rejection prevent other societies from desiring my membership, however, and in the same month.

In May, I was notified of my election to membership in the Council of the American Society for Extension of University Teaching to represent my University, and was also made a member of the American Sociological Society.[51] My own church had already made me an alternate to the Methodist Ecumenical Conference. It was also in May of that same year that I went to Atlanta to deliver the commencement address at Morris Brown College, one of the church schools, on "The Modern Drift." This young institution was founded in most part through the united efforts of Bishop W. J. Gaines and Bishop H. M. Turner—both, my friends from childhood, and both men of the "old school" of slavery, self made, rugged, powerful leaders always working for race uplift. The latter who had so quizzically praised my Greek book now introduced me "with sincere pride in my young manhood and present success."[52]

In this address I emphasized the need of a skilled brain combined with dexterity of hand, the study of languages as well as practical industry to gain culture and power. The Southern speakers present were pleased to say that no race could stay behind who followed the advice given and they agreed. As one put it, and as I have always contended that when cultured you will rise. Indeed, you will not have to rise for you will be there already. As it was my first speech of importance in the South since I had left it years before, I was naturally pleased that it should receive such comment.

In this year my friend, H. C. Smith, editor of the *Cleveland Gazette,* was elected to the Ohio Legislature. He was doing splendid work for the race in the authorship and passage of his Civil Rights Bill which [secured] these rights in Ohio. I helped in his election by various articles that placed his sturdy merits before the public.

Busy with all these things, I seemed to have overlooked or miscalculated some others. My friends did so also as it proved. It was the year preceding the General Conference of the Church that governed the University. It was the custom to elect instructors for one year at a time, a custom that rendered no position secure. The growth of the number of conferences with the years, had made a corresponding growth in the Board of Trustees which had at this time become quite large and unwieldy. It was constantly increasing and shifting. Not all, nor even the same members were present. With new men and little knowledge of educational needs and of the situation, anything was possible in managing the affairs of the University.

In June of 1891 the attendance was comparatively small and made up of nearby members. Things were already beginning to take shape for the coming General Conference in 1892 in Philadelphia and aspirants for office with their friends were busy in seeking coalitions and guarding interests in anticipation of this event. Especially, the "Old Guard," as my group of staunch friends and supporters was named by Dr. C. S. Smith, was absent. By a combination of circumstances there was found a propitious moment to carry out the desires of those to whom my presence and activities were a source of annoyance.[53] In twinkling of an eye, my Greek and Latin Professorship was turned over to the nearest aspirant, and I was without a job for about twenty-four hours.

In Payne Seminary
and at a Southern University

In 1891 almost fourteen years had passed since I began my work in Wilberforce University. They had been years of unceasing activity. I had watched with pride and pleasure the growth of the struggling institution, and had been eager at all times to unite in any effort for progress. But it seemed that I had gone "too fast and too far to suit all," as my friend J.W.H. said in a published article on the situation.[1] I had gone on with my work, finishing promised articles and preparing my philological paper for the summer meeting.

For some time the A.M.E. Church had been contemplating a plan for the better education of its ministry, a movement advocated for many years by Bishop Payne. This plan had now been approved by the Bishops' Council and the Financial Board of the Church. It included the making over of the Theological Department of the University into a separate institution. The Theological Seminary was to be governed by a separate small Board of Trustees. A meeting was at once held by this board which proceeded to organize what was to be known henceforth as Payne Seminary in recognition of Bishop D. A. Payne's long life of usefulness.

The result of this meeting, among other things, was the purchase of Dr. John G. Mitchell's property for the new seminary and the election of its first faculty. Bishop Payne was made Dean; Dr. J. G. Mitchell, Professor of Systematic Theology and Hebrew; Rev. G. W. Prioleau (my former pupil in the college), Professor of Historical and Pastoral Theology; and myself, Professor of New Testament Greek and Literature.[2]

Though the Seminary was not formally opened until September 1892, the work was begun in September 1891. It was a great change for me and I was greatly embarrassed the first year as no provision had then been made for a regular salary. Each one was expected to do what he could to raise his own for that year. Had the movement taking me from college work been an intent to cripple me at a critical time, it came near succeeding. I was in debt for my home was still unfinished. I could not obtain my back salary from the college. There was only that of my wife who held in her place as Principal of the State Department by the State Board.[3]

My pen was my sole dependence. It looked dark, but friends and creditors realizing the situation with indignation, gave a helping hand. We both redoubled our literary efforts. Magazine work came to us, and Bishop Payne placed in my wife's hands the task of compiling and arranging from his voluminous diaries and letters for the first volume of the history of the A.M.E. Church, published a year or so later. She also did the same for his personal volume of *Recollections.*[4] What at first had seemed to be an overwhelming disaster proved to be a blessing in disguise.

I had now without exception thoroughly co-operative, progressive, and congenial colleagues—Bishop Payne, learned, appreciative, Doctor Mitchell, scholarly, gentle, just, Professor Prioleau, ambitious, enthusiastic. My months spent in Oberlin Theological Seminary now proved very helpful. My classes were small and the work familiar. Advanced students were few and I had little studying to do. It was well as our new work called for the raising of money, which in turn demanded frequent absences, and the unpleasant task of begging and meeting the often humiliating experiences of travel. Oftentimes I found myself financially stranded and had to put up with most sordid surroundings and deprivations.

But I had become known to the public and found some mitigation in the situation with which I was to become very familiar in after years. One thing had long been determined upon by my wife and myself, that under no circumstances was I to cease my philological study, nor lose connection with the Philological Association. So [al]though I was in such straitened circumstances, deep in debt with but little more than salary deficits. I did as many of us did and as many do today. I sought money lenders and became doubly burdened for years.

In pursuance of our mutual resolve I went to Princeton College in July where I presented a paper on "Bellerophon's Letters." My design was to show that the art of writing was not wholly unknown in Homeric times and that the word "sema" in these writings might, aside from its ordinary meaning, also express the idea of written characters, and that these epigrammatics were real alphabetical characters. This had required much research to present both sides of the contention. I had taken the view held by Professor Tyler and by Professor Jebb also.[5] It was a subject in which I had found much interest and was gratified by the long excerpt published in the "Proceedings" of that meeting. Imagine my gratification, however, when years later after I had gone further into the subject with a paper at Harvard University, I received the following letter from a philological colleague then recently returned from Greece:

1121 University Ave., Madison, Mich.,
September 12, 1922

Dear Professor Scarborough:
In reply to yours of September 8th I would say that my remark to you at Cambridge in support of your theory referred to the fact that the art of writing was very well known to the Greeks in Homer's time as proved especially by the excavations and explorations of Sir Arthur J. Evans at Assous, Crete.[6] You many be familiar with the work done by him at any rate I will give you some references, viz Seymour's "Life in the Homeric Age," p. 35 (Macmillan); Baikies's "Sea Kings of Crete" (A. & C. Black, Soho Sq., London: p. 79–81, 234–243); A. J. Evans' "Scripta Minoa," p. 39–40; H. Browne's "Homeric Study, Ch. V Sec. 2" (Longmans, London).[7] I think you will find all you want in Seymour's book, (he is the T. D. Seymour you used to know) in Baikie's and Browne's, or perhaps in any one of the three.[8] Your college library ought to have and may have all three. They are intensely interesting. There is plenty more on the subject in various places.

Assuring you of my pleasure in hearing from you, and of my pleasant remembrance of meeting you several times, at Cambridge, notably at Sir William Ridgeway's reception,[9] I am very truly yours,

Chas. Forster Smith[10]

How little did my colleagues even guess at the paucity of research material at my hand!

I spent the remainder of the summer of 1901 in the east in my new side profession as a beggar, more rewarded by the making of new friends who were to serve me later, than in money collected, as I found the philanthropic public then caring little for our theological training. It is now (1924) seeing such a need, and schools of religion are being supported in a number of the great institutions of learning. I did make it an opportunity to move about reaching audiences among my own people.

In this new [form of personal] contact, I learned to my satisfaction, that I had plenty of friends, and had only to bide my time for vindication. I had the opportunity to learn what my chief offense had been. I "did not work in harmony" and I was a "kicker."[11] As to the "harmony" charge I plead guilty. I could not and would not be contented to live or work in a rut. I wanted to see things move forward. I wanted to be let to move them as rapidly as possible and I was willing to lay upon the altar all my powers to this end, if allowed to do so. As to being a "kicker," to that too I plead guilty. It has often been said of me, but I've consoled myself, and I think I have shown the world, that like a certain Frenchman likewise accused, "I always kicked toward the goal."

September found me back in Ohio, and giving the Emancipation address at Portsmouth which the *State Journal* termed a "brilliant effort." Then in November I addressed the Epworth League in Springfield on "The True Measure of Power."[12] It was termed by the *Springfield Republic* as a "scholarly, interesting, beneficial discourse, especially urging the attainment of education and culture by all, particularly the colored race." The development of this culture, backed by energy and character, measures the power of individuals. Character is incomplete without thoughtfulness, perseverance, and courage. These fully developed make a powerful man.

In December I went to Nashville reading a paper before the National Educational Association on "The Negro Element in Fiction" which, as I took issue with noted American novelists, "created a great deal of interest and discussion," as the press said, adding "the speaker showed a wide knowledge of philology that had much weight." I was to add in this field of research other papers for Hampton and shortly to be called to enter a wider one along the same line.

It was at this time that my new professorship called me into what was to be a life-long editorial work for the A.M.E. Sunday School Union— a department in my church, which its progressive spirit had established under the management of Dr. C. S. Smith, one of its brainiest men—a man of brilliant parts, with intellectual keenness, and far-sighted vision, who sought all intelligent aid in his efforts. With the establishment of Payne Seminary [Smith] set about carrying out his plan to provide the Church with Sunday School literature. He turned to the faculty of the new seminary for this purpose of providing a full teachers' quarterly of some thirty-six pages with the necessary exegesis.

The work at first was divided among Mitchell, Prioleau, and myself. But Doctor Mitchell soon found his exegetical part too laborious and he turned it over to me. In 1895 Professor Prioleau resigned, becoming later a chaplain in the United States Army and Doctor Smith asked me to take his share, also. It had then been enlarged with two added pages for 'Reflections' variously written thereafter, but with that exception, the entire work for this teachers' quarterly including all exegetical work has continued to be prepared by me and far in advance publication so the Sunday School secretary might utilize the printing force at all idle moments. The Sunday School Union was a success financially and otherwise from the beginning as it has been ever since and especially so (1924) under its present able and fearless lay editor, Ira T. Bryant.[13]

There was a time in 1899 when with some clamor for this position by ministers, and a false claim that I was having such work done outside the Church that he added an editorial to the *Teachers' Quarterly.*[14] Very soon it became necessary to reply to some who intimated that the work was not performed by race writers as promised, and Doctor Smith gave this reply in the *Sunday School Quarterly*: "As to the work of writing and editing the contents of our periodicals, that has been exclusively performed by our own editors since 1892; all insinuations to the contrary notwithstanding, Prof. W. S. Scarborough, the best known Negro in America in philological circles, has been, and is now, our chief aid in preparing the expository notes on the International Lessons; and if he is not competent for the task, who among us is more so?"

Later, in order to silence ambitious malcontents, the Sunday School management found it expedient to withdraw all names from its editorial headings with this explanation: "I am perfectly satisfied. Your copy is everything it should be—scholarly, correct, clear, and always promptly delivered. I shall make no change. Continue the work. You know the clamor." So I worked for three successive secretaries:—Doctors Smith, Chappelle, and Bryant for over thirty years.[15]

It has been fascinating from the start, requiring as it has much study relating to Bible times, history, and characters together with keeping pace with the light thrown by many recent explorations and discoveries. Oh, for time to read and for more money for books! Here speaks the scholar in me, whose wealth of study to this end is evident in every exegesis. Of my labors in this field, Prof. Ira M. Price, of Chicago University and Secretary of the International Sunday School lessons, wrote: "at the end, he has done a splendid work for the Sunday Schools. He was one of God's noblemen."[16]

It was in 1892 that I began to show signs of strain. I had ever feared the tubercular trouble that had carried off my uncle at about this age.

Happily for me, a vigorous and constant course of treatment and care for some months corrected this though I always watched for signs of this lurking scourge. But my work went on. I had become a public man and owed labor for public good. The year was crowded as before with literary labors, school and political activities.

Articles for a Negro history were asked for the Advance Publishing Company on the "Future of the Negro in the United States." The *Mail and Express* [asked] for a paper and the *Republican Magazine* published two articles in September and November on "Republicanism—The Federal Election Bill" and "The Future of the Southern Negro."[17] *Our Day* published my "Race Legislation for Railways" and its editor, Joseph Cook wrote, "We shall want your article on 'Resistance to White Supremacy.'"[18]

I was urged to hold a Teachers' Institute at West Virginia's Colored Institute under State Peabody Institute.[19] The American Association of Educators of Colored Youth (including both white and colored instructors) had been organized in Washington on March 27, 1890, and as one of its directors I went to Wilmington, N.C. [in 1892] to read a paper before its Conference of Afro-American Authors on "How Our Connections with Anglo-American Publishing Houses Can Be Strengthened."[20] I also reported its work for the *Manchester Guardian,* (England), which commented as follows:

> The education of the American Negro is making progress. With that passion for combined effort and social intercourse which marks the English-speaking world, there has been formed an "American Association of Educators of Coloured Youth," and the report of the proceedings at its annual meeting shows how varied are the questions involved, and how strenuous and hopeful are the effects made to deal with the problem. Now the mere existence of such an Association and the discussion by its members of the topics we have named is a remarkable fact when we remember that the Afro-Americans are not quite a generation removed from the darkness of slavery and are harassed by many unjust discriminations arising from white Americans' prejudices as to race and colour. Among the speakers was Dr. W. S. Scarborough who contributes a scholarly discussion of the "Negro in Fiction," and criticizes the presentation of the race in the pages of [William Dean] Howells and other novelists.

It was decided then to hold another meeting in Chicago, Illinois in 1893 at the time of the Exposition. Through this medium I kept before the English [speaking] public the doings and progress of the race in the United States. Then I was made a member of the New York Academy of Sciences and Affiliated Societies in 1893.[21]

In December I gave the Emancipation address at Norwalk, Ohio as "the unanimous choice of the Republican Executive Committee of Huron County" and I found myself recommended by Hon. John S. Clarkson to the Republican National Committee for ten speeches in the campaign of that year.[22] In June John M. Langston wrote regarding political matters: "I shall have something to say to you of political significance. I hope to see you soon." This bore upon the coming campaign and my future in politics, as a chance at Hayti seemed imminent. This year Kentucky State University bestowed upon me the [honorary] degree of Ph.D.[23]

Then the Editor of the *Forum,* Walter H. Page (later Ambassador to the Court of St. James) with whom I had for some time a pleasant and helpful acquaintance, wrote genially, "Send along your paper on 'The Beneficial Effects of a Force Bill.'"[24] There never was a more helpful editor and a better literary friend to me than Walter H. Page.[25] He remained a constant friend, sending me frequent letters and continually later when with Doubleday, Page, and Company, urging me to put my life and reminiscences into a book, or as he wrote, "If you've not the time, give me the facts and I will put them in shape." Later he expressed his joy in a genial letter at my word that I was beginning the work. "I am delighted you have begun your book. Strength to your hand!"

This year held two notable events that meant much to me. One took place in July when I went to the University of Virginia at Charlottesville to present a paper before the Philological Association.[26] It was the first meeting to be held so far South. The decision, reached the summer before, to hold this meeting in the South in 1892 would have made me apprehensive, and probably I would not have been present, had not one of the professors of the University sought me out at once and showed anxiety that I should attend this meeting by his urgent special invitation. I went, taking the train from New York that brought me to Charlottesville about midnight. I had wired this professor of the time of my arrival. I was met by one of the most prominent colored citizens of the city. He took me to his home saying he had been requested to take every care of me and to make it as pleasant as possible for me while I remained. Nothing had been omitted that would add to my comfort and pleasure.

The next morning the professor called to see how I was located and cared for. To my thanks for his courtesy, he replied that it was his duty and pleasure especially in the care of a man like myself and one of their fellow members in the learned association. In common with my associates I was given the freedom of the college buildings and grounds as our meeting opened and we were welcomed to the University.

I was on the program for my paper on "The Chronological Order of Plato's Works," designing to prove the order in point of time of Plato's writings by the Greek used by him and by the circumstances that surrounded him at the time of writing.[27] The [session] was held in the Rotunda of the University used as its library. The white aristocracy of the city turned out in large numbers. There was hardly standing room. On the walls hung the portraits of Jefferson Davis, the President of the Southern Confederacy, Gen. Robert E. Lee of the Confederate Army and other prominent Southern generals. The feeling that came over me was a strange one, as I stepped forward to present my paper. Every eye was fixed upon me and a peculiar hush seemed to pervade the room. It was a rare moment. Like a flash the past unrolled before my mind, my early Atlanta examinations, Calhoun's famous challenge, that no Negro could learn Greek.[28] For a moment I felt embarrassed as I faced my audience aware too that they must experience a peculiar feeling at the situation—a Negro member of that learned body standing in intellectual manhood among equals and where no Negro had ever been allowed even to enter, save as a servant—a Negro to discuss the writings of a Greek philosopher. I even fancied for a second that Jefferson Davis' portrait looked down upon me with a perplexed, questioning gaze, if not a horrified one.[29]

I recovered poise at once as I bowed to the presiding professor and looked over my audience. Yes, it was true, I was among friends, and [as] I proceeded, I never felt more at ease than on this occasion. Though my paper was long and intricate I had the closest attention and at the close I received universal hearty applause.

I know my colleagues were greatly gratified by the individual compliments given later and the young Lincoln University student whom I had invited to accompany me, and, who was one of the audience, said he overheard sentiments both of high appreciation as well as surprise.

As for myself I am sure no one would criticize me for being elated over the accomplishment—a victory for myself and for the race. I must say I doubt whether there has ever been a meeting held at any college where from first to last I received a more cordial reception and especially courteous treatment than here. I was thoroughly cognizant that there would be certain limitations for me, but these were overcome as far as possible. The social functions were such as to make me feel that a Negro could be treated well by the better classes of white people even in the South. The fact is that as the Negro advances, stands on his own feet, and acquits himself as a man in education, politics or any line of activity he is bound to obtain treatment in accordance with his deserts by the better element everywhere.

On my return to New York I called on Dr. William Hayes Ward of the *Independent* and found that friends had already apprised him of my reception which delighted him highly, for he had eagerly watched for word in regard to it.

About this time Bishop B. W. Arnett through the action of the General Education Board of the A.M.E. Church organized the Tawawa Association of the Church with sessions at Wilberforce University in the summer seasons. In this I and my wife took part for several years.

I was still writing editorials for *Leslie's Weekly* on the approaching Ethnological Congress. In reply a pleasing letter came from the editor, bearing this significant sentence, "We have a fine story on hand by S. C. Scarborough, which we [shall] publish soon. I presume that this name is closely related to yours."[30] He was right; my wife was the party in question. One of these editorials dealing with the political situation drew a reply from Bartlett Arkell, the editor: "We are heartily pleased that in this you have digressed from that one subject which naturally is uppermost in your mind, and have struck out for that love of truth and fair-play upon which the Republican party must stand."[31]

As will be later seen by the strenuous work of the following year (1893) for which much preparation was necessary, [my] activities outside [of the] classroom were more or less abandoned. I began again however in June of that year by delivering an address before the Georgia Teachers' Association by invitation of its President, R. R. Wright, Senior, my former Atlanta University classmate.

At the World's Congress Auxiliary of the Columbian Exposition

The other especial event of note, mentioned in the previous chapter, began with the preparations of the nation for the Columbian Exposition to be held in Chicago in 1893. In fact, historically these [plans] had begun back in 1889 when a World's Congress Committee was appointed in connection with preparation for this exposition.[1] In 1890 the World's Congress Committee developed into the World's Congress Auxiliary of the Exposition. Its purpose was to bring about a series of world's conventions of the leaders in the various departments of human progress during the exposition season.

This movement had brought about an effort by the race and its friends to induce Congress to make some provision for exhibiting the progress of the Negro race in this country. The failure had much to do with the resentment and aloofness of the race during the months it saw these magnificent preparations going on to completion without any opportunity to show its own progress. Congress had given its fiat however, and there seemed no way by which the colored people could take a part in the exposition.

Despite this attitude, a way was opened and the Negro did have a part. Among the congresses developed in the auxiliaries, one of the first was an Ethnological Congress. It proved to be the greatest of all congresses taking part in this, [the most] wonderful exhibition [that] America had ever presented to the world.

Of this Ethnological Congress Dr. J. E. Roy of the American Missionary Association became chairman, and Frederic Perry Noble, Librarian of the Newberry Library, Chicago, the secretary.[2] With these men in command Africa was not to be left out. The reasons for representing Africa in this congress were set forth in an article entitled "Africa at the Columbian Exposition" by the latter published in the November 1892 issue of *Our Day*.[3]

No paper to my knowledge has ever so thoroughly covered the ground nor given such cogent reasons for holding this Congress on Africa, especially at that time. These reasons—each fully elaborated in the article— I state briefly here: (1) Africa is ceasing to be the lost and hopeless continent; (2) Africa, [al]though long an alien if not an outlaw from the commonwealth of nations, has played a great part in ancient history; (3) The scientific importance and significance of the dark continent at the present time; (4) The final and crowning cause for the convocation is to be found in moral, philanthropic and religious motives.

Mr. Noble was the leading spirit in this Congress. He had studied African subjects for twenty years and his connection with Newberry Library had put him in command of rare resources for classifying human knowledge of Africa in its every aspect and relation, in order to produce the wonderfully comprehensive program put forth. It covered as has been asserted more ground than either the Brussels Conference in 1876 or the Berlin Conference of 1884. It was international in every sense with experts and specialists to tell of Africa's need and opportunity. In fact, as he said, "it was a Parliament of Man taking counsel for humanity's ward."

Early in 1892 Dr. J. E. Roy had notified me that I had been made a member of the Advisory Council of World's Congress Auxiliary, as "one of the 300 nominated and ratified from Americans and foreigners who are expert or are especially interested in the broad question, whose members are invited to suggest the vital themes of the subject under debate, with the names of suitable speakers and writers, and to be present to participate in the deliberations of the Congress." Of these 300, at least fifteen were representative colored Americans and six of these were members of the African Methodist Episcopal Church. This notification was followed shortly by the following letter from Secretary Noble relative to the program to be carried out:

Chicago, Ill., U.S.A.,
August 11th, 1892

My dear Professor Scarborough:
Since you are a member of our Advisory Council, you are aware that a Congress on Africa is to convene here next July. It is, if possible, to be the most representative African and Afro-American conference ever held. It affords me, therefore, peculiar pleasure to have the honor of inviting you to address it on "The Function and Future of Foreign Languages in Africa."

Though this may not be in line with your special study, yet I feel sure that your philological genius, when turned upon the literature assigned you, will in the long months at your disposal enable you to produce an essay of great and permanent worth.

So for the sake of poor Africa and the wronged black man of the South, I pray you to accept this appointment. Requesting the favor of an early reply.

I have the honor to be your obedient servant.
Frederic Perry Noble
Address: Newberry Library

Dr. Roy expressed in his letters his "delight at being assured" of my acceptance. Again, he wrote anxiously for further assurance of my presence "that the congress may have without fail the benefit of your presence and your service, at the date set for your paper, August 16th, the second day of the season."

I was expected to show what influence the modern languages, such as French, German, Spanish, Italian, etc., would have upon the native tongue, whether the native tongue would be so influenced by them after following the laws of language as to lose their identity, becoming in a sense jargon, like what we sometimes call "pigeon English." It was a most interesting subject and enabled me to take up language study in a new way. I entered upon its preparation at once.

To Dr. Robert Needham Cust, the noted English Orientalist and Africanist, I owed much.[4] I entered upon a correspondence with him which continued for some time. He sent me with his autographed photograph his books: *Languages of Africa* and *Africa Rediviva* with others on other subjects and suggested further material obtainable here.[5] I was also aided by letters from Dr. Sayce, the great English philologist, author of *Ancient Empires of the East,* then Professor of Assyriology at Oxford, England.[6]

In this African Congress representative scholars from nearly every civilized nation were invited to take a part. The United States was represented by a large number of its most distinguished ones—clergy and laity—white and black. In the Department of Languages and Literature to which my paper was assigned with six others I was very proud to find myself in the learned group consisting of Dr. R. N. Cust; of Lewis Grout, an ex-missionary to Zululand and author of a grammar of Zulu; of the noted great Egyptologist, Dr. George Ebers; of Yakub Artin Pasha, minister of Public Instruction in

Egypt; of Mrs. Christensen, author of *Afro-American Folk Lore;* of Dr. Rankin then President of Howard University, and myself.[7] My paper was published in fall of 1894 in the quarterly, the *Methodist Review.*[8] Dr. Cust was [later] unable to be present, but sent his paper on "African Philology."

There were other noticeable things connected with these programs that made this particular Congress the most adequate and representative conference concerning the Dark Continent which humanity has ever held. One was the additional program that included special African night services in various churches of Chicago of the churches of the world. This was fully carried out and the fact emphasized that true Christianity is the one thing necessary to solve a problem that has become here, racial, social, political, religious, and educational in its ramifications.

The other is that about half of the entire number of addresses and papers were by members of the Negro race. The *Chicago Advance* remarked of these: "Those of white men did not as a whole surpass those of their colored brethren," and the *Inter Ocean* said: "This congress will throw new light on the Negro question and surprise people with Negroes as able in debate as white men."

The welcome speech of Dr. Roy declared: "All races have had a hand in making Africa the 'pariah of continents,' and it is ours to help her advance and pay part of the debt Caucasians owe Africa." Dr. J. T. Jenifer, a leading member of our A.M.E. Church and later its historiographer, replied with dignity and ease, saying significantly among other things, "You bring the Afro-American into best position at this feast of nations. You save American Negroes from an obscurity and mortification which the failure to award them place in the Exposition has caused them to feel keenly."[9] When we consider that Douglass, Langston, and Arnett lent their eloquence and oratory to the occasion we may well be proud of our representation at this occasion.

This particular Congress closed dramatically. Our own Bishop Arnett gave the valedictory, and Mrs. French-Sheldon, the noted African traveler, called Bébé Bwana (Woman Master) by the natives, presented to the secretary an African gavel with which the Chicago Congress on Africa was adjourned *sine die.*[10]

There was still another important auxiliary congress in which the race took a prominent part, the Parliament of Religions—a splendid gathering where the Negro again and especially the A.M.E. Church took a prominent part. Bishop Arnett presided at two of its sessions, and I was honored by reading before this body because of his indisposition, Bishop Tanner's paper on "Afro-American Journalism."[11]

I have spoken at length of this congress held at the Art Institute because I would urge on the present generation of ambitious young scholars who are studying the Negro's needs and history to acquaint themselves with the factors as found in the report of this great Congress on Africa as well as with that of the other—the Parliament of Religions, also of great interest to us, gatherings that three decades ago stirred not only the city of Chicago, but the entire nation and other countries as well.

One thing was noticeable and significant of the spirit of the South in connection with this congress. Many southern white speakers were urged to take part, but unfortunately they "could not accept." I recall no one of note who appeared in its programs. This fact drew criticism from some of the leading papers of the day. I am thankful that a broader spirit seems growing today. The present inter-racial conferences, North and South, are serving to cause better understanding. But it may be as Mr. Noble then observed, that "it would not be rash to predict that for 250 years to come it may require all the accumulated forces of Christianity and civilization to root out the taint implanted by southern slavery in the character of the white man, as well as his brother in black." However, time, contact, open-mindedness, and true religion may work wonders in a century more.

While these two Congresses were the ones that created the most interest, they were not the only ones in which the race had a share. In connection with the Educational Congress held July 25–29 under the auspices of the World's Auxiliary of the Exposition there were sessions of the American Association of Educators of Colored Youth, where all phases of education in Negro schools were discussed by representatives from such.[12] Three of the professors of Wilberforce University took part including myself who presented a paper, "Traits in Negro Character," in keeping with my recent studies.

Still another meeting was held at the Art Institute at the Exposition during this time. [It was] a session of three or four days of the Philological Association. There I read a paper discussing a disputed passage in Plautus' *Captivi,* "hunc inventum inveni."[13] The Philological Association had opportunity to be cared for at Chicago University, and "with no friction" my wife and I were located in the hall, just across from the interesting Midway. This spot had its attractions for me in race studies as did the various buildings erected by different nations within the Exposition grounds, showing customs as well as products (which space cannot be made here to record) together with the many pleasing incidents which made the race feel so much less distinction on account of color, at least within our sphere of observation.

The failure of Congress to provide in its departments [the] opportunity to show race progress, led to other plans made by friends so that we should not be ignored. These plans were coincident with those of the Auxiliaries. The following letter explains the desire of the friends of the Negro's progress:

Chicago, Illinois, August 30, 1892
Prof. W. S. Scarborough,
Wilberforce University,
Wilberforce, Ohio

My dear Professor Scarborough:
The proposition to present at the Columbian Exposition a special exhibit or department showing the work of the Colored people in this country has been fully discussed, and decided in the negative. But the progress of this people since its emancipation is one of the great phenomena of the closing century, and I think it should be presented at this Exposition. The propositions before Congress were not decided adversely, but practically failed. If anything is done it cannot wait until we can see whether assistance can be had at the short session, or what that assistance may amount to.

Those who have given only casual attention know that the Colored People have made great and substantial progress. They have increased in numbers by many millions. They have acquired the ownership of large amounts of land. They have amassed wealth, which in the aggregate amounts to a large sum. They have established and maintained schools, colleges, seminaries, and churches. How can these facts be presented in the most complete and the most effective way? What mechanism is already in existence which can be utilized in this work?

Many such questions will suggest themselves to you. You have doubtless already given much thought to this subject. May I ask you to advise me as to what, in your judgment can be done, should be done, how, and by whom?

An early and full reply will be very greatly appreciated by

Yours truly,
Selim H. Peabody
Chief, Director of Liberal Arts

To this I made the reply that "because of this failure of Congress I knew of no better outlet for the race than what was already begun by the Committee on the African Ethnological Congress, that individual schools should apply for space and exhibit their work, that we could not afford to pass it by because of the part the race itself as a whole, and particularly, [that] the A.M.E. Church and Wilberforce University had played in educational progress."

The result of this correspondence was that, [al]though Dr. Peabody's department afforded the race opportunity to obtain space for exhibiting its educational work, it was thoroughly piqued and resentful at the failure of the United States Government to provide adequate recognition. [Only] two educational Negro institutions accepted this opportunity. These were Hampton Institute of Virginia and our own Wilberforce University of Ohio, [which was] the only exhibit representing the higher education of colored youth.

Our participation consisted of an attractive exhibit which shared space in Ohio's Educational Section. It was planned and erected by our own teachers and students. It illustrated completely the different phases of our work—by examination papers, drawings, and industrial products—all the handwork of our students, [and] was presided over by the different members of our faculty who saw it become a center of admiration and praise, suffering nothing in comparison with other exhibits. In the end, the university was awarded the Columbian Medal for student work.

It was at this Exposition that I formed a close acquaintance with many persons of note, together with one who was to become noted as the "sweet, ill-fated singer of the race"—Paul Laurence Dunbar. He was attached to the Hayti Commission over which Frederick Douglass was presiding in the Hayti Building. He was then eagerly trying to find an outlet for the offspring of his muse and asked my advice. As our fields of literary endeavor differed so greatly I could only suggest possible openings of which he later availed himself profitably. When better known (by William Dean Howells' mead of praise), he entered upon his brilliant, if brief career.[14]

Frederick Douglass was one of the most prominent figures connected with the Exposition. Having been Minister to Hayti he had made such an impression on the Haytian authorities that they appointed him to represent Hayti and to preside over the Hayti Building. He was a magnificent figure to observe—dignity personified in every moment. His massive frame, leonic head, firm tread attracted attention wherever he went. I have seen hundreds stop and gaze as he passed and crowds gathered round to gaze and follow in his wake whenever this distinguished man moved from place to place. It was well for the Negro everywhere that such a representative was called to be within the observation of the nations gathered here.

I also made the acquaintance here of Héli Chatelain, the French explorer as well as that of the noted English lady explorer of Africa, before mentioned Mrs. French-Sheldon.[15] The former I was to meet again soon at a Hampton Institute Conference where we both presented papers on Negro folk lore. The latter in a few weeks visited us at Wilberforce University where she entertained faculty, students, and friends in a graphic account of her experiences in Africa and exhibited some wonderful specimens of African native art—bracelets and other articles hammered from pure gold nuggets.

She had done much in letting the world know of what she called the "humanness of the natives," as she, a lone woman went into Africa for the purpose of knowing and making this known to the world. Her book, *Sultan to Sultan,* is a most enlightening book on African life, manners, and customs.[16] I felt it a great honor to acknowledge the receipt of the gift of a copy with this inscription, "Yours Faithfully, M. French-Sheldon—Bébé Bwana." We were to meet her again a few years later in London.

Friends and Helpers—Deaths

The close of the year 1893 found me with much promised literary work on hand, but saddened by the passing of three close friends. Samuel Armstrong of Hampton, who was stricken down in his great work some two years before, had died in the summer leaving to carry on his work, Dr. Hollis B. Frissell, a man who in temperament was quite his opposite.[1] Another was Professor Price of the A.M.E. Zion Church, and the third one was Bishop D. A. Payne, who had given his last public utterance at the Parliament of Religions.[2] He passed on November 29.

In these deaths I experienced a great personal loss. Hampton could never be the same to me again, though I learned to admire greatly Dr. Armstrong's successor. The death of Professor Price was the taking off of a man just standing on the threshold of life having, as the newspaper the [New York] *Age* expressed, "demonstrated magnificent ability and done work which gave evidence of greater things to be done."

On the demise of Bishop Payne, I wrote an appreciation for the *Independent* and the *Christian Recorder* where I spoke of him as "a loyal friend, abetting all constructive measures, a student of nature and of mankind, of indomitable will, broad views, and generous impulses, stern, yet affable, like a true leader, recognizing his limitations and seeking only to do the work he felt fitted to do."[3] As he had said of himself: "When God has a work to be executed he also chooses the man to execute it. He who undertakes through envy, jealousy, or any motive or consideration to reverse this divine law resists the purpose of the Almighty and brings misfortune and sometimes ruin upon himself." Daniel A. Payne's chosen work was Christian education for his race, his platform the Christian pulpit. As such he was a living example of the dignity and force of an educated ministry which he sought to obtain for his people.

It is little wonder that Doctor Thirkhield, the President of Gammon Theological Seminary, wrote me in the following strain: "I pray that the Lord may raise up some man of great intellect and spiritual Christian power to take his place."[4] "As yet," he concluded, "I have seen no other such great leader in the A.M.E. Church. Leaders are not made by man, but the race is better and richer because these men have lived and labored."

Death had shown its love for a shining mark in leveling his dart at these men, and he [was] not yet content with his prey. [A new strike was to follow] soon after I had attended the Seventh Lincoln League Banquet at Columbus, where Bishop Arnett responded to the toast, "Three Decades of Freedom."

The University had entered upon the year of 1894 with much rejoicing over the good fortune that had just come to it through its designation by the War Department of the United States as a school for military training brought about by the influence of Senators Sherman and Brice of Ohio with others.[5] In March Lieutenant John Hanks Alexander was detailed to it as Professor of Military Science and Tactics.[6]

He was the third member of the race to graduate from West Point and had been given the post of honor in the Ninth Regiment of U.S. Cavalry. He had been a student at Oberlin, but left in his freshman year to accept the cadetship at West Point. Because his life stands out as a shining example of the possibilities of the young men of the race, I may be pardoned for speaking at length of this coming young man who had conquered poverty, prejudice, ignorance, and won his right to a scholarship in West Point by competitive examination. His competitor was the son of the eminent jurist, Chief Justice Waite of Ohio.[7] It is an honor to this noble son of a worthy father to know that in the first examination at Elyria he received the first award of the prized scholarship by superiority in physique, Alexander being made alternate. This young man met his humbler rival at the depot at West Point and showed him every courtesy when the two met for the final test. We are told that the results of that examination went before the Board of Judges by number not by name, and with Justice blindfolded that she might be just, an average of 92 was made by John H. Alexander, the cadet from Ohio.

The service course at West Point was followed without a failure. His gentlemanly courteous bearing, his intellect and character in time eliminated prejudice against him and with only a few instances of discrimination he was graduated in 1887. To their credit be it said that in a few cases where differences arose even some Southern students took his part.

With such a detail we had high hopes for this new department. Within the month came the tragic end. He went to Springfield to spend a weekend. The day following, March 25, the startling message came of his sudden death in a barber's chair by the bursting of a blood vessel.

The President, the Secretary, Mr. Wallace Clark, and I at once left for that city and made arrangements for his body to be brought back to the University.[8] The esteem in which he was held showed itself at once by the offer of the Springfield white military guard to accompany his remains back to the University. Our own Arnett Guards, however, met the body at the city limits and took up the escort to the University where the funeral services were held. The burial took place in the Cherry Grove Cemetery in Xenia, Ohio.

Second Lieutenant Rhodes of the 6th U.S. Cavalry who was stationed at Ohio Wesleyan University, Delaware, Ohio at once sent his sympathy in a fine letter of tribute.[9] There also came to us by order of Colonel Biddle of the 9th U.S. Cavalry another letter, expressing sorrow and stating the respect and admiration in which Alexander was held, he was "manly, courteous, and honorable; always a gentleman with a high sense of the duties and obligations of an officer," and adding that "in respect to his memory the officers of the regiment will wear the usual badge of mourning for thirty days."[10]

It was not only a blow to the University, but to the entire race. As I review his life and the thwarted endeavors of our people in respect to the experiences of our youth in connection with this military school of our nation with only three graduates of color from it in over 130 years, I am forced to exclaim: "When will Justice again be blindfolded that she may be just to our Negro youth!"[11]

On the 21st of May Lieutenant Charles Young under a furlough from the government arrived at the University to take charge of the Military Department in anticipation of an appointment to be made September 1st, when his five years of service [would make] him fully eligible to this chair. For years to come, we were to receive at different times the invaluable services of this equally brilliant young officer. He was the third and so far, the last man of our race to survive the rigors of West Point prejudice and discrimination.[12] With these events weighing heavily upon me, it was well that I was kept busy with my literary work for which I was now besieged.

Doctor Fallows wrote for my biography for the history of the Lincoln Jubilee.[13] It was held in Columbus by the Illinois Commission on the Half-Century Anniversary of Methodism, and the Michigan Equal Rights Association called for my presence at its Fourth Anniversary Convention in Grand Rapids. Then the Whittier Historical Association of Memphis, Tennessee, desired me to address it on the anniversary of Whittier's birthday.[14] The Chautauqua Literary and Scientific Association sent for my autobiography and autographed photograph for its year book.[15] I did what I could for all, and with all was induced to write the introduction to Professor Atkins' forthcoming volume of the *Proceedings of Our American Association of Colored Youth*.[16] Along with this medley came an insistent call from Secretary Woodmansee to attend the National Republican Convention to be held in Denver, arguing the "necessity to have the state well represented" and "promising a royal good time," but though I recognized the importance of the occasion I let politics take a second place and prepared to meet the Philological Association at Williams College in Massachusetts.[17]

In the meantime the Commencement at home held a pleasing event. In the presence of many distinguished guests at the Commencement in June of this year were Governor McKinley and Frederick Douglass, who showed their deep interest in our work by their speeches, and were pleased to accept the honorary degrees the University felt honored to bestow on them.[18]

I went to Williams College in July and found myself on the way forced to put up with one of those situations so inconvenient and humiliating to the race. Unfortunately for me I reached Williamstown about midnight. The college was across the river and some distance from the station. As I did not care to risk crossing at that hour I applied to some parties nearby who I was told had hotel accommodations. They gave me the usual excuse, "all the rooms engaged." Not having any acquaintance with anyone in the place I saw but one [thing] to do. I asked permission of the traction men to remain in the tool house till morning, as there was no station house. Though seeming surprised they acquiesced, and I spent a wakeful night in the tool house from which I emerged hungry the next morning to cross the river hastily and report to the learned body of which I was a member and to find my hotel as a guest in common with the other members.

There I read a paper on a subject rather suggestive of my recent experience. I had [examined] certain Greek and Latin words of somewhat disputed meaning, expressive of the three meals of the day, breakfast, dinner, and supper.[19] My purpose was to show that in the Greek and Roman these words had variable meanings under different circumstances and changed conditions. The paper was afterwards published in *Education*.[20] An enjoyable trip to Greylock Mountain with its wonderful view was the entertainment feature of this occasion.[21] I recall the pleasant meeting with Miss Bascom the author of *Bascom's Literature,* a book I had studied in Oberlin, and whose author I had supposed to be a man.[22] At Williams [James A.]

Scarborough's mother, courtesy of Rembert E. Stokes Library, Wilberforce University, Wilberforce, Ohio

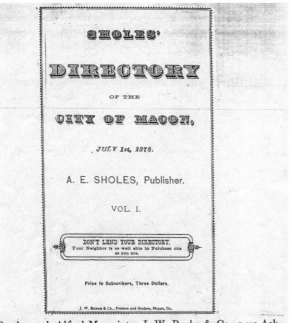

Listing for Jeremiah Scarborough, Macon City Directory, Middle Georgia Regional Library, Genealogical and Historical Room, Macon, Georgia

Scarborough as a young man,
courtesy of Rembert E. Stokes
Library, Wilberforce
University, Wilberforce, Ohio

Mrs. Scarborough as a young
woman, Western Reserve
Historical Society Library and
Archives, Cleveland, Ohio

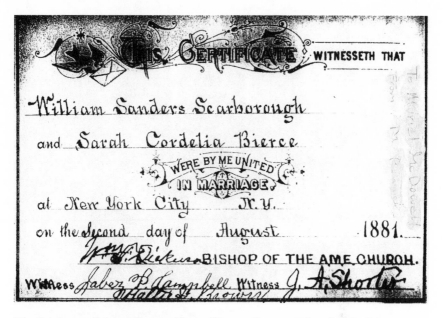

The Scarboroughs' wedding certificate, Western Reserve Historical Society Library and Archives, Cleveland, Ohio

Ivory fan carried by Mrs. Scarborough on her wedding day, courtesy of Sarah A. Grant, Mrs. Scarborough's great-granddaughter, Warren, Ohio

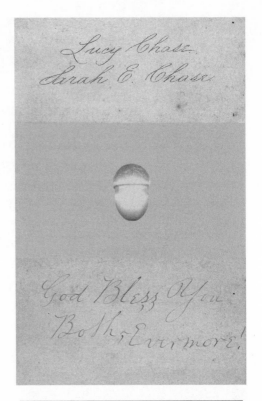

Lucy Chase
Sarah E. Chase

God Bless You Both, Evrmore!

A bead (3/4") and gift card from the necklace given by the Chase sisters to Mrs. Scarborough on her wedding day, courtesy of Sarah A. Grant, Mrs. Scarborough's great–granddaughter, Warren, Ohio

Advertisement for Scarborough's textbook, *People's Advocate,* 1881

Scarborough standing in front of Tretton Place, courtesy of Hallie Q. Brown
Memorial Library, Central State University, Wilberforce, Ohio

Maidenhair fern from
the Coliseum and
olives from Mount
Vesuvius collected by
the Scarboroughs in
1901, courtesy of
Sarah A. Grant, Mrs.
Scarborough's great-
granddaughter,
Warren, Ohio

Scarborough in his maturity,
courtesy of Rembert E.
Stokes Library, Wilberforce
University, Wilberforce, Ohio

Scarborough with a group of students outside Arnett Hall, courtesy of Hallie Q.
Brown Memorial Library, Central State University, Wilberforce, Ohio

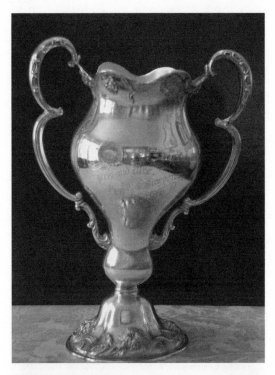

Loving cup presented by
Wilberforce class of 1913 to
the Scarboroughs to celebrate
his birthday in 1912, courtesy
of Sarah A. Grant, Mrs.
Scarborough's great-granddaughter, Warren, Ohio

Scarborough in academic
robes, courtesy of Rembert E.
Stokes Library, Wilberforce
University, Wilberforce, Ohio

Scarborough at work at his desk, courtesy of Rembert E. Stokes Library, Wilberforce University, Wilberforce, Ohio

Grave site in Wilberforce, author's collection

Garfield's sons studied and graduated.[23] And I recalled the saying that a liberal education would be "Mark Hopkins on one end of a log with the student on the other." Such was the power of this famous educator who was Williams' president for thirty-six years, dying in 1887.[24]

The occasion however was much marred for me, and I am sure for the other members as well, by the vacant chair of my old friend, Professor Whitney, whose death had taken place the previous month.[25] To honor him a special meeting was held at the University of Pennsylvania in Philadelphia in the following December.[26] Mrs. Scarborough and I were then the guests of Bishop Tanner. It was a splendid meeting with magnificent tributes paid to the distinguished scholar whom I was to miss greatly ever after. It seemed that friends were falling fast!

Here I met for the first time Dr. Talcott Williams, that active friend of the Near Eastern peoples, whose father had been a missionary among them.[27] Needless to say that I received interested attention from him in whom I found a valuable friend in the future. His entertainment of the Association was a memorable occasion.

From there we went to Washington, D.C., to be the honored guests for a few days of Frederick Douglass and his wife—a never to be forgotten visit where we were entertained most royally. The "Sage of Anacostia" in his home unbent from his dignity and played with gusto his violin to my wife's accompaniment. He even executed a dashing "pigeon wing" at the conclusion. "It is good to be out of the limelight and among real friends," he said as he sat in his library and chatted with us.

Then came the shock in a few short weeks of his death.[28] Surely my friends were falling fast. I was wired to be an honorary pallbearer and went to pay my last respects to the man of the race whom I admired and reverenced and who had risen to such eminence. A great man had fallen and his passing brought white and black, high and low, to do him magnificent honor at his obsequies. Such honor has never been given to another of our race. Truly a great man had fallen. When shall we see his equal?

Following this Mr. R. C. Ogden, the good friend and helper of Hampton and who had taken much interest in me, expressed his pleasure at the receipt of a copy of my *Birds of Aristophanes*. [But] these events of the past months together with the increasing demands on my time now nearly overwhelmed me. Hon. Asa Bushnell was now before the people [for the office of] governor. I put aside other things for a season to help on his election—a most popular one, and one that was to be of great value to our school. As I had also been asked to place myself at the disposal of the Albion

International Young People's Lecture Bureau, which promised a wider field for platform work, I spent time in preparing a lecture for this purpose.[29] For the Philological Association meeting in July at Adelbert College, Western Reserve University, I had time only to choose from my material another paper on "Modern Languages in Africa." The abstract of this paper was lost in transmission and fails to appear in the proceedings.[30]

Here the Association was given a reception by Mr. and Mrs. Samuel Mather at their beautiful home, Shoreby.[31] [The Mathers were] two noble people whose lives were being spent in good works for humanity. I was to have most cordial and helpful relations with them in the passing years. Mrs. Mather was a most noble type of womanhood. [She was] one of the few great women whose lives are a constant benediction to humanity. She and her distinguished husband leave a precious legacy to humanity in their boundless philanthropies, for which I, as one of those ever helped in our work, am eternally grateful. She was especially interested in the freedmen. In her death in 1909 we and the world lost a true [and] helpful friend.

In 1910 Mr. Mather published a handsome volume to her memory.[32] It was as its preface announced "printed for private presentation to friends whom she held dear." I have never experienced a happier privilege than when there was sent a copy with my name inscribed on its presentation page, and still more did I treasure the volume when among the host of Tributes I found my own humble one as President of Wilberforce University with those of Atlanta University and Livingston College. Such lives have our eternal gratitude. God's blessings on both these good friends!

About this time an effort was made to accomplish more for the welfare of the state supported Department of the University by a new legislative act and reorganization. The Department was now placed under a newly appointed Board of Trustees, and upon a financial basis more in keeping with other state institutions of education.[33] It also created for it the new office of Superintendent. While this movement was claimed to be the legal thing to do to correct some existing troubles, it laid the foundation for new ones in a quasi-headed department, which was to be the source of endless friction involving both officials and faculties. Because of it I passed in later years through many trying experiences.

With this change I was asked to be a candidate for this Superintendency. I declined as the duties were out of my line of work. A college colleague after hearing from me that I was not to be a candidate sought and obtained the office and transferred himself and his allegiance to this state.[34] This took place soon after Governor Bushnell went into office. As we had long been friends and I had taken a leading part in his campaign, he sought my counsel as to the appointment of some new members of the Board. I was pleased that he appointed Dr. W.A. Galloway to it.[35] I requested as it met for organization that he be made President of the Board and that Mrs. Scarborough, who had been principal of the Department since its organization in 1887, be retained as such.

With all this accomplished a long sought extension of courses was begun. This the new President of the Board forwarded in every way. I here give tribute to this friend of the race who served us faithfully and conscientiously for over twenty years. He made great sacrifices to the detriment of his [medical] practice, and even to the loss of friends in working thus for the Negro people.

I was now developing a growing interest in the Hampton Institute. Robert C. Ogden was anxious I should visit that school. He wrote begging me to do so, and to let him know when I would go so that he might secure me "such attention as will afford an opportunity for thorough inspection of the place."

I was unable to go until the following May, when I went to speak at the annual public meeting before the Hampton Folk Lore Society. I gave many illustrations from proverbs and stories, which greatly interested Héli Chatelain whom I found most affable, interesting, and scholarly. The address was published in full in the *Southern Workman* and an article on "Negro Folk-lore and Dialect" was published shortly [after] in the *Arena*.[36] This was immediately followed by my election as member of the American Dialect Society.

Of this visit Mr. Ogden wrote me:

My dear Professor Scarborough,

I am exceedingly pleased to learn from yours of the 28th instant that you enjoyed your visit to Hampton, and, although the demands upon your time were somewhat large, I am yet very glad that you were thereby compelled to remain a sufficient length of time to get a good grip on the ideas of the institution. The whole establishment has its face to the front with an intense anxiety to do some practical good for the solution of the questions that immediately confront us. You know my notions upon this point and it is not necessary to repeat them here. I hope to meet you there again.

Yours sincerely,
Robert C. Ogden

In 1896 I was again drawn back into politics, and had but little time to give to philological study, but I did so at the meeting of the Association at Brown University with a paper on further phases of African language study.[37] Here I was urged again by Professor Fowler to obtain a fellowship in the School at Athens, Greece, and was promised assistance by a leading member.[38] Again the ever pressing question of finance, increasing work and responsibilities, and new interests compelled me to relinquish the idea.

The political events leading up to the campaign that culminated in making Governor McKinley, President, [were now unfolding.] As history shows there was now much bitter feeling in the Republican ranks in Ohio. Foraker, Bushnell, Hanna, McKinley, and Sherman were all involved in the situation. I knew all well, and counted myself a friend to all. It was both grievous and embarrassing to me to see the growing breach that the situation was creating. But my mind and attention were soon to be diverted more closely to my own affairs.

Back to the Classical Professorship
and a Vice Presidency

With the closing of the school year in June 1897 I had spent six years in Payne Seminary. They were years of growth for me as well as years of a wholesome change in classwork that because of my circumscribed environment had hitherto tended to monotony. This I had realized was detrimental to real creative work of any kind. This change had brought me into a closer study of the Bible and the years had not only deepened my reverence for the Word, and increased my Christian faith, but it had made me to see more clearly that human nature has ever been the same through all the ages. My own race group has often been pictured as passing through the same experiences as had the Israelites. I have studied these similarities and they have helped me to look upon the vicissitudes of life with a growing tolerance. I even developed a patience for the vicious injustice as well as with ignorant prejudices. My faith had been strengthened in the belief that a better future will dawn for us as a people. I was philosophically following Samuel Armstrong's course as he wrote me, "I have learned what can't be cured we must endure."

There was a comparatively small attendance of the large Board of Trustees of the University at the trustee meeting in June. The General Conference of 1896 had passed by and with the next one three years ahead in the future there seemed to be no reason for any great political church activity for jobs.[1]

The small Board now assembled was made up of those who felt a deep responsibility for the University's welfare. It was a working Board, and at once it set about to acquaint itself thoroughly with existing conditions and to act for betterment. Its work quickly terminated in an unexpected manner, and I found myself summarily transferred back from the Seminary to my former position as head of the Classical Department of the College and also made Vice-President of the University. "It was a unanimous vote," J.H.M., a trustee wrote to the *New York Age,* adding, "the trend of events for Wilberforce University is in the right direction and the danger point is passed."[2] I will not quote further from this frank article, except to refer to his comment that "resignation from office," "silence in Board did much good" and "absence was another blessing,"—a reference made in a previous newspaper article by him to those "who would not play if Scarborough was in it."

Though I had liked my work in the Seminary and my co-workers, it was a pleasing vindication to be replaced in my classical chair. In these few years it had undergone vicissitudes under three successive occupants, one of whom had come to it with high ideals as I had, but who had met with some similar experiences.[3] In fact in a somewhat heated faculty argument he had once taken me to task for remaining at Wilberforce for taking "the treatment accorded you and letting the institution build up on your name," as he bluntly put it. "I would never have remained," he declared. Well, he did not remain and I had remained.

I now had much to do to build up again the department which had become much reduced in numbers. In addition to regaining my hold on my old work I was devoting some time to my old friend Flipper's cause— his re-instatement in the army, and to my own the application I had again made for the post to Hayti. In February I went to the Lincoln banquet held in Zanesville where Booker T. Washington was the speaker. At the closing of that meeting a pilgrimage was made to Canton to visit and call on President-elect McKinley.

The following incidents [were] connected with this call. After greetings were made Booker T. Washington and myself remained a while for a private talk. The conversation that followed related to the Negro people and appointments he had in mind to make. Booker T. Washington took occasion to urge my appointment which McKinley promised to consider. At the close of this interview he asked me to remain for further private talk. He told me of his desire to have Mr. Hanna appointed as U.S. Senator, as John Sherman had resigned to take a place in his cabinet. He then said he knew Governor Bushnell and I were very friendly and asked if I would have any objection to going to Columbus to see the Governor and make his wish known to him. I asked Mr. McKinley why he did not appoint Mr. Hanna to a place in his cabinet. He replied that Mr. Hanna did not want that, but preferred the senatorship. I told Mr. McKinley I did not know what influence I might have, but I would go to the Governor and do as requested. In fact, I could not well refuse. Under the strained relations then existing with Governor Bushnell and Senator Foraker on the one hand and

Mr. Hanna on the other, I could not see any success in such a mission. But I could see I might be antagonizing all parties, all of whom were my friends, and jeopardize my own interests.

However, I left Canton for Columbus and conferred with Governor Bushnell, telling him the circumstances that left nothing for me to do but come as I had. Governor Bushnell listened attentively to me and finally replied rather sadly, "If you knew all that I know you would not make that request." He then explained fully the situation giving his reasons for not making such an appointment. We talked over the desire of the Republican Party for peace and harmony, and he finally asked me to call on Senator Foraker and talk it over with him. But I already knew too much of the fights and feuds of these troublous political times which I could not tell and I concluded not to go further with the matter by going to Senator Foraker. I returned to Canton and stated as frankly to Mr. McKinley as I could without giving offense that the appointment could not be brought about. He thanked me and said he would see me again. In the end Governor Bushnell hoping to make peace in Republican ranks did appoint Mr. Hanna to the Senate, where he became, however, the Junior Senator.

I was glad to see the matter settled this way. I have often wondered what influence if any my mission might have had to do with it. I was friendly to all—standing by Senator Foraker always until I saw no hope for his ambitions, and he himself in his frequent letters to me said I had done just the right thing. [It was a thing which] "I would have done had I been in your place," he emphasized. But it was not a pleasant position to be in when he and Senator Sherman became at odds, and years later again when Foraker and Senator Burton were at variance. I honored and respected all, but had to act according to my conscience. [I used my] knowledge of inner matters, and my best judgment for the good of the party. Truly political ways and political life make a hard road to travel! I felt then and now that all respected my stand and harbored no personal ill-feeling.

It took some time for Mr. Hanna, however, to put full trust in me. He did so, however, learning that I had only the good of Republican success at heart. I was chosen as one of the committee that went to the St. Louis Convention for McKinley. And this [unhappy] incident followed.

It was whispered that the St. Louis people were not pleased with the idea of having so many Negroes stopping at their hotels. Mr. Hanna informed them if they were not satisfied with the conditions that he would take the convention to Chicago. The result was there was no further protest and we remained undisturbed at the McCleod Hotel.[4] Later, Mr. Hanna wired me as to the part he wished me to take in the campaign and I kept him advised especially as to the situation in the South.

I was a delegate to the convention that nominated Governor Foraker for the third term, to which idea his brother-in-law, Mr. W. E. Bundy, told me plainly that Foraker strenuously objected, but his nomination was put through by his friends despite him. All knew Mr. McKinley was greatly disappointed at the outcome and he arose from his seat at the close of the convention and in no unmistakable tone said, "You have nominated your man, now go home and elect him." I knew as he said it that that utterance meant Foraker's defeat. He was defeated, but with his indomitable courage held on. I worked hard for him in this campaign though I knew it was hopeless. I do know, however, that in all the political turmoil he had been true to McKinley's interests. Though he was assailed as an enemy, he was also a true friend to us. I have had reasons myself in late years to beg to be delivered from my friends[!]

Another trying experience had occurred in 1897 when Mr. Foraker entered the contest for the U.S. senatorship against John Sherman, (when such elections were by the state legislature—a method I still hold to be superior to the present one by primary). I was wired by both to come to Columbus for conference. I then felt that Senator Sherman's long and excellent service entitled him to re-election and that Senator Foraker as a young man at that time could wait. I had finally to let both know the predicament I felt myself. But feeling was running high and I've always felt that Sherman never felt quite the same toward me. Governor Foraker was defeated, but as ever he went down bravely. McKinley was elected and Hanna finally made Senator. Ohio politics were quieting down and I was assured by Elmer Dover, Hanna's secretary, that "you are entitled to a share of the credit."[5] Being a Foraker man was evidently now against me as in later years.

These episodes came near drawing me from politics altogether. I was not like so many of the politicians—ready to hide with the hare and run with the hounds. I had many good friends and it was source of great distress to me when they fell out among themselves. Ohio politics had now become dangerously stirred by these bitter dissensions among leaders, and the Republican Party in the state was almost completely dismembered, a condition that remained for a long time.

I debated the subject long before I became active to any great extent, although I did take part in state and national campaigns, especially for Myron T. Herrick, who was elected governor in 1904.[6] But I must say that my greatest political interest was centered at this time in the camp of

Warren G. Harding, who was just entering politics, and was victoriously elected state senator in 1899. This young man I gave from the first the same loyal strong allegiance I kept for Senator Foraker to death. Both men were [marked] in mind and heart with that personal magnetism that drew men to their support.

[In regard to] the system of electing senators, I must say that I believe [that] the system of nominating senators is better than the present primary. I hold with Senator Foraker, and think that there must be leaders and organizations—even bosses. In politics to have but one who is responsible is better than to have several who through agents invisibly control numbers and are for that reason less responsible as their recommendations are not open. And [al]though the people nominate, if a mistake be made the fault is theirs.

Returning to the summer of 1897 and to my application for the mission to Hayti under McKinley, I have this to say. I had a strong backing of the Ohio Legislature and I was sure of Governor Bushnell's, Senators Foraker's and Sherman's support, also of Secretary Foster's. I was not so certain of Harrison's influence, as Edward Arkell says: "I hope they all are back of you in earnest."[7] He lent his support, endorsing me thus: "Professor Scarborough is, and has been for a number of years a most valued contributor to *Leslie's Weekly* done in the columns of our paper a yeoman's work with the touches of the scholar. Cultivated to an unusual degree, I believe he also possesses those other qualities which would make him a most valued addition to our consular service."

I am inclined now to think I really cared more for the opinion of my supporters than for the attainment of my objective, especially as I was aware of so much.

Bishop Tanner said, "I'll give you any endorsement you desire but I think it will be a calamity for you to leave Wilberforce University or rather Payne Seminary. I am reluctant to see you leave. Whom can we get to take your place!" Bishop Tanner said among other things in his editorial for the *Christian Recorder:*

> Men of Professor Scarborough's stamp are not to be jostled aside by competitors among lesser lights. He embodies staying and sterling qualities in himself, and leading appreciative minds regardless of race accord him the place he so rightfully deserves. No name yet mentioned in connection with the appointment is more widely known or better qualified to measure up to the demands of the post named in point of literary eminence and all-around merit than this author, educator, scholar, and philologist of trans-continental fame.

The literary world doffs its hat in recognition of the worth and services of Professor Scarborough. It would willingly do all in its power to enhance his fortune or insure his renown. But the goal of honor is not to be thus reached . . . alone. He should be supported by those near to him and who have enjoyed the fruits of his services. But this is not the case, for his foes are of his immediate literary household. The great heart of the race is true and the people identified with Professor Scarborough will come to his relief in this hour of emergency. We believe in fair-play and would offset the advantages sought against this eminent man by suggesting a rebuke which will be no less far-reaching than effective.

Tanner was right as to foes though not exactly confined to [my] "literary household." My enemies were those who would neither do themselves, [yet] sought to keep me from doing. I have ever found in my race that men who have risen by works and worth have been uniformly friendly and appreciative. There were local aspirants for office under McKinley. And there had to be a way out of it. Geographical and political trickery finally resulted in the appointment going to another state than Ohio, [and] the state seemed to have been left for its reward only the consulship to Santo Domingo, a place for which I had never had desire.[8] It was given to another of Greene County who accepted readily. Of this the press said: "It was fully expected that Professor Scarborough would be rewarded by this appointment at least. The matter was put up to the late Hon. McKinley and he decided in favor of M. . . . Thereby hangs 'an interesting story.' " Knowing a portion of the story I've often queried what was the rest of it, but it will never be fully told. Indiana received the Haytian position.[9]

So my political aspirations were again squelched. Perhaps as I look at politics now, R. T. was right in what he said of me [that] "my sphere is in the realms of thought rather than in intrigues."[10] And R. T. knew much of such "intrigues."

A post in Washington was offered to me, but this I declined, and as I have said, I dropped out of politics for a while until Harding's campaign for state senator, and gave myself to the rehabilitation of the Classical Department after my six years of absence. I continued to write for the magazines. After another visit to Hampton I wrote for the *Independent,* an article describing the "Hampton Spirit." And I sent one to the *Arena* on "Negro Folk-lore and Dialect" which was published at once.[11]

In 1897 the Rev. Dr. Alexander Crummell of Washington City, a graduate of an English university and one of the most scholarly Negroes in America, formed the idea of founding an American Negro Academy. He wrote me concerning it and asked my co-operation. He also enlisted that of Dr. Kelly Miller, Dr. DuBois, Dr. Booker T. Washington, and a few others in what was to be an organization patterned after the French [Academy].[12]

The purpose was to form an organization of authors, scholars, writers, [and] graduates of African descent for the promotion of letters, art, literature, and science, the encouragement and assistance of scientific and linguistic scholarship and artistic powers with the aim for excellence, and to aid with all means in its power to raise the standard of intellectual endeavor among American Negroes. The movement which was at once carried out in organization indicated clearly that the Negro was thinking in those lines that make for his highest moral good and that they were planning and formulating plans for their betterment. The condition of prejudice against the Negro, the difficulties that he had in entering the fields of literature made all of those interested in this movement very anxious for the plan to become permanent, one for the betterment of our group. It was a step in the right direction and if it had been rigidly adhered to I think our literary standing would have been more quickly elevated to a high place.

Following its model, its elected membership was to be limited to a certain number and when this had been reached no others were to be permitted to enter until there should be a vacancy. Though the French Academy seemed to err in black-balling some great men, it also refused to admit those having no claim to its membership. The *Manchester Guardian* (England) to which I sent the notice commented: "Let us hope that the membership of the American Negro Academy will avoid the failing of their great exemplar." I think it has, but there is fear that like so many organizations it may have gone to the other extreme letting its standard give way to numbers rather than achievement. But it still exists and I feel I can be numbered with its founders.

At its second annual meeting I read a paper on "The Educated Negro and His Mission," which was published as one of the "Occasional Papers of the Academy."[13] A copy sent William Hayes Ward brought this reply: "I have read it through with much interest. It is an excellent statement and argument which you make. You are abundantly right in what you say about the importance of the Negro [in regard to] the higher education." It is well for us that its necessity had such advocates as he.

Early in 1898 Prof. John Williams White wrote inviting me to become a member of the Archaeological Institute of America, closing with these words: "May I express my personal hope that you will be able to accept our invitation," which I did and later enjoyed meeting with this society.[14]

In a short time Professor Kelsey gave me a special invitation to meet all classical men at his home at a meeting held at Michigan University [*sic*], begging me "to honor me with your presence."[15] Such invitations may seem too small to mention, but their worth was incalculable to me and should be to the race struggling upward, showing as they do the disposition toward equality and fraternity among men of high culture and learning. It is a sign post pointing the way to my people for the recognition they desire.

Looking forward to the Philological meeting at Trinity College at Hartford, Connecticut in 1898, I took up a theme that called for much study and research as well as a review of my French. For this I called in the assistance of my wife who at Bishop Payne's request had already translated into blank verse Lamartine's drama, *Toussaint L'Ouverture*.[16] She now translated Racine's *Iphigenia* to render my work easier. My paper, "Iphigenia in Euripides and Racine," was to be a character study of this heroine as presented by the two dramatists, the Greek and the French. This proved to be such an interesting study that in a later paper I extended my research to include Goethe's representation of the same heroine.

That I was not to remain out of politics, was shown on the occasion of the Twelfth Annual Lincoln Day Banquet at Dayton, Ohio on February 11, 1899 to which I received a pressing invitation to be one of the six or seven to respond to toasts.[17] Mr. B. said, "We will not accept 'no' for an answer. Now please write to us as an old friend and tell us you will accept. We feel that no one can perform this duty more acceptably than Professor Scarborough."[18]

I could not refuse such a friendly invitation. Immediately I received Chairman N. P. Ramsay's letter saying: "The committee on arrangements is getting up a souvenir of the occasion and have requested a number of the leaders of the party to furnish them with an autographed letter for about twenty-five to fifty words embodying their opinion of Lincoln. Will you not kindly send them at once a letter as above outlined to be placed among the collection? [I am] thanking you in advance and hoping to hear from you at as early a date as possible, and also [looking forward] to meeting you on that occasion."

To this request I also responded at once in this brief sentence: "Abraham Lincoln, the great commoner, was unquestionably one of the most remarkable men of the age—one of America's greatest and noblest patriots, a magnificent specimen of the true statesman, brave, loyal, a servant to Truth and Justice, and withal, a humanitarian."

I had felt it to be an honor to be invited to reply to a toast, an added one to be asked to be one of the few for a sentiment, but it was to me an overwhelming one, when I looked at the handsome souvenir at my plate, and saw that while the program included the toasts to be given by the Toastmaster Hon. Robert Nevin of Dayton, the seven autographed sentiments thereon were from Gov. Theodore Roosevelt, Pres. William McKinley, Gov. Asa S. Bushnell, Senator J. B. Foraker, Senator M. A. Hanna, Chairman C. W. Raymond, and myself. It was an illustrious company of which I found myself a part.

The banquet was a magnificent affair from first to last. The Toastmaster, Hon. Robert Nevin of Dayton was most happily eloquent and the responses were masterpieces. Hon. J. B. Foraker responded to "The Republican Party," C. W. Raymond of Illinois to "The Parity of Wheat and Silver in the West"; Gov. Asa Bushnell to "Ohio in Peace and in War"; Hon. Cushman K. Davis of Minnesota to "New Lands and New Responsibilities"; Bradley of Kentucky—sixth and last—to "Abraham Lincoln, a Native Kentuckian."[19] My response to the toast assigned expressed fully my own reasons for allegiance to the Republican Party.

A large group of ladies looked down from the balcony upon the occasion. As my turn to speak approached, a prominent guest at my right probably observing my nervousness said to me: "My wife is in the balcony, waiting especially to hear you, and has told me if you acquitted yourself with honor to give you a rose," [and pointed] to one in the decorations. Perhaps it is not for me to say, [but] my speech was received with generous applause, and the press, Republican of course—gave me extravagant praise. One saying, "Professor Scarborough's ability as a speaker, able to rise to the heights of eloquence as the occasion demands, was shown by the splendid response he made." And I received the rose[!] Again I felt elated that I had scored for the race.

The banquet came at a time when need was great to cement together Republican factions, a thing in which it purposed to aid greatly. But great breaches are not easily closed, some never fully in life, and this effort did not succeed in healing wounds before death overtook some of these great political figures.

In July I went to New York University where the Philological session was held [that year] and read my paper on "Extracts from Thucydides."[20] I was growing intensely interested in this author and found my students enjoying him as well.

Requests were still pouring in upon me [to speak]. I [was able to] assist in issuing an address as one of the Vice-Presidents at the Annual Session of National Afro-American Council in Detroit. At this time Booker T. Washington's book *Story of My Life and Work* had come from the press. A Boston magazine in which many of my articles appeared [asked] for my views of Booker T. Washington as an educator. On its receipt the editor denominated it as a "strong, well-balanced article."[21] The following extracts are given:

How far this work at Tuskegee is to be considered as a main factor in solving the Negro problem is a question that will arise. There can be no question that it is a vast help. The industrial idea that Booker T. Washington carries out undoubtedly has an important place in this solution. The vast numbers of colored people in these congested districts must continue for a long time a sort of peasantry. Such a class cannot rise to high levels instantly nor by the help of mere brain culture. A higher class in any race is evolutionary—a result of time and growth through lower stages. To let these learn to work wisely and well with the hand is of vast importance; to teach them habits of industry, thrift, prudence, is of equal value. These lessons learned, the higher planes are before them, and will be reached by the gradual rising of those souls with high aspiration, sensible aspirations. In just so far as the leader of the enterprise at Tuskegee keeps it in view that no great principle must be sacrificed, just so far his work is an important factor in the endeavor to reach a solution of the questions that vex us all regarding the race. He is a needed leader in this direction. But this is not saying that because of his success in this line all the race must run mad over industrial education, or that because this line is doing much good the whole world must jump at the conclusion that at last has been found the sole sort of education the race, as a race, should have.

As for being a benefactor, one who makes two blades of grass grow where but one grew before belongs to this class assuredly, and his work, in its entirety aims to just such increase, both literally and figuratively. As to leadership it is a foolish thing to discuss. A leader is known by his followers. We cannot make or unmake a leader by declarations. Mr. Washington is leading well a class along industrial lines. He has followers who are striving to emulate him in this respect, and the good work goes on. But the whole race is not absorbed in these lines, not by any means. The race has been growing in wealth, refinement, learning. All these have worked to produce another class where there may be found goodly numbers on the heights where leaders dwell, a class of which he has never aspired to speak. Mr. Washington is too conscientious a man to claim to stand for Negro education at large; he may justly claim to stand preeminently for Negro industrial education, because his efforts, his success, his well-won recognition, entitle him to this place.

The editor of the *Hampton Southern Workman,* then traveling abroad wrote soliciting urgently "something from your pen." In response to this appeal I began a series of race sketches, opening with Bishop D. A. Payne, which was followed by others on Alexandre Dumas, Toussaint L'Ouverture, and I acceded to the request for a review of Washington's article on the American Negro, which came from the American Academy of Political and Social Science for its *Annals.* At the same time I received notice that I had been made a member of this Association "in recognition," as it stated, "of distinction attained by you in education."

These constant demands began to make work extremely laborious. I was disinclined to accede to many invitations, especially, as at this time the health of the president of the university was failing, necessitating a prolonged stay at Asheville, N.C.[22] This left all administrative work of the University to me as Vice-President. One thing I was pleased to do was to be instrumental in bestowing the degree of LL.D. on my learned English friend, Mr. Axon, who established the Axon Prize for the students.

The year 1900 was to become noteworthy in several respects. In February the Lincoln Banquet was held in the Hotel Alms in Cincinnati.[23] H.C.S., the talented editor and fearless upholder of Negro rights was the chosen speaker.[24] I was also invited and spoke, and I was to meet another reminder of my color when I applied for accommodations at the Gibson House where members were to make their headquarters.[25] I was told they were full. I applied to other hotels and met the same answer. When Hon. W. E. Bundy, a relative of Senator Foraker and the U.S. District Attorney, learned I was unable to find accommodations, he insisted upon giving his room to me at the Gibson and going elsewhere. I remonstrated at such a sacrifice, but he insisted and informed the clerk of his wish, who at once assigned me to the room.

Of this meeting Mr. J. A. Howells, brother of William Dean Howells and a member of the University's State Board was pleased to say later when a guest with his wife at our home: "We were sorry to have to bid farewell to Tretton Place and the host and hostess. Professor Scarborough, by the way, is quite a politician and probably the best Greek scholar in Ohio. He made one of the best speeches that was delivered at the meeting of the Republican State League in Cincinnati."

Several such experiences in Ohio were mine. Once when attending the Modern Language Association I was refused accommodation at every leading hotel [al]though I had brought my credentials as a member of the Association, also letters from some of these same hotels asking my patronage.[26] I was told the letters were simply sent to all members of the Association, not knowing my color, and they did not take colored guests. I had to undergo the humiliation and find an obscure room with scarcely a bowl and pitcher available. In later years my own people have been able to cater to its race with good, even luxurious accommodation in large cities. And this number is increasingly large as the Negro knows better than others. I hesitated to attend the banquet given the Association by one of the leading citizens at the Burnett House, but special effort was made to have me present, and make it pleasant for me. The members were keenly incensed at the treatment and made the hotel people understand that I, as a member of the Association, was entitled to the same privileges and accommodations as extended to others.

All these incidents show that no matter what the attainments and aspirations of the Negro may be, he is bound in many instances to suffer just such treatment, because of his color. Is it at all surprising that many "cross over"? But it would stun those who so proscribe the race could they but know how many times they have catered to some of us who are still included in the race by law, but whose identity is not disclosed, not even by the servants, who do know and silently serve and chuckle.

No, we cannot all be put in one class neither in culture nor color. It is growing daily more and more difficult with the mixtures that time and relationship have brought. Really we are not a Negro race with all the different bloods running in our veins. And there are those who see great beauty in this diversity. I cannot forget Dr. Ward's observation after lecturing to our University. His eyesight was poor. He said, "I wish I could see more clearly, yet even my dim eyes saw a beautiful sight in that audience of youth of all shades of color."

Some editors have said to me they were glad to have me discuss questions that did not have to do with race discrimination which naturally had been uppermost in my mind. But I've often wondered how they or any white person would feel in my place [if] subjected to the indignities that are so frequently ours to endure.

Perhaps nothing pleased me more at this time than to learn how my students regarded me when I was wired by one in Arkansas, [saying that] "our school has this day planted a tree in your honor." And [I was pleased] when Hiram Hitchcock of the Fifth Avenue Hotel wrote me, [recalled] meeting me at Hanover and [invited] me to stop at this hotel whenever in the city.

The event of the year, with results most far-reaching, was the General Conference of the A.M.E. Church in May at Columbus, Ohio. It was a stormy session. There was much unseemly wrangling and warfare for place and position. It was well known, too, that the health of the President of Wilberforce University was waning and that he would resign in June. [And] the General Conference always took a high hand in A.M.E. school affairs.

With these facts in mind the coming election of another president for the University in June was a matter of much concern. It seemed necessary to look ahead, especially as it began to be rumored that "Professor Scarborough," as Vice-President, would seek the position. This was emphasized at one session by a demonstration in my favor by some of my students, of which I had not the slightest knowledge of their intention, nor was I an aspirant to the place, no matter what my friends desired. I knew the situation too well. I knew the President's physical condition and I had no desire to take up the burdens he was about to lay down. But suspicions had been aroused—suspicions that were never abated.

The Church believed the Presidency of their educational institution belonged by divine right to the clergy. The University had narrowly escaped having a layman at its head when Samuel T. Mitchell was hastily elected after affairs had reached a stage that caused his brother, Dr. John G. Mitchell, to resign the place to which he had been elected twenty-four hours before.[27] But this supposed disaster had been averted by the immediate entry of the incoming president into the ministerial ranks. Such a dangerous precedent must not be repeated!

The conclusion of the whole matter was reached at the June meeting of the University Board. There had been disappointed aspirants for the bishopric at the General Conference and one was solaced by election to this vacancy. The Bishop's Council met immediately after this meeting and appointed me as a layman delegate to the World's Methodist Ecumenical Conference to be held in London, September 1901. I leave it to anyone to judge who had the better supposed "plum." This was to be the third Ecumenical Conference which was held every ten years. The first was held in London in 1881. [E]xcepting this and the second in this country, I have been a delegate to each of the others following in 1911 and 1921. This conference saw the legal incorporation of the A.M.E. Church to which my signature was added.

From my own Commencement I went to the reunion at Oberlin of my Class of '75, where I responded to the toast "'75 in Pedagogy."[28] On my return I was reminded of the summer meeting of the Committee on Education at Hampton Negro Conference and had to give a few days to this. I also read a paper before the National Association of Education of Colored Youth on "The Place and Importance of Higher Education Among Afro-Americans."

September saw the re-opening of the scholastic year for us at the University with the ex-president, Samuel T. Mitchell (who died the following year), occupying the chair of mathematics, and a new president, Joshua Jones in office.[29] A formal installment into this office was not then observed with any ceremony. As vice-president I sought to extend the courtesy of an introduction to the faculty by calling a meeting for that purpose. But the incidents at the General Conference had made the president, whom I had regarded as a friend, look upon my movement now with suspicion, and my motives were misconstrued.

In September there came a call from *Pearson's Magazine* which I could not ignore.

Dear Sir:

The "Color Question" has again become so important to both the white and the colored races, that *Pearson's* has decided to publish a series of four papers on the subject by James S. Metcalfe, M.A.[30] The first of these series appears in the October issue, of which we have mailed an advance copy for your consideration. Mr. Metcalfe is treating the subject from the standpoint of the historian, and all the facts point to the terrible injustice done to the Negro by the white man—to the fearful cruelties practice[d] by them upon your forebears—the heart-rending incidents attendant upon the life of the slave. It is a thrilling, yet historically accurate pen picture of the miseries of your ancestors. There must be some moral evolved from this question of man's inhumanity to man. What is that moral? As a representative man of your race, we should welcome a few words from you on this subject, after you have read Mr. Metcalfe's article. Thanking you in anticipation, we remain,

Very truly yours,
THE EDITOR

As I could not attend the Wisconsin meeting of the Philological Association in July, I went to a special session held in December at the University of Pennsylvania.[31] For this I prepared my second paper on the story of Iphigenia—as interpreted by Goethe, Euripides, and Racine.[32] This and my former one were afterwards published in *Education* under the title, "One Heroine Three Poets."[33] I also presented another, "Observations in the Topography of Sphakteria and Pylos as described by Thucydides in Book V." Here I met for the first time Prof. John Gilbert, a scholarly, enthusiastic young man, just returned from Greece.[34] His early death was a distinct loss to the race in lines of classical scholarship. I was also notified of my election to the American Society of Naturalists.[35]

The college year of 1900–1901 was to be one of adjustments in the University with a president either cautiously feeling his way with temerity or plunging ahead to flounder in a maze. We were waiting to see. President McKinley had been re-elected and I had done my work to place Myron T. Herrick in the gubernatorial chair. In a political way I was taking a short vacation, and preparing for a longer one. But there was still class work and usual literary work. This last included acceding to the request from the editor of *Annals of the American Academy of Political and Social Science* for a review of Booker T. Washington's book just from the press, *Up from Slavery*, for its September issue.[36] There was the Commencement address at Georgia State Industrial College in June, for my old classmate—R. R. Wright, now its president.

There was [also] the philological paper for the July meeting at Harvard College about notes on Thucydides relating to use and meaning of certain words.[37] This meeting [was] an "interesting one," as a number of young Ph.D.s from the South were present and listened attentively. In this paper I took exception to the way some American editors prepared their notes on the texts edited. I objected, claiming it poor policy to discuss extensively passages students could easily interpret for themselves and handle flippantly or ignore passages more difficult. My remarks led one of these young doctors to look me over rather superciliously, as if to say, "You are very daring to say so much on that subject." He remarked caustically, "Thucydides seems to be your *magnum opus*." I had written one paper previously on the author and had entered heartily into all discussions of him. It was the first time a member had in thus manner spoken to me of my work. But Southerners were creeping in larger numbers.

What he really thought, I do not know. Some members never seemed to understand how I had succeeded so well in philological work without extensive study and access to large libraries. Even my close friend, Prof. John H. Wright expressed his wonder.[38] I can only say as before that I had studied all through the years since my college days, that the love of

Latin and Greek especially begun then had urged me to every possible research into language study, and helped by friends and discussions my philological work had paralleled always my class work in classics. That is, I had not studied texts as mere texts to read, but I had delved into the literature of these tongues, gathering up my philological learning and continued reading all that I could find on the subjects by the best German scholars.

While in Boston I was given a reception by colored graduates, living in the city or visiting ones representing different institutions in the East—Yale, Harvard, Amherst, Brown, and others. Our young men who were seeking college education were now increasing in large numbers. They were appreciative of my work and literary connections. Such recognition by my own people always touched me deeply, for as I noted in after years, the lack of wide knowledge of Negro thought and endeavor [among Negroes]. Far too many of our youth "know not Joseph."[39]

From Boston I went to meet my wife at Point Pleasant, N.J. just before sailing for the Ecumenical Conference in London. We stopped at "Berea Cottage" to participate in the summer Chautauqua, held there annually. This visit led to another opportunity to strike a blow at discrimination. The incident is preceded by a word concerning "Berea Cottage" itself.

This stopping place at the seaside had been made possible for the race by a wealthy Christian widow of Philadelphia, Mrs. Barber, whose husband, in his life had established Barber Institute in the South, a Presbyterian School for the race.[40] She had seen how proscribed even the best classes were at seaside resorts and had set aside one of the cottages at this place where the leading Negro people of education and refinement might find a pleasant resort to spend summer months. My friend, Matthew Anderson and his capable wife, a physician, were placed in charge.[41] A board of directors named among whom were Frederick Douglass, Dr. F. J. Grimké, myself and others. Here Mrs. Barber spent much time from her own cottage, sharing our company, dining with us, and participating in our meetings and bravely ignoring criticism to help the race. Here many prominent people of color from different parts of the country spent the summer weeks. My wife and I were frequent guests.

This year a party of us including a prominent man from South Carolina and once its postmaster went up to Asbury Park, Ocean Grove for the day.[42] He and I stopped at a soda fountain and asked for a glass of soda water and were refused. My indignation was great at such treatment at this renowned Methodist camping ground where so much was made of religion and Christianity, and to whose great World Conference I was on my way as a delegate. I at once wrote a severe indictment of it to the *New York Times*. The sequel followed me across the sea where I received a letter from one in authority at Asbury Park asking me go give him the full particulars which I did. On reaching London a clipping from a London paper was shown to me, reproducing the article I had written which was causing a stir in Methodist circles at home, and now in London because of the approaching conference. Later I learned that authorities boldly took hold of the situation as on my returning home the following clipping disclosed: "Discrimination against two colored clergymen because of their race by the proprietor of a soda water fountain who refused to serve them at Ocean Grove recently, is not likely to be repeated." Complaints of the treatment of the men were made in a recent letter published in the *New York Times*.[43] The matter was taken up by the Ocean Grove Camp Meeting Association, which has adopted the following resolution: "That any discrimination in business on account of race or color shall be regarded as a violation of the rules of the association and shall render the person making the discrimination liable to forfeiture of any and all rights claimed under any lease of ground or permit for the transaction of business within the bounds of Ocean Grove."

This was done after an investigation had proved the facts to have been stated correctly in a letter from William H. Willis of 138 East Fortieth Street, this city, to the officers of the association. Bishop J. N. Fitzgerald, the President, states that the association has always stood in open sympathy with colored people and that in the present instance the proprietor professed his ignorance of the position of the local authorities on the race question.[44]

This incident caused me to receive considerable personal attention from the foreign press which attention was to increase as the race in the person of the colored delegates was soon again to meet the monster, American prejudice, on British soil.

First European Trip—Delegate to the Third Methodist Ecumenical Conference—London, 1901

We sailed from New York early in August. As it was our first trip abroad everything was novel to us.[1] At that time, too, over twenty years ago, it was not a common occurrence to see persons of our group traveling abroad. Today there is much foreign travel by members of our race. We became the center of observance throughout the passage. On the English Cunard vessel—the *Campania*—we were treated splendidly.[2] We made some interesting acquaintances, too. I met for the first time Judge C. W. Dustin of our own nearby city of Dayton. His interest in us and our work which his father had always upheld began then. I shall speak of this later. Seasickness seized only one member of our party and the voyage of seven days passed very pleasantly and uneventfully. We passed a few anxious hours before we reached Queenstown, as the fog was dense and the fog siren sent out its warning continually. The stop late at night was made just outside the harbor and we watched the novel sight of transfer of some of our passengers to the tenders. The next day we reached Liverpool. The American Consul here was the Hon. James Boyle, former secretary to President McKinley. He was well-known to Bishop Arnett and myself. He had been apprised by wire of our coming. He came out on the tender to meet our liner and showed his genuine pleasure at meeting "home folks." He finished his duties at once, took us in charge, saw us quickly through the customs, and escorted Mrs. Scarborough to the boat train for Liverpool while we men of the party saw to other matters. His attention to us created quite a little chagrin on the part of some of our fellow travelers who were struggling along with the strangeness of the situation.

A four hour ride brought us to London where the novel manner of hunting out our own luggage was the first thing to strike us.[3] After[ward] we accustomed ourselves to the sight of the small engines and the compartment arrangement of the English cars. We went directly to the St. Ermin's

Hotel in Victoria Street where we had made arrangements to stop before leaving America. It was a large magnificent hotel in the fashionable West End of London only a short distance from Westminster Abbey, the Parliament Buildings, Buckingham Palace, and St. James. Many tourists were stopping there, among them some Americans from whom we were to hear later.

The artist H. O. Tanner, son of Bishop Tanner, had come over from Paris to meet his father, and after attending morning services at Westminster we spent one afternoon with them at an exhibition of Velasquez's paintings and walked down the Strand to St. Paul's, the great minster in the East of London.[4] The sight of the mounted horse guards and their change at the entrance of St. James was a novel one. They sat like statues, immovable on their black horses, a change of intervals being made with all ceremony. These old practices are among the things that make London so intensely interesting to strangers.

We had already decided upon a trip to Rome before the Conference opened, and made preparations accordingly. We chose the lower route across the English Channel, as the shorter route to Paris was forty miles from New Haven to Dieppe. A captious conflicting set of waves assailed our little steamer from start to finish of the four hours of passage. It was unceasing succession of sea-green walls and deep green valleys. Everybody about was seasick. Bishops Arnett and Tanner took to their berths at once. Bishop Derrick, Mrs. Scarborough, and I stood on the narrow deck passage and faced the wind, sea, and waves throughout the passage, the best way to do and keep your equilibrium—get the roll of the vessel and become a part of it.

We met the parade of the cross as we landed at Dieppe, the constant reminder that France is Roman Catholic. I am sure the priest who bore it wondered why our black-frocked companions did not give the Catholic recognition, for it seemed to be understood on the Continent that we represented that body. Bishop Derrick's cross worn conspicuously probably led to that impression. It was not altogether a disadvantage as we found more than once when treasures in cathedrals were disclosed quickly to our sight and hastily withdrawn from the view of tourists who might be about.

From Dieppe to Paris, this picturesque Normandy was a pleasant journey. In Paris we stopped at the Grand Hotel, just across from the Grand Opera House. Other delegates met us there who had come from America by the Mediterranean route. Mr. H. O. Tanner pleasantly went with a party on a sight-seeing tour of the city, taking in Notre Dame, the Pantheon, the

Luxembourg, the Louvre (where one of his paintings had the honor to be hung) and the Tomb of Napoleon.[5] We drove through the principal Boulevards and looked upon the bronze statue of Alexandre Dumas designed by [Gustave] Doré [made in 1883].

To us however a most interesting place was Mr. Tanner's own studio in the Latin Quarter, where he showed us many interesting objects gathered by him in the East, and his unfinished sketches. [There was] also, what I should have considered a most prized possession, a portrait of Benjamin Constant, his master in art, bearing this inscription in French, "To my pupil, Tanner, his master and friend, always confident in his final success."[6] His paintings have been nearly all of Biblical scenes, though we possess one other fine piece, presented to us by his father, *A Fishing Scene in Brittany*. To aid him in his work [Tanner had] purchased at the death of the celebrated painter, Munkacsy, all of his oriental costumes.[7]

Who have we among us to succeed Tanner today? Is the love of pure art, as well as the love of pure learning to receive no further notice by our youth in this materialistic age? I trust not. The outlook is dubious.

In art, especially in Paris, there is a general fraternal feeling for all who possess talent. Paris is so used to a kaleidoscope population that [excepting] the omnipresent American, the colored man receives no distinct treatment in hotel, cafe, or concert hall. Nor did it matter in Italy. Even the American tourists there took only a languid interest in our color, and a young man from New Hampshire greeted us in Switzerland as long lost relatives, so glad was he to hear the sound of our English tongue. One man of our color crossed our horizon at Scrivia and we only saw that he was treated as all others. They begged the *centissimi* out of his pocket with [the same] affectionate glances they served out to others. *Is not money then one great leveler?*

It is impossible to give here all that was seen and experienced in this great city, which [we] visited twice again in later years. [B]ut we gathered the bits of this tour which seem particularly [appropriate to me], as a classical student, interested in the thousand things concerning which I had read and taught for many years. One thing amused [us] both: the praise given in Paris and also London for our "correct English." We wonder what was expected from us. After a few days the journey to Rome was continued by only three of the party. Bishop Tanner was made so ill by the Channel crossing that his son took him to his home in the suburbs, and Bishop Arnett, hampered by his wooden leg, decided to return to London with friends.

The journey was of exceedingly great interest to me from the moment we left Paris. The first station at which we stopped was one of the oldest villages of France, Melum, where there was a garrison. Its origin goes back to the history of the Gauls. In Caesar's *Commentaries* it is called Melodunum. Through the Forest of Fontainbleau, through the center of the raisin culture, through fertile valleys, past great white quarries, [there are] quaint scenes on every side; an old woman on a stool, knitting as she tends her cow on a narrow strip of pasture, and another [grazing] her ducks, young women gleaning fields like Ruth. Nothing is wasted in France, every strip, every corner produces something. Our people make far more than these, but they spend or waste it. We must learn to save.

With government owning the roads and with little heaps of stones on either side ready to repair the least break, they are kept in perfect order, magnificent snowy stretches. Women work everywhere. We saw a buxom woman stand at the railway crossing with her green flag, the *garde barrière* of France. We remember that one of the world's most famous singers spent a childhood here with such a woman as mother.[8]

From Lyons the valleys grow narrower and the scenery more grand. A gentleman from this city drew us into the aisle outside the compartment to show the walls of stone which [are] now the only dividing lines in the fields. Hedges have disappeared. Great wine tanks are in sight and the tunnels begin. We emerge into a vine-clad valley as the sun sets, the most gorgeous one we have ever looked upon. It turns pink, gold, and purple as we glide down to Dijon.

The gentleman from Lyons excitedly points out to us Le Mont Afrique, the chain of the Jura, and far beyond we see a rare view, the misty top of Mont Blanc. We reached Macon, the wine center at lamplight. Its name appealed to us to stop for the night, but we decided [to] see Rome first.

After many tunnels the frontier line at Modane was reached. Our baggage showed we had nothing dutiable and we settled ourselves to the sensation of doing what Napoleon could not do—pierce the Alps. We entered the Mont Cenis Tunnel, seven and three-fourths of a mile long, twenty-six feet wide, nineteen feet high with two lines of rails, the first one of the three great bores that man has made through that mighty barrier that nature has placed between Italy and its northern neighbors. The St. Gotthard eastward leads out from Switzerland—nine and one-fourth miles long. Another is still shorter, still another was then being bored, twelve and one-half miles long, still further east. I passed through this on a later trip on the Continent.

In twenty-five minutes we were in Italy. We had read the twenty-fifth Psalm as we passed. Now the miles open up to us [with] vineyards and tunnels, chestnut orchards and tunnels, Lombardy poplars and tunnels, lofty peaks and tunnels. We slowly descended to the ancient pass where Charlemagne defeated the Lombard king [Desiderius] over a thousand years ago. Not far from here Hannibal crossed the Alps on that memorable expedition to the north that Livy describes in his Twenty-first Book, [one that] students so often have read. Soon we rolled into Turin—"Torino" as the guard calls it. [Then it was time for] breakfast and a change of cars helped by a wonderful tall figure wearing a cocked hat with a falling rooster's tail plume. In this land of fruit, peaches were eight cents a piece.

French is always spoken, and Mrs. Scarborough's knowledge [of French] helped us to all we desired to know. There were odd dresses, sober priests, cowled monks, gay lunch baskets and the inevitable bottles of sour wine, vended from the rolling wagons on the platform, and sour grapes.

With all this our good bishop's genial [and] frequent call for "aqua" was to be heard, as he trustingly sent forth his silver cup with no more certainty than Noah had of the return of his messenger. But the cup always came back with dripping contents followed by a grimy outstretched hand for "pourboire." We were in the land of which I had dreamed when I thumbed my old geography in Macon days and I delved into ancient history in Atlanta University. I seemed to tread with Addison "on classic ground."[9]

Then on down through the wine country to Allesandria [we went]. [There were] only twenty-four tunnels from Scrivia to Genoa-Genova in Italy. We feasted our eyes for the first time on the blue Mediterranean. Then we steamed away over the famous Riviera with some eighty tunnels in prospect before we reached Pisa, the city of the leaning tower whose picture in our early days had often perplexed us. There is still a long stretch ahead. We looked back and caught a view of the [mountain] Socracte, and across the plains ahead stretched curious disjointed lengths of the ruined aqueducts of the long dead Romans of past ages. With Galileo, we assent, but the world does move nevertheless, and the tourists of our group were well-fitted to observe its movements.

At last a huge wall rose before us, dilapidated and old. We passed the gates and slowly entered the station. "Roma," calls the guard with a welcoming smile and nods to us as he drops from his car behind to the platform and passes our compartment. We were in Rome and that watery streak we saw is what our beloved Horace so often mentions as the golden Tiber. It was a disappointment to my modern eyes. When later I spoke to our guide, Paglia, of the width and sweep of American rivers the shrug of shoul-

ders assured me it was only out of politeness that he refrained from expressing his opinion that I was telling a Munchausen story.

I was in the land of which I had long dreamed. We planned to see
not only regular sites, but to visit especially places that the reading, studies,
and class work of Mrs. Scarborough and myself had decided upon as providing most helpful information for future use and enjoyment. Paglia proved
to be an excellent guide with a store of knowledge beyond that of the ordinary one. I had never before heard the saying he repeated when one had a
fear of anything, "Is Hannibal at the gate?"[10]

We went to the Roman Forum where fitful excavations had been
going on since 1861 and wandered through the wonderful ruins of Rome's
early day[s].[11] The Palatine brought back Virgil and his representation
of Evander, the Shepherd King as entertaining Aeneas. Here [too] we saw
the names of a lot of Roman schoolboys scribbled on the walls of the
Pedagogium, the schoolhouse.

The vast Coliseum ruins spoke volumes to my imagination of the
days when Christian martyrs were given over to the lions before applauding
crowds. Today the runways from the dens to the arena are clothed with ferns
and grass, from which our guide secured a bouquet for Mrs. Scarborough to
press. There was the ruined Circus Maximus, too, which Livy tells us was used
in the times of the Etruscan kings of Rome for games and chariot races with
seats for 300,000 people. The Romans did everything on a grand scale, yet
Rome fell in time, a lesson for our own America. When men decay, then
empires fall.

[We visited] three of Rome's great basilicas, St. Peter's, St. John of
Lateran, and St. Paul's outside the walls. St. Peter's is too bewildering, too magnificent to attempt any description. We gazed up at the wonderful dome and
the frescoes, and stopped before the high altar where the Pope alone can sit
to hold high mass, and under it the tomb of the saint. We saw the statue of
the saint with its bronzed toe worn by repeated kissing by the faithful. Our
guide let us enter the Treasury where are kept jewels and clothes [worn] by
the saint's statue on feast days. Mrs. Scarborough was delighted to be allowed
to hold back the *dalmatica* of beautifully embroidered blue silk worn by
Charlemagne on the day he was crowned emperor. We had hoped to see
Pope Leo XIII, but he was ill and no audiences were allowed. Otherwise we
were assured it would have been possible for Bishop Derrick and his party
from America. We drove about the city past the Scala Sancta where the pious
ones were ascending the stairs on their knees. We were shown Tasso's oak, a
great old gnarled tree very unlike the tall ones at our own home.

My work in the Seminary had stimulated my interest in St. Paul, shared by the other two [members] of the party, and [we followed] the footsteps of the apostle from the time he came to Rome, a prisoner over the Appian Way. We rode out upon [that] wonderful military road of 293 miles in length, constructed so long ago from [Rome to] Brindisi, and [named] after Appius Claudius. It is lined with crumbling monuments to aristocratic Romans, and beneath are the Catacombs, a vast underground cemetery, showing the niches where the dead Christians were placed in their martyrdom for the faith.

We entered that of St. Calixtus, saw gruesome skeletons, and with lighted tapers followed our guide through a tortuous labyrinth of lanes cut from the tufa rock and lined with recesses once holding the Christian dead. Sufficient to say we kept close together and did not tarry. We came back into the city through the gate under the arch of Drusus, as did Paul, on his entrance chained to his guard. We went to the place of his imprisonment, the Mamertine Prison, overlooking the Forum, a dismal subterranean one of two stories, one over the other. I had read Sallust's fearful description of it in connection with Catiline's conspiracy. Here the war prisoners were strangled and the Numidian King Jugurtha was starved to death. And here the legends say Nero caused both Paul and Peter to be imprisoned before [being] led to death, and that Peter converted the two jailers and baptized them from a living spring that gushed forth. Bishop Derrick procured a small bottle of this water which he brought home for similar purposes.

We went to the Protestant Cemetery where Keats and the heart of Shelley are interred and—what interested Mrs. Scarborough in particular—where also was buried the heart of her former instructor in history, Mary Sheldon Barnes, the daughter of the famous American educator, Dr. Edward Sheldon.[12]

We rode out to the Abbey of the Three Fountains, which legend says was named from the fact that three fountains sprang from the three spots touched by the head of the apostle when beheaded there. Three churches were built there, one over the place where the miracle occurred. It is a place noted also by the fact that the Trappist Monks had reclaimed the land from the pernicious Roman malaria by planting eucalyptus trees. They [now] make a wine from this tree which they sell for abbey support.

We were surprised by the statement of Father John who eagerly [told] us that he had once been an inmate of the Trappist Monastery on Walnut Hills, Cincinnati, Ohio. His English was faultless and his pleasure at meeting even colored Americans was genuine. At last we followed Paul to his tomb in the splendid basilica outside the walls of Rome. This church had been rebuilt after the conflagration in 1823, but was still unfinished though magnificent now beyond description with its great alabaster columns and malachite pedestals, its mosaics and marbles, its eighty massive granite columns, revealed as we pushed aside the great leather curtain at the entrance and looked at the splendid interior. The convent adjoining the church has a most beautiful cloister with arcades ahead of us over the pavement. The third basilica which impressed us most was that of St. John in Lateran, first built by Constantine. It had been ruined by fire and damaged by an earthquake, rebuilt and modernized by succeeding popes down to Clement XII. Here it is claimed, rest the heads of both Saint Peter and Paul over the papal altar.

Only a few things can be mentioned here of the many that were seen in roaming over the Eternal City. Of the three greatest ruined arches, [that of] Titus, Constantine (which is the best preserved one), and Severus, the first held greatest interest. It was erected in honor of the victory of Titus over the Hebrews and of the destruction of Jerusalem in 79 A.D. While it is a ruin [in places,] the middle is intact. It holds two stupendous bas reliefs, one of the triumphal march of the Hebrew prisoners and the seven branched candelabrum and other objects belonging to the Temple of Jerusalem. This is said to be the only representation left in the world from which to know what this golden candlestick was like. Our guide added another bit of information—no Jew today would knowingly pass under that arch.

There was also the Pantheon that called for notice, said to be the finest and best preserved architectural monument of all Roman edifices remaining. How old and new Italy are united[!] For it was built by Agrippa, son-in-law of the first Roman Emperor, and here the beloved Victor Emanuel II, first King of United Italy rests in a imposing tomb always covered with wreaths. We looked in upon the ruins of the famous baths of Caracalla and others, those luxurious baths that helped to the degeneracy of Roman civilization. There was also the ride to the Pincian Hill where [fashionable people] gather.

We [also] visited what tradition says is Virgil's Tomb, close by which Cicero had a villa. It was as disappointing as the sight of the Tiber. The tomb holds inscriptions and a modern copy of what was an epitaph by Virgil himself when he concludes "the pastoral charge and agricultural toils, and arms I sang."[13] This certainly recalls his *Georgics* and the lines so well known to every classical schoolboy [that begin the *Aeneid*]—*arma virumque cano* [arms and the man I sing].

One thing which surprised me as we passed through agricultural portions of Italy [were] the methods of cultivating the lands. [They were] still so like those that Virgil describes in his *Bucolics;* the long-horned white oxen and wooden ploughs of the rudest kind. But we could not linger in Rome and we, as all good travelers do, took a draught of water from one of its many splendid fountains, that of Trevi, and threw a coin into its basin to insure our return as superstition promised. We were sure the nearest urchin secured it before we were out of sight. But superstition is found everywhere, and as our writer says if one is to enjoy a pilgrimage he "must have faith or perish." Holmes puts it thus:[14]

When doubt is disenchantment
'Tis wisdom to believe.

We had planned to go southward as it was decided that we must see Naples and Vesuvius and we departed for Napoli [at once]. Under Cook's guidance we made the ascent of the mountain whose fiery glare was visible that night on the sky long before we reached the city. Then the ascent was made by carriage up to within 3,150 feet of the crater through the villages of Portico and Resina. The latter was built over the buried city of Herculaneum.

A Russian *privat docent* from the University of St. Petersburg made the fourth in our carriage. Two others carried German and Portuguese parties. The law required a third horse for the ascent. To find one the driver took us through narrow, filthy streets. Curious carts and donkeys piled high with produce, goats in pavement nooks and cows with calves blocked the passage, [supplied] the real fluid to customers—dirt, unspeakable odors on every side. At last [came] a courtyard and a horse and our own demand that we proceed straight to "Vesuve."

With poverty, squalor, [and] dirt on every hand we rode along the bay, up the sloping streets to Resina and through its portal. A boy of nine darted out with bundles of green feed—"lunch for the horse" and perched himself by the driver, [speaking] English gathered by tourist contact. A band of mandolin players surrounded us at the gateway, playing airs and singing songs which aroused various emotions as we considered we were 7,000 miles from home, alone in a strange land and undertaking what was ever a risky feat, for the erratic mountain had overwhelmed a party in 1871.

We rode up a splendid road past orchards of chestnuts, olives, and figs, vineyards of grapes, tomato patches, whose pear shaped fruit was already plucked and hanging to dry in open sheds like tobacco leaves. The verdure grew scarce and at last vanished entirely as we began the zig-zag climb through immense lava beds, dark angry masses all about, [in] long coils like ropes, or piled high in swollen heaps, or like distorted giant roots, hard and immovable. We reached the observatory and rode on over the carriage road, rebuilt since the last eruption to within 3,150 feet of the crater. There we took the funicular train up the next 2,690 feet to the upper station, [which was] 450 feet still from the crater's rim. Here one must take a guide by law to walk over the fine lava ashes. The sight at the rim was awful, the smoke and sulfur fumes stifling. We remained a few moments and descended to the station a mile above sea level. It was a wonderful scene we looked upon, waste and desolation all around, at our feet lazy villages with orchards and vineyards, ships at anchor in the bay, dim islands, west, north, and south. Above Vesuvius's continual pall of smoke and over all the blue Italian skies, Pliny the Elder must have looked 1,800 years ago, when he commanded the fleet in the Mediterranean. He saw, too, a more terrific one on that awful day [August 24, 79 A.D.] when he met his fate with others, when the volcano waked and overwhelmed Pompeii and Herculaneum.

We were glad to descend to the next station [for] lunch and [to] write our postcards, stamped at Vesuvius, [and] take our carriage and go back over the long serpentine road down to sunny Naples. Back from the grandeur of nature to the sordid sight of human poverty and misery, where barefooted beggars [ran] at our wheel with a plea for *centissimi,* and cruel drivers beat struggling raw-hipped mules, [we completed] a day never to be forgotten and one whose combined sights can hardly be told.

We had seen in Italy a peasant life everywhere hard and grinding in the extreme, where the lower classes were oppressed by the burden of taxation. It is no wonder that America is the haven of distressed peoples. [But] there was more to [come]. I had hoped to be able to run over to Greece, but every plan was unexpectedly cut short.

The next morning in Naples I picked up the Paris edition of the *New York Herald* and saw my own name mentioned with others in an article headed "A Tempest in a Teapot."[15] It said that some American tourists in London had complained to the proprietor of the St. Ermin's Hotel of the presence of colored guests and had threatened to leave if they were not turned out. This settled our course. We decided to return to London at once and see what it was all about. As our tickets called for the circular route back to London we returned to Rome, got our baggage, and took the first train for Venice.

On our way we spent a brief hour in Florence, and had time for a glance at that famous earliest bridge of the fourteenth century, the Ponte Vecchio, lined with shops and we enjoyed the sight of the famous Campanile, Giotto's Tower, with its wealth of sculpture which I saw in a more leisurely manner some years later. We reached Venice at night, that noted city of the sea through which the tides of the Adriatic flow every twelve hours. There we rode in a gondola with a gondolier, [although] a modern steam one was already operating on the Grand Canal. We survived the attacks of huge mosquitoes that night and began a strenuous day of sightseeing that next morning.

We walked in the famous square of St. Mark, the heart of Venice, admired the four huge horses adorning the cathedral each of pure copper weighing two tons. What a varied career has been theirs[!] The work of the Greek Lysippus, it is said, they were brought from Constantinople to deck St. Mark's, seized by Napoleon to crown a triumphal arch and finally sent back by the Austrian emperor to be restored to their former proud position. We fed the pigeons that flocked about us, admired the beautiful campanile, which fell soon after our visit. We noted with pleasure the red granite monolith bearing the statue of St. Teodoris, the first patron saint of Venice, and the gray companion one surmounted by the symbolic bronze winged Lion of St. Mark's. We had a hurried look at the Doges' Palace, sought out the old Rialto, and looked up at the Bridge of Sighs, [which] connects palace and prison.

What a strain of historic [and] classic memories crowded upon one as the names of the great are recalled everywhere, emperors, doges, popes, painters, poets, sculptors, authors, and we saw their works all about us, an education, even to look upon. But St. Mark's itself is the center, the costliest building in the world, it is said, to which every country has contributed its wealth. Here St. Mark's body is supposed to lie under the high altar, brought from Alexandria surreptitiously in a vessel of lard as we are told. There are no words to describe the wonderful mosaics. Some were being repaired and Mrs. Scarborough was the fortunate recipient of a handful of these bits of glass. One's pen will run away with oneself if left to wander[!]

There were other things for which Venice [exemplified] for me, [namely] its books, its literary life. Here was printed the first book in Italy, the *Familiar Epistles* of Cicero. Here the French printer, Janson, set up his printing establishment in the fifteenth century and gave the world a new type, the Roman. Here was found in 1490 the Aldine Press by Aldus, the classical scholar. From his press was first published so many classical works, Aristotle, Aristophanes, Herodotus, Demosthenes, Plato, aside from Italian works.

I wanted more time. But time was short. A mere glance at the wonderful lacemaking and glassmaking was all that could be given before turning toward England. We stopped only once more at Milan to see its wonderful marble cathedral with its lofty spires upholding over 2,000 marble statues. It was but a tantalizing look and we were off through the Gothard Tunnel into Switzerland, catching a glimpse of the William Tell country. [W]e stopped at Basle to pass customs, change cars, and gaze upon the Rigi in the morning sunlight as we sat in the coach, bound for Calais. We spent the night there, crossing to Dover over a calm sea and we reached London in a few hours.

We found London stirred by the action of the Americans who had demanded the ejection of the St. Ermin's colored guests. They were a unit in denouncing this display of prejudice and the impertinence of trying to run an English hostelry. [T]hey praised the manager who had promptly told the complaining Americans that he needed no instructions as to how to run his hotel, [and] that any guest who was a gentleman was not to be thus insulted, though every white American left his house.

All honor to Harry Richardson for his noble stand![16] All this because of the prejudice against color. [They were] people of distinction at home. There were five bishops, and a college professor and author, and three ladies, then some of the forty or fifty colored delegates out of the five hundred attending the conference [who] were either invited guests or located in English homes by the management.

Some of the party would have withdrawn in disgust, but the manager insisted on their remaining. The Ecumenical Conference Committee at once endeavored to cover the situation by arranging [rooms] for all colored delegates at another hotel. But this, too, was set aside as segregation as had been attempted in Baltimore ten years before. The upshot was that the seven who had been the cause of the row remained at St. Ermins to be treated with every consideration, while some seven prejudiced Americans finally left.

No further act of this unreasonable prejudice took place. [But] delegates occupied stated portions of Wesley Chapel in City Road at the meetings, [and] some English delegates criticized this, thinking it much better to have the sections mingled in seating. It was said however that a reduction of delegates was contemplated by some for the next meeting at Toronto, seeing it a way to reduce colored representation. However, colored ministers and laymen received appointments commensurate with their numbers and were eagerly sought after receiving equal recognition with the white brethren. I, myself, spoke at one of the six evening meetings at St. James Hall with Bishop Hartzell and others. I and other colored delegates also spoke with white speakers in outlying suburbs.

I wrote at length several articles concerning this show of intolerance and hate for the American and English press. My article requested by the *London Chronicle* was spoken of as the "finest protest ever heard."[17] It found its way to America, but several dailies in Charleston, Nashville, and Washington severely criticized it and vilified me as an "impertinent Negro" and worse for uttering such sentiments. They would not publish my reply. I only wrote the truth concerning the prejudice as it existed among Negro haters in America.

My articles however made me rather conspicuous, but in a pleasant way. Russels called for a sitting for my portrait, and when the venerable Baroness Burdett-Coutts visited the conference she sent her secretary, Ashmead Bartlett, to our section to say, she "wished to meet Professor Scarborough and other colored delegates."[18] She was very gracious as we were presented to her. Later she wrote me of her pleasure at meeting me and of her great interest in my work.

Mrs. Scarborough and myself were dinner guests at the home of Rev. Scott Lidgett of the Wesleyan Methodist Church at Blackheath.[19] He took us to the Greenwich Observatory, where we stood upon the earth's meridian line, a long groove made in a stone slab on its grounds, the letters worn dim by the countless feet. It would take several chapters to do justice to this great conference of Methodists, and so only the main incidents and those things that attracted and interested us most can be included.

As to the conference itself, every subject relating to the work and welfare of Methodism was discussed by individuals assigned to places on the program.[20] Bishop Tanner and Professor Kealing of our church were representatives on it, and almost every delegate was found some place on programs for evening or provincial meetings and Sunday School services throughout London and its suburbs.[21] There were many hours, however, to devote to the attractions of London.

We had read somewhere that "if you wish to see London you should take a bus, but if wishing to be of London, take a cab." That is true, but we also found that if you wish to know London you must walk. We did all three, but the last is best if we would see a thousand things escaping the casual eye or in out of the way places, and we saw much that gave us mutual pleasure.

We made good use of these hours when Mrs. Scarborough and I could steal away from the conference together and go where we pleased. As "two is company" if there are mutual tastes, "three's a crowd." We wandered together here and there and saw a marvelous amount of sightseeing by design and by accident.

One day we were the invited guests of Mrs. Kendall Clark, formerly of Boston, to take lunch and a stroll through Hyde Park.[22] Later Mr. Clark had us take five o'clock tea at his office rooms and lunch at the Cheshire Cheese after an afternoon spent with him as a guide. We went through the Temple Garden where the white and red roses were plucked by Somerset and Plantagenet. He took us to the famous Guild Hall Museum with its curious crypt and relics. Then we wandered on through other narrow streets to the Tower where Mrs. Scarborough was obliged to leave her handbag in the warden's care. [This was] a relic of the precautions taken ever since Guy Fawkes nearly three hundred years before tried his "gunpowder plot" on Parliament.

They were grim things that we saw there in the Tower [which contained] instruments of torture and execution. But the Regalia of England in the large iron cage made a wonderful sight to look upon. What names this tower brings back[!] [So] many eminent ones imprisoned there, Raleigh and the Bell Tower, the square space where six executions took place, including Anne Boleyn and Lady Jane Grey. To see this and to read the inscriptions by famous prisoners on the walls of the towers, all make one shudder at man's inhumanity to man. I was interested to see the Traitor Gate through which prisoners entered, brought up the Thames to their death.

But there were other more pleasant trips, [as] when we stole out to Bunhill Fields across from Wesley Chapel to see the graves of De Foe and others, and read the quaint inscriptions; the hours we found [for] the British Museum, where we took notes on all we could find of Gregoire Pushkin and other noted men of the race for my future papers and Mrs. Scarborough hunted up her "Canterbury Pilgrims." [W]e lingered long in the King's Library over the cases of beautiful and rare manuscripts with their richly illuminated texts. Coming and going we often dropped into Westminster Abbey to run through the Poet's Corner to find famous graves and statues, [and] to copy the inscription over Chaucer's tomb. One day Mrs. Scarborough dared slip under the silken rope and sit in the Coronation Chair under which rest the Stone of Scone.

The social side of the conference opened with a large reception at the Portman Rooms, [where] Bishop Derrick was called upon to speak.[23] The finest was one given by Sir Robert Perks and Lady at their magnificent palace at Kensington Palace Gardens. Everything was on a royal scale. He is a member of Parliament, a man of wealth, distinction, and influence, and a loyal Methodist with strong Christian interest in all things pertaining to humanity.[24] In a long letter he wrote me after my return to America concerning the treatment of the race he had this to say:

> If I were an American citizen I should not trust to legislature to break down racial barriers. I should look to more successful causes to the love of God in the hearts of men, to the practical example and daily personal influence of Christian men and women, to the universal spread of educational and other civilizing influences, and to a frank and full concession of equal rights in the church, in the market, in the courts of justice, in the council chamber, in the schools, and in the home. In Methodism I see a change since our first Ecumenical Conference in 1881. God grant that should we be spared to attend the congress in London in 1921, we may see even fewer signs of racial jealousy, my dear Professor Scarborough.

This vigorous thinker and forcible speaker possessed [an] invincible courage and a sturdy determination to carve out for himself and his nation an ever upward path, hewing close to the line of human rights and justice. God bless the men animated by such spirit, wherever found, and God bless the countries where I have found them—countries where the Negro is as good as a white man.

It is impossible to recall the many pleasant people whose acquaintance we made. We were especially delighted to renew one with Mrs. French-Sheldon who called upon us at our hotel expressing her remembrance of our Chicago meeting and of her visit to Wilberforce after the World's Fair in 1893.

There was one event never to be forgotten. One morning we descended to breakfast to meet the startling announcement of President McKinley's assassination. This was followed a few days later by the news of his death, which owing to the difference in time reached us some hours before the people of the United States were apprised of the sad event. We had been shocked by the attack upon him, but had hoped against hope that it would not be fatal. Queen Victoria had but recently passed away. The symbols of mourning for her had hardly all been removed, now black was again draped everywhere.[25]

That morning our Bishop Arnett presided over the conference and paid fine tribute to the deceased President. Many speakers followed all showing their grief and high appreciation of President McKinley, as a man and a brother in Methodism. Many messages of sympathy were prepared and sent. From our own A.M.E. delegation Bishop Derrick and myself sent a special message. The American delegates were besieged by interviewers who sought especially the opinion of those from Ohio and those who knew President McKinley personally. As one of those, I was called upon to give my own tribute to the *London Chronicle*. The conference [members] recalled that at the last meeting held in London in 1881 [they] had been called upon to mourn a similar event when President Garfield was assassinated.

A memorial meeting was held by the conference at the same time one was held in Washington. It was a solemn and memorable occasion, as was the great one held at Westminster Abbey. All creeds and peoples were represented in the immense gathering in the great abbey. Our own bishops received here a representative part in the ceremonies. At St. Paul's also a meeting was held.

Everywhere every possible mark of respect was shown. The King ordered the Court to wear mourning for the week. Everywhere the flags of the two nations were displayed at half mast and draped in black. Everywhere was heard query as to Theodore Roosevelt who now succeeded to the Presidency. The shadow remained over the conference to the close. Such a tragedy makes the whole world kin.

Our longest excursion out of London was to Oxford where we spent the day. An introductory letter from Dr. Axon secured us the attention of the librarian of the famous Bodleian Library who pointed out its special treasures. I was especially interested in the specimens of papyrus and the reduced alphabetical characters called *minuscule* from the Seventh Century. There were the *ostraka,* polished tablets and funeral ones placed on the breast of the dead. There was a "Logia" fragment, a Virgil of the tenth century in broken Lombard, an annotation of Euclid's *Elements* dating back to A.D. 888, and the sight of Duke Humphrey's books chained to their cases was a relic of olden times. Later, I sent Mr. N. copies of our catalogue and of my own humble work for which he sent me gracious thanks "from the Curator."[26]

We climbed the dome of Radcliffe for the first full view of the "city of pinnacles and groves" and strolled out into High Street with its splendid curve of colleges. We crossed the bridge over the Cherwell and into the Botanical Gardens. We saw Magdalen College, walked under its beautiful cloisters, gazed at its quaint statues, and wandered down the shady water walk that Addison so often trod. From its ivy covered ground Mrs. Scarborough bore away leafy mementos for her class in English Literature. We looked into St. Mary's Church where Wycliffe preached and Cranmer recanted.[27] Carpenters were now making repairs. We entered Christ Church under its noble gateway and walked through its grand hall. We were wishing we might remain to hear from Tom Tower the curfew toll. We saw its old world kitchen and dining hall with the master's table at the end on a dais and the students' long ones ranged on either side below with backless benches, all strange to our American eyes and customs. Here John and Charles Wesley were once members of the House.[28]

The magnificence of the architecture was a delight to the eyes, as was the beauty of the gardens with deer browsing peacefully in the distance. We wandered down Broad Street and saw the Martyrs' Memorial, a striking one, erected near the spot where Cranmer, Ridley, and Latimer were burned at the stake for the faith.[29] We were on the ground of Methodism with its Wesley Memorial Chapel. Here it is claimed Methodism was born. John Wesley was a resident fellow of Lincoln College. We found too a Temperance Hotel named "Wilberforce."

At last we took a late lunch opposite the Sheldonian Theater where we could see curious busts on the pedestals at the entrance. We then crossed the street for a closer view. The design of this splendid building was suggested by the ancient Theater of Marcellus in Rome. It is now used for Oxford's great assembly occasions. Here prize orations are given and honor degrees conferred on eminent men with pomp and ceremony. The warden learning my position from my card invited us both to ascend to the platform and sit in the Chancellor's Chair that we might better view this immense auditorium. Then we took a last view of this noted seat of learning. It was a wonderful panorama from the cupola on the roof. Four of Oxford's Colleges are now open to women [I might add].[30]

We returned to London to find that our delegation had had its picture taken at the Wesleys' graves and we were not in it. But we had had what repaid for anything missed, our day at Oxford. At the close of the conference speaking appointments were made for the delegates who were to spend more time in England. My own was in Manchester where we went at once to my friend, Dr. Axon, although our assignment was to stop with Dr. Sherwood of the Free Methodist College. Between the two we were finely entertained. We [noticed] some English scholar customs at dinner with Dr. Sherwood. Students occupied long benches on either side of the long table, chairs at the upper end being placed for guests. The students, all studying for the ministry, read a chapter and pronounced grace.

Dr. Axon and his gracious German wife spared no pains to make us at home and show us all that Manchester offered the sightseer. The only drawback was that they were strict vegetarians and we yearned at times for a good beefsteak.[31] The Lord Mayor of Manchester gave a reception in honor of the visiting delegates. We met interesting people and received much special attention. The Lady Mayoress was delighted to show Mrs. Scarborough and Mrs. Axon the Mayoress's neck chain of gold and ivory bales, representing the great manufactures of Manchester. I was also surprised and pleased to receive a few days later a history of Manchester, a beautiful bound volume bearing an inscription to myself, a presentation from Sir John Harwood through his secretary.[32]

Manchester is rich in libraries as I soon found under Dr. Axon's guidance. The famous Chetham Library of some 60,000 volumes has many rare and ancient manuscripts—most interesting to an antiquarian. Then there is the John Rutland's Library which includes the costly Althorp Library of Earl Spencer, totaling some 90,000 volumes with the finest collection of Bibles from the sixth century. There is also a Free Reference Library of 125,000 volumes. I could have spent months among these books with Dr. Axon's enriching knowledge and comment to aid me. Add to this the small De Quincey Collection in Greenheys near Dr. Axon and we understand something of the city's wealth in books.

From Manchester we went up to Edinburgh to get a long desired glimpse of Scotland.[33] Our letter of introduction took us to the Darling Hotel, kept by Miss Darling since her father's death.[34] They were great friends of our race. The Jubilee Singers of Fisk University had stopped there to be treated royally. When a sister died they cancelled their northern engagements in gratitude and returned to sing at her funeral.

The few days spent there were full of enjoyment. Our first sightseeing began by climbing the stairs to Calton Hill with its magnificent view of the representation of the Parthenon columns and the interesting monument of Lincoln [by George Bissell in 1893]. A pleasing incident occurred that morning.

We had loitered long over the view [and at] last wandered into what proved to be the private grounds of the observatory. Two fashionable tourists had preceded us, and a gentleman approaching had civilly informed them of their trespass. They retreated, but we stopped to apologize for our presence and presented our cards. What a change! For an hour we found ourselves the guest of Professor Ritchie, F.R.A.S., of Edinburgh University, who invited us to an inspection of the observatories.[35] We looked through the great telescope and saw the workings of the wonderful instruments in their delicate calculations. No pains were spared in explanation and courtesy. He was interested to ask many questions about our own work and cordially invited our return. As we departed we could but feel certain of a royal Free Masonry among workers in education, which it has [been] ours to note often in many places. We were assured of more by the noble men who erected the first monument to Abraham Lincoln ever erected in all Europe. It stood just below us on the slope of Calton itself, worthily represented by the gracious gentleman who stood for the astronomical learning of the city.

From Calton's Hill we descended "Jacob's Ladder," the long flight of stairs leading to the Old Town and stopped at Holyrood Palace, the home of the ill-fated Mary, Queen of Scots. We saw her faded tapestried room and the one with its black stains where Rizzio was murdered. I wondered how people lived in comfort in such a palace. We turned into the ruined chapel. We then went up the long street into the heart of the Canongate leading to the Castle with history on every side. We were adventuring without a guide and stumbled upon a sign, "Free Church Normal School." Mrs. Scarborough wished at once to investigate. We entered a gate in the wall and encountered a gentleman leaving the place. We introduced ourselves and learned he was the Principal. He turned back pleased to show us what was once the tress from whose stone balcony the wedding guests of Argyll crowded to look with scornful triumph upon the enemy, Montrose, passing by to his execution.[36] It seemed little like a schoolroom with its dreary interior, its long low desks and backless benches so unlike the teaching quarters at home, but this is where the children of the Canongate were taught.

We went on up High Street passing the home of John Knox whom Mary feared more than the army of 10,000 men.[37] We stepped aside into Parliament Square, an old cemetery holding now but one grave, [that] of John Knox himself. We turned into the Advocates Library under Parliament House. Again our letter of introduction from Mr. Axon brought quick attention and we saw the historic relics of Scotland's early days when Covenanters were tortured. We were shown their protests signed with their own blood.

Out again we went to stand on the stone pointing out the "Heart of Midlothian," and looked at the spot where the Old Tolbooth stood. We stood in St. Giles Cathedral where Knox preached his fiery sermons, and Jenny Geddes began the resistance to the introduction of the English

Liturgy by hurling her stool at the head of the officiating bishop. We continued on up the street to the Castle and Esplanade. For centuries it was the place for burning witches and martyrs; now [it was] a parade ground. Here we were interested to see the Highland Regiment, drilling in full kilts and wearing the curious purse in front, which they call the *sporran*. We went into the Castle to see its relics and the famous cannon, Mons Meg. We peered into St. Margaret's Chapel, the smallest in Scotland. Then we sat on the parapet and looked out across to Calton Hill and Arthur's Seat upon another splendid view. And sitting there we could reach down to the little dogs' cemetery of the garrison where their pets were buried. Every "wynd" and every "close," every step recalls Scotland's exciting history and a host of names with literary fame.

No wonder Scott loved his "Edinboro Town" with its history, its Holyrood, its Calton Hill, its Castle Rock, and its Princes Street. It is the finest street in Europe where the beautiful monument shows the novelist sitting in his chair with his dog at his feet. Perhaps it was the "Maida" of my *Fifth Reader* days, were I to live abroad I would choose Edinburgh as my home[!][38]

There was a call on the genial editor of *Blackwood's Magazine* who expressed pleasure at meeting me.[39] The ride to Queen's Ferry was not to be overlooked, for here was the wonderful Forth Bridge, where Mrs. Scarborough added to her collection of pebbles from under its arch. A hurried visit to Scott's home, Abbotsford, gave us other pleasant memories to carry away. The lastly there was the day spent in Glasgow on Scotland's Day. A look at the University, [and] a stroll about the Exposition then in progress completed our trips in Scotland.

We went back to Manchester to find a message telling us the *Umbria,* the Cunarder on which we were booked for our return, would leave Liverpool the next day. We went to a reception at Salford and learned that the Clarks and Chubbs were sailing with us on the home trip to America. The next day we hurried to Liverpool, [and] found Bishops Derrick and Tanner already there ready to embark. Our Manchester friends came down to see us off. We steamed away at four p.m. from a real land of the free to our boasted one, America.

Yet, it was home, and after all is said and done I am convinced that the distressed people of the Negro race in the heart of our own land must stay and work out the problem through all that comes. Barring lack of prejudice, we could see no sign in our travels of a chance for the masses such as is offered here, [or] what the black man can get if he is determined. I know of no Negro abroad who owns his own home nor one who possesses the wealth that may be found among us here. Some day there will rise from this peasantry of our own a stalwart middle class which will be bone and sinew to race and country. Those who know us are already aware of a higher class that is crystallizing itself into a power even now. We cannot be suppressed. We shall have to be allowed to live, to work, and to rise. Who knows? Some day these American people may be as proud of the Negro as Rome was of Scipio Africanus two thousand years ago, as Russia of Pushkin, of France of Dumas.

Miscellaneous Activities

We returned home on the Cunarder, the *Umbria,* and experienced the discomforts connected with a stormy season on a small vessel which proved to be a "roller."[1] Only two of our party of four were immune from sea-sickness, the one lady gained the admiration of the stewards of the dining salon—now quite deserted—who smilingly passed her down through their waiting line as she made her regular, if uncertain progress to her distant table seat. The rest of us spent much time on deck or in our berths, meditating on the uncertainty of life on the ocean wave—one churchman going so far as to make a last request not to be buried at sea.

From New York we proceeded at once to our western home as I was due in Columbus to appear at the meeting of the Afro-American League of Ohio of which I was the president.[2] This organization had been organized solely for the purpose of advancing the interests of the race, though some disgruntled parties called it a "political one." Just then we were engaged in striving to prevent "Jim Crow" cars from entering Cincinnati from the South [and] we finally succeeded in doing [this] in time with the help of legal advisors of whom Senator Foraker was chief. Before this body I gave an account of our trip abroad and a detailed description of the "St. Ermin Incident."

Following this trip abroad [I was asked] for additional articles for the *Manchester Guardian* and the London edition of the *Times.* I had also made new literary acquaintances of the race, and promised my assistance for some African publications. Chief among them was *Izwi Labantu* (The Voice of the People), a Cape Colony paper of which A. Kirkland Soga was the able editor.[3] [He] was seeking all possible help from the colored men of America in obtaining better treatment in the colonies for the natives and their educational uplift. His leaflet, called *The Black Man to Conference* was one of a series of articles issued by him.[4] In this he [argues] for higher education while not belittling industrial need. This paper was issued in leaflet form in the *Colored Magazine* of New York. It used the arguments of

Professor DuBois and myself to refute the claims of Booker T. Washington. It had much to do [toward stimulating the creation of] the Pan-African Conference, which has now met for several years in Europe to consider questions of race interest and race solidarity.[5] As I have had occasion to remark frequently in lectures, there is undeniably a determination of the darker races to get together in matters of self help and interest. The world will realize this more and more as time goes on and will be forced to give more and more respectful attention and consideration to their requests and protests. The *Ethiopian Review* was another paper to which I was called to lend a hand.[6]

In November I received a pleasant letter from Dr. Winslow, vice-president and Secretary of the Egyptian Exploration Fund, with whom I had formed an acquaintance and had given circulars explaining my own work.[7] Dr. Winslow said: "Often have I thought of the pleasure of meeting you *super pocula* at the luncheon of the Archaeological Institute in Philadelphia.[8] I hope to hear from you as you suggest. Last May I had a long talk with Bumstead enroute to Philadelphia.[9] I spoke of your work in glowing terms." As Prof. Bumstead was of Atlanta, I was glad to hear such.

Still another cordial [and] understanding letter reached me in December from Senator Foraker in which he wrote:

> I write to acknowledge the receipt of your letter of the 11th inst., and to thank you for its cordial expressions of compliment, friendship, and good will. Be assured of my appreciation of it all. I had been intending to write you ever since I received a copy of the London paper, containing your article on the race problem. It was beautifully written and told a most pathetic story that is all too true. While the present situation is dark and unpromising, yet, somehow or other, I feel that light is ahead, and not very far ahead either. There is no lack of desire to remedy existing troubles, but only serious difficulties in the way. I hope when I next see you we may meet under circumstances that will allow us to talk this whole subject over. It is serious and gives me more solicitude than anything else that concerns the American people at this time. When we cannot see the way, we must all walk by faith.

It was always pleasant to know what true friends thought of us.

In June of 1902 I went to Chicago to read a paper before the American Folklore Society on "Notes on a Few Proverbs and Superstitions."[10] I was also welcomed to the Press Writers Association and appeared before the Boston Literary and Historical Society.[11] This year I had contributed to the May *Forum* this article, "The Negro and Our New

Possessions," in which I expressed my idea that these new possessions should afford openings for the race where they could do much good.[12]

There was now a steady call from race papers for articles. Several Negro magazines had sprung up. I always felt it a duty to help them on and it was an opportunity to reach directly the race. The younger members were taking more interest in such race efforts. I wrote quite continuously for the *Voice of the Negro* and *Howard's Magazine* on various subjects intended to be helpful in many ways. Among these the following go to show the scope of this endeavor through several years: "In and around Edinburgh," *Voice of the Negro* 2 (1905): 548–55; "From the Thames to the Tiber," *Voice of the Negro* 1 (1904): 466–475; "Our Pagan Teachers," *Voice of the Negro* 2 (1905): 404–406; "The Negro and the Louisiana Purchase," *Voice of the Negro* 1 (1904) 312–315; "The Negro Criminal Class: How Best Reached, Pt. I," *Voice of the Negro* 2 (1905): 803–804; "The Negro Criminal Class: How Best Reached, Pt. II," *Voice of the Negro* 1 (1904): 867–869, "White vs. Black," *Voice of the Negro* 1 (1904): 25–28; "The Negro's Duty in the Present Contest," *Voice of the Negro* 4 (1907): 531–533; "Race Integrity," *Voice of the Negro* 4 (1907): 197–202; "English Principle vs. American Prejudice," *Voice of the Negro* 2 (1905): 346–349; "The Emancipation of the Negro," *Voice of the Negro* 1 (1904): 121–125; "The Moral of Race Conflict," *Voice of the Negro* 1 (1904): 90–93; "The Negro's Program for 1906," *Voice of the Negro* 3 (1906): 47–49; "Roosevelt, the Man, the Patriot, the Statesman," *Voice of the Negro* 1 (1904): 391–393; "The Negro's Appeal to the Nation," *Howard's American Magazine* (April, 1901); "The True Aim of Education," *Southern Teacher's Advocate* (September, 1905) [and] "The Negro, West Point and the Army," *Howard's American Magazine* (May, 1901).

Hampton still claimed my attention and I continued my character sketches with talks on "The Negro as a Factor in Business," "The Negro's Duty to Himself," and "Co-operative Essentials to Race Unity."[13] In February 1902 I was invited to speak before the Boston Historical and Literary Society on "The Negro Scholar and His Mission." I felt it necessary to keep my views on higher education constantly before the public as so much wealth and influence were being brought to bear to advance industrial education. A higher culture was being thrown into the background. I stopped on this occasion at the Hotel Lenox where I have always been a welcome guest.

My address was followed by a brilliant reception given to me by the Omar Khayam Circle, a literary association composed of Cambridge and Boston ladies and gentlemen of the race. Such items, may seem very unimportant to the general reader, but I feel it well to chronicle such things as well as the discriminations, so that those who may read in the future years may know more of the life in the cultivated circles of the race at the opening of the twentieth century.

In May my article on "The Negro and Higher Learning" was published in the *Forum*.[14] In the summer I spoke to an educational mass meeting in Columbus, Ohio on "What is the Colored Race Doing to Advance Itself Educationally and What Does It Contribute Yearly in a Financial Way to the School Fund?" I found I could present some very interesting statistics showing the race was doing wonderfully well in this respect.

In July 1902 I went to Union College at Schenectady, N.Y. to read my paper, "Notes on the Meaning and Use of Philon and Zenon in Demosthenes' *De Corona*."[15] Here I found myself as a Negro, the object of unusual attention and courtesy. I met prominent people, among them Miss Kate Sanborn, who was especially interested in my work.[16] My greatest gratification came, when Dr. Sihler of New York University told me he had written for the Bibliotheca Library in Berlin a lengthy article on the Philological Association. He had mentioned me and my work as a philologist and did not speak of me as a colored man, only as a "philologist and a man of letters and standing in the forefront of scholarship."[17] He then referred to what Dr. Jebb had said of me at Dartmouth some years before. I was obliged to cut short my stay and omit the social function as my funds were too low to warrant my remaining and I went on to New York. It was often thus but none of my colleagues suspected the reasons for my departure. They knew little of the great disadvantages under which I worked for the production of my papers. It became in reality the wonder of the Association. But I studied and contrived in many ways with much sacrifice to be possessed of the necessary books.

But this particular trip had almost driven me to despair. My small salary was still being mostly paid in notes and promises. The renewal of notes gave me no immediate relief. This made my struggles very severe at times. This was one of them. Members of the Association did not always receive [reduced] rail rates as an association. It made no difference that my efforts redounded to the good of my University in the outside world. It took little interest in my part in such things. This time I had called for my money, only to be told that the sum set aside for teachers by the Board in June had been found necessary to be used for other purposes. To borrow at user's rates had been my only recourse. I had not attempted it at this time.

[Yet] there were pleasant incidents that [came to me] within the next few months. At the opening of the new year the *London Daily Chronicle* carried the following in its editorial columns:[18]

> We have to thank Dr. Scarborough, one of the leaders of the coloured people of the United States, for his kind New Year's greetings, which we cordially reciprocate. The message is written on the fly-leaf of a learned booklet on the *Birds* of Aristophanes, read by Dr. Scarborough who is considered one of the best Greek scholars in America before the American Philological Association at one of its annual meetings at Sage College, Cornell University.[19] The theory of interpretation which he supplies is a political one, quite in contrast to the metaphysical meaning which Hegel read into the works of Aristophanes. Dr. Scarborough was an honored delegate at the Wesleyan Ecumenical Conference, and our readers will remember the two-column letter which he addressed to us, constituting, perhaps, the finest protest ever heard against the treatment of his race.

I attended the Lincoln Day Banquet at the Hotel Hollenden, Cleveland, Ohio, in February and in April addressed a meeting of the presidents and representatives of the Agricultural and Mechanical Schools devoted to Negro education held in Baltimore, speaking on the "The Negro College."[20] I also delivered an address at an Educational Mass Meeting in Quinn Chapel, Chicago.[21] In August I responded to the call for a meeting of the Negro teachers in the United States held in Nashville.

With so many things breaking in upon my class duties, I complied with Dr. Simon Newcomb's invitation to become a member of the International Congress of Arts and Sciences which was preparing its program for the Exposition to be held in St. Louis in September with the proviso that "I be assigned no work to do."[22] At this Congress some English friends were on the program and the Philological Association was to hold its meeting there in the same month.

I returned hurriedly from Washington to find my English friends, Dr. Axon, Mr. Broadbent, a young literary man, and his father-in-law, Mr. Harrison, at my home. [With] Mr. Axon, as Assistant Librarian of [the] College of Manchester, [they] were on their way to the St. Louis Exposition, where Mr. Harrison was to present to the Congress a paper on libraries with Prof. Guido Biagi, Royal Librarian of Florence, Italy.[23]

No better choice could have been made. No man knew more of libraries in general, their needs and contents and how best to utilize these. The three coming at an unexpected moment, with true English love of walking, had stopped over and walked the three and one-half miles from the city to the college, especially to see us. It was their first direct contact with a group of the race, and it was a surprise that delighted them to find such a community of intelligence and such homes of culture and refinement at Wilberforce.

If true friends of the race would take the trouble to see and know more of us as a people from the inside, it would go a long way toward a solution of some of our problems. It is a good thing. One thing is true of so many of the white people who visit our schools and colleges is that they have not yet learned how to address a colored audience without making it evident that they are conscious of the "color line," and talk at us. Some few have learned the art of speaking before us, an art that has its source in the acceptance of the common brotherhood of mankind. These three Englishmen had the art.

I went on to St. Louis to hear Mr. Axon's paper, but I was too busy to take any part even in the Philological Association meeting held there.[24] I looked on but remained only a brief period as political demands were pressing for my services in the Roosevelt campaign. I sent out by request in October "An Appeal to Colored Voters" in a circular letter in which I said the "election was to be by all odds the most important since the Rebellion." There had been much ado, North and South, made over the fact that President Roosevelt had invited Booker T. Washington to lunch with him at the White House. It was recognized as an eloquent big appeal to vote for Roosevelt, "who had the courage to recognize merit and manhood irrespective of class or condition." "[Roosevelt,]" Democratic Congressman Hefflin of Alabama had declared, "should have had a bomb thrown under his table," because he exercised his personal rights to ask any man he pleased to his table.[25] I quoted from the close of President Roosevelt's speech this paragraph as showing why I felt the race should support him: "If I could be absolutely assured of my election as President by turning my back on the principles of human liberty as enunciated by Abraham Lincoln I would be incapable of doing it and I would be unfit for the president if I could be capable of doing it. I do not expect to be elected president by those who would close the door of hope against the Afro-American as a citizen. If I am elected to this high office it must be on my record as the executor of the law without favors or discrimination."

Another strong and fearless President—namely Harding—saw fit to use Roosevelt's language in his own behalf almost two score years later. President Roosevelt's act and his speech should have been kept more fully in our minds when the Brownsville affair became a political issue with our people.[26] I stood staunchly by President Roosevelt then as I did at this moment and sought to win our Negro vote. I was also active in October in promoting with others the movement in our university of the Republican College League.[27] I felt that our youth should learn to feel a responsibility to the race in understanding thoroughly [all] possible movements. I always encouraged them in debates and otherwise to this end.

I was also to hear a bit more just now about the Santo Domingo matters when the consul wrote me at length for my influence in Washington to "correct the injustice which I think has been done to me and the race in the failure to promote me to the newly created post of Minister Resident there."[28] But I was not interfering with the situation in Santo Domingo. I was too busy at home.

I put forth a similar appeal when Governor Herrick was again a candidate. He warned colored voters that the issue was "not a local one, not merely a state one, but to all intents and purposes, national in its scope and the result will have direct bearing upon our future. We cannot afford to swap horses at this time in the midst of the stream."

Governor Herrick wrote that he knew he could count on me. But there were those who opposed Governor Herrick thinking he was not a true friend. I recall well some years later when he visited our University and spoke to our students after he had been made Ambassador to France.[29] As he stood and looked back upon the institution he remarked feelingly, "How I wish the same feeling existed here toward the race as exists in France where there is no distinction and no trouble."

I did not find it convenient to attend the Philological meeting held at Cornell University in December of 1905.[30] There were other duties calling me. I had other papers I felt I should undertake, when I received the following letter from the editor of the *Southwestern Christian Advocate*:[31]

We will issue an educational number of the *Southwestern,* under the date of July 26th, and I want to ask you to write an article for that issue showing what the Negro has accomplished as a student. I mean from the standpoint of real scholarship. The *Morning Star,* a Catholic paper of this city in its discussion a few days ago concerning the education of the Negro had this sentence: "The defect of the pure blooded Negro, racially, is that he has not the creative faculty, that he never discovered or invented anything of consequence, never wrote anything extraordinary," etc. Now will you be kind enough to write me an article showing just what we have accomplished? I have referred so many times to your Greek textbook, of its being used in the North in colleges, and we have other illustrations. I am relying on your interest in the education of our people in making this request.

This year saw the death of Bishop B.W. Arnett. He had long been a stalwart figure in the Church, especially alert to its educational interests. He had also been a leader in Ohio politics always uncompromisingly battling for the Negro rights. He fell before he could participate in the Fiftieth Anniversary of Wilberforce University. [For] in June there was held the Golden Jubilee of Wilberforce University (1856–1906). [It was] a great occasion when addresses were made by Dr.W. O.Thompson of Ohio State University, U.S. Senator Charles Dick, Hon. J.Warren Keifer, U.S. Senator J. B. Foraker, and Booker T.Washington.[32]

A reception was given for the last at my home, [where] Dr. Washington said, "We find one day all we can stand. How do you ever get through with seven?" But we always had seven and had accustomed ourselves to it. At this time our Carnegie Library was dedicated. It had been gained through the efforts of the Secretary of the University, Dr. Horace Talbert. [It was] the first building to be erected since Shorter Hall.

The invitation to attend the Twenty-Fifth Anniversary of Booker T.Washington's school carried me to Tuskegee in May. In July I gave the commencement address at the Kentucky Normal and Industrial Institute. I also went to Detroit to address the National Afro-American Council on "How Shall We Reach and Improve the Criminal Classes."[33] This address was repeated in Springfield, Ohio the same month.

In July and August I was in the east taking part in the program of the Negro Young People's Christian and Educational Congress in Washington. I spoke before the Educational and Ministerial Chautauqua in Atlantic City, and at Mother Bethel A.M.E. Church in Philadelphia.[34]

With the change from the summer to the mid-winter sessions of the Philological Association meetings, the Pacific Coast division held its meeting in December. A joint meeting of the Eastern division and the Archaeological Institute was held in January, 1907 at the George Washington University in Washington, D.C.There was a large attendance, some three hundred representatives from the best universities and colleges of the country.This university was thoroughly Southern, but I have always been treated well by it. I read at this meeting a paper on "Notes on Thucydides—Kateklesan," a passage where I took exception to the translation given by a certain English editor who had no basis for his interpretation of it, as neither the text nor the verb which constituted the pivot of my discussion, warranted his conclusions.[35] In my argument I compared the verb used by Thucydides with the same verb wherever used by other Greek authors, both as to meaning in its simplest form and as to its meaning in compounded words. [And] my paper was received with warm applause by a large and enthusiastic audience.[36]

The Association was invited to meet President Roosevelt at the White House. At the hour named the Association adjourned to pay their respects to the head of the nation. We were escorted to the Blue Room. Professor Seymour of Yale presented the different members.[37] I stood midway in the line. When President Roosevelt saw me his eyes twinkled. He showed both surprise and delight at my presence in such a body. He greeted me heartily and asked me to remain, saying he desired to speak with me when the others had withdrawn. I did so and he asked me to call the following day as he had something of importance to say to me in regard to a position he had in mind. I thanked him and withdrew.

Of course I was curious. From what I could learn later he was so much impressed by my presence there with such a distinguished body that it was hinted he saw in me one whose appointment to a high place might mollify the race. I was then most resentful at his hasty action in causing to be dismissed without honor 270 soldiers of the Negro 25th Infantry accused of "shooting up Brownsville." The innocent had been made to suffer with the guilty. If indeed any were guilty, [for this] was doubtful as no evidence was ever educed to prove the case against any of the soldiers. In this trouble Senator Foraker as usual had come to their defense and fought the battle to the end, opposing sturdily President Roosevelt's action. The ensuing hostility of the two is a matter of history.

My appointment with President Roosevelt was not met as his secretary sent me the following letter the next morning: "Your letter of the 7th instant has been received, and in reply the President requests me to say that the matter he wished to speak to you about he has gone over with Mr. R.W.T. and he will not have to take it up with you, at any rate not at present."

There was nothing for me to do but thank him courteously for even considering me. I never learned for a certainty just what "gone over" meant but from previous and after occurrences, it was safe to conjecture that T. had shown I was an "out and out Foraker man" which was enough to make me *persona non grata* for honor at that time. I have well grounded suspicion however that T. did not stop there, it was not the first time he, being desirous to control Ohio politics, had sought to thwart my ambitions and my personal endeavors for the race.[38] It was also not to be the last as investigations proved when a despicable attempt was made to spread rumors that would deter high officials from taking part in our program, even intimating I had dined at the White House with President Taft.

Senator Foraker was soon to retire from public life. During all these years I had very close associations with Senator Foraker, closer than with any other public man of the day except Warren G. Harding after he entered public life. My files hold many letters bearing on public questions and they disclose full his confidence in my friendship and right doing. Senator Foraker wrote me as to his own actions and reasons in affairs touching the race, especially when he was opposed by some of them in certain movements. He made explanations and sought confidentially to know what course was best to pursue in the various things he sought to do in its interest. In one he wrote pathetically: "I strive so hard but hardly know what to do at times to please." The Senator's confidence was never violated. He wrote me on one occasion when I feared my actions in an election might be misunderstood: "You were doing exactly right [...] I did the same thing and I would not find fault with you without condemning myself. It was not necessary to make explanation. I know a true man when I see him, especially after I have known him as long as I have known you."

I especially cherish words from letters he wrote me from the United States Senate in January:

My dear Professor Scarborough:
I do not know what the future may have in store, but I hope it is full of blessings for you. Your life has been one of great toil and usefulness and it should be, as it doubtless is an inspiration to the young men of your race, who know of your work and are ambitious.

I sincerely hope I may sometime find opportunity to show in some other way than by mere words how much I appreciate your long time friendship and good will.

Yours sincerely,
J. B. Foraker

When the Senator had written asking for a copy of my Greek book, he wrote on its receipt, "I wanted the book in order that I might have a token of what you have accomplished, as a testimony in favor of the capacity of your race not only to make progress, but to do the most difficult deeds. Surely there is nothing more calculated to test the intellect than the preparation of a Greek work." I knew well the rare worth of the man who clung to our cause to the end at the risk and cost of every political ambition.

About this time it was necessary to fill a vacancy by placing a Democrat on the State Board at the University and I was connected with it. It has been my good fortune to be on most friendly terms with the Governors of Ohio from Governor Foster's day and I had been confidentially consulted many times in regard to matters pertaining especially to the race, and its interests. Now Governor Harris sent for me, and said he "knew many Democrats," but was not just sure that he knew a man he "would like to appoint to fill this position." He asked me if I knew any Democrats that I could recommend. I replied I thought I did and named Judge M. W. Beacom of Cleveland, a graduate of my own Alma Mater.[39] He then asked me to go to Cleveland and see if Judge Beacom would accept the position. I did so telling him I was looking for a good Democrat and that he was the best representative of the party that I knew for the place mentioned. He replied, "I will be glad to accept the place if Governor Harris appoints me." I reported this to the Governor and Judge Beacom was immediately appointed to the position. He served us well for a few years when his health caused him to retire.

Mr. Ray Stannard Baker visited Wilberforce this year seeking material for his new book, *Following the Color Line.*[40] [But] like many others who seek to know race life from the inside in a few hours visitation, he failed to get fully into the real heart of things, generalizing from too few particulars, and like many who interview our people he learned only what the few interviewed chose that he should learn. When the Negro chooses he can be as non-committal as any race.

At this time I had sent my article on "Greek Learning and Human Liberty" to Doctor Ward, who hastened to say [that it] pleased him greatly, coming from such a learned source: "My dear Professor Scarborough, I thank you for your paper. It is a fresh and valuable presentation of the value of Greek study and especially appropriate for your students."[41] At the close of the year I went to Chicago University to read before the Philological Association my paper on "The Greeks and Suicide."[42]

Made President of Wilberforce University

As indicated in the previous chapter, I went to the Philological Association in December. Because of this I had been unable to accept the invitation to Atlanta University for the inauguration of its new president, Edward Twitchell Ware, son of Edmund Asa Ware, the founder and first president, and my instructor in Atlanta school days. The occasion was to be a memorial as well to this founder. Doctor Ware wrote me of his great disappointment that "you could not be present at the inauguration."[1] Again it had been a matter of finance, so I chose the Chicago meeting [al]though I too was disappointed. But in April I was present at the anniversary of the founding of Tuskegee. [I also involved myself] in issuing an appeal to the Negro citizens of Ohio to vote "No" for the Home Rule on the Temperance Question. Instead I proposed and voted "Yes" for the state wide prohibition of the liquor traffic, [for I] was always on the side of temperance though never a fanatic. I was convinced as time passed that the enforcement laws as they stood were not accomplishing the desired end.

[Al]though I had felt unable to go to Atlanta in December I was not to be let off easily. At once I received the invitation from the new president to deliver the address [on] May 28th at Dr. E. T. Ware's first commencement.[2] I could not refuse. It was an aspiring occasion with many prominent Northern friends present. My address on the "Mission of the Negro Graduate" was called "a masterly presentation." It was a day of thronging memories, and as "Atlanta's First Graduate" as I was introduced, I indulged in recalling them in my opening words as follows:

> So to me this invitation to address the graduating classes of 1908 comes bringing thronging memories. More than this, it comes with a peculiar emphasis, standing as I do the first student sent out from these walls ready to enter higher work. I feel therefore that I may lay a just claim to being Atlanta's first graduate. [I was] the first prepared under the personal training of its distinguished founder and first President, Edmund A. Ware, a man who

stood as a father to me in the years I spent here, a man who was one of the salt of the earth.

Because of this, in accepting this invitation I have been deeply impressed with the thought that this occasion must be made to form a most fitting link of present with past, when the product of the illustrious father's training addresses the first class sent out under the eminent son. I am charged, as it were, to bring you a message from that experience that means so much to me, a word from the life of one who laid it down in consecrated service for the race of which you and I form a part, a word that shall serve to guide your footsteps and mold your actions in that future upon which you launch your boats tomorrow.

[Then] after speaking of "Education and Usefulness," of "Acquirements Expected," of the "Mission and Boundless Opportunity for Service," of the "Importance of Versatility," and "The Need for Toil and Sacrifice," I closed with this charge: "Go forth with a fixed determination that you will make your service tell on your day and generation. Act wisely, cultivate tolerance and forbearance, while not abating your manliness; make friends, but do your duty regardless of enemies; teach all virtues and condemn all vices. Go forth, determined to convince the world of the worth and necessity of scholarship and learning, to lead our people to higher and better lives, and to an honored place among races."

Here I met that noble woman, Miss Jane Addams, who out of her wide experience in our community life gave much practical advice coupled with this suggestive conclusion to the graduates.[3] [She said:] "After all, the families in one place or another, of one nationality or another, must be founded on somewhat the same lines, and if it is given to you, as I believe it is, to make a fresher start than some of the other people I have been able to meet, to make your adaptation with the advantage of knowing something of the best, by restraining yourselves by some sort of training and belief in the better things, you should count yourselves most fortunate."

Concerning my own address, President Ware wrote me: "It was especially gratifying to me to have you, one of the first who ever studied under my father, to be present and take part in my first commencement."[4]

In this same month my own church university in Atlanta, Morris Brown, conferred on me the degree of Ph.D.[5] I may be mistaken, but I do not recall any occasion in Atlanta University's history when it conferred an honorary degree. It was still a university in the South, [al]though controlled by Northern philanthropy and was ever cautious. [But I] was not through with commencements. I returned from Atlanta to prepare for the closing of my [own] class work at Wilberforce, little thinking a great change was to come to me which would alter my whole life. The General Conference of the A.M.E. Church had been held in May [which] I had not attended. As L. H. Reynolds wrote me: "There was many a 'deal' even in church politics that left you and some other good men out of delegations to it."[6]

My own commencement was now to take place. The growing dissatisfaction of the Trustees and friends with the management and condition of University affairs expressed itself in the decision to retire the incumbent and elect another head. This was done and the Vice-President was made Acting-President *pro tem.* In a few days the Board changed this and made me President of the University.

Knowing the real state of the internal affairs [I knew] there was little desirable in this promotion, but there were friends interested in the University's welfare who insisted. One wrote, "Take it. You are the only available man who by acquaintance, influence, and prestige can rescue the school and bring it up from the depths into which it has fallen." But many advised me against it saying: "You will never be able to put it on its feet again," [and] "It is a position that sooner or later will cause your death."

There were some other things to consider. The University owed me a large sum on accumulated back salary and interest secured only by notes. I had been told by moneyed men that these were worthless, and so they were unless the University could be released from its situation of overwhelming debt and public lack of confidence. I would be the financial loser unless the college could be placed on a sound financial basis. It is well perhaps that we cannot look into our future, but go on by faith and prayer.

I had faith as Bishop Payne had once had faith that friends in the outer world would come to my aid, that I could add to their numbers, perhaps regain much that had been lost, and save myself and others equally [from] embarrassment, while strengthening the school in moral and educational lines. Even so, could I have foreseen all that was to come to me in the next twelve years, I doubt if my courage would have held out. I accepted, [and] to speak truthfully, I really expected my tenure of office to last at the longest only to the close of the quadrennium.

[As Caesar did in 49 B.C.] I had crossed the Rubicon, come what [would]. In that acceptance I took upon my shoulders a burden that never lessened. Thereafter my whole thought and endeavor were to be continually centered on my labors for the University. Eventually [they] shortened my years.

My correspondence [about this] was not all pessimistic. Congratulations came to me from all sides. "Congratulations on the honor done you."

"Richly deserved for your years of unceasing labor," wrote one. Senator Foraker was among the first to send his, saying, "I heartily congratulate you on the well merited honor that has come to you. I am sure Wilberforce will prosper under your administration. May the good Lord give you wisdom, strength, and courage, and may His blessings attend your great institution in all its undertakings."

Hon. W. H. Taft, then the Republican Presidential candidate, wrote: "I am delighted to congratulate you and Wilberforce on your election to the Presidency." President Ware wrote: "I heartily congratulate you and Wilberforce University upon your promotion to this office of responsibility and opportunity. It means too another honor for Atlanta University for her 'first graduate placed in so important of a position.'"[7] From Oberlin came this: "It is an honor which your prominence there has long made highly probable and which I am very glad to see has been given you."

Dr. Ward said: "I congratulate the University and yourself. You have a heavy and most honorable task and I am glad to put in a word for Wilberforce." One ex-member of the Trustee Board appreciative of the trying situation, wrote: "I look for a brighter future for Wilberforce with such men as yourself in command. I see no reason why improvement cannot be made and confidence restored. I congratulate you on the position you will now occupy at Wilberforce and feel that the interests of the institution will now be advanced by and through your efforts." Still another member of the State Board wrote: "The Lord has surely heard the prayer of his saints for deliverance of the University."

From Tuskegee came this: "I think you are the right man in the right place and we feel proud of your appointment." The Secretary of the Epworth League said, "I am simply delighted at your recent election to the Presidency of the University. You will remember that I said at your table that you would some day be President of the University. It ought to have been so long ago. It means something to have a man of your reputation at the head of the chief university of your church."

The Negro press generally sent congratulations, though some wondered if the "scholarly Scarborough would be able to make an administration that could pull the University out of its difficulties." I always realized the power of the press [however], and from the first set out to enlist its co-operation for my campaign. Dr. Ward's columns were always open and encouraged me. The *Forum* and *Leslie's Weekly* gave me a prominent place at once with my portrait in its editorial column saying:

One of the leading educators of the colored race is Dr. W. S. Scarborough, who was recently elected to the presidency of Wilberforce University, Ohio. The doctor has long been connected with that institution as its vice-president and as head of its department of ancient languages in which he distinguished [himself as a] graduate of Oberlin College and is a member of numerous learned societies in America and Europe, before which he has read many papers. He has written much also for the press having been a frequent contributor to *Leslie's Weekly,* and has traveled extensively in Europe. He is broad-minded and cosmopolitan in his views, cultured, and of pleasing address, and there is no finer representative of his race. There is no doubt that Wilberforce University will take on new life under his administration, and become one of the most potential agencies in the amelioration of the condition of the Negro people and in promoting their elevation through sound educational courses.

Throughout the summer such cheering words drifted in, and had much to do with heartening me for the task before me. I took time a few days later to run up to Oberlin to the Thirty-third Reunion of my Class ('75) and received the warm congratulations of my classmates and the college. I spoke at the Memorial meeting in honor of the first to fall, my old friend and comrade, I. W. Fitch. Over three decades had passed since graduating from Oberlin. It was now decided that a Class Book should be published to commemorate the class and the reunion. Its completion, however, was not reached until the close of the year.

I observed that Rogers, our energetic and generous class president, edited and published it. It was a splendid memorial volume of some two hundred pages with portraits and brief biographies covering the years since our graduation day. The roll call sketches closed with a paragraph picturing a scene which not one of us could forget. It tells of the "boys." Let memory paint the picture of one scene in the last act of college life. In the little room under the organ in the old First Church, the boys were marshaled, ready to march to the platform to receive their diplomas. Professor Ellis stands before them, his eyes fill, and laying his hand on the shoulder of one near him he said: "Boys, I've scolded you sometimes, but I have always loved you."[8] With such a benediction, who could choose but to go forth into life's work with all the earnestness of a high purpose? Surely not the "boys" of '75. So, as a business man, teacher, journalist, doctor, lawyer, and minister, each has made for himself a place in the great field of life. We may rank McClelland, distinguished; Chamberlain, our true great-heart; Scarborough, teacher, author, statesman; Bradley, a factor of high degree in the unlocking of the Orient;

Ryder, Hatch, and Burnell, active agents in the solution of one of the greatest problems of the age; Rogers, the man who "thinks in iron," and whose deeds are loving kindness. Yes. We have lived and these words at that time strengthened me beyond expression.

From this reunion with its encouragement I had returned to lay my plans for the campaign for friends and aid for Wilberforce. No one knew better than I the Herculean task before me. But I had faith that it could be accomplished and I set to work. With no funds to draw upon, I from the first saddled myself with a number of obligations for University debts and needed repairs, and pushed ahead. I recognized that I must leave no stone unturned, no contact neglected in order to interest the public and to keep myself and my work constantly before it. In many respects, as one said, "I needed no introduction, but my work did."

My first aim was to reach the great educational philanthropic boards. Influential friends at Hampton and Tuskegee generously gave advice and endorsement, as did others. Among these were President King of Oberlin, President McClelland of Knox College, Ill., Senator Theodore Burton, a classmate at Oberlin, ex–State School Commissioner O. T. Corson, John B. Peaslee, one of our former state trustees and Superintendent of Cincinnati Schools, James R. Garfield, and Governor Harris of Ohio.[9]

Armed with such credentials I went east for the summer, aiming first to approach Mr. Carnegie, whom I had previously met at Tuskegee, for help in erecting a badly needed dormitory for girls. I was at once successful in placing the need before this great philanthropist. Every spare moment was given writing for the press and magazines, arranging for the publicity I knew to be necessary to gain success.

Realizing my many new responsibilities I decided it best also to retain my place to a certain extent in political life as an aid to my financial endeavors, and before the University. So when the Republican National Campaign opened in Youngstown, Ohio in September, I accepted the most cordial invitation to be present. On the program I found myself listed as Reverend as well as President to give the Invocation on the program where Governor Harris of Ohio and Governor Hughes of New York and Senator Beveredge of Indiana were speakers. I was jovially told it did not matter, for "you will give a good one." I was constantly being looked upon as a minister[!]

In a few days I prepared for the opening session of the University, where I gave a formal address, "inaugurating myself," for there had never been a formal inauguration ceremony established by trustees. In it I pledged myself irrevocably to the task before me in these closing words:

> And now as to my policy, as I take up the reins of government of Wilberforce University, I promise with the help of God and as far as in me lies:
> To bring friends to its aid.
> To reduce its burdens.
> To add to its equipment and endowment.
> To raise the standard of scholarship, demanding good and thorough work.
> To make it especially the Mecca of students desiring classical, scientific, professional, and industrial training.
> To bring all departments into a harmonious whole, working for the best interests everywhere.

This duty over I plunged east again to continue my campaign for aid. I gave up going to the Philological meeting in December held at Toronto, and returned home to give a report to my board of my first administration.[10] I had set numerous wheels in action, as my report to my executive board shows. I quote a few extracts showing the situation I had faced and my efforts:

> When I accepted this responsibility in June last, matters, as you well know, were in a chaotic condition which despite numerous Board meetings were found almost next to impossible to straighten to our satisfaction. My summer was spent in counteracting many adverse influences, in planning, and in improving conditions. To this end I pledged financial aid in grading the grounds about Carnegie Hall, and putting in concrete walks. I pledged funds for gas in the laundry, in Shorter Hall, and my own office. I must insist that the appearance of our grounds and buildings must be made a matter of constant care. It speaks much for us to the world.
> Aside from the above improvements I also prepared to follow some lines looking to financial betterment, such as obtaining a grant of money from the General Education Board in New York in soliciting for a girls' dormitory from Mr. Carnegie and adding to our meager endowment.[11]
> I reached Mr. Carnegie's ear and met Mr. Buttrick of the General Education Board who assured me of his deep interest. Blanks were received from both calling for exhaustive details, concerning our University affairs. These Mrs. Scarborough in my absence gave her personal attention and labor so that they were completed and returned in November. I have obtained pledges of aid and have brought in several hundred dollars toward current expenses. Friends have helped us carry notes in the bank. The promised organized aid from [the] Bishops has begun.

But suits have been brought for old debts and we have lost in several test cases because, as our lawyer said, the Board made settlement without taking these old debts into consideration. We have avoided some suits by payment and notes. As will be seen most of our new obligations have had to be incurred for these old debts which we have been facing all along.

After going into many personal details I concluded my report thus:

Our losing experiences show us that we should be most careful as to legal measures in all our future financial transactions. Summing up, I wish to say that we are striving to build up our impaired credit in every possible way. We have paid interest where demanded, renewed notes where possible, cut down some, taken up some, paid on running accounts of last year, and avoided unnecessary new expenses. We have also succeeded so far in almost paying up all of our teachers for the past four months. Some are fully paid. We hope to square up accounts with all very soon. This we mean to keep doing so as to avoid one huge deficit that has heretofore confronted the school annually. We have decided to closely look after these things: keeping down expenses, paying teachers, keeping our paper in proper shape, and winning public confidence.

Considering that in September there was not a dollar in the treasury, that debts pressed on all sides, [and] that we were really ignorant of our actual indebtedness, [progress has been made]. Not a scrap of paper showing records of previous transactions of the president's in regard to school or dining hall was turned over to me by my predecessor. We began on nothing but faith, hope, and determination to win, based upon the promised aid by good friends and on [the] return of [banker's] confidence, individuals and the general public. For six months we have literally ploughed our way through, groping largely in the dark in many things, held up by unexpected claims in many quarters. When we consider all this through which we have passed since last June, I feel [the need] to thank God humbly that He has given us strength, hardihood, and courage to push forward in spite of all obstacles. He has let us enter upon the new year with a fair measure of success already achieved and renewed hope for the future.

I returned to New York in February at the invitation of a committee of representative colored citizens of Brooklyn who were arranging a movement to commemorate the 100th Anniversary of Lincoln's Birth.[12] They had [asked] me "to honor them by delivering the oration on that occasion." The meeting was an inspiring one, the public notices were many and most complimentary, and they were very helpful in forwarding my plans.

My efforts for publicity now drew the attention of Mr. W. N. Hartshorn whose Clifton Conferences were making better known the race efforts and progress, and were improving race relations.[13] Up to this time, Wilberforce University's work seemed not to have received much attention. Now Mr. Hartshorn wrote to me for help in gathering information. This I hastened to give. Later I was called upon to furnish the chapter on the University for Mr. Hartshorn's book, *An Era of Progress and Promise*.

True to my determination to keep in touch with politics I had taken every possible spare moment to forward the presidential candidacy of Honorable William H. Taft against William Jennings Bryan. I had seen with pleasure the victory of a man I had long known and admired. I was therefore naturally pleased to receive the invitation from the Marshall of the Third Division to become a member of his staff in the inaugural parade in Washington in March of 1909.[14] But my work would not permit me to attend.

I deplored also having to be absent when in the same month a public reception and presentation by the colored people of a loving cup to Senator Foraker took place in Washington. This was given as a token of appreciation for the senator's noble stand for the race in the Brownsville Affair. [Foraker] had fought continuously and valiantly to the end the long battle in behalf of the men so hastily and unjustly dismissed without honor. The end had been really to array such active hostility against him that he had not only been put out of the race for the presidency in 1908, but had lost out in a senatorial contest as well, and had retired two days before this reception. To him, principle and right were more than political preferment. He should have our eternal gratitude. I wonder if again we will find another such friend and supporter.

As March drew to a close I was made happy as I saw the fruitage of my efforts when I received the following letter:[15]

New York
March 24, 1909
President W. S. Scarborough
Wilberforce University
Wilberforce, Ohio

Dear Sir,
Responding to yours of December 14th and other letters regarding Wilberforce. Mr. Carnegie notes that you wish to erect a

Dormitory Building for young women at a cost of thirty-five thousand dollars and he will be glad to provide the second half of such sum, when the first half has been contributed by others and expended. If the building is complete, ready for occupancy and for the purpose intended is to cost more than thirty-five thousand dollars, it will be necessary for you to have such balance in hand and expended before calling for Mr. Carnegie's subscription, so that when same is paid there will be no debt left or further calls for money.

Respectfully yours,
(Signed) Jas. Bertram
Secretary

Then my special work was mapped out for me. I began planning for it while preparing for my first commencement in 1909. [But] I committed the error of making a Baccalaureate address, [and] taking a *text* as basis of my remarks. It was a shock to the Trustees and I was privately admonished that only an "ordained party could preach." I was not anxious to preach, but I did claim the day to be mine, and used my prerogative by obtaining the best speakers possible. I was not to be challenged again as long as I stuck to "preachers." Thereafter while my ordained visitors held forth on "texts," I sat and listened properly humbled and chastened.

The home press remarked of the commencement: "The first year of President Scarborough's administration shows marked improvement along all lines not in a reflective sense, but in a real progressive way. There was a new departure from the usual way of conducting the exercises and this, too, was appreciated and refreshing."

Shortly afterwards I took part in the unveiling of the monument to Paul Laurence Dunbar in the Woodlawn Cemetery at Dayton, Ohio. I had been invited by the Committee through Judge C. W. Dustin to be the "orator of the day."[16] It was a notable occasion. A large assembly of people, white and black gathered to do honor to the "sweet singer" of the race.

The Dayton papers united in publishing a full and glowing account of the exercises, giving in full my address in three columns. Of my part the *Dayton News* said: "President Scarborough of Wilberforce College is a man of fine presence and great gifts as an orator. It was fitting that he should be chosen to make the principal address." Another paper said: "It was a splendidly eloquent tribute." The two distinctively impressive features of the ceremony [to me] were the transfer of the deed of the lot to the mother of Dunbar and the planting of a willow over the place where he lies, as he wished, "Down beneaf de willows [*sic*] in de grass."[17]

It is to be regretted that in the length of these Memorial Exercises only a part of my address could be printed with that of Dr. Davis Wasgatt Clark of Boston, President of the National Dunbar Memorial Association.[18] It was not long before Doctor Clark wrote me that the Dunbar Scholarship had been voted to Wilberforce University.

After this time my acquaintance with Judge Dustin grew into most friendly relations. His father had been one of Wilberforce's early friends and much interested in the progress of the race. Judge Dustin was now to become a very helpful friend in my future efforts and promised me many times that he would not forget my school. His last promise was made in July of 1926 when he had just returned from a trip around the world. He drove over to Wilberforce to see me. He talked over the situation and again said, "I'll not forget." He did not, but chose to do it in his own way, as his will revealed at his death in 1919. He left several thousands to Wilberforce University for the "Dunbar Scholarship Fund Committee to administer."[19]

My hands were now full with many irons in the fire. It was more than I could handle alone. Eastward I went in May and was an invited guest at the meeting of the Century Club and addressed that body. I also had a conference with Booker T. Washington, and had already secured pledges of help to meet Mr. Carnegie's offer. While in New York I was present in October at a complimentary dinner given to a member of the race, Mr. Matthew Henson, by the colored citizens of New York.[20] I was glad to honor this intrepid man and give a toast to him, for the part he had taken in assisting Peary on all that explorer's Arctic expeditions but the first.

There were honors to come to me this fall. I was elected to the Archaeological Institute.[21] The Secretary, Mr. Carroll, notified me and added: "Will you kindly permit me as an officer of the Institute to welcome you into our membership and to express the hope that you may find much satisfaction in the relation."[22] I was also elected to the National Geographical Society.[23] The President of the American Civic Alliance wrote stating his delight "to learn you will be present at our Congress in Carnegie Hall. Delegates from thirty-four different states will attend. The following evening we shall hold a banquet in their honor, and I hope you will honor us with a short address, either then or on the previous evening at Carnegie Hall."

I was also the recipient of the honorary degree of F.Ph. from S. Columbia College of Durham, England. This came unexpectedly through a certain gentleman with whom I had had a long literary correspondence, Dr. Charles Forshaw of Hull.[24] He was a man of much culture and learning, the author, also of a number of works, and in high standing in Masonic Orders. He was also a friend of the Negro and like William Wilberforce, appreciative of its efforts and progress. He was pleased to send me materials pertaining to the great abolitionist and to the noted Wilberforce Museum at Hull.

As I had not attended a Philological meeting since my election to the presidency of Wilberforce, I took time to prepare a paper on "Some Disputed Passages in Cicero's Letters," for the meeting at John[s] Hopkins University at Baltimore in December.[25] The outcome [of this meeting was unpleasant, and here is what happened.] The local committee had sent invitations to the members who subscribed to the Anniversary Dinner. Before this took place after the opening, I received the following letter: "I regret to inform you that the Hotel Belvedere will not undertake to serve a dinner at which members of your race might be present. It therefore becomes my painful duty as Chairman of the Local Committee to recall our invitation to subscribe to the Anniversary Dinner."

I did not [of course] attend the sessions and my paper was read by title. I received shortly after a letter from Dr. Kelsey in which he said:[26]

No one can regret more keenly than I the unfortunate circumstances in Baltimore. If the banquet had been held in any one of several Northern cities you would have been welcome. Baltimore, however, is in a Southern state, and my understanding is, that after the banquet had been arranged the manager of the hotel gave it as his ultimatum that if any except white persons were to participate in it the contract would be annulled. No blame of any sort is to be therefore attached to the officers of the Association, who did the best they could, and who personally would have been glad to have you present.

This was the first time I had been the subject to a discourtesy since my connection with the Association. It did not hold another meeting at John[s] Hopkins until 1920.[27] Sufficient to say I did not attend it.

Back at Wilberforce from the moment I was assured of aid from Mr. Carnegie in March 1909 I began work to meet conditions and had the necessary sum nearly pledged when Miss H. Q. Brown went as a delegate to the Missionary Convention in Scotland. While in London she was able to interest Miss Emery, a former resident of Cincinnati, in our work.[28] Miss Emery wrote for literature and documents and expressed willingness to give a sum equal to the cost of one of the buildings she had given to Tuskegee. This brought Mr. Washington into the correspondence. He aided by suggestions and endorsements.

We received $13,000.00 for buildings. This sum, promised by Miss Emery, and added to that obtained by me more than met Mr. Carnegie's condition. The building committee then decided to enlarge its plans beyond the original sum of $35,000.00. In the end over $50,000.00 were expected to build and equip "Kezia Emery Hall." By agreement it was named after Miss Emery's deceased sister. I feel it due myself here to say that aside from the $13,000.00 coming through Miss Brown's solicitations the entire balance of cost was obtained through my own plans and efforts. I deem it necessary to make this clear because of a widely spread impression that Miss Brown obtained the entire amount needed to build and equip Emery Hall. The committee was pleased to give Miss Brown an honorarium for her good service as an agent in behalf of the University.

As 1910 opened I began to plan for a final effort to meet the sum now needed by changed plans. In this the Wilberforce University Club of Washington, D.C. opened my campaign by a mammoth meeting to be held in the Capitol City under the auspices of the Bethel Literary and Historical Association. The club desired to gain the presence of President Taft and other distinguished men. As I had known the President for many years, the committee desired me to accompany them to the White House and introduced them to the President. It was perhaps an unprecedented thing to approach the President of the nation with such a request. But we went to the White House by appointment. I introduced the committee who made known the object of the call. Later the President's Secretary informed them of his acceptance of the invitation to this "Wilberforce Night."

It proved to be a wonderful meeting with such dignitaries as President Taft, Chief Justice Harlan, Senator Charles Dick, Bishop W. J. Gaines, Bishop Derrick and several others of our own Episcopal Diocese, Dr. John Hurst, one of my students of an earlier day, now Financial Secretary of our Church. Hon. W. T. Vernon, our race representative as Register of the U.S. Treasury and Miss Portia Sprague, granddaughter of Salmon P. Chase, once Governor of Ohio, who had given our school its first large bequest of $10,000.00.[29] Many notables of our race were present, including congressmen, professors, lawyers, doctors, clergymen, and laity, [making] a representative audience of which any race might well be proud.

In my address, I set forth succinctly the history of Wilberforce, its accomplishments, its strategical situation for Negro education, its growth and equipment, the endorsement of friends from its beginning, the work of its more than 1,000 graduates, high positions attained by many, and its needs, ending with this special plea: "Let us remember that education is the saving power of the nation, that Negro education is the absolute necessity for the good of all, that to have good schools we must have leaders of thought, and that no one school, however great, can accomplish all this. There must be many strong centers and Wilberforce University is one. There should be no vying but co-operation of all existing forces to one end, the education of the Negro, the elevation of the race."

Register W. T. Vernon introduced the President of the United States, the Honorable William Howard Taft, closing with these words [that] happily characterized the nation's chief: "On this night, epoch-making for Wilberforce, I present one, who whenever and wherever requested to assist institutions committed to the education of the race, has responded; whose world-wide influence has been extended to us for those things of soul, things that endure; a member of the Jeanes' Fund Board, doing a work that will eventuate more into racial weal as the years pass; the patron of education; the preacher of moral excellence; the philanthropist and friend of the aspiring, the President of the United States."

President Taft in his splendid and appreciative address [said]:

First, I want to congratulate Wilberforce University on having the influence to bring together so large and so intelligent an audience. I am sure it augurs well for the cause which President Scarborough is pressing. Of course, when I see him in a week or two and he comes to see me, I will ask to put it down in figures, and perhaps then he will think he will have to call two or three other meetings for the purpose; but what I am anxious to do is to testify by my presence to the deep interest I take in the progress of [this] institution of learning, which for fifty years has been in my state, and has been full of usefulness for the race and the country.

And again:

[What] I want to call your attention to is the amount of money that is devoted to the higher education of the Negro, as compared with the ten million Negroes in this country, [for it] is not enough, if you were to divide it among that ten million, to make any great amount per capita. President Scarborough can tell you I went over the figures once or twice, and instead of being enough to indicate waste there is an indication that there is not enough money to even educate the leaders of the race, which the race must have if it is going on to progress, as it is. Therefore, whenever I hear of a movement toward Negro education, whether it be primary, secondary, industrial, or university, I am in favor of it from the ground up.

After continuing in this impressive strain, and after saying that "there is nothing that comes from Ohio that is not worthy of your consideration," he concluded genially with these earnest words:

I presume that presidents of colleges realize that their chief function is begging, just as I have come to realize that the chief function of the President of the United States is not to preserve and defend the Constitution, but it is to increase the box receipts. And when I find a president of a university around on the errand that has brought President Scarborough here, my heart goes out to him. I can conceive of no work at times more discouraging than that of opening a man's pocket. It is easy enough to get speeches, easy enough to make speeches, easy enough to get a crowd, if you only have the speeches, but to get the money that is necessary to run a university, that is real difficult work. I look upon a man of that sort as a man who is bearing a burden for his fellowman, that ought to call out the sympathies of all those who sympathize with the object that he is seeking to attain and who know the discouragements and valley of humiliation that he has to go through in securing sufficient funds to make the university what it ought to be.

From Chief Justice John M. Harlan of the U.S. Supreme Court came words equally pleasing, paying high tribute to Douglass, "a man more able than any other man I ever met in American public life to dominate any crowd before which he spoke and induce them to listen to him."[30] He insisted that the white people should not fear being overwhelmed by equality, but it should "march along in the lines of duty," his own responsibility being "to do my part to enable the race to meet the opportunities that are upon it." [Harlan] added: "We are in line of duty when we are standing up for Wilberforce University; it is a university in Ohio. When we find an Ohio university with the personnel of which Ohio public men are acquainted, endorsed by such men as our honored President and Senator Dick, we may be satisfied that if we want to help it, we are helping a good institution."

U.S. Senator Charles Dick spoke in glowing terms of the progress of the race and said the race question "is not a sectional question; it concerns the whole country, yes, the whole Christian world."[31] He continued:

It is not for Ohio to settle within her boundaries, and she has not sought to confine her efforts within her jurisdiction. She has sought in every struggle that looked to the establishment of human freedom to spread her influence around the globe, and she is as proud of Wilberforce tonight as of any other institution within her boundaries, and in the effort that my friend, Dr. Scarborough, is making to broaden the field of usefulness by giving better advantages and greater opportunities for the hundreds who seek admission, but for whom there is no place. It is just as much the white man's part as it is the black man's part to contribute to that end, and by contributing to let something speak more eloquently than words. Let it be cash. You can hire orators for ten dollars a night, but you cannot educate scholars at Wilberforce on oratory. It is to all this that Wilberforce and like institutions are contributing, contributing more than any of us know, contributing more than some of us are willing to admit, in a struggle that ought to brand every man engaged in it as a hero of his time. And in it all, it is a part of the duty of every American citizen to help along in that struggle men like Dr. Scarborough and Booker T. Washington, and every other man who is taking up the work for better things.

It is impossible to quote further from the orators who so ably and generously pleaded the cause I presented that night, words I would wish to record fully here, if space permitted. However I have this regret. If only those who have desired to be helpers had been willing to continue to be such in a wisely helpful, unambitious, and unselfish way and had not been misled, much dissension and effort wasted in controversy might have been saved.

With this send off I continued my labors as a "mendicant," interspersing them with attendance on the other duties of my office. I went to the inauguration of President Gates at Fisk University in the same month of March.[32] I was also present at the dedication of the Carnegie Library at Howard University.

I wrote home jovially, "I must surely have arrived as the Rockwood Gallery has asked me to 'pose for their series of great men, who more than any others shape the destinies of our nation.'" A letter from Tuskegee assured me that "the advertisement and publicity which you have given the college surpasses all its past records. I trust they will leave you alone for the next decade for I believe you will bring Wilberforce into its own soon."

My name also headed the signatures to a strong address to the American people issued by the Negro National Education Congress held in St. Louis that August. It called attention to the problems still before the people, setting forth a declaration of principles favoring all that was best for the race, and condemning unjust legislation and holding the race responsible for individual crimes. I also sent my endorsement at Booker T. Washington's request for a National Negro Exposition.

In the autumn of 1910 I was again in Boston endeavoring to enlist philanthropy in my work. I was again and again to meet the wonder why we had not come to them before. It seemed that since Bishop Payne's day our schools had been lost sight of. So many now declared they had all the schools on their lists that they could carry.

On this trip which at the moment was not a successful one, I suffered a nervous collapse and was ordered home at once by the attending physician. I started but sturdily refusing to give up, and though weak I stopped long enough in New York to secure some promised aid to the school. On reaching home my physician forbade any further exertion. All business was kept from me for a couple of months. Gradually I began to resume my activities as the new year opened.

My friends, alarmed over my condition, could now rejoice over my recovery. Hon. Jeremiah Brown wrote: "Knowing of your many struggles for the success of the University and how you have been so often met by unscrupulous and malicious persons, it is a pleasure to learn of any success that comes to you and [it is] equally a regret to learn of anything that may interfere with your work. I hope you will soon recover completely." My former Oberlin school fellow, C. J. Cox of New York, wrote warning me: "Try not to push your powers too far. It does not pay." I took [their] advice and began to work very slowly. I did not leave home until May when I lectured to the Kansas City Club to arouse the Wilberforce Alumni.

Another honor I highly appreciated [came] when I was informed in March by Governor Judson Harmon that I had been "selected a member of the Board of Trustees of the Ohio Lincoln Memorial Association." I was, he said, "the only colored member to receive the honor on this board of twenty-one," having Governor Harmon and Mr. Zeller, State Commissioner of Common Schools, as Ex-officio members and, headed by Hon. Brand Whitlock. It bore such other prominent names as S. D. Fess, O. C. Baber, George B. Christian, J. G. Schmidlapp, H. E. Eavery of Xenia, Hon. T. S. Hogan, then Attorney-General of Ohio.[33] The board was a representative one of many classes. The Honorary Members were four ex-Governors of Ohio, including Foraker, Campbell, Herrick, and Harris, six Supreme Court Judges of Ohio, Speaks of Warren, Davis of Marion, Shauck of Dayton, Price of Lima, Johnson of Springfield, and Donahue of New Lexington.[34] There were also three ex-Judges of the Supreme Court, Bradbury of Pomeroy, Crew of Cleveland, Summers of Springfield. To these were added an ex-member of Congress, Isaac R. Sherwood, and two ex-members, Generals Grosvenor and Keifer.[35]

It was a goodly company and a high honor to be placed with it. My regret is that it functioned but a short time for lack of adequate financial support. It deserves historical mention here, however. I was affiliated with the Lincoln Memorial Association of later days as with those of Presidents McKinley and Harding. The movement to honor Lincoln became national and I was pleased to be with it in Washington in 1922. It is to be noted that in these many selections [as a] representative of the race, I was looked upon as the "peer of any man."

During the spring there were other calls upon my time. Dr. John Wesley Hill, President of the International Race Forum, sent for "a written expression of opinion as the value of the movement" and begged me "to accept an honorary membership and so far as time would permit help by suggestions and otherwise."[36] Then the Alpha Phi Alpha Fraternity which had made me an honorary member of Wilberforce Chapter called for some attention which took some of my time.[37] For my third Commencement I was honored by Dr. William Hayes Ward's acceptance of the invitation to speak before the Literary Societies on "Forces That Make For Civilization." Ward was delighted to see our work. We were equally pleased to entertain him in our home during his altogether too brief visit, which was to be his only one. [H]e never ceased to keep his interest in us and the race generally. Following the commencement, I made preparations for my second trip to England as a delegate to the First Universal Races Congress to be held at the University of London in July where I was to present a paper.

Second Trip to Europe—Delegate to the First Universal Races Congress— [A] Rhine Trip

The First Universal Races Congress was scheduled to be held at the University of London, England in July of 1911. The Rt. Hon. Lord Wearsdale was the President of the movement, which was sponsored also by other prominent men.[1] Mr. G. Spiller was its enthusiastic active Honorable Secretary.[2]

The object briefly stated was "to favour cordial relations between the various races of the world." I fully agreed with a friend of color who "marveled that Christianity should have existed for nineteen centuries and that the First Races Congress should only be held now." In a letter written to me by Dr. DuBois, one of the American Secretaries, asking me to be one of a special delegation of one hundred of our group to attend it, he said, "In this gathering the Negro American will receive full recognition."[3] I [entirely] agreed with him that it was [very] important that a representative delegation of our people should go and by mingling with the races of the world impress upon them the justice of our cause and the worth of ourselves. I promised to help forward any plans to this end and to be one of the Negro American representatives to go and take part in any programs arranged. One of our college professors was also designated to attend, and Chaplain T. G. Steward, retired from the U.S. Army, made a third who would be present together with his wife, Dr. Maria Steward, and her sister, the widow of Dr. Richard Garnett.[4] Mrs. Scarborough also accompanied me. [She was] needing a change, as she was over-worked and deeply depressed on account of death in her family.[5]

We sailed on the *Carmania* early in July in a torrid wilting heat, and welcomed the first breeze down the bay.[6] It grew cooler as we reached the Banks. Weather generally was good, the liner steady as a rock. There were days when the water did not move in our glasses at the table. We were one of two couples enjoying tables for two, close by the captain's.

Our service was excellent. It came to our ears that the captain had informed the waiters that if we were not properly served he would wait on us himself.

We met a number of interesting people and discovered how small the world is after all, when Mrs. Scarborough made the acquaintance of a Scotch lady doing settlement work in Brooklyn and now going to Keswick. She learned by accident that one of our former students, a resident of our own village, who had been laboring in Africa as a missionary, was taking her place while she was abroad.

The American Consul to Hayti, Dr. Peres was one who helped to make the voyage a pleasant one.[7] For some time I was [mis]taken for this distinguished gentleman and was thus greeted until I made it clear that this title belonged to another. So curious were passengers as to myself that I saw many consulting *Who's Who* from the ship's library. We soon learned that he was well acquainted with Major and Mrs. Charles Young, with whom he had been brought in touch frequently by his diplomatic relations in Hayti. He was a most interesting companion as he knew Hayti well and also the most distinguished Negroes in that country, native and foreign born. When we left Fishguard for the special, (the ocean express for London) he was in our compartment and took dinner with us in the dining car as we rushed through Wales. We parted from him at Paddington Station with regret that we were no longer to have his genial company.

Those who read *Harper's Monthly* will recall a series of articles on Mark Twain by Albert Bigelow Paine. Mr. Paine was one whom we were delighted to meet on board the steamer. I had many pleasant talks with him, and learned that Mark Twain was much interested in the Negro people and had helped to educate one young colored man because he believed in the possibilities of the race.[8] Mr. Paine had been appointed Twain's biographer, and was on his way to visit the former haunts of this great man of letters to obtain material to aid him in the preparation. He was pleased to speak of my *Forum* articles and articles for other magazines which he had read and which he said made him anxious to meet me.

Another interesting passenger on board was Mr. W. Horton, who became interested in us both and talked freely about his literary future. He told us that he was illustrating the forthcoming book by Ryder Haggard, *The Mahatma and the Hare*. The Macmillans issued the book later.[9] It is a fine piece of work, the etchings very spirited and idealistic.

Colonel Anderson, a veteran of the Civil War, from Quincy, Mass., and one who took and held Fort Mobile under General Butler, was another charming man.[10] He told us much of his life in the army. He had once visited Wilberforce in Bishop Payne's day and had met him.

Still another person with whom we became acquainted was Miss Locke, a young English girl who had distinguished herself in Greek literature at Oxford, especially in poetry and philosophy. When she learned that I was the author of a Greek text book and a treatise on Greek comedy, she sought me out and became especially agreeable. I found her a young lady thoroughly enthusiastic in her line of work.

Another gentleman, who from his connection with the labor unions and because of his mission abroad, attracted much attention, was James Duncan, also from Quincy, Mass., and Vice President of the Labor Federation in America.[11] Much that he told me in confidence I afterward saw and realized in the great labor strike in England in the month of August after I returned to the continent. He believed that the Negro should be welcomed to all labor organizations.

It had been our intention to go directly to Liverpool, but as we reached Queenstown, we decided to leave the steamer at the new port, Fishguard, and take the journey to London through Wales. The disembarkation of the passengers at the Irish port at Queenstown is always a novel sight, and we remained on deck as we did some years before to see it.

The next morning it was our turn and a crowded tender left the *Carmania* outside reluctantly to take the luxuriously appointed special train for London. Four o'clock found us at our hotel, the palatial St. Ermins. London has beheld many great events in its existence as a city, and this year was a most remarkable one, because of four things: the great political crisis, the coronation, the Races' Congress, and the National Strike.

The meetings of the Congress were held in the great hall of the University of London from July 26th to the 30th.[12] Preliminary meetings or conferences were also held previous to this time. Various papers, some sixty in all, had been presented and published and these [were] on the wide range of topics, scientific, practical, and philanthropic, with the branch topics, gave full opportunity for a discussion of the relations between the races of the East and the West, and of the "color line." Sixty-two nationalities were represented, Chinese, Japanese, Egyptians, East Indians, Turks, Persians, Italians, French, Spanish, Germans, Jews, Africans, and Americans, eminent men and women of all colors and races, a world of movement.

The gathering in action and movement was in itself, one that called for scientific study in its bearing, its evident earnestness, its watchful attitude, and the indescribable something that bespoke the fact that all had problems and a consciousness that here was the opportunity to see how far people would be understood. [We wanted] to learn if beneath it all there could possibly be brought about that inter-racial friendship that would lead to the destruction of prejudices that have been so detrimental to the proper and just treatment of the backward or subjected races.

As far as the Congress was concerned there was an endeavor to present the situation fairly and to set forth hopeful views for the future. Men of science, noted men such as Von Luschan of Berlin, Sergi of Italy, and Myers of England took part.[13] The anthropological side received close attention from such as Jean Finot, the author of *Race Prejudice,* a book that has received much attention in America.[14]

One thing that impressed all was the use of the French language, the polite language of the nations, [that was] used by a large majority of the speakers. Lord Wearsdale, himself, who presided at the opening, gave the welcome in both English and French. Among the interesting personages who appeared on the platform was General Legitime, former President of Hayti, a stately and highly cultivated representative of his people.[15] He presided on the day that I addressed the Congress on the "Color Question in the United States." All creeds and dogmas had their representatives. Mrs. Annie Besant was one to appear before the people.[16] The position of women in various lands was one theme that interested all.

One incident made quite a dramatic scene [namely] the appearance upon the stage of a Turk and a Armenian together. The North American Indian had one sole representative, Dr. Charles Eastman.[17] Duse Mohammed, the Egyptian historian, was also an interesting figure.[18]

A correspondent of the *Christian Herald* said of it: "Never was there such a gathering since time began. From every country in Europe, from far India, China, Japan, South Africa, America, and the islands of the South, came twelve hundred earnest men and women of all races. Each one paying a guinea for admission and faithfully keeping up the attendance until the close of the last session through days of excessive heat. German professors and highbred English women and Americans sat down to lunch with men and women of all degrees of color."

But the keynote of this wonderful assembly was the unity of the human race and the brotherhood of man. Whatever the subject discussed the brotherhood of man was never lost sight of. It was advocated and emphasized by the followers of every sect and creed and all from the same platform. With this as a basis of equality of rights and opportunity, fair play in the race of life was urged by both Jew and Gentile.

Among other prominent representatives of the race from the States were Dr. and Mrs. Moton of Tuskegee, Archdeacon Russell and son. I was disappointed that more of our leading people were not present. The social arrangements were very fine indeed. An official reception was held at Fishmonger's Hall, where we made the acquaintance of many distinguished people of other nations. We received a shock when to our surprise Mrs. French-Sheldon greeted us there for her death had been heralded in our papers the year before. She had been very ill and looked very frail in mourning for her husband. Mr. Milholland of New York also entertained the Congress at his palatial Kensington home.[19]

The reception at Claridges, the hotel of royalty, was especially notable, [and] the most elaborate of all the entertainments. It was given by Mrs. Elmer Black of New York in special honor of the President of the Congress, Lord Wearsdale, and for all visitors.[20]

The most interesting of all, however, undoubtedly was the invitation of the Countess of Warwick to spend the day at Warwick Castle.[21] At the close of the conference a special train conveyed us to the ancient seat of the Earl of Warwick. We were served both a luncheon and tea under ancient oak and hoary cedars of Lebanon by the butlers from the castle. We were taken through the castle and its grounds to see its wonderful treasures, the sword of the legendary Count Guy of Warwick, the paintings, the beautiful inlaid table, and the famous Warwick vase, found in Hadrian's Villa at Tivoli. We went down into the dungeon and climbed to the top of huge Caesar's Tower, the oldest part of the castle from which we had a splendid view.

We lived in the past on those great lawns where last spring one of the May old fashioned pageants was held. We wandered about the beautiful gardens, looked at hoary battlement towers, and had to pinch ourselves to be sure we were awake and that we were of the present. We left as we entered through the old gateway, over the moat and under the portcullis of feudal days. It was a wonderful trip of commingled old and new, but it left no desire to possess or live in such castles, no matter how historic. Lady Warwick later sent me a beautiful letter in connection with the public work she was seeking to accomplish. Much credit is due Mr. Spiller, the Honorable Secretary, for his successful management of the Congress and the splendid service rendered it. There were other pleasant hours spent at homes of new-made friends.

One disappointment was met by my failure [as president] to meet the benefactress of Wilberforce University, Miss E. J. Emery, who was sojourning at the seashore. She died in 1913, mourned by thousands to whom she had shown munificent kindness.[22] She left her wealth to the Salvation Army by whom she requested to be buried, which was done with simple rites and tender tributes.

I took one day to go to Cambridge University, but as it was my good fortune to spend more time there some years later I will not speak of it here, but reserve my impressions when I write of that most auspicious occasion. I was, however, much impressed by the beauty of architecture and surroundings. As Mrs. Scarborough was ill at the time, I did not remain long. Her illness also prevented us from accepting Mrs. Clark's invitation to her home at Asgard. I did not meet the Lydgetts. Mr. Lydgett had passed on and his family had removed from Blackheath.[23] Ten years had already made many changes.

Our tickets read from America to Paris and return, so that when the Conference had ended we went over to Paris to spend the time before we were due at Manchester where our friends had returned from vacation at Clovilly. In Paris we joined a Cook excursion to Versailles one day, and went through the palace, saw its beauties and to our modern eyes the discomforts of ancient days. We were pleased with the views of the long galleries [and] of the mirrors which lined both sides all within the hall being duplicated, giving the effect of illimitable space. One of the battles was most interesting, the walls covered with immense historical paintings, and busts of great men set at intervals. The room was to be made famous later when the scene of the signing of the Armistice took place there. But if the glory of France is portrayed in its palaces, the beauty of Versailles is in its parks and gardens with its immense worth of art shown in its statues and vases and fountains, all on a most magnificent scale transcending any description.

We attended a service at the wonderful, windowless church of the Madeleine. We took a bus and rode through the Great Boulevards to the Place de la Bastille to see the monument commemorating the French Revolution of July, 1830. We were interested to learn that the key to the Bastille hangs in the hall of Mount Vernon, given to Washington by Lafayette on his first visit to America. We were interested to note the figure on the summit of the monolith which is 154 feet high. It represents the genius of Liberty, standing on a globe carrying in one hand a bird, in the other the broken chain of slavery. The medallion at the base represents Justice, the Constitution, Strength, and Freedom. May France ever hold to her heart the sentiment for which such symbols stand[!]

One thing I must mention [which] we greatly enjoyed as we walked about was the sight of these grotesque creatures of art, the gargoyles.

Those of Notre Dame should never be missed. We are told their primary origin is to be traced to the Apocalypse. A study of them is most interesting. We have some in our own country, but none like those found in Europe. The ["]hideous["] pictures have deep [d]evout meanings. This representation is combined with the practical for we learn Gothic art had no useless ornament, so they are made to be water spouts. The word itself has two derivations, one from a French word signifying sound of running water and another from a word meaning a dragon.

Another day we went with Cook through the Boulevards. We saw much we had seen before [as described] in [chapter XVI]. This excursion took in the Trocadero Palace with its immense dome, to which we ascended by an enormous elevator, a "lift" in Paris, to see the splendid view of the city. This dome is wider than St. Peter's in Rome or St. Paul's in London.

Our guide in these excursions was an English professor who taught his language in a Paris school. He perfunctorily filled well the office of guide, but seemed bored, probably by such frequent repetitions. His face did light up as when he entered the Cemetery of Père Lachaise. Mrs. Scarborough asked if he would not point out the tomb of Abelard and Eloise. He was one of the great founders of scholastic theology and she, the French abbess whose love and marriage came to the tragic sacrificial end, that history has so often repeated. He stopped, looked at us in astonishment, and then ejaculated, "You do know of it? So few do!" As he guided us to it near the entrance, he added in a disgruntled undertone, "So few bring any knowledge with them."

That is what renders tourists the subject of ridicule, even contempt. If one is to enjoy travel thoroughly and profit by it, he must carry knowledge with him. A person brings back in proportion to what he takes with him.

With further time on our hands we decided to spend the remaining days in an individual tour of the Rhine from Cologne to Strasburg. The splendid arrangement of Cook's provided for those who do not care to be hampered by a party, securing everything for us in advance, hotels, and guides. We reached Cologne, the Colonia Agrippina of Caesar's day, but Caesar is now spelled Kaiser. We were met and taken to our hotel, the Dom Hof opposite the great Cologne Cathedral where we could see its splendid outlines and easily enjoy its beautiful interior. We had now to master the German currency just as we had learned something of that of [the French]. One day we went to Bonn to see the university there and saw the house where Beethoven was born. We crossed the river to

Königswinter and climbed the Drachenfell for the fine view of the river and noted points.

Another day we leisurely steamed up to Coblentz where Rhine and Moselle meet and where stands the fine monument of Emperor William I. We enjoyed the view on either side, ruin after ruin, and castle after castle, and turned to the legends as we passed. To see the Mouse Tower, Bingen, and the Lorelei Rock recalled our *Fifth Reader* days.[24]

At Coblentz our hotel was but a step from the river, where boats [sailed by] constantly and a bridge of boats led across to the famous Fort of Ehrenbrietstein. We could not understand then why this fort was struck from our itinerary at this point, and a boys' training school substituted where we saw some simple athletic exercises. We do now.

Germany was then making ready for war. The Algeciras incident had only just been quieted down.[25] We were told there was to be a review of troops by the Kaiser in Mayence. All that night troops from the Fort marched across the bridge to entrain for that city. Their footsteps mingled with the music from the excursion steamers and the band on the pier carried my thoughts back to early years in Macon when I heard the strains of my favorite, "Il Trovatore," float on the air. Yes, I had gone far since my childhood when I had first heard them.

We reached Mayence to find 50,000 German troops in the city and Emperor Wilhelm himself. There was little opportunity for sightseeing because of the immense crowds in the streets. The next forenoon when we took the carriage for the station, from which we were to take the express to Strasburg, we were fortunate in seeing a long and imposing parade with cavalry and the emperor at the head, followed by many distinguished people.

At Strasburg our hotel was fine, but Baedeker [spoke] truly when he said it was "rather noisy." Here we found a new atmosphere of repressed excitement. We well understood it. We took a long ride through the city provided with a French guide. The reason grew perfectly apparent.

It will be remembered that Alsace-Lorraine is that territory that France was compelled to cede to Germany in 1871 as a result of the Franco-Prussian War. Strasburg is its capital. Germany's effort ever after was to Germanize everything, the people being made to learn German and the schools to teach it had forbidden French language. But French did not die out. Schoolmasters taught it surreptitiously and parents preserved it in families.

How I admired their pluck and determination. Today as I write, the territory is again France as the result of the World War. I hope our guide is alive. His face would be full of joy [rather] than [the way it was] when he so carefully yet earnestly told us of that first war and showed us what havoc the Germans had wrought and what the French had suffered. We carried as a last remembrance of Strasburg his impassioned French speech, the ride through [the] Orangerie, a most beautiful park with rows of orange trees. After pointing out a stork's nest on the top of one of the many quaint steep roofed houses, our carriage crossed and recrossed so many bridges, that we asked what water it was. "Toujours c'est Ill," was his reply, "always the Ill."[26] Then he brought us to the Strasburg Cathedral, which in the war had suffered greatly from German shells, spoiling magnificent windows, one piercing the organ but happily missing its wonderful clock. How the Germans loved to wreck such [places] was shown later.

The cathedral was beautiful with its sculpture, its painted windows, its chancel turrets, and its astronomical clock, a noted piece of workmanship and mechanism, where the Wise Men bend every hour before the Virgin Mary, and the clock crows and flaps his wings. It would take pages to describe it. The tall Swiss guide who explained it was, however, more interested in me, and asked in an aside if I was from Africa or India.

From Strasburg we proceeded to Paris. The only incident was when a stout sleepy German in our compartment hearing us speak straightened up and blurted out, "You from America. So am I. I live in New York. I've been to the Baths. I travel with my daughter and husband. I meet them at Basle. But they may stay, I am going home, home in America where I can find comfort and not have to pay a fee every time I turn." He had certainly become Americanized.

We proceeded straight to Paris and London. It was a disappointment to me that I could not go to Rothau only twenty-eight miles from Strasburg where John Frederick Oberlin lived his self-sacrificing life among his backward people for fifty-nine years.[27] We reached London to find Victoria Station so deserted and dirty we were puzzled until we learned that the great labor strike was on and was gripping [all of] England. We had not seen English papers.

We soon found it a grave matter. No trains were running out of London and steamship companies could give no certain date when their boats might sail. Their offices were besieged by stranded tourists, business men who must get back home, teachers who must get to their schools, and worse still the hundreds whose funds were exhausted. Happily we were not worried over these things, [al]though we desired to proceed to Manchester. That being impossible we were determined to make the best of it. Talking with a newspaper man whose acquaintance I had made, we received an invitation to go out to his apartment in the suburbs to spend a few days, his family being absent at Brighton Beach, to rest and see what English housekeeping was like. Our curiosity led us to accept Mr. R.'s invitation.[28] I meanwhile went into London daily to learn the situation.

Over a week later I was apprised of the first train out for Liverpool. We gathered our trunks and hurried away almost fearing it would prove untrue. However, we found a train that took us through Wales with its unspeakable names everywhere, not daring to stop at Chester to see its walls as we had planned, we reached Birkenhead and ferried to Liverpool, finding the same short service and dirty conditions everywhere.

We left all luggage at the Cunard office which was to notify us when the *Carmania* might sail. She was then at Plymouth trying to coal, but feared coming onto Liverpool, as her crew might possibly be interfered with. We learned later that Chaplain and Mrs. Steward and sister had sailed on another boat which left [the] docks with mounted guns on her deck.

Our stay in Manchester was to be brief this time. We stopped with Dr. Sherwood. His students serenaded us that night. We took tea with the Axons at Mr. Harrison's. Mr. Broadbent had died the year before as had Mrs. Axon. Mr. Axon was much enfeebled in health. "What shall I do with my library?" he asked. I knew how he felt. I ask myself today, "What shall I do with mine?" His in the end was given to the Manchester College Library. Four days later we took leave of these friends—never to meet them again.[29]

The return voyage was restful, entirely uneventful until three days out. Then we were met in the morning at breakfast by the announcement by several, "We are going to Halifax." We took it as a joke at first, but soon realized that we were really going to enter that port, an unheard of thing. The question "Why?" aroused curiosity, even alarm and some grew unreasonably angry at the delay.

The captain wisely replied to all that the ship had not put in enough coal at Plymouth. The next morning we found ourselves anchored at the dock in Halifax, a bleak place, in a drizzling rain. He then made known to the passengers that some damage had been done to the machinery in entering the harbor. No large ocean liner had ever done so before, and that aside from coal we must await the necessary repairs, the time uncertain. The notice said that all first and second class passengers who desired to proceed to their destinations by rail would have passage thus arranged. Again there was much confusion and fear of panic in the steerage, as rumor spread. One wise helpful first class passenger went into the steerage and helped reduce the excitement by declaring he and his party were going to stay by the ship to New York.

A few, mostly westerners who felt the necessity of being at home on given dates, took the train from Halifax. The majority remained. The ship coaled day and night, women and men going up and down with baskets of coal on their backs. We stood by the ship and waited after wiring our friends of the delay and our safety.

Two days passed. On the third day notice was given that we would leave after midnight. We woke the next morning to find ourselves on the sea again. We gladly welcomed the sight of the sea gulls as some forty-eight hours later we steamed into New York Harbor. Really, the old Statue of Liberty looked good to every one, [al]though she seems a fraud so often. We docked, hurried through customs, failed to meet friends, who were uncertain as to time of arrival, [and then] arranged for homeward tickets before we sought a stopping place.

The morning papers told the story of a dangerous break in machinery, that really we had been running from Liverpool with one engine disabled, that the break necessitated entrance of a man into one of the large pipes to close a valve before damage could be determined or repaired, of volunteers for the job, and of pulling out three times from exhaustion the man selected before the work was done.

There are heroes in everyday life of which the world knows little. We perhaps never learned the entire extent of danger. But we had a wise cool captain and a courageous crew. Our lives were in their hands and they nobly did their duty. In the end we were at home again to receive a glad welcome and to report the Congress to school and friends, back from the great Races Congress, hoping that the men and women who claim to be such firm believers in the brotherhood of man will practice what they preach, and will help hasten the day when there will be no race problem. The future will show whether there has been any real substantial gain by such a concerted movement.

Labors for Wilberforce University— Incidents

New friends and new literary connections resulting from this second trip abroad only augmented the tasks that became mine on my return. But the change had also given me added strength, and encouragement for the pressing duties of my office. It was well that it was so, as these were automatically increasing daily.

Then a very pleasing event occurred. Again I was to go to northern New England after twenty-seven years from the time I made my entrance into philological circles in 1884 at Dartmouth, an unknown but ambitious young colored man. There I had received what was to me my "accolade." The ladder had been a long one, but I felt that I had mounted at least some of the [rungs], when I received from my old friend, Dr. Guy Potter Benton, formerly President of Miami University of Ohio, the invitation to his inaugural as President of the University of Vermont at Burlington. A letter followed announcing that I together with President Thirkield of Howard University and Principal Booker T. Washington's brother as representative of Tuskegee Institute was to be the guest of the brother of General O. O. Howard.[1] General Howard was well known for his bravery in the Civil War and for the part he took afterwards in the education of the Negro by founding Howard University at Washington, D.C. I felt indeed honored to be thus located.

The occasion was a most dignified and inspiring one. The academic procession to Convocation Hall was gorgeous in color. The more than three hundred colleges participating were in line according to their founding. This placed Wilberforce University quite far ahead of both Howard and Tuskegee. As this was one of so many attended I cannot give space to any further description. While in Burlington I took occasion to make a visit to the Tenth Cavalry, [and to] our colored troops at the well known fort nearby. President Benton had written me the year before that his heart was in Miami, but it seems he had decided to cast in his fortunes with the University of Vermont.

No man knew better the trials of a university president than did Dr. Benton, [which he set] forth in his book, *The Real College,* published the year following my own induction into a similar office.[2] I agreed heartily with his statements as defining what I had long considered to be the relationship between the president of a college and its other officials. His views were in complete accord with my own, upholding my stand from the first as I battled for my right not to be a mere figure head, though the institution was under church control. I know that my church did not stand alone in thinking that the president should be entirely under control of the trustee board. My race had not yet had sufficient time to gain that knowledge that comes from long experience with educational institutions. I wish it to see here that I was not alone in my views as to my rights as head of its chief college, so I cull a few of Dr. Benton's statements for coming generations to ponder over and appreciate their truth. I would urge that a copy be in the hands of every college president and his trustee board. Note how true this first quotation I make is: "The president of a church college who succeeds is a professional beggar." For such an executive there is no surcease of toil from the morning of his installation to the evening of his effective resignation. Speaking of trustee boards, Dr. Benton says that in recent years it is notorious "that in the last analysis their choice of a college president has been governed by his ability to control a financial following." He adds, "Sad is the day for a student when looking for a lofty ideal, he finds in the president of his college nothing better than an expert ability to multiply shekels." Again he remarks what I sorrowfully found to be true: "Presidential duties will undoubtedly require abandonment of reading and research on the special line that absorb the interest of the professor in the college chair." He asserts that "administration is a line of specialization as eminently respectable as Philosophy or Linguistics, and that devotion to problems of administration will make his deliverances accepted as the product of scholarship."

With any of the points made in Dr. Benton's book I am sure college presidents in general will concur: "Time was when boards, not only chose the president and faculty, but prescribed curriculums," but now "no self respecting college president would submit for one moment to the suggestion that matters purely academic should be taken from his faculty and committed to the board of trustees." This is wherein I had sad experience. "Today it would be difficult to find a trustee presumptuous enough to entertain the thought of passing judgment on the quality of trustees. The president is charged with this responsibility and the reputation of his institution must stand or fall on his ability to meet this responsibly." We rightly argue that "to hold an executive responsible for all the work of an institution, including the teaching done would be unfair unless therewith should go the privilege of choosing his colleagues for whose work he must answer."

The pitch is that "no limits should be set for his despotism by a board so long as his power is not abused and while his institution thrives. He should be a leader without being a dictator, an executive not an autocrat in his relations to his faculty."

Again, "the president who knows how to put men to good uses will realize that one of the valuable assets of a successful administration is a devoted body of alumni." No president can afford ever to intimate tò the alumni that he wishes their "hands off" [because] he is running things. And Dr. Benton realized what we all must, concerning the financial situation of a college, that "nothing so oppresses or retards growth of an institution as an incubus of debt, prosperity cannot be found by living beyond income."

One of the first greetings I had received came with the information that I had been enrolled in the work of the National Economic League as a member of the Council.[3] As I had been unable to attend the Philological Association at Brown University in 1910, I deemed it best to be present at its meeting at Pittsburgh University in December, 1911.[4] Here I stopped at the Schenley House, a hotel that had accepted but one other colored guest heretofore, B. T. Washington.[5] I received the best treatment, though I think they did not know my race until I arrived, but unlike some other hostelries, they did not insult me by refusing. Can we ever get away from color? Should time bleach out the race, what then could be made the stigmatizing mark? Perhaps nothing, for white is white and many Negroes are yearly included in the white census and, yes, social life.

Early in January 1912 I received the sad news of the death of my life-long friend and supporter, Bishop Wesley J. Gaines, a man of strong personality.[6] I hurried from an eastern trip to go to Atlanta to pay my last respects to one who had stood by me unflinchingly from the beginning of my career. One by one I see my "Old Guard" departing, I sadly wrote home.

The year 1912 opened with a request by Dr. Paul Monroe for an article on Wilberforce for the *Cyclopedia of Education* to be issued by Macmillan Company.[7] [It concerned] the editorial work [that] he was directing, [and] I was pleased to accept and receive Dr. Monroe's enthusiastic approval for the article I sent in.

My birthday this year was remembered by the seniors of the class of 1912 when it presented me with a beautiful "Loving Cup."[8] Invariably my students had remembered this season since my earliest days in the

University and some pleasant memento was brought to me. Mrs. Scarborough looked forward to these events with greatest anticipation. I was an ideal host as all could testify, even my colleagues who often enjoyed the hospitality of Tretton Place, whether it was a lawn picnic, a "Caesar" evening party, a Thanksgiving dinner for all Seniors and Juniors, a Christmas candy pulling, or an evening with friends.[9] I always bore in mind my own college days and the influence on young lives of such occasions. It was a pleasure to make my students happy.

In the early part of this year I did not go far afield on account of the condition of my mother's health. She passed away the night of the *Titanic* disaster, laying upon me a grief from which I found it difficult to recover.[10] My work was a god-send.

I had made many new acquaintances, among them Duse Moham-med, editor of the *African Times and Orient Review* published in London and author of *In the Land of Pharaohs*. At his request I wrote an article for this paper, concerning which Jean Finot said he "greeted with pleasure any attempt to make the coloured people better known [and] to cause them to be received without the least restriction as equal brother to the rest of mankind."

Such an expression from the noted French author of *L'agonie et la morte des races* was to be expected from the man I had met at the Races Conference and who was doing valiant work in his many books, some of which had been crowned by the French Academy, to dissipate the race prej-udice, and who believed as I do that by "union of common efforts will be created germs of esteem and affection between the brothers of mankind." For this reason, I [have] endeavor[ed] to write for both white and colored papers and mingle with both peoples, in fact with all people regardless of color.

In May I went to a reception in my honor and reunion of visiting Wilberforcians in Kansas City, [and] I wrote an article for the new book [of my friend Culp], *The Twentieth Century*.[11] In July I attended the Negro National Education Conference in St. Paul to which Governor Harmon had sent me as a delegate.[12]

Reports to my board and the General Conference of 1912 showed that these first years of my administration had been successful ones despite problems and debts. The previous General Conference had acted on my rec-ommendation and reduced the number of the trustee body. [I had] always pleaded for the church to recognize fully the place of its school and support it accordingly. Especially did I call for church help in paying more attention to Payne Theological Seminary and restated my determination now to bend efforts toward a school building, a college chapel, a "New Wilberforce." Also, I reported help toward remodeling the first old hall, [and described] the progress of the new dormitory in the process of erection. The good news [was] that the debt of the university had been so cut down that only a small sum had been needed from banks. Best of all I could report what I had determined on from the first that for the four years past the salaries of the teachers have been almost fully paid, and no new notes given except in one instance. This policy of avoiding note-giving to teachers was another thing I had determined upon. The student body was increased, the admission requirements raised, curriculum enlarged and made more thorough, and the strength of faculty looked after. [Furthermore] in these four years we have built up most cordial relations with other schools both in a literary way and in athletics. In short as the church paper said, [I] "had won signal success in placing Wilberforce University before the world as never before." The press, white and black, were cordially opening columns to my pleas.

I and others had not forgotten Senator Foraker, now in retirement. They were desirous of seeing him brought back to public life and higher honor. [To this end] I ventured to write President Taft asking that the Senator be appointed to the U.S. Supreme Court.[13] A letter from the Senator showed me that he was not in the frame of mind to accept such, when he wrote in reply, "I thank you for the friendship and goodwill so manifested. At the same time I am sorry you did so. I am not a candidate and I do not want the President to imagine I am, as he possibly does in view of the fact that others appear to have written him as you did."

No one regretted more than I that he had not attained the highest place in the nation, and I am sure the race would have been glad to have seen all animosities wiped out by such an appointment to the Supreme Bench. But Senator Foraker sturdily stood aloof from overtures. We all felt thereafter that further efforts were useless.

An incident [then] occurred at George Washington University in Washington D.C. I recall that when the question came up in taking my membership in the Archaeological Institute of America, which has local branches in leading cities, I was somewhat solicitous as to the treatment I might meet, as a large number of these local branches were [made up of] wealthy business men, who needed to be interested in the work in a financial way, and who as a rule were not interested in the race question. I took my membership in the Cleveland Branch, and I must say that at this time it is gratifying to remember that I have always been cordially received wherever I have attended its meetings.[14] So it was pleasing to receive the attention that was mine at this university as intensely southern as the University of Virginia where I had also received the best of treatment.

At this meeting the headquarters of these joint associations were the aristocratic Shoreham Hotel.[15] There the members gathered for social converse and their smokes. Some lodged and dined there. I was stopping with friends but I was urged to share the hospitalities wherever offered. I have never tried to make myself offensive in the case of such, but I did attend a smoker and met not a particle of discourtesy nor was any prejudice evinced in any way against my presence wherever I was.[16] The President and professors of George Washington University accorded me every respect. A card issued by the University Club of Washington conferred its privileges upon me, sponsored by Mitchell Carroll.

As was the custom, a reception was given at the beautiful residence of Mrs. Charles Foster.[17] Mr. John Foster came to me at one of the meetings, thinking probably I might hesitate to attend this function and earnestly urged me to come. He sought me the second time and repeated his request saying he hoped nothing would interfere with my attendance. The President of the University also came and repeated that Mr. Foster had especially desired that I should be present and enjoy the hospitality of the local branch of the Archaeological Institute. He gave an added announcement that I would meet Dr. Edward Everett Hale, then chaplain of the United States Senate.[18]

I attended the reception and met many distinguished men and women. All of whom treated me with all cordiality befitting my position as a member of the Association. It was a pleasure to meet Dr. Hale, grown venerable since the early years when in connection with Antioch College, the Unitarian Institution near us at Yellow Springs, Ohio. He also was an early member of our own trustee board when our school was in its infancy. He recalled this with pleasure and hearty interest. Later he gave me and my work his hearty endorsement when I stood as its [representative].

I have written this at length because such exceptional incidents show the possibility when people can rise above race prejudice and color. I have known little of it wherever I have been with these associations. It causes me to determine that it is on the higher rungs of the ladder we are to find prejudice eliminated and respect accorded us.

In September I addressed the National Congress of Colored Educators on "Institutions under Colored Management" and attended the Educational Congress in Philadelphia, held under the auspices of the Emancipation Commission of Pennsylvania, appointed by the Governor.[19]

Dr. Fallows also wrote that the Commission appointed by the Governor of Illinois to conduct the National Half-Century Anniversary of Negro Freedom cordially requested me to become an Honorary Vice-President of the Commission.[20] I was also asked by the President of the National Emancipation Commission to act in advisory capacity for the Fiftieth Anniversary of Emancipation to be held in St. Paul. I was appointed a delegate to it by Governor Harmon.

It was simply impossible to attend all these, but at some of these held in the east, I was present and aided all possible. In December I went to the inauguration of Dr. Stephen Newman at Howard at his urgent request not to fail to come.[21] I was one of the five university presidents to deliver an address at the Trustees' Reception. I did not neglect my home work nor Ohio's claim upon me and accepted the invitation of the Ohio State Commissioners of Common Schools to meet a gathering in Columbus, when President Wilson and Governor Cox were to speak, and to have a seat upon the stage. Nor did I fail to keep in close touch with my student body.

My great regret, as my work became more and more confined to administrative duties, was my severance from classroom work and from close contacts with my students. The former had to be relegated to others, but I was always ready to meet and hear whatever my students as a body or as individuals had to say. I endeavored to give impartial justice to all. I felt as I often expressed it to a friend: "We older ones do not always understand youth. We misunderstand and misinterpret their shyness and seeming curtness for impertinence when brought before us for discipline." To me it has seemed an endeavor to hide embarrassment under jaunty airs. I may have erred in this and was doubtless imposed upon at times. But there were others who thought as I did and the student body respected my attitude and decisions. As a whole they obeyed what I said. By [then] I was adored which did not add to my popularity in some other quarters.

To me they turned when in want, when in debt, when in any trouble. If dining halls failed, then I fed the hungry in my own home, if funds failed, I stood for their debts. At one time I was confronted with a bill of several hundred dollars for meals made years before. When I stood for students, until they received remittances and forgot all about them after they graduated or left school, strangely enough these bills were not sent to me until years later.

At this time my English friend, Mr. Axon, who had died early in this year, [was] honored at the last, as his son wrote, by a degree "from Manchester University to which he gave his valuable library."

The Dayton Flood in March 1913 brought disaster when our school was cut off from telephone, telegraph, and railroad connections with the surrounding country for ten days. It affected many of our students as their families had later to withdraw them from school. It affected seriously our financial efforts for education, as philanthropy was poured out for the distressed districts.

[Furthermore] it became my sad duty in my report of 1913 to chronicle other deaths. Two Bishops, M. [B.] Salter and W. B. Derrick of our Church, died. Both were strong helpful friends, though the former had been incapacitated for a long time. In the latter I found not only friendship, but that good sense which recognizes limitations, and knew that ignorance of work [coupled with a] determination to rule could only hamper and destroy. When he said to me as Bishop of the district as I took the presidency, "Scarborough, you are a school man with college training, I am not. You know what to do, go ahead and do it. I'll help in all ways as Bishop." He kept his word. How few have this good judgment when elevated to high command! Another [death] that affected us deeply was that of our benefactress and friend, Miss Emery.[22] It occurred in London where the Salvation Army, in which she was intensely interested and to which she left large bequests, gave her a royal funeral.

I was much pleased to receive in July a gift for the University from a former student then doing missionary work in Germany. [It was] an ancient and valuable clock, 192 years old. My report in June showed a strengthening of the Theological Department by adding an instructor. I did not withhold my meed of praise to any who were doing worthy work. I also gave notice of the opening of Wilberforce's Summer School. It was first since the early days of the University in the '80s when a "Chautauqua" flourished for several years under the leadership of Bishop Arnett and auspices of the Tawawa Association.

At this time President Wilson had bestowed high honor on Walter H. Page by appointing him as Ambassador to the Court of St. James. To a letter of congratulations to this friend of [many] years, the following response came:

Dear Professor Scarborough,
I wish you to know how heartily I appreciate your kind congratulations and good wishes. The President has great courage to trust such a mission to a man out of the working ranks of our

democratic life; and the confidence of my friends is now very helpful, and I assure you very pleasant, too.

Gratefully yours,
Walter H. Page

It was an appointment that I was especially delighted to see made. From the time of my first acquaintance with him, he had proved a loyal friend. Though a Southerner, he was thoroughly democratic. He was ever ready to receive me when I went east and to accept for his magazines what I had to say on the questions of the day. He was also constantly urging me to write up my life. Now he was at the top of the ladder of success and like so many ready to give his life to his new duties into which he threw all his heart, soul, and body, as *His Life and Letters* reveal.[23] Those whose life-long prejudices cannot be overcome, those who unrelentingly hate the Negro and fear social equality, and especially those who have not secured social status, those are the ones I've found averse to according courteous treatment to the members of the race who merit it.

Increasing duties were now making it impossible for me to continue my philological researches and to attend regularly the meetings. I went to Harvard in the winter, however, where I read a short paper on "Semion" to which reference has been made in a preceding chapter.[24] I did not attend another meeting until 1916 when business took me to St. Louis where the Association held its session at Washington University in that city.[25]

The year 1914 opened up at a period that was henceforth to call for every ounce of energy and all co-operation possible. It opened with notification of appointment as one of the honorary vice-presidents of the International Longfellow Society.[26] As two other engagements claimed me in May, I could not accept the invitation from Dr. Mott to speak in Atlanta to the Negro Christian Student Endeavor Convention.[27] Instead I went to Boston to lecture before the St. Mark Musical and Literary Union, a splendid club of cultured people of our group.[28] I returned to Ohio to attend the meeting of the World's Court Peace Congress to which I was an honored delegate.[29] Its banquet was held at the Hotel Statler in Cleveland.[30] The world was then becoming filled with apprehension of coming war. Of this meeting I wrote at the time: "If war can be averted for the world it will be due to just such gatherings of men of wide influence throwing [their] full weight for peace. But my observations in 1911 in England and Germany have led me to feel that war was inevitable."

I was right. My work too, was now to begin dimly to see the deepening shadow of the coming conflict. [This appeared] first in my unsuccessful endeavor to get reappointment of an army officer to the university, "owning to the exigencies of the service," as the Secretary of War wrote. The University had to take the services of one trained in the institution, an instructor, Prof. L. Palmer, a young man I am proud to mention.[31] [He was a] man of excellent mind, an inmate of my own household during his entire college course, and who had made good in the educational world. He gave good service as a military instructor until relieved later by a regular appointed army officer.

The commencement of 1914 was an enthusiastic one, [with] Hon. Frank Willis delivering the address.[32] My report to the Board of Trustees in June was optimistic. It showed a strenuous year, but outstanding debts were gradually being met. I pleaded the importance of new systems of bookkeeping, that I might better approach philanthropy, and my plans were broad for the future. Standards had been raised and courses had been lengthened. I wish to repeat what I then said because it may be of worth in the future. I abbreviate here:

> Our faculty deserves special commendation for willing work in so many different fields in which each has been asked to labor from time to time because of our limited means. But modern scholarship forces all to keep up activity all along their respective lines and we expect freshness of material offered by teachers of wide preparation as well as for those with special training in special lines, and there should also be a demand for piety as well. Schools seek men who can inspire as well as instruct those who can make their students anxious to learn and enter upon special lines of research and investigation. But we cannot get good teachers and hold them unless there can be some certainty of tenure of office when no valid charge can be sustained against them. Good teachers will not place themselves in a position to be humiliated or crippled annually by any who may feel inclined to use influences to oust them. The same is true of the head of the University, his term of office should be indefinite. He must be able to be free to look ahead to the carrying out of plans and purposes for the upbuilding [sic] and strengthening of the institution over which he presides. There should be no such uncertainties and we are too far advanced in age and dignity as an institution to keep up practices to which no high grade colleges, except those among ourselves, adhere.

This had been considered before, but the situation was a tangled one as my report shows. In 1912 the President was elected for an indefinite term, and then re-elected in 1913, either by inability to recognize what was needed, or by a fixed habit of opposition, or by reluctance to relinquish a practice, giving opportunity for exercise of many bad traits of human nature. But I had learned there could be many ways used to impede and instruct.

I [also] pleaded continually against a practice allowed to grow up in the University, that of a member of the faculty drawing salary as such and also being made a member of the Trustee Board. It was against state law, forbidding such except in case of the President. It was a bad practice and unjust to other colleagues not members, for to my personal knowledge and experience it has always been a prolific source of trouble. It was some time, however, before this practice was discontinued.

The next winter while in Boston I had a unique experience which [had a pleasant outcome]. While writing a card in the Boston post office lobby, I was approached by a stranger who after begged my pardon for speaking and said, "I don't know who you are, but if I had seen you sooner I would have asked to paint your portrait as the face of the model man of your race instead of the one I chose for the picture I am painting." He then introduced himself as Darius Cobb whom I was to learn later was a famous Boston artist, one of two brothers both artists and sons of Sylvanus Cobb, the author. He invited me to his studio and begged me to sit for a portrait. I consented and learned also that he was one artist who worked reverently in the conscious presence of God.[33] [His painting,] *The Master,* his life ambition which he had just completed at eighty years, was considered a wonderful work of art. [Other] paintings hung in the art galleries of France, England, and America and he had painted the portraits of many eminent Americans.

It can be seen that I felt this request to be a great honor. In the sittings I gave him and the many letters that passed between us I learned to revere the man who had possessed most lofty ideals and had done such wonderful work. The portrait was completed and delivered to me richly framed with his compliments. Of this meeting and the portrait Darius Cobb said: "I was so impressed by the power of this man mentally and physically and by the dignity of his appearance that I was irresistibly drawn to him. I have painted the greatest men of our country but not one excelled Dr. Scarborough in powerful expression of both face and form."

The portrait was exhibited in Boston and received unstinted praise from the press, the *Boston Transcript,* praising it in its art column saying that "the artist had a very strong character to portray."[34] It was a splendid bit of publicity as well for my work in which Mr. Carnegie was greatly interested. Had he lived longer I feel his influence would have enabled me to gain more aid from Boston philanthropists, but their philanthropy had been pretty well pre-empted by others.

In August 1914 I gave the welcome address to the Colored Women's Federation, which by invitation held its biennial session at Wilberforce University.[35] This was attended by some five hundred prominent women of the race. It was a marvelous meeting. Prominent women of both races were present. Mrs. Harriet Taylor Upton, represented the Ohio Federation. Mrs. B. T. Washington, Mrs. Nellie Langston Napier, wife of our U.S. Register of the Treasury, Bishop Gaines' daughter, [and] Bishop C. S. Smith's wife were our house guests for the week. Together [with the group was] Mrs. Shears, the head of the Douglass Center of Chicago, an organization having for its object, the bringing together of the best elements of white people in contact with that of the colored people so as to adjust misunderstandings.[36] With her came Miss Zona Gale, already well-known as writer and soon to become famous through her novels so analytic of character.

There is no surer way to break down prejudice than in such a gathering where the worth of mutual work for the advancement of womankind can be recognized by all having a common aim in humanity's advance irrespective of race or sex. I believe in woman's suffrage, and was glad to voice that belief in answer to the request from the Ohio Woman's Suffrage Association for a brief expression to find a place in its leaflet, saying: "I believe there is no good or justifiable reason for withholding the ballot from woman while there are innumerable such reasons for granting it to her." A few years later Miss Gale sent us her *Peace in Friendship Village.* The chapter, "Dream," is one commanding attention of every man and woman, even Ku Klux men and women, who are open to the conviction of the innate worth of people, educated and cultured, though carrying the varying strains of colored blood.[37]

In September I opened the university session with an address on "The Use of Means to the Best End." I then proceeded eastward to give an address to the race on "Education" at Bethel A.M.E. Church, Passaic, New Jersey.

The declaration of war was now shown in various ways. An enlarged foreign correspondence, increasing continuously, began in November when

Sir Gilbert Parker who had sent me many official papers, wrote graciously in reply to my letter of thanks, "It is a great comfort to know that men of influence, like yourself, sympathize with Great Britain in the fight which she is making."[38]

Then Dr. John Wesley Hill, ever ready to enter into any movement for peace and who had "taken a most friendly interest in me," begged for my co-operation and membership in the International Peace Forum. Later Dr. Hill sent me his splendid characterization of *Abraham Lincoln, Man of God,* and with the inscription: "To my esteemed friend, Dr. W. S. Scarborough, with my sincere regards."[39] In December my interest in the Panama-Pacific International Exposition brought me these words from President Moore, who wrote: "Its inspiration and influence shall go forward. Your own interest and assistance have helped to make this possible."

A year later when "the lights went out" and the ceremonies closed, the volume *The Legacy of the Exposition* was sent [to me] by President Moore.[40] I had been honored on the closing day. My sentiments were:

> The Panama-Pacific International Exposition, conceived by a magnificent people and held in the magnificent gateway of a most magnificent state, has not only commemorated fittingly one of the most marvelous achievements in the world's history—the Panama Canal—but by presentation of all that symbolizes America's unparalleled progress, it has also commanded the admiration and respect of the nations for this great country, has linked all together in closer bonds, has stimulated all to higher endeavor, and has laid the foundation for that growth of fraternal world relations, necessary to the fullest understanding and the highest conception of the true brotherhood of man.

These courtesies, seemingly small, were appreciated at their full worth. I saw in each one not only personal tribute but openings for extended influence not to be undervalued which would serve to push forward my work.

On the first night of the new year, 1915, I suffered an accident when called to attend a duty that really devolved upon others. They seem to think I must be proctor and chaperone as well as President and money-getter. I slipped on the ice and fell heavily, but attended to the duty and returned to a meeting where I presided the remainder of the evening. When I reached home I complained of a pain in my back, but refused to allow a physician to be called. In the morning I insisted upon going to the office. At noon I sent for the physician who found two broken ribs and a fractured one. This was only one of several instances when grit and determination led me to do my duty though heavens fell. So I was incapacitated for some weeks which caused my physician to forbid attendance in February at the Bishop's Council in New Orleans, and told me that when I was [able] I should spend a few weeks in Florida to regain health and strength.[41]

It was unfortunate for me, as at this time internal matters at the University were reaching a crisis that demanded drastic attention. To add to my manifold duties I found that I must ever be the first to contend for rights of the University and reply to its calumniators. My pen was kept busy replying to signed and unsigned articles that had found their way into the Negro papers [that were] tending to foster ill feelings between departments in the University.[42]

Trips—South, West, and East

The visit to Florida served both to recuperate health and gain knowledge of the educational facilities of the state for the Negro people. I found a decided increase in our education which was making rapid progress. I spoke enthusiastically of the fine school created by Mrs. Bethune, destined to become a powerful factor in education.[1] One of our graduates had also built up a strong public school of high grade at West Palm Beach, the first of its kind in Florida. The Edward Waters College, our own church school, was also striving bravely to keep to the front.[2]

The early spring brought the news of the death of another old and constant friend from boyhood. Bishop Henry Turner was a man of singular strength and of progressive ideas, another self-made man coming out of slavery, a stalwart pillar of the church and my staunch supporter.[3] How these were falling by the way!

In May I attended, as delegate, the meeting of the World's Court League in Cleveland and the luncheon given by the city's Chamber of Commerce at Hotel Statler.[4] Early in June I went to the Fiftieth Anniversary celebration of Worcester Polytechnic Institute in Massachusetts with its banquet at the Bancroft Hotel, where among other speakers were Senator Weeks and Major-General Wood.[5] I could not go to the inauguration of Dr. McKenzie as President of Fisk University at Nashville, Tennessee, though Dr. McKenzie had sent an urgent personal invitation to be present.[6]

This year I was invited to the celebration of the Half-Century Anniversary of Negro Freedom by Dr. Samuel Fallows, President of the Illinois Commission for this purpose, who wrote, "May I add my hearty personal invitation to you to be associated with the Commission as requested in the accompanying official communication." To this anniversary held in Chicago I was sent as delegate by the Ohio Commission.

At the commencement in June I had as house guest and commencement orator, my close friend and Oberlin classmate, Dr. Hastings H. Hart, brother of Professor Albert Bushnell Hart of Harvard. Dr. Hart was a public spirited man, a scholar, a theologian, and a humanitarian, known for his work for prison reform in connection with the Russell Sage Foundation.[7] He spoke on Prison Reform, the work nearest his heart. He often jokingly claimed to have been in prison more times than any member of our class. My enjoyment of that visit was very great indeed. Dr. Hart's admiration, respect [and] pride in me, his classmate, showed itself in many ways in endeavors helping my cause with people of influence and in his persistent endeavor to put me on the Carnegie Foundation Pension list.[8]

In the summer I set out on a trip to the Pacific Coast. This was a pleasurable and restful one, going by the way of Denver and Salt Lake City and returning up the coast by the northern route which enabled me to see the most possible, visit friends, and speak in several places. Ex-President Taft was on his way westward on the same train. Seeing me in another Pullman he came to my car several times and spent some time in general conversation on the political situation and other topics. He was a man I had always admired for his democratic friendliness and uniform kindliness always shown to me personally and to my work.

I saw something of the Great Exposition, and in Los Angeles through the courtesy of an old friend, Professor Alexander, formerly associated with our university, I was given a reception at a rousing meeting at the Los Angeles Branch of the N.A.A.C.P., while the papers most kindly mentioned my presence and work.[9] The trip resulted in making contact with friends who were to be helpful in the future. It brought me also renewed physical strength.

I stopped over in Chicago to meet an engagement with the Alumni Association and reached home in time to open the school year, as usual with my annual address on "The Educational Value of Environment," a practice I had not failed to keep up [wishing] to make it a dignified occasion.

My return brought me face to face with continued ambitions and endeavors to interfere with the harmony and work of the departments. This called again for rejoinders which I was forced for the second time to make through the Negro press. This time I felt it necessary to reply with considerable vehemence, which put an end for a time to such attacks. I was able to divine the source of all these attempts to hurt our work. Later I was to be assured of the correctness of my conclusions by the writers themselves of the articles in question. Murder will out.

Though forced to decline some invitations, in October I attended the inauguration of Dr. McCracken of Lafayette College at Easton, Pennsylvania.[10] I was brought again in touch with eminent men, philological acquaintances, and [I] delighted to see my special friend, Dr. Sihler of

Columbia receive the honor of [a] doctor of law.[11] Here, too, I was much embarrassed as my academic costume, expressed from home, had not reached me, and I may add it never did, having been lost or stolen en route. It was too late to obtain another. My friends, however, insisted that I take my part. Therefore when among some two hundred others my university's name was called, I rose and went forward as the others to acknowledge this courtesy.

In the summer I found myself honored by being made an Associate Member of the National Arts Club which urged me to "join to make it a center of intellectual, aesthetic, and educational activities."[12] Early in November I gave the address at the dedication of the Washington Avenue School in Glendale, Ohio.[13] From there I went to Tuskegee, Alabama to serve as an honorary pallbearer at Principal Washington's funeral on November 17.[14]

The occasion was a sad one. Dr. Washington's death was untimely. We needed him. Just such men as leaders are not readily found. In fact each has his work, his niche to fill and no one else can fill it fully. He was the recognized leader of industrial education. Dr. [Robert] Russa Moton, brought from Hampton to take his place, has done admirably, sustained by Hampton's and Tuskegee's eastern friends.[15] Still there can be but one Booker T. Washington. We were always good friends though our work lay in different lines.

At Wilberforce we were feeling more and more the growing financial stringency, though long-standing obligations were being cleared off, as these had taken much of current monies raised from my efforts. We were forging ahead in spite of it. The Fourth Educational District of our church had never done better toward support of the university than during the quadrennium in 1916. Bishops Shaffer, Lee, and Tyree worked together to aid through the faithful men of their respective Episcopal districts. Bishop Derrick had also passed away and I missed his loyal support.

We had become a member of the Association of American Colleges and Association of Ohio Colleges despite our limited means.[16] A commander, Captain B. O. Davis, had been assigned the university by the Secretary of War, departments had been reorganized, [and] our faculty had been increased, a research club under the professor of mathematics had been established, the summer school was prospering under strong management, the library was being reorganized, our secretary's books were being kept in accord with plans outlined by educational authors, Founders' Day was growing in inspiration and interest and helpfulness, and I was still begging and pleading the church for help for scholarships, for worthy endowment, for harmony, [for] the wiping out of both sectarian and state lines, and for proper recognition of Wilberforce University as the Mother School of the Church by adequate support and [the] appointment as Trustees, men [who would be] fitted by education and experience for such a task, [able] to make a representative body in both numbers and efficiency.[17] I carried this plea to the General Conference which met in Philadelphia in 1916.

With the opening of 1916, I began to find my mail laden with calls for my assistance in many organizations as the conflict in Europe grew more and more intense with the United States. [I was] torn between watchful waiting and a desire to see the end, [and I] planned more and more how to best prepare to meet the situation. The *Independent,* the official organ of the National Institute of Efficiency in Washington wrote me of its pleasure at my acceptance of membership in it and assurance of personal co-operation. The Religious Association in Chicago sought my membership.[18] My name was also recognized by the Scientific Department of the *Encyclopedia Americana* as seen in this extract from a long letter addressed to me:

> We are about to revise *Encyclopedia Americana* and, as you will observe from a perusal of the enclosed clipping, much of your later life and activities have not been touched upon in your biography.
>
> We would like you to complete this biography and bring it up-to-date, as much has occurred since the last revision of this book and the later developments of your life are of increasing interest to the national public.
>
> Will you favor us with this, or arrange to have someone else, who is properly qualified, do so, and advise us when we may expect it in our new edition, which we are now preparing?

The early part of the year I was at the inaugural of Dr. Watters as President of Gammon Theological Seminary in Atlanta, Georgia.[19] In April I addressed a body of alumni at St. Paul's Church, St. Louis at its "Scarborough Evening," [that] it had arranged in my honor.[20] The city paper quoting from the eighth biennial publication of *Who's Who in America* concerning my life and work added, "He has been more highly recognized in educational circles of America than any living Negro." In May I was present at the Second World's Congress in New York City to which I had been made a delegate by its Board of Governors. From here I went by invitation to attend the First Annual Assemblage of the League to Enforce Peace held at the New Willard in Washington, D.C. over which meeting Ex-President Taft presided. In May I attended General Conference of the church in

Philadelphia where I urged in my report what has previously been stated. I was invited guest of the Teachers' and Officers' Alliance of the A.M.E. Sunday School Union of the First Episcopal District at a banquet in honor of General Conference guests. I had been writing the Union Teachers' *Quarterly* for over twenty years.

I mention these official courtesies to show that in the higher realms of learning prejudice was not shown and I was welcomed and treated according to my position. In every instance save at Baltimore I have had the honor and pleasure of invitation to and perfect freedom in the various clubs, which extended courtesies at such times. These occasions, however, I wish it understood, were not seized upon to force myself into white society, but because I deemed it courteous and right and best [to] accept invitations to maintain the dignity of my position, to honor my race, and to make friends for my work.

Despite these demands I felt I must keep in close touch with the political situation. Hon. Myron T. Herrick, later the highly acceptable ambassador to France, was a candidate for the U.S. Senate. To this candidacy I gave unqualified support, issuing by request a special [appeal] on his behalf to the Negro voters. The following letter shows the cordial relations existing between us:

June 16, 1916
Prof. W. S. Scarborough
President of Wilberforce University
Wilberforce, Ohio

My dear Prof. Scarborough:
I have your kind letter of June first which I found on my return from Chicago and am deeply sensible of the honor you have paid me personally by your acceptance of a place on the Executive Committee of the Herrick Voters League in your county. Please believe I shall esteem anything you may find it convenient to do that will make for my advantage in my candidacy for the Senate. What you tell me as to sentiment in your community is indeed encouraging and I shall watch returns from there with a great deal of interest.

If my memory serves me, you hold your commencement exercises some day this week. It is a keen disappointment to me that I was not able to accept your kind invitation to be present, but I hope the opportunity will [arise] later for me to meet you and my other friends there.

With best wishes for the success of your splendid educational institution and with kindest regards for you personally, I am

Very truly yours,
Myron T. Herrick

In July of 1916, Chairman Wilcox of the Republican National Committee wrote expressing his pleasure at my willingness to take active part in the National Campaign and later called upon me for the distribution of the personal appeal to Negro voters that he had prepared.[21] Because of these demands coupled with those of the university I was forced to cancel the acceptance of the invitation from the President of Wooster College, Ohio to give a chapel talk at its summer school session.[22]

There was one call, however, I could not nor would not refuse to accept, no matter how heavily pressed by duties. My own commencement over, I had been very busy through July into August when the last of the month I was apprised by Dr. Hamilton Holt, the editor of the *Independent,* of the approaching death of Dr. William Hayes Ward, its [founding] editor.[23] He wrote: "I am writing to a few of his friends to send in a brief appreciation of his work in the special lines that appealed to them and I trust you will be willing to write me a brief appreciation of Dr. Ward as a friend of the Negro."

This letter was followed the next day by a wire bearing this message: "William Hayes Ward died yesterday. Asking a few intimate friends for brief appreciation on various phases of his life's work. Will you not send 3,000 words in a letter of service for the Negro cause?"

I complied, saying: "I appreciated fully the honor of being thus singled out to be the spokesman for my race, and to give my tribute to one who had been a strong personal friend for years."

The article appeared in the next issue of the *Independent* and as spokesman for the race I insert it here:[24]

> With keenest sorrow I learn that a valued personal friend of the Negro race has passed to the great beyond, and I gladly accept the invitation to give a brief appreciation of Dr. William Hayes Ward's work for the Negro. He has virtually devoted his life to the interests of the race to its emancipation, to its education, to its struggles, to its ambitions, to its possible future, without a particle of prejudice.

Believing that God made mankind all one blood and that the Negro should have free enjoyment of the rights and privileges of any human being and of any American citizen, Dr. Ward arrayed himself always on that platform and fearlessly fought the battles of our race.

Proscription, segregation, mob violence, lynchings, denial of vote, all race distinctions, all the thousand and one indignities, persecutions, cruelties, and crimes against the Negro wherever practiced, have found in him one who denounced vigorously and unsparingly all such as unlawful, unjust, unchristian, and inhuman.

His work did not stop with his strenuous endeavors to right the wrongs done the Negro, but he maintained that the education of the race should be the highest type, declared and demonstrated its intellectual capacity through many Negro contributions to be independent on all lines of thought and encouraged all its ambitions and aspirations as a people.

Everything connected with the race won his personal interest, and he never wavered in his allegiance. Public opinion never warped his convictions. Nor did personal interest ever cause him to swerve from the course he deemed right in regard to the race.

There was no mere sentimentalism in this. He was a humanitarian of the most royal type, espousing our cause because he believed it a just one and because we were lowly, defenseless, weak, and friendless. So his warm heart, his keen brain, and his facile pen have united for over fifty years to declare through the *Independent* and every other possible channel that he was the Negro's staunch friend. The Negro people have lost a most noble, loyal champion, one they will ever hold in grateful remembrance. May his mantle rest upon and forever enfold the *Independent*.

Dr. Ward died at his home in Berwick, Maine, August 28, 1916, in the eighty-second year of his age.

Dr. Holt answered: "I want to thank you most sincerely for the letter in regard to Dr. Ward which appeared in last week's paper. It was a splendid tribute to a great man, and all who loved him will thank you for it."

A few months later I put forth an effort, sponsored by the *Independent*, to erect a science building at Wilberforce as a memorial to this noble hearted friend of the Negro. The exigencies of the war period, however, soon made it evident that we must postpone our efforts to a more propitious time for such a philanthropic endeavor. The strenuous activities connected with the war and its aftermath and our own needs forced me to abandon the project so near to my heart. Perhaps someday Wilberforce University may be able to erect such a memorial.

At the close of the year I went by invitation to Durham, S.C., to the Conference on Progress of Negro Education at Prof. W. G. Pearson's

Training School which was attaining a worthy [and] wide reputation. This conference had been made possible through the generosity of a Christian woman in New York City, so that the educators of Negro youth may come in closer contact and study the real needs and seek to find a plan among themselves to better existing conditions.

My address was on "What Should Be the Standard of the University, College, Normal School, Teacher Training, and Secondary Schools."[25] On receipt of a copy, Superintendent Pearson of Ohio wrote, "This is excellent in all particulars and does honor to yourself, your institution and the State."

My interests were world-wide. I let no opportunity pass to make connection that would serve to establish such friendly relations everywhere as would advance and aid mankind generally.[26] So the students from the Chinese University of Honolulu on the tour of their athletic team through this country were invited to play with the Wilberforce team. Though the Chinese team had made a record of sixty-five consecutive victories, they were now defeated, but took it gracefully and enjoyed much their short stay with its social activities. Wilberforce boys played at times with many university teams—white and black—with the best of good feeling. I felt that athletics could thus be wisely made to serve a double purpose. But I deprecate any such over indulgence in sports as would lead to neglect of the purpose to train our students in mental pursuits.

I also accepted a membership on the Provisional Jewish Committee with a desire to be helpful in stamping out racial injustices, intolerances, and persecutions wherever found, and to forward racial good fellowship everywhere. This attitude was appreciated when an American Jewish Congress was held for the first time in the history of American Jewry in Philadelphia.[27] The Committee sent me their "Bill of Rights" begging my signature in a letter from which the following paragraph is taken: "It is our purpose to obtain the approval of these human principles from the most prominent Americans in political, social, civic, educational, and religious life. Knowing your broadmindedness and religious tolerance, we trust that you will lend your name in this worthy movement, which would eradicate religious discrimination and anti-Jewish laws in those countries where they still abound."

World War I Work

The year 1917 opened up a new era for the university and for the race when the United States entered the world conflict in April. From that moment I found my work laid out for me in many new and varied channels. My long and intimate acquaintance with public men and long participation in public affairs now stood me in good stead for successful management of tasks confronting me. The College Board now wisely allowed me to take the lead, backing up my plans and suggestions with commendably little friction.

Immediately the university offered to the national and state government its entire resources, school and faculty for use in the crisis in whatever form might seem best. Both President Wilson through the War Department and Governor Cox made a grateful acknowledgement "for your generous pledge of co-operation and support," and assured the university that "you will be called upon for proper service in case of need."[1]

The university thus placed itself in the forefront, ready to do its "bit" to insure victory for the Allies and to give the world over to true democracy, a democracy that means freedom for all the people. We have special reasons as a race to desire this; and no matter what the conditions in this country savoring of inconsistency, we as a race and a school propose to wave aside any insistent dwelling upon our grievances and by our attitude, words, and works show our loyalty and determination to be a helpful factor in the great struggle which is going on in behalf of freedom for suffering nations. Hoping that by loyal devotion to this country, even to the laying down of life itself, to gain the rights and privileges of other true Americans, and do away with the discrimination, insult, and torture that is our lot on account of race and color. No world is safe for democracy until this is done.

There was another reason for this prompt offer to the government. Our institution was especially prepared for its work as its students since 1893 had had military training. It was [one] Negro school in the country with a military department supported by the national government and with a regular detailed military officer as instructor.

At this juncture, Captain Benjamin O. Davis was at the head of the list of officers available for foreign service, and Secretary of War Baker could not see his way clear to retain him in this country for such or any other service at the present time.[2] He was ordered to report at once to the War Department, but at my request and by the assistance of U.S. Senator Atlee Pomerene of Ohio his departure was deferred until June that he might give necessary drill for our coming inspection on April 30, the report of which became highly favorable to us.[3] Then he left leaving us for the time being dependent on a cadet's service as noted in a previous chapter.

By this time an Officers' Training Camp had been established at Fort Des Moines and the university had been designated as one of the centers for examination of applicants. At this critical moment Colonel Charles Young, the third West Point graduate of the race, was at his Wilberforce home. He had been recently retired from active service through a medical board examination. Most of the race, however, looked upon it as an injustice, a scheme to be rid of him in this war, preventing him from promotion and the participation which promotion would lead. As one of the race papers said: "The step from Lieutenant-Colonel to Brigadier-General is not a great one and should Young remain in active service he would be in line for promotion which would have to be made in the near future."

Such a storm of protest arose at this retirement that the War Department was compelled to take notice of it.[4] On closing a lengthy letter on the subject to Professor Kelly Miller of Howard University, Secretary Baker wrote in July saying that another board of officers was directed to re-examine the question of Young's disability, and expressing the hope that "the board will find Colonel Young still able to perform active duty, and have at least the hope of being able to have his assistance for the present."[5]

The [New York] *Age* correspondent made this comment: "That one examining board will render a report declaring that the first board was in error in its findings is not regarded probable by those familiar with the inner workings of the War Department. The attitude of the present administration at Washington on the Negro question is generally known, and for this reason many construe Secretary Baker's statement, 'have his assistance for the present,' to mean that his retention in active service will be but temporary."

I did not agree with those who criticized Secretary Baker unmercifully. It was a Democratic administration it is true, but I never felt the secretary should be held personally responsible for this.

As an Oberlin man I knew Secretary Baker well and always found him both friendly and co-operative.[6] I believe he tried to be just, but he was only one man. When later there were hurtful rumors concerning our 368th Infantry of colored men he made a statement (which unfortunately I cannot find now). I wrote him my personal thanks for it to which he replied as follows:

War Department
Washington, D.C.
November 18, 1919

My dear Doctor Scarborough,
I am very glad to have your letter of the fifteenth and to learn that you think my statement with regard to the 368th Infantry will help to quiet the hurtful rumors and prejudiced discussion which has been going about. Happily, I am not a candidate for the presidency, or any other public office, and therefore, able to speak my mind freely and frankly without having ambitions which can either be hurt or helped by my course.

Cordially yours,
Newton D. Baker
Secretary of War

However, the university was to profit by this allowance—to have his assistance for the present—as the Government allowed Colonel Young to give it his service at this moment when haste and efficiency were required. It was in a measure a great relief to him to render this aid though he did not become a direct detail. To Colonel Young [we] owed much for the willing and hearty service rendered in preparing the boys for readiness for prompt entrance into the army service at the call of the government now at hand.

In reply to my telegram to the Adjutant-General in Chicago, Captain Tilford of Ohio State University was ordered to proceed to us. He spent three days examining our cadets and any [who were] desiring to go to Fort Des Moines Training Camp.[7] Thirty men were taken and became Class C men. It was made clear that our boys would finally have advantage over others as they had been trained by officers detailed by the national government.

Though Colonel Young's help was incalculable, he was not regularly detailed to the university as a ranking military officer and there was thrown upon me the responsibility for all plans and correspondence with the national government relating to the situation. This was a great burden with a small office force. The situation continued until after the armistice, whereupon repeated requests and with Senator Pomerene's assistance, a detail was secured for military instruction in the person of Lt. Col. John E. Green, another member of the race who had risen from the ranks of the Regular Army.[8] Senator Pomerene was kind enough to congratulate me on my "success," but I know the worth of his assistance in the matter which I always found him ready to give.

Despite added duties and responsibilities, peculiar and exacting, every demand made upon the school was met promptly and with satisfaction to authorities. Some disorganization in school work was at once inevitable. State schools and departments were by action of State Superintendent of Public Instruction agreed through their presidents to dismiss students at once with the urgent request that these make the best use of this time in promoting increase of food production in the state. This led to the withdrawal of a considerable number of male students.

As days passed, we, in common with other schools, organized and entered into all war activities, everyone finding representation in the university and its closely allied community, Red Cross work, nurse training, special relief, courses in conservatism, extension work, lecture series, boy scouts, bond buying, as rapidly as requests and directions were received from War Headquarters. The government assisted wherever possible, giving to us a Y.M.C.A. detail and the faculty united loyally in all that came to hand to accomplish.

We were fully launched upon war work. The calls were now constantly coming in from various quarters for our students to engage as clerks as members of 351st Heavy Field Artillery. In the end quotas were sent to the Second, Third, and Fourth Training Camps.

Added to all these there still poured in pleas for my enrollment in patriotic societies, with many of which I felt it best to make affiliation, as it would help to award proper recognition of my people and the part they were taking. So when the American League for National Unity sent me its letter of such appeal, the paragraphs I quote made me hopeful that "real unity" might be attained in the end. It sounded well:

> I am directed by the Executive Committee to extend to you an invitation to become a member of the American League for National Unity, which has been organized for the purpose of conducting a nation-wide campaign

for a more thorough and deep-rooted Americanization of citizens of all classes, both native and foreign born.

If we are to be a homogenous people and the men and women of foreign lands who are coming to America to share our freedom are to be assimilated, we must assume an entirely different attitude in the future in dealing with these new-comers. Lines of racial and class distinction must be broken down, and a genuine spirit of brotherhood must be displayed by men and women who have never known any other fealty or allegiance in their relations with our new citizens.

Nor could I disregard the request of Dr. Albert Bushnell Hart, Chairman of the Committee of the National Security League on "Patriotism through Education," who wrote begging my presence at Chautauqua, New York in July at a Conference of Representatives of Organizations Engaged in Patriotic Service.

The work was strenuous, but there now came pleasing recognition of management and help when the following letter was received from the Governor of Ohio:

State of Ohio
Executive Department
Columbus
August 8, 1918
Dr. W. S. Scarborough
Wilberforce, Ohio

My dear Scarborough:

It gives me pleasure to hereby formally notify you that you have this day been appointed a member of the Ohio Branch, Council of National Defense, to take part in future deliberations of that body, and to act in an advisory capacity to the Governor and his aides in all matters which properly come before the Council.

As you are aware, this organization is in reality the Governor's War Cabinet. This selection of yourself is due to the position you occupy as a leader of your race in the state, and because we feel the race deserves this recognition in view of the fact that so many thousands of Negro soldiers are now at the front or preparing to go to the front in the battles for world democracy, and in recognition of the hearty co-operation of the race at every turn.

I am sure that your service in this cabinet will be of the highest order and in keeping with the record made by you in your labors in behalf of the race in other fields.

With every good wish, I am,
Very truly yours,
James M. Cox

I feel that I may be easily pardoned, if I say I felt very proud of this recognition. To be the one man of color called to the cabinet of the Governor of the state was a great honor. I received many congratulations. Among them I prize Senator Pomerene's words when he wrote me: "I am sure you will merit to the fullest extent, the confidence placed in you by the Governor. I think you are both to be congratulated. You have just reason to feel proud of the splendid work being done to win the war by representatives of Wilberforce University."

This appointment was now succeeded by another from the Federal Food Administrator for Ohio, Mr. Fred C. Croxton, who said in the closing report of his department:[9]

> Negro churches and Negro lodges joined the ranks of co-operating organizations in Ohio under the leadership of Dr. W. S. Scarborough, colored, President of Wilberforce University, Wilberforce, Ohio, who was appointed on the staff of the Federal Food Administrator, and who made a tour of many cities and towns in Ohio, addressing colored organizations. Dr. Scarborough was also appointed as one of the three Labor Advisors in Ohio to represent colored labor in the interest of food conservation.

He also wrote me a personal letter at the same time saying:[10]

My Dear Dr. Scarborough:
In closing up affairs of the Food Administration of Ohio, I must render you my praise for your co-operation in organizing food conservation morale which enabled us to do our part in Ohio.

The fact that you and your people were able to play so creditable a part in the common undertaking must be a source of great satisfaction and pleasant recollection to you as it is to me.

I was called to the Southern Migration Conference in July to help adjust the labor situation and provide plans for the general welfare.[11] This migration, intensified by riots, and lynching, was rendering labor problems more and more complex. Mr. Croxton as Vice-President of the Ohio Branch of Council of National Defense, wrote the following:

> My dear Dr. Scarborough:
> At the conference held in Columbus under the auspices of the Department of Labor two or three weeks ago, it was decided that there should be a Committee appointed for the state consisting largely of colored members but with a few white members. I am enclosing a list of names of those suggested for members of this Committee. I am asked to approve this Committee or to make such changes as may seem advisable.
>
> I therefore would very much like to have your opinion of the general makeup of the Committee.
>
> I am very glad to know that you have been made a member of the Ohio Branch Council of National Defense.

Added work came when I was informed that the War Department had approved the designation of myself as a member of the special "Committee of One Hundred" in the work of mobilizing the Negro public opinion in enthusiastic support of the war aims of the nation. I was also informed that I was made a member of the Greene County [Ohio] Advisory Committee and of the Negro Circle of War Relief.

[On] June 3, 1918 I received a wire from District Educational Director, P. R. Woodworth asking: "Are you interested in training colored soldiers for the War Emergency?" An immediate affirmative answer was sent, a telephone conference followed, and he came to us to arrange details. The work necessarily was at that moment placed largely in the State supported department which had the immediate facilities to meet requirements. There came to us in July 180 soldiers for such training to be known as Wilberforce University Training Detachment, National Army, [and] to remain for sixty days training under command at first of Captain Ostermaier, an efficient white officer.[12]

When the Student Army Training Corps (S.A.T.C.) was planned by the government, I at once made application for such a unit at the University. This was granted after an inspection of our college facilities by men sent for the purpose who found us "admirably located and fitted to meet the requirements, our educational standard meeting full approval."

It was this order that changed the status of all vocational detachments, wherever located, to that of "Unit B" of the S.A.T.C. [and] all college units becoming "Unit A." Captain Ostermaier was then relieved of his command and the two units at the university placed under the command of two colored officers, "A" under First Lieutenant P. R. Piper and "B" under First Lieutenant M. H. Curtis, both efficient soldiers who now continued in charge until the demobilization of the S.A.T.C. took place. The latter returned to civil life and the former was retained to take command of the R.O.T.C. instituted at that time in the colleges of the country.

With the establishment of the S.A.T.C. there had been an unfortunate display of prejudice that was always ready to seek segregation.[13] We were soon advised by the War Department Regional Director for Ohio that it was the policy and ruling of the Department not to allow white and colored students to occupy the same barracks in colleges having the S.A.T.C. This statement, sent to other colleges in the state as well, led to advice [given] to colored students by many heads of colleges to come to Wilberforce under the situation. Oberlin College true to its colors declared it would welcome such students. Many students chose to come to us. I was emphatically opposed to such a policy and entered protest as did other heads, [al]though at first there was nothing to do but accept the situation until investigation could be made and the wrong righted if possible.

This investigation was undertaken by Dr. Emmett J. Scott of Howard University, who had become an advisor to the Secretary of War. [He] found that certain men with more zeal than wisdom had brought about this undesirable condition with the confusion that followed, and that there had been no such real ruling made.[14] Some of the men returned to the colleges from which they came, others remained declaring themselves satisfied at a school of their own people.

These confusing instructions at that time brought about by the unsettled policy of the government together with the consequent [and] frequent changes made, resulted in new and difficult problems. Yet we were able to settle them adequately and to the satisfaction of the inspector who had feared our ability to manage necessary adjustment of war work to literary work. In fact we learned that there were other institutions which had not mastered them before demobilization took place.

Then came not only the call for clerks for France, but our quotas of professors and students were sent to Washington to the Training Camp at Howard University to take the forty-seven days intensive training.[15] The draft too hit us and caught up a goodly number of students who were carried over seas swiftly and cautiously. On the return of one junior, a member of my own household, I was to learn of the gravity of the situation when on the brink of defeat just before the Armistice every available soldier of the Allies was ordered to the front.[16] As he said, "It was horrifying as many of our group to my knowledge had never handled either gun or bayonet, their occupation being in labor battalions and mostly in burial of the dead, concerning which many a tale of horror could be told."

On the signing of the Armistice, the unexpected closing of a scheme so elaborately and auspiciously begun as the S.A.T.C. caused sudden changes in the plans and purposes of all the institutions that had undertaken the training of these men. Financially we suffered little, but it left us with some undesirable situations which in turn created new problems that took time to solve, together with patience and hard work. It left a distaste for military drill which showed itself in a strong disinclination to enter the R.O.T.C. that was offered as a substitute for the S.A.T.C.

We accepted the offer, but the young men did not take well to it, due in part to their experiences in the S.A.T.C., and also to other disappointments relating to the status of colored officers. After a time it was accepted more readily when the students saw it was but a reversion to our pre-war military life.

As always I was intensely and personally interested in the students. I had not failed to visit home camps to which Wilberforce officer quotas had been sent. I was received with every courtesy by the commanding officer (white) and given every facility for speaking to the men, seeing how they fared and how they were trained. No fault could be found with housing, food, or treatment. It was admirable, and the training most efficient. It might seem heartless, cold-blooded, but it was to be remembered that they were being trained in these same dugouts and trenches for the actual experiences being met by the men "over there."

The boys everywhere were overjoyed to see me, especially so at Camp Funston where I went by special invitation of the Knights of Columbus to speak and to be present at the boys' commencement when officers were to finish training and receive commissions. Among these General Ballou singled out two as having done splendid work. He spoke highly of the entire group, which finished with a higher rating than those from other schools. Of course I was proud! I made the occasion in two instances. At Forts Des Moines and Funston where in both cases I found General Ballou in command, [I had] the opportunity to solicit his influence in obtaining Colonel Young's return to active service.[17] I [noted that]

General Ballou was sympathetic both times, but could not think the medical board in error, so I was forced to cease my pleas.

It was lamentable that there should have been such delay in forwarding to these colored young men their commissions. They were not received until some were already in France, and not until I, assisted by our Ohio Senator, had insistently taken up the delay with the War Department. As there could be no pay "until commissions received," the loss to the boys was considerable in both money and possible advancement.

As demobilization took place, our students gradually returned, but there were some who could not find themselves ready to resume academic life after the strenuous life overseas and in cantonments. In connection with the effort of the War Department to rehabilitate the disabled soldiers, Wilberforce University was also selected as a place to which some were sent for instruction in special lines of vocational work.

It is humiliating to say that the treatment of our colored troops on their return after demobilization, now after their heroic services in defense of their country, has been evidenced so often and so widely in a persistent refusal to grant them their manhood rights. [B]ut I admit that this treatment was somewhat mitigated in local instances whereas at my home in Ohio we shared in the county's welcome, [one] extended [to] all returning soldiers.

My indignation grew. I emphasized this further as I sought the American public as I always did hoping to arouse public conscience to right wrongs. This time it was by an article on "Race Riots and Their Remedy," published in the *New York Independent,* August 16, 1919.[18]

I asserted [that] the Negro returned from the war was altogether a new man, with new ideas, new hopes, new aspirations, and new desires. I drew attention to their treatment, many going to their homes with laurels won in their country's defense, and not permitted to ride in other than "Jim Crow Cars," many of them assaulted and thrown off cars, all of which are under government control, simply because of their color. Many have met death because they sought better treatment. Only the Negro's love for good government prevents serious trouble. The Negro only shows occasionally a retaliatory spirit. Negroes are not rioters but can be made so. Will not the American white people come halfway, put aside their prejudices and play fair with this people that has done so much to help win this war? There is but one remedy for race riots and that is justice, a willingness to accord to every man his rights, civil and political. [It is] the only solution of the vexed question called race prejudice.

My article received wide notice and favorable comment. A president of a noted Ohio university wrote me: "I was very much pleased with your article, not only pleased, but I approved and quite agree with you." The writer went on to say, "I believe there is a little envy at the prosperity of the Negro. I've evidence of this."

A thorough-going Southerner said to me last fall: "The niggers," as he called them, "had taken their part in the war better than most of the white men." He spoke with much enthusiasm of the way in which these men had met their obligations, not only as soldiers, but as residents [who] had come forward and done their part locally in all matters. He added, however, that it would raise a serious problem after the war and said, "They will say we helped to win the war, now what are you going to do for us."

Dr. T. was not the only one who saw the only solution must in *Justice* [be] done.[19] Another writer wrote congratulating me on the "terse and fair handling of the question," and added, "the more publicity that can be put in the hands of the white people of the country by such men as you who are known to have only the interests of your people at stake, the sooner will we be able to deal with this question as it should be dealt with."

In spite of all war difficulties and the fact that I had found my efforts to raise funds for the school much hampered by existing conditions and my inability to give as much time to such field work, my reports of 1918 and 1919 showed that the university had been able to pursue its normal course throughout the war period. It was not an easy thing to do, but it was fortunate in many ways in that no doors were closed and our fuel problem was met and quite readily solved. I could say that notwithstanding these things I could report phenomenal growth.

Never had our financial condition been in better shape. Several bequests had been left by members of the race in gifts of money and real estate by alumni. This gave much help and encouragement for such aid in the future. When our alumni [will have begun] to serve us thus, we [shall] have entered upon a new era. Upon their support and influence all our institutions must in time depend for gifts.

The greatest help however came now through the settlement of the affairs of the Avery Institute of Pittsburgh preparatory to closing it [down] as an institution. In the progress of events from the year following its establishment, [the Institute] was not now serving the interests in the best possible way for our people for whom it was designed. Pursuant to carrying out the wishes of the founder, a suitable institution was sought to which the funds might be turned. The attorney, knowing of our work and Mr. Avery's interest in it long ago (he had given it $10,000 in its early years), came to Xenia [and] quietly inquired into our present business conditions.[20] Receiving the assurance of leading business men and bankers as to our growth and progress, [he] came and laid before me his intentions and plans. The result was that the university [would obtain the assets of the defunct Avery Institute.]

Local and Closing War Labors

War activities throughout this entire period were not confined to the United States Government situation. Local war ones seemed continually to keep pace with the other, in fact these grew sometimes to a state almost beyond endurance, as I strove to keep the balance true.

For some time we had been as a people and a school under one of those periodic attacks of insane infamous prejudice that was endeavoring to put back "Black Laws" on Ohio's statute books.[1] We had to meet the underhanded Ku Klux Klan's efforts to rouse race hatred, and check its display wherever found. In this we had the united assistance of all school authorities, the Negro press, and white friends of the race—individuals and press. We won, though we knew the flame was fanned by unscrupulous ones within our ranks.

To add to the already overwrought situation a long seething undercurrent of local ambitious jealousies and rivalries came to the surface with attacks on the college department.[2] It went through various channels, having gained a following of a few of our devoted, but misguided alumni, who with mistaken zeal and a limited knowledge of complexities of the problems gained from garbled information, conceived in their duty to help keep up a jangle between the church supported department and the state supported one. They thus lent themselves to be made a cat's paw for private ambitions, which were constantly hatching up schemes for sole control. To all these attacks carried on mostly to still and thwart the Negro press it fell almost exclusively [to me] to reply.

I could wield a caustic pen when necessary and the writers of such articles did not care to renew the attacks after my vigorous and logical rejoinders, "hitting straight from the shoulder," as one eastern editor said, "and making the bull's eye every time." One of such several replies closed with the following remark which struck to the root of the local situation: "As for 'harmony,' we submit that it is the experience in any enterprise that nothing will throw any machinery out of gear so quickly as the insistence of individual cogs in the work on doing duties belonging to others. And as for 'reorganization' every one knows that this usually means only getting out those that are in and getting in those that are out."

Growing directly out of this plotting it seemed for these disturbing elements to be the opportune time to instigate legislative investigations. I reported to the board: "These got into politics through designing men who were not interested in the future of the University as a unit. As a result the differences of opinion as to methods and policies were spread abroad and made a basis for much newspaper gossip and misrepresentations in order to attain desired ends. The president himself was made the subject of many false attacks."

At this juncture as the new [national] presidential campaign was getting under way, I had been the recipient of the following letter, which I felt to be a distinguished honor and [a] recognition of the part I had long taken in politics.

Ohio Republican State Executive Committee
Columbus, Ohio
January 31st, 1919
Mr. W. S. Scarborough,
Xenia, Ohio

Dear Sir:

The Committee named by the Republican State Central Committee to select a State Advisory Committee, by unanimous decision, urges you to accept a place on the Committee, and has taken the liberty of announcing your appointment.[3] We most earnestly urge your acceptance and your active participation in the work which the organization will undertake.

We are not unmindful that some sacrifice is involved in giving needed attention to the somewhat ambitious plans of the Committee, but we are sure that you realize the importance of Republican victory in the State and Nation, and the necessity of the fullest Republican restoration to power. To win in 1920 we must begin in Ohio now, and Republicans will turn to the Advisory Committee to point the way.

Mr. George H. Clark, whom we have asked to accept the responsibility of the chairmanship, has asked for a meeting of the Committee at once, so that there shall be no delay in getting plans for the organization under way, and your attendance is requested for Tuesday, February 4th, at eleven a.m., at the State Headquarters, 709–710 Hartman Building, Columbus.

W. G. Harding
N. H. Fairbanks Committee on Appointment
E. M. Fullerton

The appointment was immediately followed by two letters from Senator Harding:

United States Senate
Committee on Commerce
February 1, 1919
Dr. W. S. Scarborough
Xenia, Ohio

My dear Dr. Scarborough:
The Committee appointed to name a new Advisory Committee for the Republican Party in Ohio was unanimous in wishing you to accept a place on that Committee.

I am only writing to express my personal interest in having you arrange, if possible, to attend the first meeting of the Committee to be held in Columbus, Ohio, on Tuesday, February 4th.

I feel every assurance that you will be delighted with Mr. Clark, who has been chosen to take the executive responsibilities of the Committee.

Assuring you of my personal regards, I am,
Very truly yours,
W. G. Harding

Will H. Hays wrote [as] Chairman of the Republican National Committee:[4]

I have just learned of the appointment of the new Advisory Committee in Ohio. I am glad that you are on it. I know you will give the attention to the matter which the situation warrants and all things will work out well.

With very warmest personal regards and cordial good wishes,

Sincerely yours,
Will H. Hays

I was now in a position to help most effectively [to] stem the tide of legislation threatening the University at that moment.[5] The first attempt to cripple our work was by a legislative bill to cut the $5,000 annual appropriation to the University for services rendered by the same. This failed of passage.

Then a bill found its way through the Legislature, reducing the number of our university trustees so that the college would have but two out of seven men on that board, but the governor vetoed this bill.[6] Thus another victory was ours.

Our third victory took form in the defeat of a measure that seemed impossible to accomplish. It was a measure to make the C. N. & I. Department an independent institution with a head of its own. A legislative and an educational committee spent two days in our midst with a view to that end, but their efforts failed, as the Legislature dropped the matter and took no further action, letting the status of the institution remain as before.

I was assured by letter from the Chairman of the [Ohio Republican] State [Advisory] Committee that "there will be no trouble about your appropriation [of] $5,000 and I feel that the House and Senate Finance Committee will follow your recommendation in regard to the Normal Department."[7]

In another letter from the same source:

Hon. W. S. Scarborough
Wilberforce, Ohio

My dear Doctor:
Your favor of the third inst. received. Answer has been delayed owed to my absence from this office on fieldwork.

We congratulate Wilberforce University that its status has remained unchanged and its usefulness for the great, constructive work it performs unimpaired.

It is true that legislation was introduced in the legislature the effect of which, if enacted, would have been to retard measurably the progressive and constructive tendency of the work. Happily, however, your interest in the institution, your knowledge of its needs and your clear and unbiased presentation of the questions at issue to those in authority in the legislature averted what might have been a great mistake.

Concerning your loyalty, interest, and intelligent constructive treatment of the difficult questions arising because of the peculiar status under the law of Wilberforce, we can always testify.

With cordial regards, I am,
Yours very truly,
Geo. H. Clark, Ch'r.

With such conditions facing the University, it was like living a life between hawk and buzzard, trying to steer a straight course, keep the balance true, and carry on the work safely. I thanked my Maker that I had been given intelligence and understanding, experience and sympathy, also, to uphold my hands. Without these, the burden would have been too great for mortal man to carry. But it required all my energy and patience and it took full toll of them. I was heartsick of it all, but many friends encouraged and bade me to ignore these efforts. I could not ignore all—[not] out of self-respect, nor self-protection, nor duty to the University.

These things coupled with unceasing war work, too, drew heavily on my strength, so heavily that, not having been a most robust man since my previous breakdown, my health was now threatened. Friends grew anxious, especially when the flu broke out among the soldiers, and every available hall was turned into a hospital. They advised me to take inoculation against the epidemic. A curious result followed after I had had two injections of preventive serum.

I began to experience frequent spasms of coughing. These grew into such violent paroxysms as to threaten strangulation at times. Twice at home I was so overcome that I fell to the floor. I kept at the office tasks and would allow no one to know this, except my physician, family, and the office force. As a drink of water seemed to check the attacks, a glass was constantly kept at home and office within my reach day and night. I even carried a flask of water in my pocket at all times after I once came near falling on the street. I never knew when my enemies [would] begin to accuse me of the "drink habit." In short the attacks which wore away as summer advanced were deemed due to whooping cough developed by the inoculations.

During these war years the demands of scholastic life and its accompanying functions were met, [all of] which had to be maintained. In March of 1917 I went to carry greetings and speak, as I reported, in a very happy manner at Howard University's celebration of its semi-centennial.[8] I took the occasion to assert anew that the "future of the race lies along the lines of scholastic training that Howard and Wilberforce Universities had been following."

I had already attended the International Arms Conflict Congress called by President Wilson in Washington in January and had at the request of Albert Bushnell Hart gone to the Conference of Representative Organizations Engaged in Patriotic Service. I was even asked by the Fusion Committee of 1917 to lend help to Mayor Mitchell of New York City, and I was asked to support Mayor Mitchell and other Fusion candidates in its efforts to show New York City's loyalty to the country in the great conflict.[9] It was suggested that I draw up a list of names of some one hundred people I knew "well enough to approach personally or send letters."

In July I felt that I must meet the Association of Teachers of Colored Schools at Harper's Ferry at its twentieth annual meeting. I was asked to address it on "Negro Colleges and the War." This was followed in the fall by [my] visit to New York as a delegate appointed by Governor Cox to the twentieth convention of the Negro National Educational Congress.

As 1918 opened I received this letter:

The A.M.E. Church Review
Editor's Office
Oceanport, N.J.
Jan. 4, 1918
Dr. W. S. Scarborough
Wilberforce, Ohio

Mr. President and dear friend:

I appreciate your good letter, not only for its expression of personal appreciation, but also for the heartening evidence it bears of the substantial manner in which your labors in behalf of Wilberforce are being crowned with success. No single individual has, on the whole, so completely identified his life with the intellectual and material development of Wilberforce as have you.

My dear Doctor, be of good cheer. In this new morning of

the world you are splendidly adorning your high and responsible station. May that fellowship with Jesus which gives poise of spirit and illumination of mind, be yours constantly in all the duties and opportunities that await you. Mrs. Ransom joins in kind remembrance to you and Mrs. Scarborough.

Cordially yours,
Reverdy C. Ransom[10]

Early in the year I accepted the invitation to represent the University at the Congress of Constructive Patriotism held in Washington January 25. I also acceded to the request of the League to Enforce Peace to speak in May before one of the Philadelphia schools on "Win the War for Permanent Peace."[11] In May I was invited to be a guest at the Allied War Dinner in connection with the great "Win the War for Permanent Peace Convention," held at Bellevue Stratford and Hotel Walton in Philadelphia.[12] I was assigned a place with nine other delegates at one of the one hundred forty-three tables set. And the heavens did not fall. While in Philadelphia I filled an appointment as speaker at one of the most prominent white churches.

In March I opened the Colored Y.M.C.A. in Columbus and [in] the latter part of the month went to take part in the Easter program of St. John's A.M.E. Church in Frankfort, Kentucky. In Kentucky I swung around to speak at both Lexington and Harrodsburg. The last of the month found me at Camp Sherman, [Chillicothe,] Ohio in attendance at the Memorial Day services with [the] 317th Engineers and the 325th Field Signal Battalion where some of our students were in service.[13] In the meantime the faculty series of lectures just brought into being had scheduled me to open the series with one on "Greek Learning and Human Liberty."[14]

All of these activities called for every moment even on trains, penciling articles on scraps of paper as I traveled to and fro. I turned them over for typing to the ready hands of my secretary and my wife, whose understanding, co-operative aid was always at my service to relieve me at every possible point.

The pamphlet, *Wilberforce in the War,* was issued as my 1918 address at the opening of the school session that September.[15] I received congratulations by Secretary M. A. Atkinson, executive secretary of the National Committee on the Churches and Moral Aims of the War. On behalf of the Committee, Mr. Atkinson wrote me in December:[16]

I have the honor of extending you a cordial invitation to be present as our guest at an institute to be held at Louisville, Kentucky, Thursday and Friday, December 19th and 20th for the purpose of discussing and conferring together upon the beginning of reconstruction and the part churches and religious organizations must take in this crisis of the world's history.

The Central Powers have been defeated but we have not won the war in the best sense of the word unless we achieve the great moral ends for which the war was fought. We are face to face now with the rebuilding of civilization and each one of us must take a hand. We must do more than follow the reports in the daily papers. There are tremendous problems ahead and we must talk about them and work our way through them.

We need your presence and your help. This is purely an education and inspirational meeting designed to deepen the spiritual life of all and help us meet the pressing problems in our various communities.

I must not fail to recognize here the assurance of the editor of the *Christian Herald* that it was a pleasure to give your work publicity.[17] The Unitarian Church grows in its devotion to your cause.

Since my election to the Presidency of Wilberforce in 1908 I had been unable to prepare papers for the Philological Association nor even attend the meetings, except twice in 1912 and [19]13. In fact my attendance in 1909 at Johns Hopkins and the treatment accorded me by Hotel Belvedere's refusal to serve a banquet if I were to be present, had so wounded and incensed me that I felt no inclination to attend, especially, as few of my old friends were left in it. A pleasing reminder of past days, however, was received in the following letter from the secretary of the association when he wrote:[18] "Our members of thirty-five years standing, who have reached the age of sixty-five, are exempted from payment of dues. It is therefore my pleasure to inform you that you will continue to be a member of the Association without receiving the annual bill."

When I joined the American Philological Association many years ago the personnel of its membership differed largely from what it is today. The men and women of those days thought more of scholarship and less of prejudice; the color of a man made no difference with them. It was his standing as a scholar and as a representative of American scholarship that counted. The Harvard, Yale, Columbia, New York, Cornell, and even some of the Princeton men vied with one another to make me, the only [active] Negro member of the Association of that time, feel at home. It was then that I read most of my papers on classical subjects. It was then that I felt that an American scholar was an American scholar, be he white or black. I did some of my best work in the Philological Association in those earlier

days, but as the years went by, and as young men from the southern institutions, and there were many of them, became members of this association, I noticed a different atmosphere. My interest in that association became
less, so that in later years the papers read by me have been fewer in number. Some of these men would not adjust themselves to conditions. They
could not forget that they were from the South, representing a civilization
far different from that we have in the North. I met these young doctors
and scholars in hotels where I stopped, and on steamers. In fact I met them
in all avenues of life, social and intellectual, where I saw it was difficult for
them to adapt themselves to existing conditions.

[I pressed on.] In January of the next year I was asked to attend a
series of nine Congresses for the League of Nations and was also appointed
by Governor Cox as delegate to the "Great Lakes" one held in Chicago in
February.

The close of March 1919 brought a message that startled and
shocked all at the University. The Bishop of the [Third] District, Dr.
Cornelius Shaffer, had passed away quite suddenly shortly after he had left
the University where he had presided over its Founders' Day exercises.[19]

Bishop Shaffer had served the Third District of the A.M.E. Church
for eight years. He came to it when the University was laboring under
tremendous financial burdens. With the aid of officials and the other bishops in charge of the "First Educational District" of the Church he began
an organization of his district to clear off the debts of the University. This
last Founders' Day Rally had with such help exceeded any previous amount.
To this Mrs. A. Malone had individually given us $1,000, a splendid gift
from one who had built up a great business in St. Louis that is an honor to
the race.[20] With Bishop Shaffer's death we were to miss not only a dignified presence and an able organizer, but an unselfish interest that it would
be difficult to replace. Our great loss was soon to be made very evident.

In the midst of war work and that going on to prevent unfriendly
legislation as noted in previous chapter a pleasing invitation came to me in
the following letter. It constitutes one of the most appreciated ones in my
career. I may be pardoned in giving full names in connection with such
courtesies. I would let posterity know of such a noble act from a fellow
President in Ohio.

Cleveland, Ohio
May 27, 1919
President Wm. S. Scarborough,

Wilberforce University
Wilberforce, Ohio

My dear Mr. President:
The formal opening of the new gymnasium of Western Reserve University is to occur the evening of Monday, June 9th. It would give me great pleasure to receive you as my personal guest at dinner in the gymnasium at half past six. Despite the numerous and imperative duties of the season, can you not give me the happiness of receiving you? Believe me. . . .

Ever yours,
Charles F. Thwing[21]

In July President Demos of the American Association of the Greek Community in Chicago addressed a letter to me in reference to a matter of great interest to all Greeks and friends of Greece, desiring my opinion.[22] He wrote:

> Under Greek control, Constantinople would develop free speech, religious freedom, guarantee life, liberty and property rights, irrespective of nationality or other affiliations. It would be a free port, thus assuring the neutrality of the Dardanelles, while peace in the near East, and particularly in the Balkans, would be an accomplished fact.
>
> Many prominent citizens have expressed an opinion with reference to Constantinople and that it should be maintained by the Grecian government and as a part thereof. Our association is now soliciting the opinion of American men of distinction and of all professions, in the hope that the association may have the benefit of an entirely American viewpoint. We, therefore, respectfully ask that you favor us with such comment upon the subject suggested as you may deem worthy.

I was very glad to reply as I never allowed an opportunity to pass to lend any support where the cause of freedom was involved. A few paragraphs are given from the reply made showing my deep interest in matters then agitating the world.

[My] letter to President Demos [read]:

> I gladly comply with your request. I am thoroughly in sympathy with Greece. My long study with its language and literature has made me decidedly Greek

in spirit. My admiration and good will have always been unbounded for the country that first gave to the world the full idea of human liberty.

The city of Constantine (Constantinople) is undoubtedly Greek and not Turkish, Greek by name, by a multitude of associations and by inherent rights to exclusive Greek control. It should be given to its rightful owner. Any other disposition of this famous capital would be rank injustice.

The Turkish dominion extending from 1453 makes some 466 years since this city has been occupied by this barbarous people and the time has now come for a change. Turkey does not deserve any favor on the part of the Allied Forces. That country has by its numberless atrocities and inhumanities put itself outside civilization. To place Constantinople under Greek control will be to help on the final accomplishment the long sought freedom of nations, the true world democracy and world peace. A Treaty of Peace that does not include this change is defective. By all means let Constantinople be given to Greece.

I was elected in October as one of the representatives of the A.M.E. Church to the Interstate Commission of the Ohio State Federation of Churches with the assurance that "we welcome you to a place in our midst." In December I was made a member of the Interchurch World Movement of North America and asked to conference in Home Missionary Boards as representative of independent institutions, [in a] survey of Negro institutions held in New York which I attended in December.[23]

I was also made an associate member of the American Asiatic Association.[24] Even the National Medical Association begged me to accept membership in its society and the Horticultural Society of New York elected me to that body.[25]

Though I had not been able to be in the field soliciting contributions as much as before, I had been able to keep up creditable contributions. With the bequests obtained and added church interest, the Secretary was able to close his 1919 report showing an excess in current receipts of more than $5,000 over the preceding year. With increased assets as President I reported that debts had been reduced. "We owe the banks not a penny for the first time in the history of the institution, and the University now has confidence, credit, and a bank account. Our Founders' Day receipts were considerably over $4,000, the largest sum ever received on that day." I also expressed in the same report high hopes of the University being accounted in the near future among the beneficiaries of some of the great educational foundations of the country. I had good reason for this last, as appended to a letter from one such to which I had applied and which was delaying to accede to my request, was the penciled private note of the secretary: "I think you will obtain it later as they are favorably impressed."

In connection with the financial situation there had been conceived a "Betterment Plan" by the President of the State Department Board, who personally was always desirous of helping the college for the good of all.[26] It was designed to make the College work more efficient by this board taking a share in some control and meeting some expense thus enabling it to become "strong enough financially to meet our demands." The plan provided for a specified period when the former status would be resumed automatically. It passed all the Boards and State authorities, up to the Legislature, where it failed in passage.

As President, I had labored without cessation to bring success to the University over which I presided. This was recognized by friends who had watched through the years, one of whom, a noted Detroit lawyer, wrote:[27] "Ever since I learned the extent of the burden Wilberforce bore I have been greatly concerned for its future. Others connected with it felt as I did and wondered in the time of this world stress if sufficient revenue could be obtained to meet pressing demands. You have accomplished what many thought the impossible. You have worked a miracle and deserve our richest commendation."

I reported in June of 1919 that the University business matters [were] being conducted in a strictly business way. There is nothing but ourselves that can impede our upward and onward progress.

Close of Forty-five Years in the Field of Education

While some of the incidents following the death of Bishop Shaffer in 1919 have been [described] in the previous chapter, there were others more closely connected with [the] future course of events. The continued success of the University had been such as to make [the office of the president] now a desirable position. This for some time had led to ambitious covetous eyes being fixed upon the presidency.

I was informed by friends watching the situation that there was a silent grooming of [a] candidate for the place. [Knowing] that the power of a bishop in his immediate diocese was practically unlimited, I foresaw things that might happen—many of which did happen—as plans began to take shape. In my mind there was now no question as to the outcome when the Bishops' Council was soon convened in Chicago [in order] to appoint one from its bench to take charge of Bishop Shaffer's diocese until General Conference a year hence. I was approached by a leading presiding elder in this diocese, who was a member of both College and State Board of our University with a petition prepared to ask for the appointment of my predecessor in the presidency (who was also the father of the present dean of the University) to fill this place.[1]

I was no sycophant. My self respect called for my refusal to sign it. I knew that because of a bishop's power over presiding elders and the power of these over pastors, this petition would receive sufficient signatures to ensure its being granted. I was not disappointed in my conclusions, nor was this presiding elder, whose son before many months was to succeed to the superintendency of the State Department. After, in the throes of an upheaval ending in a vacancy of that position, I was warned that it would be my turn next. I knew it. However, it did not deter me from doing what I felt to be my duty for the good of the school. Knowing the genesis of the situation as I did, I added another enemy to my list.

I knew other things also: that though the debts of the college department had been now greatly decreased during my administration, it still had debtors and I was one with notes for unpaid salary through deficits dating back for a long period when salaries had never been fully met. I knew that something would have to be done to remedy this before the end came to me. I was not wrong and waited. It was a time when [fund-raising] drives were in their prime. One was instituted to wipe out all indebtedness of the University. The fear of state control as well as ecclesiastical spur now administered lent wings to this drive through the Third, the Ninth, Fifteenth, and First Church Districts, [all] lending a hand. To this drive I contributed $1,000 of the University's indebtedness to me, and the Faculty also made noble sacrifices.

I had already been warned by friends who knew as to impending movements in the General Conference of the Church which was to meet in May. [It was] a time when cabals were entered into and heads of schools of the church so often were "butchered to make a Roman holiday."[2] I had been advised not to contribute my $1,000, that it would aid a purpose in the [fund-raising] drive that would spell my own finish. But I gave it nevertheless for the cause of education. I had also been told that no matter what sacrifice I made no faith would be kept with me.

All these friends were right. But I had decided. I knew my work was done and I had no desire to continue in a situation daily growing more distasteful, embarrassing, and humiliating with the son of the presiding elder both Dean of the College and the candidate for the presidency.

My resignation was typed and known to my friends before I went to the General Conference in St. Louis in May.[3] There I clearly saw the handwriting on the wall as power rode rough shod over laws and courtesy and decency. I returned to hold my last Commencement and to make my last report. At the Board meeting the Secretary had been able to report for the quadrennium ending September 20, 1920: "For the first time in the history of the school Wilberforce University is free of the incubus of debt ... more than $44,000 was turned into the coffers of the University." And so I could give the Board the following retrospect of my administration:

> It has been my lot to serve as the head of Wilberforce University for three quadrenniums. It is not out of place at this time to present a brief summary of what I have been able to accomplish in these twelve years aided by Divine power and faithful friends.
>
> When I came to the presidency in 1908 I took charge of an institution that was virtually bankrupt in many ways, no money, no credit, no public

confidence. We did not know where we stood. We only knew that the out-look was dark, that we had deficits and debts, and clamorous creditors, banks and individuals.

The first year was a horrible nightmare of work and worry as we groped in the dark to find a way out and up. I need not go into the harrowing experiences of the period. There were, however, faithful, helpful trustees and friends who knew and shared the burdens and anxieties, and whose combined efforts, advice and credit helped to secure the necessary assistance to keep the institution afloat. Personally I went hither and thither to make friends and secure aid. The details of that mighty struggle to keep above water financially while we presented a brave front to the world and kept pushing up our standards, possess elements that reach to the tragic. But grit, pluck and work won and gradually we pulled upward to a firm footing.

In June 1919, after eleven years of ceaseless, untiring, tremendous efforts, the following could be pointed to among the things achieved:

The University affairs had become clearly straightened out and well organized.

- An up-to-date system of accounting had been established.
- An investment committee had been appointed.
- Bank credit had been restored and general public confidence regained.
- The college teaching staff had doubled, with increased salaries, and prompt payment, from a teaching force in combined faculties of 30 which included officers and employees (in 1908) to 42, not counting officers and some instructors in mechanics and extension work which would make 55 in all today.
- Offices had been aroused, associations formed over the country, bringing union, solidarity, and financial help.
- Founders' Day had become an organized event when loyal alumni, students, trustees, and friends vied to make it a great financial success, receipts increasing from $402.80 (in 1908) to $4,556.57 (in 1919).
- Helpful friends had been made; contributions came in; prestige was won; the name of Wilberforce had reached the front mark.
- The curriculum had been revised, standards raised, courses everywhere enlarged and increased in number, and the preparatory department was made into an academy under a separate faculty.
- The attendance in [the] College department alone had increased from 22 (in 1908) to 141; it now reaches 200.
- The combined number in the University had risen from 400 to 1,542, counting in those served by extension work. (Today we have 1,000 regularly registered exclusive of the extension work and the soldier body.)
- The State Department had grown in many ways as a strong arm of the University.
- Cordial and reciprocal relation had been established with other institutions.

- The C. N. & I. Board had, at my request, increased its appropriation for our aid in teaching from $3,500.00 annually to $5,000.00 annually.
- Debts had been reduced to $25,000, although expenses had almost doubled.
- Our assets had received large additions. Investments had been made and endowment increased. Emery Hall had been erected with fittings at a cost closely approximating $50,000.00, all but $15,000.00 of which were obtained through my unaided personal solicitations.
- The Avery estate portion had come to us after the lawyer's consultation with me and after his being assured by bankers and friends of the great growth of the institution.[4] Its value is about $28,000 in bonds, mortgages, and equipment. Shorter Hall had been rehabilitated at a cost of $2,500.00 and an electric light plant put in for it, Emery Hall, and the Library.
- With the establishment of the college unit of the S.A.T.C. granted by the War Department at my request, its successful operation had brought both financial aid and prestige.
- Contributions and requests in money and real estate, amounting to over $10,000.00 had been received, and we had bought one of the cottages on the campus long held by other parties. Last June also saw the cancellation of all notes in [the] bank against the University and in hands of scalpers, together with a mortgage of $3,000.00 paid, which had been running for twenty-five years.

Aside from this with what I have turned in for the purpose this year, I had secured some $1,100.00 set aside in a separate fund by the treasurer as a nucleus for a science building. And here I feel I may chronicle my own personal gift in April of $1,000.00 which I deducted from the University's indebtedness to me for years of accumulated salary deficit.

I recall all this growth with gratitude and pardonable pride that those eleven years of my administration as head of Wilberforce University have been blessed in so many ways. I am grateful to all friends, to the Bishops and members of the First Educational District, to the Educational and Financial Departments of the Church, to Bishops Derrick and Shaffer of the Third Episcopal District, now gone to their reward, and to Bishops Coppin and Salter, both of whom have encouraged, sustained, and given aid to all my efforts.[5]

The twelfth year (1919–1920) has seen the financial drive already mentioned in my General Conference Report. With this we have wiped out the last vestige of debt and we hope that the report from it will show a large surplus to the credit of the University.

Today the university is immensely richer in many ways than it was twelve years ago. In looking back I can but maintain that an institution with such a record may truthfully, rightfully, justly, and undeniably claim the twelve years of my administration to have been years of phenomenal progress and unquestioned success.

It is also due to myself to say that this success has come despite tremendous opposition. While friends have been loyal and helpful, opponents have hampered work in many ways, and conflicts have ever been present because of the complex workings and relations of Church and State.

Had I not known the situation intimately for years—known the rocks and shoals, the opposing forces, and how to carry the load—I am sure that I could not have survived twelve years of such strenuous effort as I have been compelled to put forth to make a greater Wilberforce.

Had these years been years of failure I should rightly and would inevitably have been held strictly responsible as President. As they have been years of success it would seem that at least some need of praise were due to my personal efforts, position and influence. I have given Wilberforce University my whole untiring service—my very life and all that my influence could bring—and with very meager compensation comparatively speaking, except the consciousness of duty done, the good will of friends is the Church and throughout the country, and the friendship of thousands of students whom I have served.

My conscience is clear. I have done ever what I saw to be my duty. I have sought only the just rights of every department and its upbuilding and have stood to hold the balance true and impartial in trying situations. I am perfectly satisfied to let the world, that has been looking on, give its verdict as to the worth of my labors in these three quadrenniums.

But Wilberforce now stands at a crucial point in its career. . . . Money alone cannot save it. Words alone cannot save it. Disaster in some form is sure to come, unless we adhere unflinchingly to the right path of progress, giving justice everywhere, demanding efficiency and working righteously for the perpetuation of the entire plant as a harmonious unit.

There must be an end to dissension and hampering, and instead an aim at uplift and progress if Wilberforce University is to hold the place it has won. Wilberforce is situated as no other school of the race, blessed in location and environment, and holding potentialities to be the leading educational center maintained by the Negro. Shall its great opportunity for service be destroyed? Very much depends upon this Trustee Board in determining the future. My prayer is that it may know how to direct wisely the affairs for a progressive future.

With an eye single to this future I closed this report with these words:

In the hope that my long and intimate knowledge of some present necessities may be of worth in this endeavor and in that we are in a position to systematize and plan for the future, I make the following recommendations. I give only the most important here as showing proposed growth. These call for the creation of a budget and a new office—that of Registrar—classification of professors and instructors, according to experience and length of service with an increase of salaries on this basis, and new buildings, among these a science building for which I had already made a small beginning in funds turned over to the Treasurer for that specific purpose.

My report made, it was at once evident what the chair designed a [specially elected] committee should proceed to do. I had been prevailed upon over my good judgment to withhold my resignation for the time by a group of trustees who considered the situation a grave one threatening the best interests of the University. My acquiescence was unwise as it gave opportunity for my being butchered by the committee for that purpose. The contending forces then battled for nearly two days one to thwart schemes, the other to carry them through. I begged my friends at last to withdraw my name, which they had doggedly represented. It resulted in a compromise candidate being brought forward in the person of Dr. John Gregg who was elected to the presidency.[6] The meeting was then abruptly adjourned *sine die* by the chair, which refused consideration of any motion that considered my name in any form. Revenge at least was complete; though victory was delayed not defeated [as] it was claimed.

Thus ended my career of forty-five years in the field of education, forty-three of which had been spent in the service of Wilberforce University. I announced my "graduation" with the class of 1920 as I bestowed on them their diplomas. Of this a spectator wrote the press:"Those who were present will not forget the shocked murmur that spread from the class to the audience. There were even sobs, and at the close a crowd pressed forward to grasp the hand of the 'beloved president,' as the class had designated him in their published annual the *Archiviste* and to express its sorrow at his retirement from the office he had so long filled with signal ability."[7]

At the dinner table that day the Commencement speaker and guest, who had been shocked at the announcement, said to the group of trustees gathered there, "Gentlemen, does your Board know what it is doing? President Scarborough has the ear and consideration of influential philanthropic boards in the east. It is a species of suicide it will find."

A reply to my letter sometime after congratulating another prominent retiring university president on his labors bore this significant phrase, "You, too, have trod the wine press alone."

Of my retirement [and about] my address at the alumni meeting following [the press said]: "It was appropriate—the broadminded educator's words to his successor, wishing him well and pledging support. The audience gave him such an ovation that it all but lifted the roof." The press universally united in praise for my administration and regret that it was terminated. Among these many expressions, the following which was highly appreciated as coming from the editor, [Reverdy Ransom], of the *A.M.E. Church Review:*

> After more than forty years of continuous service as either professor or President of Wilberforce University, Dr. W. S. Scarborough was *relieved* of the presidency by the Trustee Board in June past. During the years of his fruitful activities there he has given to Wilberforce world-wide recognition in the realm of scholarship, through text books he has written, addresses he has delivered to learned societies, and his scholarly articles in the leading magazines of the country, and his informing lectures and addresses upon the public platform. Aside from all this, during the number of years of his Presidency, Wilberforce has gained much in material strength and outward beauty, and through his personal efforts a large portion of the money needed for the completion of beautiful Emery Hall was raised. The student body has grown from two or three hundred to more than a thousand. College atmosphere pervades the campus and halls of the University, more from his character and personality than from any other cause. If Wilberforce has had anything to do with shaping his development, he has had silently and indirectly much more to do with the bringing of Wilberforce up from the grade and atmosphere of an academy to the spirit of a college. He was and is the outstanding example of a Negro Scholar, emancipated from the leading strings of the white man, giving character, support, and direction to the higher intellectual life of his race. This is not adieu, nor the rose that is given at parting. In order to honor Dr. Scarborough and to preserve our honor, proper dignity and self-respect, we shall as we should, at the first opportunity, hail him as President Emeritus of Wilberforce University and cherish him in life while ever joyously opening the door of opportunity for him to give to us the benefits of the culture and classical erudition which he has been storing up throughout the fruitful years.

[My] wide circle of friends knew that it was indeed not only a "relief" but immeasurably welcome, though all depreciated with hot speech the method employed. Payne Seminary stood by me as it always had. At its Board meeting the next day I was elected for the second time a lay delegate to the Fifth Ecumenical Conference to be held in London [in] September, 1921.[8]

There has been no intent to give the detailed history of Wilberforce University [here], save as I found myself and my work inextricably connected with it. [This account] treats the termination of my labors with it, which I feel necessary [to give] as [a] vindication of myself, my work, and my course.

I had turned my attention to politics again soon after April, 1919. Two men whom I counted as friends to be sustained by me personally and by the race were now in the public eye. One was Hon. N. H. Fairbanks, brother of Vice-President Fairbanks, who was on the Ohio Republican Advisory Committee with me where we were thrown into close contact that caused me to learn to admire him greatly.[9] He proposed now to enter the race for Governor of Ohio. I pledged my support to him and stood by him loyally in his canvas until when after the campaign had begun he withdrew.

This drew from him a long letter from which the following paragraph is given: "I appreciate your interest in me and the support given by the colored folks generally, [al]though some have not chosen to do so. But always, my dear Dr. Scarborough, I have a fond interest in you and wish the best shall always be your reward."

In this connection an incident occurred that summer in Atlantic City while attending the Convention of Education over which Dr. John R. Mott presided. I received a wire from Mayor H. L. Davis of Cleveland, Ohio inviting me to be his special guest at a dinner to be held there.[10] I was obliged to wire that while it would give me great pleasure to accept, my duties at Atlantic City made it impossible for me to be present to accept his gracious invitation. I then wrote explaining more fully my reasons for absence. A reply brought the statement that Mayor Davis was contemplating running for the governorship of Ohio and desired to talk over the matter with me with a view to having my influence and support. On my return to Ohio I went to Cleveland and talked over the matter. I told him frankly that I had pledged myself to Senator Fairbanks, but I also added that if for any reason the latter should decline to run he—Mayor Davis—should have my cordial support.

With the final withdrawal of Senator Fairbanks I informed Mayor Davis that I would give him my active support as soon as I returned from New York where I was then obliged to go on business connected with the University. I came back and entered into the campaign to bring about the election of Mr. Davis who was successful in November.

Because of my previous support of Senator Fairbanks and because of some double crossing of me by certain colored parties desirous of assuming to control in colored politics I write of this the more fully as I have felt assured in his campaign that his manager, perhaps he himself, was led to think my efforts had not been vigorous in his behalf. At any rate I was treated accordingly though I had kept my promise and had worked faithfully where and how I knew it would do the most good. My conscience was clear. I helped launch the Republican campaign that year at its meeting, being on the program for opening prayer. But in politics we are often misunderstood as well as maligned.

The second friend to whom [I] gave perfect fealty at this time was U.S. Senator Warren G. Harding. Sometime before the primary election I went to Senator Harding in Washington. His Secretary, Mr. Christian, took me to his committee rooms on Foreign Relations and we had a long talk.[11] It was then that I told him if he should become a candidate I would give him my hearty support. As soon as he decided to do so I laid my plans to that end. Shortly he sent me to the Chairman of the Republican National Committee with the following letter:

United States Senate
Committee on the Philippines
November 13, 1919
Hon. Will H. Hays, Chairman
Republican National Committee
New York, N.Y.,

My dear Mr. Hays:
This letter will be presented to you by Dr. W. S. Scarborough, President of Wilberforce University, Xenia, Ohio.

Dr. Scarborough comes to National Headquarters to confer with you and ascertain what service he can render in contribution to Republican success. He is not only a member of the Republican State Advisory Committee in Ohio, chosen by the unanimous vote of the Committee authorized to name the advisory board, but he is universally recognized as the leading colored citizen of our state. I wish you to know these things so that you may be able to appraise him at his real worth during his visit with you.

Very truly yours,
(signed) W. G. Harding

At his and Mr. Daugherty's request I became a special advisor in this campaign, and operated between the two headquarters in Chicago and New York occasionally making speeches where my services were needed.[12] To the Convention in Chicago Mr. Marcus Shoup of my home city had been elected an alternate in the Republican Primary of the county.[13] He found he could not go and asked if I would serve in his stead, should he commission me to act as alternate by turning over to me his credentials. He said he thought my position in the country and the Republican Party made it very fitting for me to have this honor. I accepted and thus became an alternate in the convention that nominated Senator Harding for the Presidency.

It was an exciting convention and a long hard fought fight because of the strength of General Wood, Senator Johnson, and Governor Lowden and their financial backing.[14] But I had from the first an unshaken faith that Senator Harding would be the final choice of the convention. It was my work to try to convince colored delegates especially of this and I insistently kept it before all. I know I had success.

There were colored delegates who were bound to others; there were some wavering, but to our credit as a race I know of but one who unscrupulously broke his faith as a worker for Senator Harding's nomination. This was known to Mr. Daugherty who wrote me later of it and expressed his opinion of such despicable conduct in no uncertain terms.

As I wrote the press later I feel I can claim to be the one man of color who long before and from first to last in the convention had centered not only hopes, but connections and efforts on his star as the one in the end to be ascendant over all. As I had predicted Senator Harding was nominated on the tenth ballot. Being assured of victory, I left just before the close to fulfill my last obligation to my University in reporting to my Board and holding my last Commencement.

Efforts were now put forth by schools and individuals to have me to enter into cooperative work for the advancement of educational causes in which they felt my influence would be of great help. Nothing tempted me. I felt I was done with educational labors and wished rest.

Free now to do as I pleased I began at once to arrange my affairs that I might give full time and effort to the coming presidential campaign. Despite dastardly attacks on the Republican nominee, it ended successfully in November when I saw the man I esteemed highly in every sense made the President of the United States. I knew that in him the race I represented had a staunch friend.

I was present on that eventful day at Marion when Senator Harding was officially notified that he was the people's choice. I heard his magnificent acceptance speech given with that same dignity, serenity and poise shown afterwards throughout a long and trying campaign, I noted the deep undercurrent of feeling bringing sincerity to every word, and I was proud of the eloquent and emphatic words and manner as he gave his dictum on the Negro question: "I believe the federal government should stamp out lynching and remove that stain from the fair name of America. I believe the Negro citizens of America should be guaranteed the enjoyment of all their rights; that they have earned the full measure of citizenship bestowed; that their sacrifice in blood on the battlefields of the Republic have entitled us to all of freedom and opportunity, all of sympathy and aid that the American spirit of fairness and justice demands."

[My friends], Senator J. B. Foraker and President Harding, were friends [themselves]. The sturdy unswerving loyalty of this mutual friendship had been an exceedingly fine thing to note. In fact it stands in the character of both these great men as a most knightly characteristic. Of all the public men I have ever known, I have yet to find a superior to either of these two stalwart Republicans and representative Americans.

A restful winter at home followed the election varied by the usual annual address to my boys of the Y.M.C.A. in New York. This was followed by attendance in the spring at the inaugural of President-elect Harding. I also busied myself with arranging material for future articles, making preparation for the trip to attend the Methodist Ecumenical Conference in London.

Third Visit to Europe— Again Delegate to the Methodist Ecumenical Conference in London—Scotland—Continental Trip

O n my third trip to Europe, I went in advance of the party of the American colored delegates to the Ecumenical Conference for whom Secretary John Hawkins of the A.M.E. Church had booked an itinerary with Cook's Agency.[1]

Mine was made a personal affair. I wished to cross earlier on the *Carmania* on July 16th as I was due in Cambridge, England, August 2 to 5 as one of the representatives of the American Philological Association to the Classical Association Meeting in an Anglo-American General Meeting. I was to join the other delegates on their arrival on the 19th at Cherbourg. Mrs. Scarborough felt it necessary to give up the trip at the last moment because of illness in her family.[2] This was a great disappointment to both as we had counted much upon the mutual pleasure in seeing Europe after the war. We were particularly interested to observe the changes in the country, its people, and conditions.

We had crossed on the *Carmania* in 1911. Since then this ship had seen a remarkable war service with others of the Cunard fleet of twenty-six steamships. It was thrilling to look over this ship now refitted for passenger service, and recall how she [and] others were ruthlessly stripped of their luxurious furnishings, armed, equipped and munitioned for battle. She was one who carried 28,135 members of the American Expeditionary Forces over seas. Of her service I must quote what Philip Gibbs said of her meeting with the German Auxiliary Cruiser *Cap Trafalgar* off the island of Trinidad on September 14, 1914: "It was a duel between two liners armed as cruisers which lasted an hour and forty minutes, until both ships were on fire and the *Carmania's* rigging, masts, derricks, and ventilators had been raked by shell fire, a shell had passed straight through the cabin under the forebridge. She

had 304 holes from seventy-nine projectiles before the enemy cruiser cap-
sized to starboard and went down bow first with her colors flying."[3]

Now she was calmly catering to peaceful conditions, but bearing
evidence everywhere of that terrific struggle. To the passengers these scars
were pointed out with great pride.

The trip across was a calm one but a rather lonely one, until I met
a young Japanese who was equally lonely. We were both first class passengers and sole representatives on board of our respective peoples. We were
attracting considerable attention and causing much speculation among the
passengers who grew very curious concerning us. Three of these made conversation with me at different times in the first two days concerning the
young man—one a Harvard man, one a Wall Street banker, one a student
of the University of Pennsylvania. All were asking the same peculiar questions: "Whether I knew the Japanese, where he was going, his mission, and
all wondering what he was thinking about." I had not yet made his acquaintance and replied that I knew nothing and added that I was not even a student of telepathy and could not fathom his mind[!]

The young man made my acquaintance one night as we stood
together by the rail. In broken but melodious English he told of his loneliness as a yellow man—which I could appreciate as no Nordic can. I learned
that he was from Tokyo. He had come to Honolulu, thence to California,
and across the continent to New York. He was at one time a student in
Berlin. He was a chemist by profession and was on his way to Bombay to
enter business. On my part I told him of myself and my mission abroad.

From that time we were inseparable companions and our Nordic
fellow passengers soon learned about us both. We thereafter received much
friendly attention. On parting on the other side, the young Japanese
besought me to go with him to the East. I should have enjoyed the trip in
his company, but my plans could not be changed. As we separated he
expressed the fervent hope that we might meet in Paradise. The yellow and
the black may meet some day [soon]. The dark races are tending to know
each other better [and] to draw together in mutual understanding.

We docked at Liverpool on July 23rd. I took the train directly for
Edinburgh. My itinerary covered the days preceding the arrival on August
19th at Cherbourg of the group of delegates. These days I had planned to
spend in Scotland and in excursions out from London before the
Cambridge meeting.

I reached Edinburgh and made my headquarters for my week in
Scotland at the North British Hotel. The next day I sought out the Darling

Hotel near Calton Hill where we had stopped twenty years before. I found Miss Darling still carrying on her Temperance hostelry, but grown feeble with the years. She gently chided me for not coming there at once, but I had not known whether she was still living. One day was spent in wandering over the grounds we covered in our previous visit and resting a bit. If I had not been alone it would have been a most delightful stay, where in that northern latitude the days were so long that I could read my newspaper at ten p.m. without artificial light.

A trip to the Trossachs seemed the best way to spend one day. This valley region in the Highlands is full of romantic scenery between Lochs Katrine and Achray made celebrated by Scott's "The Lady of the Lake" [1810]. The word means "rugged scenery." We went by the Caledonian railway over the Forth Bridge. As we crossed it a gentleman, Mr. Dunbar of Edinburgh pointed out to me a wrecked ship in the Firth. To my surprise I learned it was the *Campania,* the ship on which we crossed the ocean in 1901. He told me it was used in the war as a British auxiliary ship and that it sank in a storm in the Firth of Forth off the island of Inchcolon.

Autobusses awaited us at the end of the rail journey of about an hour and we drove through an interesting country to a fine hotel by the side of a lake and took dinner. It reminded one of Switzerland. Then we took [the] busses again to a boat landing together with a number of tourists from different places who were to make the trip. After about an hour and passing the island where Scott is said to have received his inspiration for "The Lady of the Lake," we reached a landing. Here we were met by several red and green tally-ho coaches with four horses and drivers wearing scanty coats and tan high-topped hats and carrying long whips. We mounted to our seats by little green ladders and were off through a beautiful country of mountains and waterfalls to Loch Lomond where we rested and took lunch, before taking the little steamer to cross the lakes to take the train back to Edinburgh.

It is impossible to describe the wild rugged beauty of this journey. I leave it to the guidebooks. It was intensely picturesque.

The last day of July found me back in London where I had made arrangements to stop at the Hotel Cecil. My old hostelry—St. Ermin's—had been converted during the war into Government offices as had so many other buildings in the West End. The Headquarters of the Ecumenical Conference were not yet opened for assignments for accommodations, though it was generally understood that the colored delegates would be provided for at the Westminster Training College, thus avoiding any repetition of the incident at St. Ermin's in 1901.[4] I may as well say here that a few accepted this arrangement, but a number sought hostelries. I located myself at the Hotel Cecil. During the ensuing weeks only myself and one other were guests. There was no hesitancy in accepting, [and] no protests. We received the same treatment as any other guests at this aristocratic hotel.

I went out to Cambridge University to meet the Classical Association at the Anglo-American General Meeting.[5] I stopped at the University Arms.[6] The meeting was designed to discuss the place of the classics in our system of education and to ascertain as far as possible the sentiment that was causing the universities to discard these subjects. A very interesting program was presented. Prof. Charles Forster Smith of Wisconsin University brought the greetings from the American Philological Association. Academic dress was the rule for Cambridge University members and it made a very brilliant scene.

There were papers on a wide variety of classical subjects, lectures, concerts by Choral Scholars of King's College, military band program in the Fellows' Garden, a visit to Ely Cathedral, personally conducted visits to the Colleges and the exhibition of the famous Lewis Collection of Gems at Corpus Christi College, and receptions. The first was [hosted by] the Vice-Chancellor, Dr. P. Giles, at Emmanuel College where evening and academic dress were the rule; another given by Sir William and Lady Ridgeway, and the final one in King's College by the Provost and Fellows. A special performance of the Oresteia film was arranged as a closing feature at the Cinema Theatre.[7]

The debate on the best method of strengthening the position of the classics in English and American education was opened by Prof. John Harrower, LL.D. of Aberdeen University.[8] This to me was the most interesting and important part of the fine program, second only to Dr. Leaf's strong paper on "Classics and Realities," who maintained well that the qualities required for the "higher administrative and directive posts" in business are "fastened in a high degree by a strong classical element in education," and that we need "the large humanism based on the classics."[9]

Of course I fully agreed with this. Our own President Calvin Coolidge had placed himself on record also on the side of retention of the classics in a strong paper which every educator should read.[10]

This meeting was carried on and all pertaining to it with the customary dignity of all English meetings of this character. I only wish we had more of such among educational meetings at least of our own group. But time will aid us, I hope, in attaining it.

While at Cambridge I was delighted by an honor that can come but once in a lifetime. It was a special engraved invitation from Cardinal Mercier of Belgium to the ceremony of the laying of the corner stone of the Louvain Library—destroyed by the Germans in the World War—the rebuilding of which was made possible by American philanthropy.[11] This to me was a crowning point of my trip. It with the volume wherein my own name is inscribed as one of the guests are among my library treasures.

Returning to London I revisited Oxford and went to Stratford on Avon—Shakespeare's home—took in all the sights the tourist sees, but without much pleasure in a loneliness that was growing rather unbearable. On the 18th of August I left for Southampton and crossed to Cherbourg to meet the *Olympic* with other delegates of our group all of whom were to proceed to the Continent on the itinerary arranged. We were met there by a managerial guide from Cook's—Mr. Luigi Dombre, who spoke many languages and was to remain with us throughout the Continental tour, taking entire charge of our party. It was to be my first experience with a party of tourists and here I must say that though every care was taken for our comfort and convenience, [and] there [certainly] were advantages [to the group system], yet I prefer for many reasons the individual service such as taken on my two previous trips.

From Cherbourg we went to Paris, where our accommodations were all that could be wished for at the Hôtel Louvre. Then the regular sight seeing excursions began. Versailles was visited—the gardens and fountains as beautiful as when I saw them ten years before. A new interest to me was the two day auto excursion to the war zone. Starting by train, Château Thierry was our first stop where cars met us for the 126 miles of the worst sectors of the World War. It was the American Cemetery that naturally attracted us most. There our own black boys rested among the others, sleeping on French soil. We walked through this cemetery with its many graves, noting names on the slabs. One of our party found the grave of one whose parents did not known of his death. We saw too the spot where the youthful Quentin Roosevelt lies.[12] We stood where "Big Bertha" was planted—the great German gun that threw shells into Paris. We saw Belleau Woods, and ate dinner at the Hôtel Soissons, the headquarters of General Von Kluck. Several hours were spent along the 600 mile Hindenburg Line. Then we went into the real trenches where the soldiers lived sheltered from shells. We had to enter these backward down steps to the dirt floor, on which rocks and poles, anything [at all] was used to make a bed.

"No Man's Land" was a desolate area, only dead trees and ground riddled with shells, [with] not a trace of a habitation. It was horrible to look at. It did not seem possible that it ever could again become a habitable area. But time works wonders. We went last to Rheims whose magnificent cathedral was bombed and shelled—a wanton outrage.

Everywhere there was horrible devastation. Yet the people were slowly rebuilding here and there with a courage that is wonderful when we consider the lack of material and of manpower. With so many men killed, the women were forced to do most of this work while they labored pitifully to support their children. It was a most pathetic sight. One thing touched us deeply—everywhere we went men, women, and children hailed our dark-skinned company with loud cheers and waving hands. They knew that our group helped to strike the staggering blow that saved Paris. Yes, we had much to do with the World War. Not only our American boys, but there were the thousands of black troops—Sengalese, Somali, Algerian, and Moors with others—all fighting for liberty. Indeed 3,000 had served in the Franco-Prussian War. Surely the nations owe us something other than efforts to retard our progress, a progress that means much to the world at large. As the Field Agent of Hampton says in an article on our part: "No group has already been affected by the war more than they have. Their development is fraught with possibly more significance than that of the Negroes of any other country. Their economic and social attainments set the standards for the Negroes of the world."

From Rheims we returned to Paris for a night's rest. Then we took the long two days' journey to Rome, made as comfortable as possible by sleeping cars and diners. This journey has been covered in the most part in a previous description of the trip as has the Eternal City itself. I found little variation from our former sight seeing program, either here or as we proceeded on the circular tour which took us first to Florence. Here I had opportunity to see the church in which Americus Vespucci is buried, the one where Dante was baptized and where all children must be baptized. We saw the famous bridge with its shops. One other church held an item of special interest to us as American—the Santa Crucis where stands the statue from which Bartoldi made our Statue of Liberty that we see as we enter New York Harbor and which the French presented to America.

From Venice to Milan, with the usual sights, we took the train for Geneva through the Simplon Tunnel. We visited the Peace Council Hall where a session was soon to be held, saw John Calvin's Church, his pulpit and his chair, circled Lake Geneva; and saw the Castle of Chillon made famous by Byron.

We took the train for Paris, spent the day, and went on to Brussels in Belgium, where Germany committed so many atrocities. The fine immense State Hall with its massive columns, built by King Leopold, recalled his merciless oppression in his African Colonies which we hope will never be repeated. We visited the American Embassy, and rode to Malines and Louvain to see the awful destruction made by the Germans. The burning of the Louvain Library was an irreparable loss to the world, destroying as it did its priceless contents. It was now to be rebuilt by American generosity, and Dr. Butler of Columbia University laid the corner stone at the ceremony to which I had been invited. Sunday was a gala day. The people seemed almost to have forgotten the horror of the war time, as they danced and sang, and drank.

A ride to Waterloo, Napoleon's place of defeat, followed, with an ascent of the mound surmounted by the British Lion where the party was photographed. Then we were ready to go to Ostend and take passage to Dover, England, and from there to London by rail, ready for the Ecumenical Conference.

The assembly opened on September 6th.[13] Though a new building for Wesleyan Methodism had been erected directly opposite Westminster Abbey since our meeting there in 1901, the opening session was held in the City Roads Chapel. The Wesley Chapel, a hallowed spot, was where we had met twenty years before. The sermon by Dr. Rose of Canada was preached from the appropriate text: "The old things are done away. Behold I make all things new."[14] Other general sessions were held in the new Central Hall. There were some 500 delegates from all over the world including a Japanese bishop.[15] The discussions were able and participated in by the delegates of color. Some of our own bishops gave addresses and presided at some sessions. Our laity was represented by addresses from Drs. Jackson and Hawkins on interracial brotherhood.[16]

The topics covered every conceivable phase of human interest. Brotherhood was the central thought. Peace relations, missions, and temperance received special attention. Ministers occupied pulpits in many churches on Sunday, and lay delegates had appointments to speak in many quarters. I was scheduled for two such and found appreciative audiences.

The entire conference was a success in showing the strength, the growth, the spirit, the tendencies of Methodism the world over. It could result in nothing but good, a better understanding, and a determination to work unitedly for world peace. The greetings sent [by] President Harding especially emphasized this desire, referring to his inaugural address when he declared, "America is eager to initiate a program to lessen the probability of war and to promote brotherhood of mankind."

The war has had a tendency to humble all the peoples taking part. It is hoped it will bring an altruism to the fore. One fear, however, is that because of the need of American influence and financial help the prejudiced American traveling abroad may delay it for this very reason. We saw no discrimination in accommodations, though here and there a thinly veiled feeling was often perceptible, even in the conference which closed its sessions on the 16th of September.

I met but few at those whose acquaintance I had made twenty years before. Dr. Burkilt then of Manchester told me of deaths and removals of the Sherwoods and family to Australia.[17] Hearing these facts I did not care to visit Manchester. I met again, however, Sir Robert Perks, Bart., who greeted me gladly, and inquired especially of my wife, recalling the meeting of both of us at the reception at Kensington Gardens in 1901.[18] He spoke with pleasure of his visit to America, when he visited Bishop Derrick at his Long Island home. It was a pleasure to meet him again, though grown older, yet the same affable, interested, unprejudiced gentleman.

There were social functions, too, the greatest being that Garden Party given as before by Lady Perks at their magnificent residence in Kensington Gardens. The first was given to delegates at Miner Hall, Westminster by the Presidents of the three Methodist conferences in England. The Freemasons were invited by Epworth Lodge to a fine dinner at Hotel Cecil, and a complimentary dinner at the same place was given to all overseas delegates. There was a difference in speeches made and of a visible attitude at times that indicated that the war would have been won even without American help.

I was, as before, interviewed by reporters in regard to many things. I had kept in touch with the Pan-African Congress to which I had also been appointed a delegate, and the London correspondent of the *Chicago Daily News,* Mr. Edward Price Bell, sent to that paper the following interview:[19]

"Force, in my view, never can advance the cause of the coloured [*sic*] people," said Dr. William Sanders Scarborough, formerly President of Wilberforce University, to myself. Dr. Scarborough has come to England on several errands. He has just returned from Cambridge where he attended the meeting of the International Classical Association, and heard impressive advocacy of the classics as educational media. He will attend the Pan-Africa Congress in London, Brussels, and Paris towards the end of August, and the Ecumenical Conference in London from September fifth to seventeenth.

"We, like other peoples, have our radicals," continued Dr. Scarborough. "We have those who believe in force as a method of progress. I am not among these. Interracial, like international questions, I think, must be settled, if ever really settled, not by violence, but by reason. My advice to the coloured people would be to rise gradually but invincibly. I would tell them to make such intellectual and moral progress, and such progress in manners, that other peoples cannot help liking them. For my own part, I never expect any man, white or black, to like me unless I can make myself likable. I long as feelingly as does anyone for justice and happiness for my race. But I can see no hope in endeavoring by physical means to advance more rapidly than cultural development warrants. What we gain we wish to hold, and we can hold nothing unless we are mentally and morally strong. It is easy to destroy, but hard to construct and perpetuate. Look at Russia.

In the principle of Africa for the Africans I believe, but between most principles and the practicability of their summary application, there is apt to be a great difference. I am convinced that any progress towards realization of the ideal of Africa for the Africans can be achieved only slowly and by the use of the weapons of the mind and soul. For us there is much virtue in good argument, and in the silent but mighty force of justice; there is none, in my judgment, in any political agitation predicated upon a threat of war. Believing this, I naturally hope the ultra wing of our Pan-African organization will not get the upper hand in our councils.

There are bright patches in the dark sky of interracial contact. Educators, for instance, are drawing together. My black skin has not kept me from warm friendships with white colleagues in scholarship. Even southern scholars take me warmly by the hand and tell me how glad they are to have me with them. During my experience in England and Scotland, I have not been insulted, not so much as slighted, by either Britons or Americans. It was the same on the boat coming over. If certain Americans treated me somewhat aloofly, they were within their right, just as I assume I am within my right in choosing my company.

Of course, as the number of my people in any community or situation increases, so friction between them and the whites increases. This is a fact which both races must recognize, and upon which they must bring their good sense to bear in the interests of peace. I am all for peace. I see only disaster in strife. I would not have the Negro movement called revolutionary, for revolutionary agitations smack of war. My vision is that of my own race because of intrinsic merit becoming ever more powerful and charming until the races now more fortunate and stronger than we, themselves will elect to meet us in comradeship, and give us justice."

After the Conference I made good my promise to see Colonel Charles Young's family in Paris. I returned there for a few days before sailing for home. Mrs. Young had come from Liberia to France with her children and to wait the coming of the Colonel who was expected daily, then all would return to America. My arrival was at first heralded to her as his by the mistaken messenger. Mrs. Young and her daughter helped me to do some shopping for Mrs. Scarborough and we spent a pleasant day at Versailles.

But the Colonel did not come to Paris as he was ordered to Lagos on special Government business. She returned alone to America. A short time later the news of his death at his post came to shock her as it did all of his friends. It was an untimely end for this brilliant soldier who, despite all obstacles thrown in his way against merited promotion, served his country in loyal silence to the end. His remains were brought a year later to this country and buried at Arlington by the United States Government with great honor and ceremony. It was a tragedy.[20]

I returned to London and made preparation for my return voyage on the *Adriatic* which I took at Southampton on the 21st along with other delegates.[21] I was pleased to have Bishop C. S. Smith express his desire to share my stateroom in preference to the one assigned him. Our voyage was without any special event. We were glad to reach New York and speed home by rail.

Europe is changed. It is impossible to go through that experience of the terrible war without change. The recovery must be slow and will tax all the endurance that can be summoned. The nations are not yet settled into acquiescence of the results of the Peace Treaty. The question is whether because of human nature this will be possible no matter what may be ceded by anyone. There has ever been war, and this one has left so many warped minds and tortured bodies that it will take a long time to reach a normal attitude by the nations that suffered. I wonder sometimes with others whether it is not true that Nordic civilization has reached its peak and in all this aftermath of oppressed nations, the despised ones are not going to rise to place and power. The years with their generations will alone give the answer. One thing is certain, all present movements tend to make the darker races understand each other better and see the strength in union. We may stand in the far future, if we progress as in the past since freedom. A thousand years are but as a day in the Almighty's scheme of creation.

A New Field of Labor

The last of October, 1921 I returned from abroad on board the *Adriatic* with other members of the delegation. Bishop C. S. Smith had [asked] to share my stateroom rather than the one assigned him with another party—a circumstance of significance later on.[1] The home voyage was devoid of any special interest. I rested on the return trip which restored my natural resiliency and helped me recover from the unpleasant occurrences that had wounded me so deeply.

As usual the first thing to cope with was a call to work. A telegram from the *New York World* awaited me, drawing attention to the International Arms Conference called by President Harding at Washington for November 11th, and asking for a contribution to a "symposium of disarmament sentiment." I was asked to send a brief statement "for the special disarmament number to help crystallize public opinion of the necessity that the conference achieve definite results if peace is to be made less insecure and the financial burden of military preparedness is to be lightened." I responded, closing my statement to the American public with these words: "If disarmament, at least to a large degree, is not secured, then the conference will not have accomplished its mission. If the broad spirit of world brotherhood and mutual helpfulness permeates the discussions, if the resolution to achieve definite results in keeping with this spirit is adhered to, and if the great end is never lost sight of, then, and only then, will success be attained. For this every true American is begged to pray."

My services in the campaign of President Harding had been such that friends and foes alike expected immediate recognition by a government appointment. It was true, however, as a Washington correspondent of the press said, that my absence from the country had operated for delay in looking after my interests. The United States Senators from Ohio stood by me faithfully, one writing, "I have said I would extend no aid to any Ohio applicant until you are placed." And again, "You must have a place in keeping with your ability and worth."

I knew that such movements were unavoidably slow. I saw, too, that many things stood in the way. However, I soon received a call to report to the Veterans' Bureau. I wrote home: "There is further delay and some impertinent inquiries, and C——— has already asked me, if I am here to take his job, which probably accounts for the impertinent inquiries.[2] At any rate the position has not materialized."

Again I wrote:

> I know it takes a long time for the President to iron out many things with so many seeking office. The President has shown both impatience and indignation at the obstacles seemingly thrown in my path. I know, too, that he is handicapped in what he intended to do. I was summoned by phone yesterday to the White House. I was told that a position awaited me and I was to report at once to the Department of Agriculture. I find I am to be an assistant in the Bureau of Economics to specialize in a literary way in obtaining for a future bulletin information concerning Negro farmers and farming in Southampton County, Virginia, the richest farming county in that state.

There had been much feeling among Negro farm boards that the farming interests of the Negro race were not being sufficiently looked after. This was a new position opened up and I understood from the President himself that I was to be allowed to develop it into a strong working bureau as an aid in this direction.[3]

Though it was not what I had looked for, I recognized all the exigencies of the situation and I saw opportunities where I could serve the race as need came along as well as in the Capitol City itself. It, too, would divert me by affording a new outlook and keep me well occupied.

But immediately I became an object of denunciation by some race papers and some race individuals. There were those who insisted that I should have demanded the highest position available such as Register of the Treasury or Minister to Hayti. But I knew more than they did of the entire matter. Though these had been the perquisites of the race at times, present circumstances, not all of which were known to the public, did not make these now available. Then there were those who were eager for positions, and determined that they should be first served, who did all in their power to influence me to "throw it up." One political understanding friend of color, however, wrote me, "You remember the old fable of Aesop, 'Don't be fooled into dropping what you have.' The whole raft of your critics stands with open mouths ready to grab it the moment you let go." I held to it as a matter of my own personal business.

I never regretted the decision, and entered on the work whole-heartedly. My work was outlined for me. My white colleagues in the department were very helpful. One went into the field with me, spending some time in showing me about and making suggestions, concerning what is to me a new kind of work. My headquarters were at Hampton Institute while in the field.

I wrote home to my wife:

> I find it very interesting. I am getting a new acquaintance with my people—seeing their life from a different angle. One thing that really astonishes me is the prosperity of these Negro farmers in this county. There are many splendid farms and good homes. Many of these farmers are far ahead of white ones. All this is hopeful, and shows that it is desirable that they hold to the land in the South where the masses are as yet best fitted to work. They treat me splendidly and I already see how I can do more for them than simply gather statistics. I can place their achievements before the world and extend help in another way to those gaining farms and those doing business in varied ways.

I set to work at once. I wrote articles for the press. Many of these farmers were either ignorant of the possibilities of the Federal Bank Loan aid, or did not know of the mode of procedure to obtain it, or as was claimed, prejudice stood in the way, though the banks asserted to me that no discrimination was made on account of color. However, the fact remained that the Negro farmer was not getting proper attention to his wants. Many needed money to save their holdings and to develop them.

Aside from obtaining statistics to figure in my bulletin I at once went to work to remedy this situation. I discovered one local obstacle that made it difficult for these men to get recognition. The local Farm Loan Association excluded the Negro membership. I set about to overcome this. A list was obtained of some two hundred deserving Negro farmers and was transmitted to the local white associations. Duplicates of the same were sent to the Federal Land Bank of Baltimore. I went to Baltimore myself, talked with the bank secretary, and urged immediate attention to these needs.

As a result of my efforts I received the following letter:[4]

The Federal Land Bank of Baltimore
Southampton County, Virginia
Mr. W. S. Scarborough,
U.S. Department of Agriculture,
Washington, D.C.

Dear Sir:

I was glad this morning to receive your communication and, furthermore, am pleased to state that since your visit to the office we
have loaned a considerable sum of money to the colored farmers
of Southampton County, Va.

I hope that everything is going well with you. We are doing
everything we can to assist the farmers in that county, but it appears
that both the white and colored farmers are so seriously in need
of money that it is difficult to get sufficient [funds] to keep up
with the demands.

I want to assure you again that we will do everything we can
to assist in the matter.

Yours very truly,
C. R. Titlow, Secretary

In the few months devoted to this work I was informed by this
secretary of loans "aggregating some $200,000, one alone being secured
for $9,000, only $1,000 less than the limit."

I wrote home jubilantly: "I really feel that I have done a greater work
than I could have done as foreign minister by helping them to gain means
to send, as so many of them were doing, sons and daughters to schools for
higher education, that I ever have maintained must in the final analysis be
the deciding factor in placing the race in high scale of comparisons with
other races. The acquisition of wealth in moneys or land alone cannot do
it, but it can aid materially to this consummation."

When the bulletin was published and I was at liberty to use the
material as I wished, I wrote several articles for Negro papers, using statistics gathered in the field. One of these closes as follows:

The Negro farmer needs an advocate at court and since he has no representative of his own group this advocate must be the friendly white man—
the white man who is willing and able to help him in his struggles. He must
depend upon him for a helping hand and for sympathetic co-operation until
the time shall come when the color line is less sharply drawn and race prejudice less acute.

Figures show that the part that colored farmers are playing in rural districts and in our agricultural life is by no means small. It is quite possible
then that here on southern soil and on southern farms the outlook for future
success is more optimistic than elsewhere. The Negro farmer is the back-

bone of the South. It is upon his success and his prosperity that the prosperity of that section largely depends. The South will yet awake to the fact that in the ill treatment of the colored farmer it is making the mistake of its life. Conditions are bound to change. The acquisition of land and the accumulation of money will be powerful levers in bringing about these changes.

The Negro should be brought into the closest touch with the Department of Agriculture. A bureau should be established to the end that the best trained minds of the race in scientific and agricultural lines may operate for their own group as others of another race cannot do. This bureau should constitute the point of contact between the Government and the field as it pertains to the Negro farmer. We already have trained specialists and experts who could meet these conditions and who could furnish the Government with valuable information making for the good of the Department of Agriculture and the country. There is much now that cannot be known because it cannot be gotten at except through scientifically trained Negro investigators. The Negro farmer is now too [full of] potential to be longer ignored and neglected.

From my experiences in Southampton County I wrote home the following letter: "My opportunity to mingle with the white people of Southampton County was a unique one. I had always contended that one great obstacle to the understanding and recognition of the race was because there was so little friendly contact between the two races that the whites as a rule knew practically nothing of the classes of Negro society."

This was evidenced when after a few months an oyster dinner was given by the Bank of Southampton in Courtland to all its patrons—white and black. [But because it was] in Virginia, the races were served in separate halls. [Nevertheless] it was an unusual occasion that merited praise.

I received three separate invitations to this from [the] president, vice president, and cashier to come and speak. I did so and gave a fifteen minute speech along with these officials. The local papers said I made "a most helpful speech along the line of opportunity in agricultural development." My own people were especially pleased. One repeated to me a remark he overheard from an official which held a doubtful compliment. Speaking of me, the party said, "He is no Negro, he is a white man with a dark skin."

I must say that despite my race, everywhere I went in that section I was accorded respect. It supports my contention that when we gather wealth and intellect and culture we can command respectful treatment from the better classes at least.

It was not intended that I was to spend my entire time in Southampton nor at Hampton. The latter place I found much changed in its atmosphere—very different from that of the days of General Armstrong and Dr. Frissell. There seemed to be a catering to Southern prejudices unknown in former days, and the relations between the races in the school were strained as never in earlier times.

I gathered my literary material and returned to Washington.[5] There an office was prepared for me in the Agriculture Department and I set about putting the field statistics into the shape necessary for the bulletin. There I had as helpers the employees trained to such work.

I was now hopeful of pushing on to success the plan of development of the work into a special bureau, which would carry out President Harding's idea when he appointed me to the position.

I had worked out in connection with some others of the race interested in such development a full and comprehensive plan for such a bureau. The President was pleased with it, but it must meet the approval of the Chief of the Department. When submitted to him he complimented me on its form and provisions, but as time passed I found no inclination to take it up for acceptance. This attitude was courteously but firmly adhered to. One of the Ohio Senators had told me that the difficulty would be to obtain funds from Congress for it, though he said he felt sure it might be done if President Harding desired it. Still it could not then be brought up until the next session as it was too late for its present consideration.

There was nothing more to be done though I knew President Harding was deeply interested in the agricultural situation as a help to the race. This had been evinced in another way when he wrote me hastily at one time asking me to name two Negro experts [on] agriculture whom he could appoint to positions in Hayti. I had named two in Tuskegee who were doing admirable work in this line. It [was fated] that the President should have no opportunity to carry this into execution as well as never to know more about my own developing plan before he entered upon that fatal western trip. I had not but just now learned that politics as well as kingship "doth hedge" a man about, and I grew more and more loath to trouble one already harassed on many sides.[6]

I have thought that lack of acceptance by the Department of my plan was largely due to the fear that it would result in more racial problems in the Department by an influx of colored employees. The Southern sentiment was still showing itself in efforts of segregation of colored employees in various departments. To this I was bitterly opposed, but

Washington is a strictly Southern city to all intents and purposes. The South is still strongly entrenched there. I recognized the futility of our group demanding the impossible. What made it more difficult for me to accomplish much in overcoming this was the fact that I must admit that I as an individual was not being subject to such discrimination. I was not withdrawn from contact with others at any time in my office situation, and any complaint of mine was met by the unanswerable question: "You are not finding yourself discriminated against are you?"

Aside from the individual appeals to stem this tide, I was being continually besought to obtain positions for people—in fact, blamed almost because of my own. I did create places for others. No wonder I appreciated President Harding's situation. However, I was able to help some cases that came to my notice through philanthropic friends.

There was another plan now under consideration for a commission to study the race situation and problems. It had been brought before Congress under different sponsors in one form or another for some time which I may as well mention here in this connection. I refer to a bill to create a Negro Industrial Commission to study the race situation and problems which came up for hearing shortly after I left Washington before this Commission on the Judiciary House of Representatives in the session of the 68th Congress in the form of two bills: the Celler Bill by Hon. E. Celler of New York for nine members, consisting of three groups—three men in each—two white, one colored—three white men from South, three white men from North, and three colored men, and the Foster Bill by Hon. I. Foster of Ohio, calling for five members with three at least to be of the Negro race.[7]

Such a Commission had been strongly favored by President Harding in his address to Congress in April of 1921. In fact, he had written me confidentially shortly after his nomination in 1920 concerning the Spencer Bill, then before Congress, along similar lines. A commission for this purpose was commended by President Coolidge in his message to Congress in December of 1923.

In fact, similar legislation was proposed to the Senate by Representative Cummins of Iowa in January 1922.[8] Its work would be along the lines I proposed to the Agriculture Department. The Washington correspondent to the *Columbus Dispatch* says of this Foster Bill: "It was generally agreed that if the resolution had passed Dr. Scarborough would have been made chairman of the commission. President Harding recognized Dr. Scarborough as a potential figure in colored circles."

I favored the Foster Bill and at the hearing in April and May 1924 I sent my approval. This letter which follows was incorporated in the proceedings when many prominent men of the race advocated either one or the other.

Wilberforce, Ohio, April 9, 1924

My dear Mr. Foster:
I greatly regret that a previous important engagement prevents my coming to Washington in time for the hearing on your most excellent industrial bill. I regard it as being both timely and opportune. I am anxious that it should pass.

It covers fully the demands of the situation and will meet a long felt want. It will greatly help to bring about a more amicable relation between the races and also a better feeling than now exists between them.

It will largely remove the causes of restlessness on the part of the Negro so apparent everywhere in that it will aid in readjusting present undesirable industrial conditions by getting at the crux of things and at the same time it will have much to do in regulating Negro migrations from the South northward, or from country to city.

This bill if passed will be the beginning of a new state of things and it will help all along the line in its benefits. If it is administered as well as it is framed, it will mean justice for all alike—a square deal for every man industrially and otherwise—let us have it; it is a good one.

Faithfully yours,
W. S. Scarborough

One woman of our race appeared to argue against it. She claimed as "National Legislative Chairman of the Federation of Colored Women's Clubs" to represent "161,000 women organized in forty states," and also presented a Baptist Ministers' Conference report from Maryland, protesting against it, claiming it as "representing 4,000,000 colored people."[9] Her contention seemed to be centered in the argument that such a commission was needless as it would handicap Mr. Davis of the Department of Labor, and as she claimed these "masses" she represented "did not want it."[10]

A careful study of that hearing shows the weight of argument to be [in favor of] a commission. We needed a commission and it seemed to me a presumption for anyone to assume to speak for so many people as this one did with no further evidence than her statement as to their opposition. I could never see just why neither bill was reported out from the Committee. But one thing always handicaps one's movements for race betterment—there is not full enough agreement among us as a people as to what we want.

Still, experience has shown me that massed opposition or advocacy, actual or suspected, representing votes, is a strong factor in disposing of any measure, political, national, local, or church. And women can now vote as men to prevent others from obtaining positions. As one party in discussing it bluntly put it the reason for appointment opposition [was] that there were "not enough positions to go around." So we often play "dog in the manger." I still hold with others that both a commission and the bureau contemplated are necessary if the welfare of our group is to be properly studied and looked after.

Other than my work I did not withdraw from society in the capital but became more or less of a recluse not caring to enter in the "Club" activities which I was solicited to share. I spent my vacant hours in the Congressional Library and at odd moments doing book reviews and articles to help on the Negro publications—the *Messenger* and *Opportunity.* I found my activities circumscribed by a government position which made me miss my former freedom. This prevented my presence with great regrets at Tuskegee on the occasion of the unveiling of the memorial to Dr. Washington to which Dr. Moton had urged me to come as "his loyal friend." I did find myself able to attend Tuskegee's Thirty-first Annual Conference in January and gave an address on "Self-Respect and Self-Reliance," maintaining that the Negro's future depends largely on further development of these two traits.

I attended the Lincoln Memorial dedication as a member of the Ohio Association. I was present at the dedication of the Douglass Memorial Home in the August following the appointment to Washington.[11] I attended church regularly and called on a few friends, occasionally I ran over to Baltimore and New York on weekends to speak as asked. One such address in New York [was] on "Some Aftermaths of the World War" in the colored Y.M.C.A. Auditorium.[12]

However, I was forced to decline Judge Allen Parker's invitation to the Fourth Conference to discuss the League of Nations.[13] It is certain, as a Christian nation possessing the spirit of altruism, we cannot live too far away from our neighbors and still be our "Brother's Keeper," but I am opposed to entering the League, making ourselves in any way responsible for European conditions, or becoming a party to their broils. I think we can act in justice to ourselves and in justice to humanity in an advisory capacity, if none other.

Early in the March of 1923 I gladly accepted the urgent invitation to be the principal speaker as an old friend at the Colonel Charles Young Memorial services held in New York under the auspices of the Colonel Charles Young Post of the American Legion and the 135th Street Branch of the Y.M.C.A. Here I gave tribute to the soldier I had known so well in a speech [titled] "Colonel Young as I Knew Him."

I was in Washington when the remains of Colonel Young were brought from Lagos, Africa, where he died in government service. He was buried in the National Cemetery at Arlington.[14] It was a most impressive military event, in which white officers took part to render tribute with every military honor to a fellow officer.

Though I was unable because of my position to take the active part in politics as I had heretofore, I kept close track of all such movements as others also did for me. My political friends missed my co-operation. One from Ohio wrote, "We need you. I have written the President's Secretary to get you a leave of absence." But that was not feasible. I did attend meetings in Washington, however, and at one such met with an unpleasant incident in connection with the meeting of the Republican State Voters' Association on Ohio night.

This meeting was held in the Willard Hotel.[15] When I presented myself I was told I must take the elevator used by the servants—the freight elevator. I did not take it. I reported the incident to the Republican Headquarters and received a reply from Secretary Chaffee who wrote that a change of location was being made, so "there can be no repetition of the unfortunate occurrence." Hon. N. Longworth also wrote assuring me of a "welcome, hoping you will find it agreeable and convenient to call."[16] The Register of the Treasury denounced the "treatment accorded as an outrage."

Another incident was of an opposite character when a chance meeting brought me again in contact with the whole-souled Mr. John E. Milholland—whose guest I had once been in London, and by whom now I was invited to call and "chat of many things." I did so, meeting a delightful reception and afterwards receiving a letter, showing his pleasure, in which he says: "It revives the pleasant memories of years ago when we met and had luncheon together in Old Kensington," adding, "I am glad that Father Time has dealt so lightly with you and wish you many more years of continued usefulness."

Despite all pleasant courtesies, I longed for home. I missed my own fireside, my books, and my wife. I hoarded my vacation days and on July 1923 came home for a month of rest. I was unusually reluctant to leave its cool shade and comforts for the heat and lonesome life in Washington. I returned to my post at the close of the month impressed by a sense of some impending trouble and fully resolved that, should I remain much longer, I would establish a home there.

Retirement from Public Life—
Fiftieth Anniversary of
Oberlin's Class of 1875

O n the second of August 1923 the entire nation was stunned as the wires brought the news of the sudden death of President Harding in San Francisco. To me, as to thousands of others, this came with a shock of personal loss. I expressed it in an immediate telegram to my home paper in these words: "The death of President Harding is painfully shocking. He was a good and great man. History will reveal all of his virtues and good qualities and he will be found in the front rank of the world's greatest statesmen and one of the best of American presidents."

In a letter home I wrote: "Words cannot express my grief. I have lost a staunch and valued friend, kind, sympathetic, patient, and tolerant in the midst of all the cares and prejudices. I can never forget one day I called at the White House, where I am proud to say I was always made welcome. I was ushered to the cabinet room where a meeting had just been held and a few members were lingering. When I entered President Harding greeted me with his usual hearty manner and somewhat to my embarrassment threw his arm over my shoulder, and turning to the members said, 'I want to introduce Dr. Scarborough to you. Here is a 100 percent American.'"

Again I wrote: "I have seen the funeral cortege as it reached Washington at the close of that long sad journey across the continent, I have made my condolence call at the White House, I have paid every possible respect to the friend I have known so long, I have looked for the last time upon the face of the man I have loved and mourn now like many others. Washington holds no further interest for me. In reality I have no more desire for public life." I could do but one thing more and that was to be among the first to become a member of the Harding Memorial Association.[1]

My course was now decided upon. It was true. Washington seemed a lonely place ever after. I paid my respects to President Coolidge with whom I had had some correspondence when the latter was Governor of

Massachusetts, but whom I had not before met. I felt that the man was a capable and safe leader, fixed in his purpose to do the best for the nation and all its peoples, and fit to wear the mantle dropped from tired shoulders. I pledged him my whole-hearted support in the task before him. Then I turned to my work to see that the material I had gathered was taking form for publication.

Then I sent in my resignation from government service to take effect at close of year. It was a surprise to friends and to President Coolidge's Secretary who wrote: "I am both surprised and shocked to learn of your decision. I am sure the President intends to provide a place for you."[2] But, I was through with public life. In a letter home, I wrote: "It is a fact that I have held but two government positions in my life—one as postmaster at Wilberforce at the beginning of my career and this one at the end. That I really never ran for any office is perhaps the reason I have never obtained any other public position. Greener said, 'I walked when I should have raced,' but that was not my way, office or no office and I am satisfied as it is."

Before I left Washington I wrote of an incident wherein the new first lady of the land figured graciously. It was a part of the Oberlin College plan to plant trees in many places: "I am sending what the camera caught of the first planting of an Oberlin Tree. The ceremony took place in the Lincoln Memorial grounds, and you will see Mrs. Coolidge braving the rain to place the first shovel full of soil about its roots with President King at her side.[3] A few Oberlin men were present, including myself, but the camera refused to show anything but the top of my hat behind her."

I returned home early in December having vacation days to my credit and began to readjust to a quiet home life. I was recalled to New York in the following February to deliver a lecture on "Race Problems Home and Abroad" to the Y.M.C.A. I gave the opinion that the darker races would ultimately get together, unite in the future for the best things for all. I was then watching Mahatma Gandhi's movements in India. The press said it was a "thrilling address."

[My] political services were again in demand as the National Convention met in Chicago in May and I went to it with renewed enthusiasm. The campaign was directed and expected that the colored committee in Chicago should counsel with me and plan work for me. On learning that no such movement was made, President Coolidge's Secretary wrote me: "I am shocked that you have not been given the work intended. We shall see to it at once." It was a deserved rebuke of the parties whose handiwork I recognized as leading to the situation. In the end I took part and aided in President Coolidge's election.

In the meantime I was kept busy preparing articles for the press. I had sometime before been honored by election to the Japan Society and was never omitted when receptions were held to high officials of that country.[4] In accepting this honor the press had been pleased to say:"This organization founded some years ago, contains a membership of 1,200 eminent American and Japanese citizens. One of its objects is to foster and promote a closer and more friendly relation between America and Japan. It is not political, but social, in its object and intent. In accepting this able race man, nothing but good can be extended in all directions, because he is fully capable of representing America in any country."

I was much interested in that country and my sympathies were all with it when the questions involving Japanese exclusion and naturalization of Japanese residents were agitating the country and especially the Pacific Coast.

The editor of the *Forum* now wrote me for a paper on my views for a symposium. I gave them gladly, placing myself upon record for unqualified admission and naturalization as the only fair thing to do. Because of delay in mails my article did not reach the editor in time for publication which gave rise to the following letter:

The Forum
247 Park Avenue
New York
September 29, 1924

Dear Dr. Scarborough:
Unfortunately, your letter to me on the naturalization of the Japanese now in this country reached me too late to be incorporated into our symposium. By the twelfth of August, when your letter was written, the symposium had been edited and had gone to press. We regret that your views could not be quoted in these pages, as we had looked forward to an expression from you and had asked our assistant editor to reserve space for you. Perhaps you can send us something at another time for our Rostrum. Or, if you have time to write us again, on the subject of Negro Migrations in this country. This debate is to be an important feature of the November *Forum,* and we will ask the assistant editor to send you a letter concerning the debate.

As you will see in the October *Forum,* the majority feel as you do, that the Japanese do present desirable material for citizenship. Your quotation of Theodore Roosevelt is most apt. Surely, few things are more important to the world than the heartiest goodwill and complete understanding between the Empire of Japan and the Republic of the United States.

I am very glad that you are enjoying the magazine.

Sincerely,
Henry Goddard Leach[5]

After the election in November 1924, the New York Alumni and friends conceived the idea of giving me a rousing reception in honor of my visit to that city in December. The Negro press writer reported it thus:

Dr. W. S. Scarborough, the noted scholar, and educator, author of a Greek text-book that is widely used in colleges throughout the country, and the former President of Wilberforce University, was honored at a public reception, tendered by the colored citizens of New York at the Public Library, 103 West 135th St. on Tuesday evening. A large audience of representative citizens were present, and joined in the tribute that was paid to the distinguished educator.

Dr. Scarborough was praised as a scholar, as a distinguished citizen, and one of the most prominent educators of the country.[6] Prominent educators like Dr. Nicholas Murray Butler of Columbia University and Dr. Henry Churchill King of Oberlin College, together with Prof. Franz Boas, Prof. Ella Woodyard of Teachers' College, and Prof. Kelly Miller of Howard University sent letters praising Dr. Scarborough for his service in the field of scholarship.[7]

The reception was arranged by Cleveland G. Allen of the *Harlem Home News* staff. In his introductory address he told of the place that Dr. Scarborough has won in America as a scholar. Miss Ernestine Rose made an address on behalf of the library, and said that she was glad to open the doors of the library to such a scholar as Dr. Scarborough. Walter J. Stevens spoke on behalf of the citizens and said that the colored citizens of New York were proud to honor him in a public way. George A. Fleming spoke on behalf of the Association of Trade and Commerce, and said that the association was glad to number Dr. Scarborough among its members. Dr. Gustavus Henderson, a prominent physician of New York, told of the inspiration he received from Dr. Scarborough when he visited Howard University while he was a student there. Lieut. Herbert Julian, a young aviator, said that men like Dr. Scarborough had brought honor to the Negro. J. Egert Allen spoke on behalf of the

Johnson C. Smith University, and said that the young college men of the country reverenced the name of Dr. Scarborough. Rev. John R. White told of meeting Dr. Scarborough at Wilberforce University. Richard B. Harrison, the noted dramatic reader, gave several selections from Dunbar.[8] Musical numbers were given by Nelson B. Scott and Miss A. C. Weston, a pianist.

Dr. Nicholas Murray Butler, President of Columbia University, and one of the most distinguished educators of the country, in his letter said:

> I am highly complimented by the invitation conveyed in yours of the first and wish that I could be present in person to welcome Dr. Scarborough at the reception to be tendered him by our colored fellow-citizens on the evening of Tuesday, December 9. Unfortunately I am definitely obliged to be elsewhere at that time and must lose the pleasure of greeting Dr. Scarborough in person and of bearing public testimony to the force of his personality, the soundness of his scholarship, and the excellence of his influence in our land. He is most deserving of the compliment to be paid him on the evening of December 9th. With cordial regard and renewed expression of regret at my enforced absence.

President King of Oberlin College wrote: "Oberlin College has regarded itself as honored in the fine academic record of Dr. Scarborough as student and scholar, as teacher and executive."

In my response to the many greetings I said that I was glad to meet the citizens of New York. In the course of the address I said that "the Negro needs a historian to be able to place the Negro where he belongs. I would like to recommend that a fund be created for the purpose of sending to Africa ten of our best trained young men, after being educated in the best schools of America and Europe. Our history lies in digging up African lore and finding the missing link." I told of my researches into the ancient languages, and of my desire to contribute to the scholarship of the world.

At the reception Professor Kelly Miller of Howard University said: "Dr. Scarborough represents the first expression of Negro scholarship on the highest level of culture and attainment. He has stood for a generation as the best exponent of Negro learning before the white races of both Europe and America. We cannot too highly honor and extol him for his great service to the race in the field of intellectual endeavor."

In December, I was invited to address the graduates of the Shaw Junior High School [in Washington, D.C.]. I recalled the fact that I was one of the orators listed on Flag Day to "laud Old Glory" in the public schools of Washington and assigned to Bruce School at the exercises the preceding June.

It was a pleasing thing just now to receive membership in the Hellenic Travellers' Club of London.[9] I was among the first to be included in a series of articles on "Greene Countians," who have achieved distinction. The press said: "Greene County has furnished more than its share of people who have later gained renown." It was not only pleasing, but an honor to be included with such men as Whitelaw Reid, Coates Kinney, the author of "Rain on the Roof," and Dr. McCracken.[10] After all, I feel I am not quite out of the world.

True to my determination to forward all movements for race betterment, I entered my protest with others against the showing of *The Birth of a Nation* in Ohio theaters.[11] To Governor Donahey's effort in the same direction I gave unqualified praise, and wrote him accordingly.[12] I received the following reply: "I want you to know I appreciate the interest and assistance you have always manifested in my administration. I have tried my very best to do what I believed to be right. I might say that I have been having a hard time to keep *The Birth of a Nation* from being shown in Ohio. I believe this picture incites racial prejudice. However, you may rest assured that so long as I am Governor of Ohio it will not be shown."

Governor Donahey represents all that is highest and best in our American life. He is an honor not only to his party and state, but to the country at large. Though a stalwart Republican I always recognized the personal worth of many in other parties and considered myself especially fortunate that I had the respect and friendship of Ohio's Democratic Governors from Governor Hoadly's time down.

Wherever my old students were found, I received admiration, reverence, and honor. In May of this year I was asked to present the diplomas to the class graduating from East High School of Xenia, the faculty of which was composed of eight, seven of whom have graduated under my administration in Wilberforce. It proved to be my last address [given] to my former pupils.

June brought a happy change. This was the event to which I had looked forward with most pleasurable anticipation, the Fiftieth Anniversary of the Oberlin College Class of 1875. I had attended various reunions at different times as my work and leisure had permitted, as that of 1908, when I responded in its program to the toast "Looking Forward."

Dr. C. J. Ryder, one of the secretaries of the American Missionary Association, had managed this affair of 1908. Now the reunion was under the management of Mr. J. R. Rogers, the successful head of the Mergenthaler Linotype Company of Brooklyn who wrote:[13]

May 13, 1925

Dear Classmate:
A rich program is being prepared. I most earnestly hope that every living member of the Class will be present at our last Reunion. The Class of '75 has been a great Class. Let us gather together to honor those of our number who have gone before, and look into each others faces, clasp hands, and say "Hail" and "Farewell."

This reunion ought to be and will be the greatest days in the lives of all of us in remembrance. None of us is any longer young. Some of us are feeble or in poor health, but, if possible, let us gather together once more, give our class yell, sing our class song, listen to a poem by Wood, and words of wisdom from other members of the class, receive honors from the college, and say "farewell" to meet again and hold a full and glad reunion in some fairer clime where we can remember our college days and the trials and triumphs of our earthly lives.

Do not let anything except absolute necessity prevent your being with us. The Reunion will be happy and glorious in proportion to the number of us that gather.

Yours in '75,
J. R. Rogers

President King gave the Baccalaureate sermon on "Patience." Hon. Newton D. Baker was the Commencement orator, speaking on "Education in Action," laying stress on "the duty of the college *trained* man and woman to make a contribution to the public welfare and to the solution of problems of world import."

There was the parade of classes on Illumination Night, and the singing on the chapel steps. [W]e were young again. But it was the Alumni Dinner that was the crowning event. Some twelve hundred guests sat at the long tables in Warner Gymnasium, where the older returning classes with their thirty-six representatives from 1861, 1867, 1870, 1871, 1872, 1873, 1874, 1875 occupied the limelight. President King was toastmaster. Hastings H. Hart made the speech for our class. Then came the announcement that we had won the silver cup offered to the class having the largest percentage of attendance. Fourteen of its living twenty-five members were present. Of course an enthusiastic demonstration followed. We were the first to give our yell:

Chapter XXVII

Bet your life we are alive,

Oberlin, Oberlin, '75.

Who are these, who are these?

We gave Oberlin six trustees.

The six trustees were Dudley P. Allen, William F. Chamberlain, Hastings H. Hart, J. R. Rogers, Charles J. Ryder, and Merritt Starr.

The fourteen present came from opposite ends of the country. From California came John F. Peck, Miss Anna M. Jones, and Mrs. Elizabeth Kimmel; from New York, Hastings H. Hart, and John R. Rogers; from Texas, Mrs. Emma Bishop; from Minnesota, Dr. Florence Nichols Baier; from Maryland, Harlan P. Roberts; from Illinois, Merritt Starr and C. S. Wood; from Iowa, Miss Althea R. Sherman. Ohio had three representatives, Mrs. Mary Ament, Miss Mary Kinney and myself.

Here I insert a clipping from an earlier number of the *Alumni Magazine* giving more specific information concerning some of our members:

> The class included Dr. Dudley P. Allen, in whose memory the Allen Art Museum was built; Miss Calista Andrews, who gave her home on Elm Street to Oberlin College; Dr. Florence N. Baier of Minneapolis, educator and physician; Dwight Bradley, who was advisor to the King of Siam; Prof. William F. Chamberlain of the Theological Seminary; Judge David Flett of Kenosha, Wis.; President Thomas McClelland of Knox College; Prof. John F. Peck of Oberlin Academy; Harlan Roberts, a prominent member of the Minneapolis bar; John R. Rogers, the inventor and a trustee of Oberlin and Berea Colleges and of the American Missionary Association; Dr. Charles J. Ryder, for many years senior secretary of the American Missionary Association; Pres. W. S. Scarborough of Wilberforce University; Merritt Starr of the Chicago bar; Henry Stone who was the Speaker of the House of Representatives in Iowa; George Thompson, a prominent member of the Kansas City bar; C. S. Wood, for many years a journalist in Chicago; Miss Sherman, an authority on ornithology; Hastings H. Hart, the prominent penologist; and Mrs. Ament, missionary to China for many years.

At the last there was given a fine reception in honor of our own John Fisher Peck, "the friend of boys." We sang our college song, "Gradatim," and added two more lines to our college yell:

And once again, yes, by heck,

We gave Oberlin John F. Peck.

So ended the 87th Annual meeting of the Alumni Association of Oberlin College which has ever been a loyal friend and supporter of the Negro race. It was a great occasion and ours a great class with a great history covering a half century's work of which we all may be proud. I feel we cannot be said to have been remiss in our duty to our fellowmen.

After my return from the Oberlin reunion I seemed almost unconsciously to begin to set my house in order, especially after I had been east in November to give my usual annual address before the Y.M.C.A. where I spoke on "Social Near East Problems" and met a reception by my old students that touched me as "unusually enthusiastic." I did not know when I should go again.[14]

During the winter I put in shape my philological papers for publication. This pleased my early philological colleagues, Dr. Sihler, Professor Emeritus of New York University, who warmly commended the effort, saying: "I am very glad to know that you are putting your work into a permanent shape. It is worthy you should do so."[15] Dr. Charles Lanman of Harvard University, who was my sponsor when I entered the Philological association nearly 40 years before, promised to write the introduction "should health permit" then added, "but you need no introduction to our guild."[16]

I busied myself now with this work and with the voluminous dictations of material designed for my autobiography. I also wrote several articles for *Current History,* one published in January, and another published in the December following.[17] These dealt with migration, the lure of city life, the baneful credit system, and civic progress. Both articles gave an optimistic outlook because of accumulation of homes, wealth, successful cooperative marketing, and educational progress.

The result of my studies while in government service, "Tenancy and Ownership among Negro Farmers in Southampton County Virginia," drew this response [from the press]:[18] "The bulletin contains a keen analytical review of farming conditions in the section stated, with particular reference to activities among colored farmers, who constitute 27% or so of the so-called Southern states. The bulletin is very complete and is a review of the subject from every possible economic standpoint. Dr. Scarborough is a scholarly and charming writer and he had made a contribution of decided value to the literature on agriculture."

I also had my *Sunday School Quarterly* work to occupy my hours. On these I worked feverishly to keep a long way ahead of publication as I had done for years. There were still calls for help by many I had served—

protégés I had long aided gladly as I could. Despite all these things that helped to make my readjustment to a less active life a somewhat easier task, it was now that I began to evince the desire for a rest from labor.

I replied to those importuning me to lead in a new movement for race betterment in words from my beloved Greek, so aptly used in a chapter heading of William Evart Gladstone's biography by John Morley:"I am too old, O King, and slow to stir; so bid thou one of the younger men here do these things."[19]

A noticeable sadness began now to replace my usual joviality, though it never deserted me. The months since the Oberlin reunion had brought news of the passing of several of the classmates present on that occasion and with news of each I would say, "Who will go next?" As the winter closed in I turned more and more to quiet chats with near friends, and to the peaceful evenings in my library among my books when my wife would read aloud to me.

A new book by Sir Arthur Quiller Couch, *On the Art of Reading,* was just now a most pleasurable diversion.[20] In the closing paragraph the author told of one who, long in doubt as to what motto he should use to decorate his library chimney piece, had at last "cast away choice" and had written up for the purpose two Greek words, ΨΥΧΗΣ ΙΑΤΡΕΙΟΝ, that is, "the hospital, the healing place of the soul."[21]

I, too, had long desired a motto for my library and had been in equal doubt. Now I exclaimed, "Eureka! Nothing could be more appropriate. We will use it."[22] There was not [much] time, but my library had ever been indeed my soul's healing place and remained so to the last. I had long hoped for a pension from the Carnegie Foundation for the Advancement of Teaching, although Wilberforce University was not in the accepted class of colleges.[23] But there had been quite a number of exceptions made whereby professors outside of that class had been made pensioners. Influential friends had worked long to place my name there and I had been made to feel very hopeful.

The last effort was made at this time and taken up by Dr. Nicholas Murray Butler himself. But Secretary F. was forced to reply to my renewed application that the Foundation had reached a point where its income could not keep pace "with the steady increase of pensioners from 'accepted colleges' and no new outside applications can be accepted this year."[24]

To me, and to all my friends as well, it was a bitter disappointment. As Samuel Mather, [the] prominent philanthropist, who had made a final effort in his behalf wrote me: "You have from your record every right to expect it." But it was not to be, and then and there I abandoned the long cherished hope not only of its recognition, but the assurance of ample provision for my last years.

About this time I received two books just issued from the press, the reading of which produced two diametrically different effects upon me. One was [a volume on] the history of the A.M.E. Church of which Bishop C. S. Smith had been the historiographer until his death in February 1923. He was succeeded by another appointee who had since had charge of the work. Of what I found in the chapter relating to Wilberforce University I have this to say: Justice to all concerned calls upon me to leave a statement in reference to the paragraph at close of [the] chapter [concerning] the presidency of Wilberforce University. It then proceeds at once to speak in eulogistic terms of the great growth of the university in subsequent years. It utterly ignores my own following connection for twelve years and finally overleaping this entire period, it adds one brief sentence saying, "Dr. Gregg is now president."[25] I preface what I have to say by this declaration made out of regard for the honor of the deceased historiographer and the truth concerning my work.[26]

Bishop Smith was not the author of this paragraph as it stands. This is attested by both external and internal evidence, which I give here:

First: Bishop Smith was a man with too high a sense of an historian's obligation to truth; he thought too much of his duty and reputation to commit or allow by omission or commission such deliberate distortion of facts.

Second: Mrs. C. S. Smith and Dr. Joseph Gomez, both of whom were the biographer's assistants in preparing the work for publication have declared he did not write it.[27]

Third: The volume bears on its prefatory page the statement that the manuscript was presented by Bishop Smith to the committee of publication in *June 1922* and *accepted* by it.

Fourth: The paragraph in question includes a reference to the burning of Shorter Hall, which took place in *late December 1922 after the manuscript was accepted*.

Fifth: Bishop Smith died in February 1923 and for some months had been too ill to write after Shorter Hall burned, even had the manuscript been in his hands.

The evidence is complete. What impression was intended to be conveyed by this particular paragraph is plainly evident.

Truth crushed to earth shall rise again

The eternal years of God are hers:

While Error wounded writhes in pain
And dies among its worshippers.[28]

A bishop of the church indignantly wrote me, "This wrong must be righted. The great church of Allen cannot afford to rest under such a stigma." Another wrote with equal indignation, "Neither malice nor enmity can wipe out the splendid work of your administration. The church and the people know." Of this added hurt, I made no effort myself to make rectification, though it wounded me deeply. It has hurt the author of it more than anyone else. A future, able, honest, church historian will rectify it, and the world knows. But it was a cowardly act to endeavor to shield the perpetrator under the shroud of the dead.

The other book came to me from the Japan Society, and its reception helped to soothe the wounded feelings. It was a copy of *A Daughter of the Samurai,* a limited edition of which had been printed and autographed in American and Japanese characters for all of its members by the author, Madam Etsu Inagaki Sugimoto.[29] This Japanese lady of high rank was at the time a professor of Japanese in Columbia University. Her father was a member of the Samurai or high military class with high ideals and unswerving purpose, and progressive withal. Disappointed in the career of his son, he had given this daughter the education such as only boys received in Japan. He called her "Etsu-bo" when she lived up to the Samurai ideals of courage, endurance, and heroism expected of a boy. When she failed she was addressed as "Etsu-ko," the termination "ko" meaning "girl" and that of "bo" meaning "boy." This daughter he adjured ever to remember that "the eyes of a Samurai never know moisture."

The training of this lady and the life she afterwards lived, as an American and a Japanese, with the purpose of the book—to bring about a better understanding between the Japanese and the American peoples— impressed me deeply. At the close of a later talk with [Mrs. Scarborough] concerning possible future events, I said, "Should anything happen to me, do not break down, remember you are "Etsu-bo." And thereafter I continually called her by that name. She soon had cause to remember my solemn charge.

The latter part of June for the first time in six years I attended some of the Commencement exercises at Wilberforce University. In fact after my retirement from the presidency whenever I made my appearance in the auditorium on a Sabbath the students made it an occasion to greet me with such applause as to embarrass me and I felt that officials were equally embarrassed. I therefore had refrained from attending exercises. Now at the earnest solicitation of friends and by special invitation of authorities I was prevailed upon to be present at a Board meeting where I was presented to the members by the presiding officer and forced to say a word in response to the greeting given me. On Commencement Day I was literally compelled to sit upon the stage—*for the last time.*

Looking Backward and Forward

The Oberlin reunion led me to much retrospection. I began to jot down my thoughts at fugitive moments and varying intervals. These are given here as I mused disconnectedly over the past and of the future.

Over seventy years ago I was born under the blight of the strongly entrenched system of iniquitous injustice that still cursed this land in the early fifties of the nineteenth-century. It was a time when there seemed to be no bright outlook for the future of the Negro race. Yet even then there were mutterings and rumblings that threatened an overthrow, and there were constant, agonizing prayers going up to God's throne from the people wrestling for freedom. He heard and answered.

As I look back over the years from my earliest recollections I am astounded at the marvelous changes that have taken place. I see a long and rugged road traversed by my race in the sixty odd years since emancipation. It could not be otherwise. But the momentous fact is that this road has led us up and on in an unparalleled progress.

Statistics are not in my line, and I shall not give them nor will I pretend to write history. I shall simply indulge myself in a cursory review of some of the changes that in my lifetime have taken place, rendering our group today one of the dark skinned races to be reckoned with wherever there is refusal to recognize our rights as men and women.

We have grown in strength in every direction. This is shown in literature, [both] prose and poetry, in education and journalism, in music, sculpture, and painting, on the stage and the pulpit, in medicine and dentistry, in law and business, in scientific and literacy research, in politics, government, and diplomacy, even in the army. In brief we have representatives in almost every field of human endeavor where individuals stand forth as having won recognition and honor—all these where a little over a half a century ago we had comparatively none.

We have acquired land and homes. We are showing ability to manage well industrial enterprises. We only need daring and money to meet competition successfully. With growing wealth, education and culture, we are rising too in a social scale of our own.

Race members are also eagerly entering into sociological study of our problems, or history, and our relations to the world at large. Admittance has been gained to take part in world movements to a rapidly increasing extent. The recognition that our group must have representation in social, civic, national, and even international affairs is most encouraging. The contact that comes from inter-racial gatherings is going to be one of the greatest factors in racial understanding, in breaking down prejudice, and in bringing tolerance and recognition of worth. As I have repeatedly said, to know the race one must do more than casually visit here and there. [One] must see more even than a close examination of our schools and churches, instructed, supported, or aided by white philanthropy will disclose. The toadies, servile ones, the politicians, the dependent ones—all must be passed by *and the people found* and known.

We have gained in civic recognition with representatives in councils of many cities, in congressional halls of state and nation, even serving foreign countries as well. In educational fields we have won greatly. Schools, universities, and colleges once closed to us are now open to us with few exceptions throughout the North and are being very liberally patronized considering our means. But still we bear the burden of Atlas in a mass of illiterates that must be reduced by constant effort on our part. Our schools are being manned by many of our race, and we are learning how to manage them more successfully by recognizing the necessity of broader views, broader courses, by demanding greater efficiency in our teaching forces.

We have made many mistakes in traveling this upward road, but we have learned as others by our errors. We have our criminals, but no more, even less of the latter than other groups. The guilty we would not shield. We only ask they be afforded their rights to be judged according to law. We have organized our group for legal protection and investigation of all such, and are more and more able to defend our rights as citizens and obtain justice for the innocent among our defenseless brethren who are so often unjustly and maliciously accused, persecuted, and mobbed. We welcome the growing sentiment that condemns such inhuman practices.

We have innumerable faults common to both white and black. These are to be recognized and overcome. We are too apt to slander without cause and attribute ignoble motives to high actions, and as a group we are prone to seek to pull each other down in personal endeavors to reach the top. This is manifested in jealousy, neglect, indifference, and unwillingness to honor those who succeed or damning with too faint praise the successful ones. Not all can reach the top, and we are sure to fail if we try to do so by wasting time, talent, and energy in pulling each other down. A certain Frenchman once said, "Mediocrity alone is jealous."[1] It is well to remember this and admit the truth in the saying which will help to correct this fault.

We do have virtues. It may not be becoming for me to relate them. There are, however, traits of patience, persistence, endurance, and faith in God, born of the dark years of servitude—traits that helped in those days. We will do well not to lose these in the coming years, still to be crucial ones.

In short we are simply human beings, no better, no worse than other groups. We ask only to be rated and treated as such and allowed to go on and work out our salvation. We have gone a long and enviable distance in these past years, and we have hopes for the future though we still meet many discouraging vicissitudes.

These hopes for our future must lie in education, in our schools, our homes, our churches—and this means in our youth. These must be trained aright through these agencies.

Our churches have not kept pace with our schools and homes. There has grown to be too much of church politics, too much greed on the part of some high in its offices—a greed for office, power, and money which has dragged in the mire the robes of some in ecclesiastical positions. This has reacted upon the schools under their care. More have been created than can be adequately supported. My hope is that some day my own particular denomination will merge its efforts and center upon one great university and theological seminary worthy of the Church of Allen.

As to the general education of our youth, I have for some time seen a danger in turning away from the cultural studies. I am not alone in deploring this. Many wise educators also see the necessity of the study of the classics for breadth of thought and higher life. I have always maintained, and must still do so to the end, that these must in the final analysis be the source of that knowledge, discipline, and culture that will lead us to a high place in the world's civilization. This material age is one of danger in this respect.

Youth seeks the new. It is impatient. It is likely to rush forward too rapidly. It does not yet fully understand the past of the race in which it had no part, nor does it fully sense that real freedom lies in following truth, and that heights are reached only by long unswerving endeavor. This I have ever essayed to imprint upon it and I may be pardoned if I re-emphasize it here by repeating a passage from one of my annual addresses to the student body as President of Wilberforce University. The *Boston Transcript* was pleased to select it for reprint as "The Road to Fame:"[2]

> We wish you to obtain here the best so that you may be able to live best, do best when you leave for the world struggles. We want you to make truth-seeking your object. How are you to do this? I reply that it is not to be done by play and easy work. Youth comes but once; early manhood passes quickly. The present is your working day—the day to fill full the reservoirs so that when life draws as heavily upon your resources they shall be almost exhaustless. So waste not the hour—your hour—the present. Simply whiling away time in social pleasures and in sports never made a scientist, a philologist, a mathematician, a linguist, a philosopher. The road to acquisition and to fame is a rugged and steep one of pure labor.

Concerning the press, I can truly say with Dr. Gladden that if one has the mind to use his pen in the service of the public, it is a great thing to have a medium of communication whose clearness and integrity are unquestionable, and I have always esteemed it an honor to have been permitted to work with men whose journalistic aims were never below the highest. And like him I always found it good to get from these the verdict of "O.K." upon my work from such men as Dr. Ward, [W. H.] Page, W. B. Shaw, Joseph Cook, Dr. Axon, Bishop Tanner, as well as from the many newspaper men of both races.

I never underrated the power of the Negro Press. In a series of articles in various race papers I have rated the race newspaper as a civilizer and an educator on all questions.[3] I have called for good papers and better support of them by our people. The press, white and colored, has quite uniformly used me well. I have escaped much of bitter invective that has been showered on other men prominent in public life of the race. I recall here the words of Frederick Douglass who knew what opposition was. He wrote me as early as 1884 in reply to my appreciation of his article in the *North American Review*.[4] As it fits my own experience so will I quote from it: "It is gratifying to find that while the colored newspapers in some instances can find nothing in me to approve, and much to condemn, that I have the confidence and approval of gentlemen and scholars like yourself. Although a true man can afford to stand alone with the truth and the right, it is pleasant and agreeable to the strongest to have the sympathy and support of his thoughtful contemporaries."

It was and still is an encouragement to know that I was not the only one to receive rebuffs. These I am glad to say have been few. I feel that on the whole I have been generously supported by newspapers and magazines, and only here and there has a reporter tried to malign and undermine me. Douglass once wrote me, "How have you escaped?" I do not know. I only know I have tried to aid the efforts made by ambitious editors and reporters to keep our cause before the world, realizing that the press, newspaper, or magazine is always a powerful agency to uphold our rights and advance individual efforts along all lines.

As I grew older I grew more conservative in my views, more tolerant, less aggressive. My opinions even often changed—mellowed by time, experience, and knowledge. Because of this some claimed I was inconsistent. My reply was: "Years bring wisdom as life opens up wider views. A wise man can consistently change or modify his opinions. It is only a fool who can never do so."

If I could be said to have had a hobby it was "Youth." I loved youth and it loved me. My heart never grew old and I could enter into its pleasures with hearty zest, either as host or guest. I have had a rare pleasure in instructing young people. It has been a delight to aid their fresh open minds to discover the beauties of the Greek and Latin tongues and literature, and I gave all possible of myself to the task. Their companionship has been an inspiration to me, and I learned from them as they learned from me. Yes, I can truly say I lived with my students, as they clustered about me in classroom, in dormitory, and in my home. I recall for them here the many pleasant hours when they were gathered under our roof or on our lawn for an evening or afternoon of jollity, and I can see in memory the long line passing at ten o'clock down the stairway and through the long hall, a happy throng, grasping our hands with an appreciative word as they said goodbye—each made happier by bearing away from the large basket at the door an apple, an orange, a huge popcorn ball as they left us, an uplifted company to live on higher planes and eagerly look forward to another gathering. How well I knew their higher education was being added to by this contact with ourselves, our books, pictures, and games.

Often in these later years they have recalled to me these incidents of the classroom, showing equal pleasures in these memories—incidents I had forgotten, when I had requested a student translating too glibly to get off his "pony" and walk for a while. In fact some of these incidents related of me seemed rather apocryphal. One thing never failed to amuse my Greek class nor seemed to fade from recollection—the endeavor to pronounce the Greek word that can be called our equivalent for "hash."[5] It is found in the [play,] *Ekklesiazousae* of that incomparable comedian and satirist, Aristophanes, and is found spelled thus in some editions "Lopadotemachoselachogaleokranioleipsandrimypotrimmatosiphiopara-bomelitokatakechumenokichlepikossuphophattoperisteralektryonopteke-phalliokigklopeleiolagoosiraiobaphetraganopterugon." I confess here that I fully believe with my classmate, John Peck, that a youth should be "allowed to stumble a little."

Yes, I can truthfully say that I lived with my students and that I am proud of the product. To call by name those who have risen to eminence would seem to make invidious comparisons. I have mentioned some else-where. The list is long—college presidents, bishops, teachers, journalists, missionaries, clergymen, scattered throughout this country, in Africa, and the West Indies. I have found them everywhere almost invariably engaged in useful, constructive work for the race. This is my tribute to them.

Concerning my friends and their helpfulness throughout the years I have this to say. I have had many friends—white and black, members of different political and religious faiths, rich and poor, young and old. I have been immensely rich in this respect. The advice and cheer of all these have been invaluable. Yes, I believe I could count my real enemies on the fingers of one hand, but I also really believe that I [would] need many times the hundred hands of the giant Briareos to count my friends.[6] To those who from the beginning of my career constituted themselves as my "Old Guard"—all now passed on—I pay tribute of profound respect and thanks for all their devotion in my behalf.

Perhaps no one individual exercised so continuously through these years a more salutary influence on my career than did Prof. Richard T. Greener. I feel he was one of the chief agents in holding me to my work in education. He wrote: "You may think you are doing little, but it is some-thing worth while to have proved Calhoun's statement false, and by your philological success alone you have lifted us all out of the ditch where he proposed we should always lie." Again he encouraged me when he wrote: "You have demanded without ceasing nothing less than opportunity for the highest intellectual development of the race and you have inspired our young men and women to reach out for it not only by your enthusiastic classroom work to which all testify wherever met, but by your own philo-logical studies and literary achievements that have given you place, pres-tige, and influence that the race may well bless you for."

Still again in a letter of much later date he wrote me: "Scarborough, as I see you now at the head of a university I congratulate you on the path you have followed. You have not only held a solid course and fought valiantly with pen and voice for our civil rights, but you have upheld the educational side in a royal manner."[7]

It was Professor Greener, too, who wrote me in the last letter received from him after he had been our Commencement lecturer before the Literary Societies—the last time we two ever met and when I had shown discouragement at the continuous fight I had had to make and which had worn greatly upon my sensitive spirit: "Don't forget, my dear Scarborough, our old Greek classic story of 'Aristides and the Peasant.'[8] Get it out from 'Plutarch's *Lives*' and reread it." It [related an incident of ostracism]. "[W]henever the people of Athens became uneasy at finding one of themselves risen to extraordinary honors and distinction, they voted banishment by inscribing the name on the oyster shell [or on broken pottery called ostraka]. So when Aristides, long loved and respected for his surname—the 'Just,' and afterwards envied as much, was accosted by an illiterate peasant who did not know him and asked [him] to inscribe the name of Aristides on his shell, he asked [the peasant] if Aristides had ever injured him. [The peasant] answered, "No, nor do I even know him, but it vexes me to hear him everywhere called the 'Just.'"

Greener [added]: "Your opponents may see the day which may force them to remember you as Aristides prayed the Athenians might *not* be forced, and, Scarborough, you are just humble enough to pray that same prayer. We shall see."

Of politics I felt that many of my strong friends have been made in the field of politics. I have said enough of my part in this elsewhere. I found it a relaxation, a change, and considered it a duty to take as prominent a part as I could because race interests were so continually in jeopardy and my help seemed needed. It was an example, too, for coming generations.

Concerning my ambition to go to Hayti, Greener advised me strongly in these words: "You can serve the race far better here doing just what you have done. Keep at it. In these political places you always have dogs at your heels. There is no money in them. It is more or less an empty honor and in going abroad anywhere you lose working contact with the race at home."[9]

I was advised by others—all were right. You can have dogs at your heels, however, at home. Still I am now gladfully satisfied that I was not successful in obtaining the only foreign appointment I sought and that I refused to consider the consulship to Santo Domingo suggested by McKinley. As I review the past I see clearly my work lay here. I had surely followed Booker T. Washington's advice in the Atlanta speech that won him fame—"to let down your buckets where you are."[10]

But to have taken part in the political movements of the day has left me with many pleasing memories of many important events and of a throng of stalwart men, white and black, who have played a part in the drama of political life and have passed off the stage forever as we all must do. A new generation is now on the stage of action. May it have the vision, wisdom, and strength of those gone before and work for peace and the Federation of the World.

My literary life and the research work I have been able to do in philological studies has been a pleasure and a constant stimulus to me. I sincerely hope the record of it found in these pages may induce others to enter similar fields. We cannot afford as a race to neglect this. Any recognition of honor I may have received I can only trust may inspire others. If I am to be remembered for anything I may have done, I hope to be known best as an educator and a scholar.

As a layman in the A.M.E. Church I felt that whatever I may have written concerning the weaknesses of my church has been written with the purpose of stimulating it to the endeavor to eradicate these and strengthen itself of the things that make for dead spirituality. I do not criticize the ministry, we have splendid representatives in it, but I do criticize any who enter it for any but the noblest reasons and who use it for selfish ones. Our avenues are not limited as in the early years of freedom. They have widened and these who are not really called to the pulpit should have courage enough to make a path for themselves in other lines. The Christian layman is a strong force today and is destined to wield a strong influence over the destinies of the A.M.E. Church.

I believe, too, that the Church today prefers to be represented by well equipped laymen rather than by poorly equipped clergy. In my years of service I have ministered in every way though not a minister. In fact my years in Payne Seminary as instructor, coupled with my other church activities have served to fix me in the minds of many as a minister. As a layman I have received honors from my father's church which I appreciate. It was an advantage, too, as I could be a free lance.

I could maintain my own self-respect by doing what I felt to be right irrespective of what any ecclesiastical head might demand. That it has been a disadvantage, also is true. It was so often made the reason why I should be scalped as head of a Church University. As few laymen were on the Trustee Board, it really was a miracle that I did hold the position for these years.

As for my fellow laymen, to them must be attributed much of the progress in the Church. It owes much to their foresight and management in the various departments where they have functioned. The women, too, must be awarded praise for the growth in all their efforts, and the organizations they sustain so nobly and which have grown to be a power.

Summing up the church work, though as a race we have progressed greatly, the Church must demand less of selfish unholy ambition in its leaders, less worship of Mammon, and more real Christianity so that pulpit and pew, ministers and laymen, may have and hold a mutual respect for each other, and work harmoniously for the common cause. Our ministry must be an educated, cultured one. Bishop Grant truly spoke when he made the declaration that if the "pew is passing us, we had better get out of the way."[11]

Speaking of organizations we have been charged with too great a tendency to organize—to have too many societies. This will correct itself in time and with growing knowledge of real need. All however have had as a reason for being a desire to be helpful. We shall merge more and more, eliminate here and there until the proper balance is found, and those worthwhile will gather strength in special work. Many such have served their purpose for the time, politically and socially, and have given place to concentrated effort and stronger organization as found today especially in the Women's Federation and the National Association formed [for] the protection of individuals, guarding their life, their rights, and their interests.

Speaking of leadership, there was need of leadership as we emerged from slavery. With the many movements started for our advancement there has ever been a hunt for a Moses. Since the death of Frederick Douglass there has been no one outstanding leader in all things. What I then wrote for the press of the situation is pertinent today and embodies fully my ideas of leaders and leadership:

> The leadership of Douglass was born partly of the times, partly of the man … He was fitted for the task both by nature and by training in a school through which few would be willing to pass today in order to obtain a diploma of merit. . . . He possessed a tempered rationalism mingled with prudent conservatism that was an absolute necessity in counseling and acting for the best interests of all—black and white . . . Who is to continue the work he began? . . . The one who is to occupy the place must be no demagogue, no extremist, no office seeker, not one thirsting for power, possessed of ambition that seeks only self-aggrandizement, not one on the sole track of wealth, not one

whose destructive powers are superior to his constructive—one who would build barriers by fanning the flames of prejudice even of his own race.

On the contrary the leader must first of all possess the elements of true manhood, his integrity must be unquestioned, he must have breadth of views, be open to conviction and have the courage of the conviction he holds. He must be discreet and farseeing with such confidence in movement that he can afford to face criticism, calmly secure in the well grounded belief that the course of events will in due time prove the wisdom of his action. He must be one who knows when to lead and when to follow and with all he must be able to command the recognition of his position on the part of other races of men.

It is not an enviable position when it is looked at in all its phases; and it would be well for these inspiring to Negro leadership to halt and ponder well and seriously before ruthlessly appropriating the mantle and posing in that character. It is a case, where it is not enough to be a born leader, not sufficient simply to achieve leadership which may savor too much of trickery, and where solely to have it thrust upon one causes a fear of the influence of ignorance, that most disastrous power for evil.

Shakespeare's suggestive ideas must be blended if the two races most interested are to find a future of mutual benefit.[12] The Negro leader must not only possess innate qualities of a born leader, but he must also achieve leadership through having accomplished something worthy of himself and race; then he must have leadership thrust upon him as an outgrowth of all this and of his mental and moral fitness. This last must be done by the consensus of opinion lodged in the intelligent, broadminded classes of both the Anglo-Saxon and the Negro. The fortunes of these two races have been joined in this country for too many years of a lamentable past to think that they can be rudely sundered in a near future. They must go on together for an indefinite time and that future for both depends in many ways upon the one who shall essay to take the place of Frederick Douglass.

It is not to be wondered at after reading such utterances and similar ones made in many published articles, that many public men spoke of me as "a safe and sane leader of his people—one of the level headed men of the race." My work extended beyond classroom and college walls to lead the people to think and act intelligently on all things affecting them. Nor did I belong to that class of leaders who are as Peloubet says of Christ, "ahead of their age in their ideas and hopes, but behind the age in that they do not see how to prepare the age and guide it to the realization of their visions," but I did belong to the class that "though beyond their age in visions and hopes, yet are in their age in applying them to it—types of true leadership."

So I worked in my particular field of higher education laboring to make the race rise from within, from culture of mind and heart as well as of hand. Letters from those who have listened and read through [my work over] the years are full of recognition of the worth to the race of ideals thus formed. Like Douglass I desired greatly and worked persistently to bring about a better understanding and feeling between races.

I have often wondered why so few white people comparatively can meet the Negro or stand before a Negro audience without showing in some way by reference or manner a sense of "Nordic superiority"—without making us feel that we are Negroes. Some excuse this attitude as an inheritance. To say the least it is a lack of tact for people who address us to refer constantly to "your people," "your folks," "your race." Yet, there are many royal souls who never offend the most over-sensitive among us. All that I can say is that if Christian brotherhood is to mean anything, our white friends must close their eyes to color and race, clear their minds of a conscious superiority, and see only the worth in man. It will not matter in the life to come whether one is white, yellow, brown, or black, and even in this world who knows what the future real American is to be with all the blending of races that is going on here, and will continue despite blatant demagogues who shriek so hysterically about "race integrity," and "Nordic superiority."

In the strenuous life that I led there had to be moments of relaxation [and] of amusement. I never used tobacco in any form. I did not play cards nor was I ever known to dance even in my youngest days. I was a strong advocate of temperance and at banquets my glass was always turned down. I took pleasure in old fashioned games and my croquet ground on my lawn was the scene of many a friendly contest, and my indoor pastime was [a] game of checkers. These with music and the never-failing companionship of my books together with pleasant moments with friends helped me to gather strength for the outside struggles of life.

Of music I was especially fond. When I became the president of the University I did not rest until I had secured an adequate equipment of instruments for a student band and whenever its strains were heard I endeavored to snatch a moment to listen. At that time I said in one of my circulars concerning the school:

> The buildings of the "Tawawa Springs" period have nearly all disappeared from the old Shorter Hall campus. One of the three cottages left may be said to be of historic value—the one built by George H. Pendleton, of Cincinnati, who later became Senator Pendleton and finally Minister to Germany.[13]

Here he and his family spent summers during the brief period of the existence of the Tawawa Springs resort, but it may not be generally known that Mrs. Pendleton was a daughter of Francis Scott Key, the author of "The Star Spangled Banner."

Today in the rear of that cottage the flag waves daily from the tall flagstaff on O'Neill campus and there is no more thrilling sight in the evenings than that at the close of guard mount drill, when the Stars and Stripes are gently lowered to the strains of Francis Scott Key's patriotic song.

An incident is recalled in this connection. When I had invited for an evening at my home the soldiers sent to the University for rehabilitation where by music, speeches, conversation and refreshments, it was sought to bring some happiness to these shell-shocked, sad-faced, silent men. At the close [of the evening] the notes of Key's hymn broke upon the air, and every man—some sitting on the floor of the crowded rooms—struggled to his feet. As the host of the evening, I sought the library to conceal my emotions.

My home was my haven. I sought it for the minutes of rest that I could enjoy there, the quiet from outside cares and turmoil. I always found there consolation, companionship, and helpfulness, also there I always gathered strength for further struggles. My friends gathered there about me for pleasant hours in happy days and for comforting ones when sorrow came. Blest is the man who has such a home and such a companion as the Giver of Gifts has vouchsafed to me.

[To my last day I lived] with the thought ever with me of work undone. My physician friend who sat hours at my bedside [as my energies failed] assured me of a life even here lived abundantly.[14] My struggle has been a long and hard one. I did not expect smooth sailing, and I cheered myself by the old saying that a head-wind was better than none at all. There is nothing to inspire one when entering a dead calm. I feel that I have fallen far short of accomplishing what I wished—that after all I have done little. I only know [that] I [have] done what I could.

Some may ask if these many pages reminiscent of the struggle upward of one man of color are worthwhile. Perhaps not as relating to the individual alone, but as relating to one of a race aspiring to rise from the darkness of injustice and oppression to a place in the sun with other races, [these pages] may be considered as worthwhile.

- Anything is worthwhile that teaches the lesson that all heads and hearts must ever combine to settle racial questions.

- Anything is worthwhile that impresses the world with the belief that with one blood all nations are created, making God our Father, and all mankind brothers.
- Anything is worthwhile if it but inspires other individuals to do their part in achieving this great end.

I look ahead into years to come, when out of all our efforts there will appear a triumphant day for our future generations. When the melting pot—America—will have melted away racial lines, hates, and prejudices, changing, mellowing, assimilating, obliterating even the memories of a shameful, painful past—a thing this country owes to its honor. We as a people cannot be blotted out, cannot be deported, cannot be segregated forever, cannot be ignored, cannot be wronged. Once a nation's wards only, we now are by law one of this nation's peoples to be considered in the solution of the so-called problems with which the world seethes today. In the words of rugged President Roosevelt, "Laws must be so framed and so administered as to secure justice for all alike, a square deal for every man."[15] Thus, and thus alone, can any nation hope for peace and security.

Someone has said we spin the threads of our lives, but it is God who uses the shuttles of his purpose to carry out his own designs. So I say as this writer says:

Spin cheerfully
Not tearfully,
Though wearily you plod;
Spin carefully,
Spin prayerfully,
But leave the thread with God.[16]

I believe that a Divinity shapes our ends rough hew them as we may, and I can say with Job as did Senator Foraker: "Though he slay me yet will I trust in Him, but I will maintain mine own ways before Him."[17]

The End [Mrs. Scarborough's Record of Professor Scarborough's Last Days]

The combination of disappointing occurrences [over a period of] some months had brought about [an] increasing languor.[1] He grew thin and rheumatic trouble crept upon him. His physician noted his symptoms, but could not reach the source. Those nearest him felt confident the cause was other than physical.

A few days after his attendance at Commencement he attempted to remove a broken limb from a cherry tree. The exertion caused a fainting spell. From this he seemed to recover easily, but was warned against further strenuous exercise. He grew more silent, and when a few days later a severe wind felled a gigantic oak on the lawn, he watched it measuring its length upon the ground and turned to smile faintly as he said, "That is myself." It seemed a prophecy.

A few days later restless for work, he stole out with a saw, insisting on repairing the grape arbor which had suffered in the storm. Though he was begged to desist, he persisted in the task till it was nearly completed. Then looking it over, he remarked, "I'll finish it tomorrow." He never finished it.

The next day an increasing lameness and an attack of nausea led him to agree that his physician be called to him. On August fifth he was told he must go to bed and rest quietly. It was the beginning of the end. Only once thereafter did he leave his room—then to creep painfully into his library, where for a few moments he gazed around upon his beloved books, and then slowly made his way to the door where he stopped and gazed back for a last look.

Nausea rapidly increased until be became unable to retain either nourishment or medicine. At first his spirit fought rebelliously at the condition and he forced himself daily to rise to his chair. Then as weakness increased he accepted it. He said one day as he waived [*sic*] away the daily paper brought to him, "I have no further interest in the outside world."

Through the remaining days he passively and patiently awaited the end. He welcomed the many friends who came to see him with his old pleasant smile until he said pathetically, "I cannot see them, I cannot talk." With his life-long thoughtfulness he had one worry—his constantly expressed fear to me, who had cared for him day and night that [I would] wear myself out.

He took comfort in the calls and prayers of his pastor and friends and in his physician's presence who spent hours at his bedside, watching him closely and ministering to his soul though he could do nothing more for him. His strong heart from a temperate life had sustained him amazingly as he lingered, daily growing more serene—the serenity that comes when one is at peace with God, his conscience, and the world—in the consciousness of duty done, and with faith in God's care and justice and the approving verdict of the world—a peace that any might covet.

Early in the afternoon of September ninth he had slowly turned his head to gaze long out of the window murmuring at last, "It is beautiful out there."

There were wavering moments in these hours. In one of these he looked up at me with a puzzled expression, then uttered but one word—his last one, "Etsu-bo." Was the endeavor only recognition or a last gentle reminder or both? Whichever it was, it was kept constantly in my mind to give strength through the days that followed when strength was sadly needed.

The end came at sunset. With his eyes fixed upon me he raised my hand to his lips, drew one last peaceful breath and passed into the Great Beyond, like one who wraps the drapery of his couch about him and lies down to pleasant dreams.

His wish had been to be buried with the most simple service at his home, but he [had agreed that] "I may be overruled so do as you think best." Friends and the university authorities protested, insisting it was due to him, to the public he had served so long, and to the many friends who wished to honor him in death, that other arrangements be made.

Therefore on September twelfth when his casket had been placed in the library of his home that he might lie last among his books, and the family take its last leave of him, it was borne with escort to Galloway Hall to lie in state during the morning before the platform on which he had so often stood. There it was surrounded by the many floral tributes that had come from family, community, and faculty of the university, and alumni associations east, west, and south. At head and foot of the casket stood a university cadet.

At 1:30 p.m. the last services were held—simple and brief as he had desired. Quite all who participated had at some time been his students. Dean Woodson of Payne Seminary came from his Detroit Conference to preach the brief sermon emphasizing the faith that had upheld him to the last.[2] [Woodson] told of his announcement to the Conference on receiving the wire telling of Dr. Scarborough's passing, how it was met by tears and sobs, many present being old students, [and how] the Conference business was [immediately] suspended. He called forward to the altar these students—ministers and visitors—and gave a brief talk on Dr. Scarborough's life and services. In three other following conferences of the church a service was held in commemoration of him and his wide recognition by the world, [which was] a most unusual tribute to give a layman.

Bishop Reverdy Ransom of the A.M.E. Church and Dr. Caldwell came from Nashville, Tennessee, the former to deliver the eulogy, the latter to represent the Sunday School Department of the Church and speak of his service to it.[3] Mr. W. A. Anderson, one of his early pupils and a member of the College Trustee Board, read the biographical sketch and tribute prepared by Dr. W. A. Galloway, his co-worker for years on the State Trustee Board, his physician and [his] friend to the last.[4] Reverend Howe, pastor of the Baptist denomination, represented Xenia in a few words, emphasizing the trait of kindly [and] friendly bearing to high and low alike that had endeared him to so many.[5] Miss Hallie Quinn Brown, life-long neighbor and friend, read two poems that he had liked— "Emancipation," and "The Upper Room." The choir sang his favorite hymns—"In the Cross of Christ & Glory," "Jesus Lover of My Soul," and Miss Ferguson sang "There Is No Death." Telegrams and resolutions of tribute and sympathy were presented from faculties, student bodies, and many organizations at home and abroad.[6] Dignified in death as well as in life, he was then borne to his last resting place in the peaceful rural cemetery there to await the resurrection morn.

Dead, my lords and gentlemen:
Stilled the tongue and stayed the pen;
Cheek unflushed and eye unlit—
Done with life and glad of it.
Ye who fain had barred his path,

Chapter XXIX

Dread ye now this look he hath?
Dead, my lords and gentlemen—
Dare ye not smile back again?
Low he lies, yet high and great
Looms he, lying thus in state.
How exalted o'er ye when
Dead, my lords and gentlemen![7]

NOTES

INTRODUCTION

1. Michele Valerie Ronnick, "Francis Williams: An Eighteenth-Century Tertium Quid," *Negro History Bulletin* 61 (1998): 19–29. For details of Wheatley's experience see Henry Louis Gates, Jr., *The Trials of Phyllis Wheatley* (New York: Civitas Basic Books, 2003) 5–16.

2. In part, quoted from a previous essay by the editor. See paragraphs 2–4 and 19–20 in Michele Valerie Ronnick, "Racial Ideology and the Classics in the African-American University Experience," *Classical Bulletin* 76 (2000): 169–70, and Ronnick, "'A Pick Instead of Greek and Latin': The Afro-American Quest for Useful Knowledge, 1880–1920," *Negro Educational Review* 47 (1996): 60–61. For further information on the argument over the study of the classics, consult chapters 2 and 4 of Meyer Reinhold, *Classica Americana: The Greek and Roman Heritage in the United States* (Detroit: Wayne State University Press, 1984).

3. Reinhold, *Classica Americana,* 35–36, 63, 72. See also Carl Richard, *The Founders and the Classics* (Cambridge, MA: Harvard University Press, 1994).

4. See Ronnick, "'A Pick Instead of Greek and Latin,'" 60–72.

5. Samuel J. Barrows, "What the Southern Negro Is Doing for Himself," *Atlantic Monthly* 67 (June 1891): 810. These paragraphs are quoted from my article "12 Black Classicists," *Arion* 11 (2004): 86–88. See also my article "Early African American Scholars in the Classics: A Photographic Essay," *Journal of Blacks in Higher Education* 43 (2004): 101–5 containing the same images, but with a different essay.

6. Ronnick, "Racial Ideology and the Classics," 169–80. See also Eric Anderson and Alfred Moss, Jr., *Dangerous Donations: Northern Philanthropy and Southern Black Education, 1902–1930* (Columbia: University of Missouri Press, 1999), on the effect that the money from Northern philanthropists that funded the industrial programs has had.

7. Judith De Luce, "Classics in Historically Black Colleges and Universities," *American Classical League* 21 (1999): 10–12.

8. See Michele Valerie Ronnick, "After Martin Bernal and Mary Lefkowitz: Research Opportunities in Classica Africana," *Negro History Bulletin* 60 (1997): 5–10. See also Robert Fikes, "It Was Never Greek to Them: Black Affinity for Ancient Greek and Roman Culture," *Negro Educational Review* 53 (January–April 2002): 3–12, and Fikes, "African American Scholars of Greco-Roman Culture," *Journal of Blacks in Higher Education* 35 (2002): 120–24.

9. See Frank Snowden, Jr., *Blacks in Antiquity: Ethiopians in the Greco-Roman Experience* (Cambridge, MA: Harvard University Press, 1970); Snowden, Jr., *Before Color Prejudice* (Cambridge, MA: Harvard University Press, 1983); and Lloyd A.

Thompson, *Romans and Blacks* (Norman: University of Oklahoma Press, 1989). On this debate, see Martin Bernal, *Black Athena*, 2 vols. (New Brunswick, NJ: Rutgers University Press, 1987–1991), Mary R. Lefkowitz, *Not Out of Africa* (New York: Basic Books, 1996), and Mary R. Lefkowitz and Guy MacLean Rogers, eds., *Black Athena Revisited* (Chapel Hill: University of North Carolina Press, 1996). See also Jasper Griffin, "Anxieties of Influence," *New York Review of Books* 43 (1996): 67–73, and R.S. Boyton, "The Bernaliad: A Portrait of Martin Bernal," *Lingua Franca* 7 (November 1996): 42–50.

10. In 1996 at the annual meeting of the APA held that year in New York City, the editor introduced this idea, Classica Africana, to the members of the organization with a panel that she organized, which was sponsored by the APA's Committee for the Classical Tradition. The panel was titled "Classica Africana: The Graeco-Roman Heritage and People of African American Descent." The following papers were given: Denise McKoskey, "'An Inclination for the Latin Tongue': The Classical Education of Phillis Wheatley"; Shelly Haley, "Peculiar Triangle: Nineteenth-Century Black American Women, the Gentleman's Course, and the Civic Ideal"; Joy King, "'An Incurably Perennial Student': Ruth Cave Flowers"; Edmund Cueva, "The *Medea* of Countee Cullen"; and Michele Valerie Ronnick, "William Sanders Scarborough: The First Professional Classicist of Afro-American Descent."

11. See Michele Valerie Ronnick, "William Henry Crogman," *Classical Outlook* 77 (2000): 67–68; Ronnick, "John Wesley Gilbert," *Classical Outlook* 78 (2001): 113–14; Ronnick, "Wiley Lane (1852–1885): The First African American Professor of Greek at Howard University," *Classical Outlook* 79 (2002): 108–09.

12. Black classicism, a.k.a. Classica Africana, is not limited to works of scholarship or literature. Consult, as one example, the Odysseus Collages of Romare Bearden (1914–1988). These collages in a set of twenty were based on Homer's *Odyssey* and Bearden was inspired to do the work after returning to his hometown of Charlotte, North Carolina. The editor discusses the concept of black classicism in similar language in her forthcoming article "Black Classicism," *Encyclopedia Africana,* 2nd ed., Kwame Anthony Appiah and Henry Louis Gates, Jr., eds. (New York: Oxford University Press).

13. See Michele Valerie Ronnick, "William Sanders Scarborough," *Classical Outlook* 74 (1997): 139–40; Ronnick, "William Sanders Scarborough: The First Professional Classicist of African American Descent," *Negro Educational Review* 47 (1996): 162–68.

14. Susie King Taylor, *Reminiscences of My Life in Camp* (Boston: Susie King Taylor, 1902), 5.

15. Alexander Crummell, "The Attitude of the American Mind toward the Negro Intellect (1898)," *The American Negro Academy Occasional Papers, 1–22* (New York: Arno; reprint, 1969), 10–11.

16. See Michele Valerie Ronnick, *The First Three African American Members of the American Philological Association* (Philadelphia: American Philological Association, 2001), 11–15.

17. By this I mean men such as Richard T. Greener at the University of South Carolina, William Henry Crogman at Clark University, John Wesley Gilbert at Paine College, and a group of educators at Howard University that includes Francis

L. Cardozo, Wiley Lane, James Monroe Gregory, and George Morton Lightfoot. None of these men, as distinguished as they were in their time, reached Scarborough's level of professional attainment and public stature, both of which extended far beyond the classroom.

18. Ronnick, *First Three African American Members*, 8–10.

19. See Michele Valerie Ronnick, "William Sanders Scarborough: The First African American Member of the Modern Language Association," *Publications of the Modern Language Association Millennial Edition* 115 (2000): 1787–93. As a result of the discovery the MLA established the William Sanders Scarborough $1,000 prize for a new book on an African American topic.

20. Henry Ossawa Tanner (1859–1937), African American artist, won international acclaim for his religious, genre, and landscape paintings; Paul Laurence Dunbar (1872–1906), African American poet and novelist, is remembered today as a dialect poet and poet of his people; Alexander Sergeevich Pushkin (1799–1837), Russian writer and poet, was the great-great-grandson of the African Ganibal about whom he wrote an unfinished novella, *The Negro of Peter the Great;* and Johann Wolfgang von Goethe (1749–1832), poet, dramatist, and natural philosopher, was a dominant force in European literature.

21. William Sanders Scarborough, "The Negro and Higher Learning," *Forum* 33 (1902): 355.

22. William Sanders Scarborough, "The Negro Graduate—His Mission, 1908," clipping file, item #10, William R. and Norma B. Harvey Library, Hampton University.

23. See Scarborough's obituary in the *Christian Recorder,* September 30, 1926, p. 3.

24. William Sanders Scarborough, "The New College Fetich," *A.M.E. Church Review* 3 (1886): 126–35.

25. Charles Francis Adams, "The College Fetich," *Three Phi Beta Kappa Addresses* (Boston: Houghton Mifflin, 1901), 11, 14, 21–22, 48.

26. Scarborough, "The New College Fetich," 127.

27. William Sanders Scarborough, "The Educated Negro and Menial Pursuits," *Forum* 24 (1898): 439.

28. William Sanders Scarborough, "The Educated Negro and His Mission," *American Negro Academy, Occasional Paper No. 8* (1903): 10.

29. W.E.B. DuBois, "Negro Education," *Crisis* 15 (February 1918): 173–78.

30. Andrew Sledd, "The Negro, Another View," *Atlantic Monthly* 90 (1902): 65–75.

31. See William H. Crogman, *Progress of a Race, or the Remarkable Advancement of the American Negro from the Bondage of Slavery and Poverty to Freedom and Citizenship, Intelligence, Affluence, Honor and Trust,* coauthored with J. W. Gibson (Naperville, IL: J. L. Nichols, 1902); Melba Joyce Boyd, *Discarded Legacy: Politics and Poetics in the Life of Frances E. W. Harper, 1825–1911* (Detroit: Wayne State University Press, 1994); William Pickens, *The Heir of Slaves* (Boston: Pilgrim Press, 1911); and Pickens, *Bursting Bonds* (Boston: Jordan and More, 1923).

32. Cornel West, unrecorded conversation with the editor, December 2001, Harvard University.

33. Library of Congress, lot 11308, "Photographs Depicting African American Owned Businesses and African American Union Members, Primarily in the Southern United States, ca. 1899."

34. Central State University, founded in 1887, developed out of the state-funded Combined Normal and Industrial Department that was established at Wilberforce University in 1877.

35. Lathardus Goggins, *Central State University: The First One Hundred Years, 1887–1987* (Wilberforce, OH: Central State University, 1987), 93–94.

36. On the fire, see *Macon Telegraph and Messenger,* March 27, 1877. There is a small oil painting of the burned building at the Sidney Lanier Cottage in Macon, Georgia, given by Sarah A. Grant, Mrs. Scarborough's great-granddaughter. It measures 81/2 inches by 14 inches and is signed, "F.S.F., Dec. 15, 1876."

37. Helen Hooven Santmyer, *Ohio Town* (Columbus: Ohio State University Press, 1961), 89–90.

38. "Intermarriage Bill Would Break Up Homes," *New York Age,* March 13, 1913.

39. "Closing Exercises of the Colored Schools," *Macon Daily Telegraph,* June 16, 1866.

40. W.E.B. DuBois, *Autobiography of W.E.B. DuBois* (New York: International Publishers, 1968), 100.

41. William Sanders Scarborough, "The College as a Source of Culture," *The Sodalian* 4 (October 1909): 4.

42. Microfilm (hereafter MIC) 179, William S. Scarborough Collection, Ohio Historical Society, Columbus. The front pages contain these details.

43. MIC 179, William S. Scarborough Collection, Ohio Historical Society, Columbus. The front pages contain these details.

44. See "Announcements," *Journal of Negro History* 56 (1971): 65. Robinson (1912–1983) was born in Pensacola, Florida, on November 12, 1912. She earned an M.A. from Columbia University in 1934. She taught for thirty years at Central State University and was named professor emeritus in 1974. After a two-year illness she died in Daytona Beach in November 1983. She was a prolific writer and lecturer on black history. See her obituaries in the *Xenia Daily Gazette,* November 15, 1983, and *Yellow Springs News,* November 16, 1983.

45. In an official preface for this work, Gibson stated in the endnote the following:

> This paper is based on the unpublished life story of William Sanders Scarborough. Mrs. Sarah C. B. Scarborough and Miss Bernice Sanders, a close friend of the family, put together the unpublished autobiography that Scarborough had written before his death. Through the aid of Mr. Truman K. Gibson, Mr. William Savoy of Columbus, Ohio typed the manuscript under the supervision of Miss Sanders who tried in vain to find a publisher in the 1930's. Upon the death of Miss Sanders the manuscript was left in the hands of Mr. Gibson who gave it to this author. After carefully editing and retyping the document for publication, the original copy was deposited in the Hallie Q. Brown Library of Central State University, Wilberforce, Ohio. The page references in this chapter refer to the re-typed document which is now in the possession of the Association for the Study of Negro Life and History where it is being processed for publication.

The life of Dr. William S. Scarborough in its present narration, represents the joint painstaking labors of Mrs. Sarah C. B. Scarborough, widow, and Miss Bernice Sanders, confidant and member of the Scarborough household, also Professor of Economics and Mathematics.

Both of these women have passed, but just before Miss Sanders' death she asked and received cooperation of myself and one of our mutual friends and associates, Mr. William F. Savoy, placing the life of this eminent scholar in permanent form. Mr. Savoy most ably edited, and in many cases, revised the manuscript without changing essential facts. He did a fine job. In addition, he was able to enlist active interest of at least two eminent historians and to bring to fruition the hopes of Miss Bernice Sanders. (Wilhemena Robinson, "William Sanders Scarborough: Scholar and Disillusioned Politician, 1852–1926," Pamphlet Box 358 26, Ohio Historical Society, Columbus.) The item is dated February 2, 1972.

46. In a telephone conversation with the editor on August 18, 2003, Truman K. Gibson, Jr. (1912–), recalled visiting Wilberforce University with his father in 1924 or 1925. He was taken to meet Scarborough in his study at Tretton Place. He described Scarborough as having a "low and measured voice."

CHAPTER I: PARENTAGE

1. In 1860 Macon, located on the Ocmulgee River, included 5,042 white people, 21 freedmen, and 3,069 slaves. Bibb County, of which Macon was the county seat, contained 8,838 whites, 84 freedmen, and 7,030 slaves. See Richard W. Iobst, *Civil War Macon* (Macon: Mercer University Press, 1999), 4.

2. Jeremiah Scarborough (ca. 1822–1883) died on October 28, 1883, at 9:05 p.m. in Macon.

3. Frances Scarborough (ca. 1828–1912) died on April 14 or 15, 1912, at 12:05 a.m. Two photos of her exist, one from her youth and another from her later years. See box 9, Scrapbook, Miscellaneous Photographs, William Sanders Scarborough Papers, Rembert E. Stokes Library, Wilberforce University (hereafter WSS Papers).

4. See David J. Hally, ed., *Ocmulgee Archaeology* (Athens: University of Georgia Press, 1994), for information on these points.

5. Records from Frances Scarborough's church, the Washington Avenue Presbyterian Church, mention a preferred charge by Sister Aldine Hall against Sister Frances Scarborough for using her name with malice: "[T]he clerk was directed . . . to serve Sister Scarborough with a summons and a copy of the charge to meet the Session at its next meeting." Minutes of Session, March 4, 1870, p. 19, Genealogical and Historical Room, Washington Memorial Library, Macon, Georgia (hereafter GHR).

6. The Georgia Central ran from Macon to Savannah. Its president, Richard R. Cuyler, supervised the system from Savannah. The line had a branch to Milledgeville and another to Eatonton. *Sholes' Directory of the City of Macon* (Macon: J. W. Burke, 1878), lists Jeremiah as a switchman. His name appears as "Jerry Scarborough" in the *Mulberry Methodist Church Minute Book, 1838–1878,* among a list of those who had "passed." The church was located in Macon at 719 Mulberry Street.

7. Daniel Alexander Payne (1811–1893) was one of the founders of Wilberforce University and a leader in the A.M.E. Church. See his *Recollections of Seventy Years* (Nashville:A.M.E.Sunday School Union,1888).Its contents were organized by Mrs. Scarborough.

8.This is the Steward Chapel, founded in 1865.After a fire in 1869, the cornerstone for the new building was laid on April 5,1869.Dr.Henry McNealTurner and the Reverend Woodlind were speakers on that occasion. Since then both Mary McLeod Bethune and Martin Luther King have given speeches there.

9. *The Church Register of theWashingtonAvenue Presbyterian Church of Macon, Georgia, Bibb County Georgia* lists Scarborough in the Register of Communicants, p. 59 and in the Baptism Register,July 1, 1868, p. 77, GHR.

10. John Mercer Langston (1829–1897), Booker T. Washington (1856–1915), and Richard R.Wright (1855–1947),men Scarborough knew, were also born into slavery.

11.She is buried in Massie's Creek Cemetery nearWilberforce with her son and his wife. See the 1912 *State of Ohio Death Index* file #21427, which lists her mother, Louisa Scarborough, and her father, Henry Gwynn (both of Savannah). She died at age eighty-four from "carcinoma of the right breast."The attending physician was "S. Maria Steward" and the informant was "W. S. Scarborough."

CHAPTER II: BOYHOOD DAYS

1.The DeGraffenreids (also spelled DeGraffenried) were an old and distinguished family with roots in North Carolina. William Kirkland DeGraffenreid (1821–1873) was a lawyer and served as local counsel to the Southwestern and Central Railroads in Georgia for many years. He married Mary H.Marsh on May 19,1847. His firstborn daughter, Mary Clare (1849–1921), was known for her work on behalf of women and children.The writer Ellen Glasgow (1873–1945) was a descendant of this family branch. For more information, see Thomas DeGraffenried, *History of the DeGraffenried Family 1191 A.D. to 1925* (NewYork,1925).See a notice about his death, *Macon Telegraph and Messenger,* August 2, 1873.

2.John C.Thomas was a native of North Carolina but had lived in Georgia for a number of years. He was a merchant, and he married MariaV.Julien on August 29, 1867.They were Presbyterians. See "Death of Mr.Thomas," *Macon Telegraph and Messenger,* January 8, 1884, p. 5;.and *Bibb County Marriage Book D (1865–1869),* 190, GHR.

3. On the influence of this book by Noah Webster (1758–1843), see E. Jennifer Monaghan, *A Common Heritage: Noah Webster's Blue-back Speller* (Hamden, CT, 1983).

4. Truman K. Gibson, Sr. (1882–1972), who earned a B.A. from Atlanta University in 1905 and a B.A. from Harvard in 1908, passed this manuscript on to Wilhemena S.Robinson in 1970. Gibson believed that he was related to Mr. Gibson.

5. See *General Index to Real Estate Conveyances,* which lists a deed (HH 132) dated February 13, 1866, transferred to F. & J. Scarborough on January 2, 1883, and then to W. S. Scarborough, pp. 29, 55, GHR.

6. In 1860 there were five military units in Macon. The Floyd Rifles was organized in 1841 and was the third oldest unit in Macon. It had regular parades several times a year.

7. James Harrison Wilson (1837–1925) was one of the most skillful cavalry commanders in the Civil War. George Stoneman (1822–1894) had a distinguished career as a cavalry officer.

8. For a picture of Macon's turmoil, see Iobst, *Civil War Macon,* 384–90.

9. For information on Howell Cobb (1815–1868), see John E. Simpson, *Howell Cobb: Politics of Ambition* (Chicago: Adams Press, 1973).

10. A resolution adopted on October 21, 1838, established the Washington Avenue Presbyterian Church. It was one of the churches that resulted from the separating of slaves from their owners.

11. J. W. Burke was a printer in Macon. His shop, J. W. Burke & Company, Printers and Binders, was located on Second Street. He produced many official publications including the city directory.

12. The *Macon Telegraph* was founded by Myron Bartlett in 1823. It merged with the *Macon Messenger* in 1869.

13. Davis was captured on May 10 near Irwinville, Georgia. He was brought to Macon on the thirteenth.

14. Henry McNeal Turner (1834–1915), author, civil rights activist, and Republican, became the twelfth bishop of the A.M.E. Church in 1880. Upon his appointment by Lincoln in 1863 to the First Regiment, U.S. Colored Troops, he became the first black chaplain in the U.S. Army. See Stephen W. Angell, *Bishop Henry McNeal Turner and African-American Religion in the South* (Knoxville: University of Tennessee Press, 1992). John G. Mitchell (1826–1900) was later an educator in Ohio. He became dean of Payne Theological Seminary in Wilberforce, Ohio, in 1893.

15. The A.M.E. conference was held in March 1868. John Mercer Langston was an African American abolitionist, reconstruction leader, and later a representative from Virginia in the 1890s. A branch of the Freedmen's Savings and Trust Company opened in Macon in 1868, but there are no records for it in the National Archives Microfilm publication 817, *Indexes to Deposit Ledgers Branches of the Freedmen's Saving and Trust Company, 1865–1874.*

16. Three books published in this period bear the same title: D. W. Bartlett, *The Life and Public Services of Hon. Abraham Lincoln* (New York: Derby and Jackson, 1860); Henry J. Raymond, *The Life and Public Services of Abraham Lincoln* (New York: Derby and Miller, 1865); and Richard J. Hinton, *The Life and Public Services of Hon. Abraham Lincoln* (Boston: Thayer and Eldridge, 1860). It is not clear which volume Scarborough purchased.

CHAPTER III: MACON AND ATLANTA SCHOOL DAYS

1. Laws preventing the education of slaves carried severe penalties for owner and servant alike. About the situation in Macon then, see Titus Brown, "Origins of African American Education in Macon, Georgia, 1865–1866," *Journal of Southwest Georgia History* 11 (1996): 43–59.

2. Emeline S. Kidd, a Macon resident, taught at Lincoln School No. 1. See Titus Brown, "African-American Education in Central Georgia: Ballard Normal School, 1865–1949" (Ph.D. diss., Florida State University, 1995), 18, 21. Theophilus G. Steward, who was pastor of the A.M.E. Church in Macon from 1867 to 1870, says he tutored Scarborough. See Albert G. Miller, *Elevating the Race* (Knoxville: University of Tennessee Press, 2003), 3.

3. For a broad history of education in Macon at this time, see Titus Brown, *Faithful, Firm and True*. For background see Titus Brown, *Faithful, Firm, and True: African American Education in the South* (Macon: Mercer University Press, 2002), 41–42, 47.

4. For the original letter from Sarah Proctor Ball dated July 10, 1881, see box 8, Correspondence, Various Persons to WSS, WSS Papers.

5. John Randolph Lewis worked for the U.S. Bureau of Refugees, Freedmen, and Abandoned Lands established by an act of Congress in March 1865. He was appointed by Governor Bullock of Georgia to the Freedmen's Bureau and served from 1868 to 1869. See Susan F. Preley, "'A Past to Cherish—A Future to Fulfill': Lewis High—Ballard Normal School, 1865–1900" (M.A. thesis, Georgia Southern University, 1992), and Paul A. Cimbala, *Under the Guardianship of the Nation: The Freedmen's Bureau and the Reconstruction of Georgia, 1865–1870* (Athens: University of Georgia Press, 1997).

6. John R. Rockwell arrived in Macon in 1866 to oversee the American Missionary Association's schools in southwestern Georgia. In 1868 he became the first principal of Lewis High School. His wife was Martha D. Ayres, matron of the Teacher's Home of the American Missionary Association (AMA) in Macon. Papers concerning his activities from 1865 to 1867 are held by the Amistad Research Center at Tulane University. On the opening of Lewis High School at which Rockwell officiated, see "The Dedication of the Lewis High School," *Macon Telegraph*, April 3, 1868. In a letter dated 1868 to AMA officials, Rockwell mentioned an unnamed student who fits Scarborough's description. He noted "that we have one young man studying Latin and algebra besides a small class in Harkness' *First Latin Book*." Quoted in Brown, *Faithful, Firm and True*, 35–36. Sarah Cordelia Bierce (April 3, 1851–July 1, 1933), Scarborough's future wife, trained to be a teacher at the Oswego Institute after a broken marriage. She then went south to Macon with the AMA to teach at Lewis High School. See Scarborough Family Papers, Western Reserve Historical Society Library and Archives, Cleveland (hereafter Scarborough Papers).

7. No records at Dartmouth College match the description of "Mr. Haley." For more information, see Brown, "African-American Education in Central Georgia," 34–36.

8. "Closing Exercises of the Colored Schools," *Macon Daily Telegraph*, June 16, 1866.

9. "A Macon Negro's Piece," *Macon Telegraph*, March 21, 1901.

10. An undated letter to Lillie Hill from Henry M. Turner describes the early history of the A.M.E. Church in Macon, and among the names and officers he recalled "Jerry Scarborough." GHR.

11. A copy of Scarborough's *First Lessons in Greek* (1881) at Rembert E. Stokes Library at Wilberforce University bears a dedication to her by the author. See the entry, "Smith, Mrs. M.E.C.," in Daniel W. Culp, *Twentieth Century Negro Literature* (Napierville: J. L. Nichols, 1902), 246–53.

12. Michael E. Strieby (1815–1899), Augustus F. Beard (1833–1934), and Gustavus D. Pike (1831–1885) were executives in the AMA for many years.

13. Scarborough must mean here Edwin D. Mead (1849–1937), author, editor, and prominent peace advocate.

14. Jean de Bloch, a.k.a. Jan Bloch (1836–1902), was the author of *The Future of War in Its Technical, Economic and Political Relations.* I. C. Long's translation of its six volumes in Russian was published in Boston in 1903.

15. This is probably the League to Enforce Peace, whose principles former President William Taft explained to the Arbitration Conference in 1916.

16. Atlanta University opened in 1865. See Clarence A. Bacote, *The Story of Atlanta University: A Century of Service, 1865–1965* (Atlanta: Atlanta University Press, 1965).

17. Adrien-Marie Legendre (1752–1833), French professor and mathematician, published *Eléments de géometrie* in 1794, which became the most popular elementary text in geometry for the next one hundred years. John Farrar of Harvard University completed one of the first translations of the text in 1819.

18. See *Catalogue of the Normal and Preparatory Departments of Atlanta University, 1870–'71* (Atlanta: V. P. Sisson, 1887), 9, 14, held in the Robert W. Woodruff Archives, Atlanta University Center. Among the student body, which numbered 170, Scarborough was the sole member listed under the rubric "senior class."

19. Edmund Asa Ware (1837–1885) graduated from Yale University in 1863. Under the auspices of the AMA he became the first president of Atlanta University in 1867 and served until 1885.

20. Thomas Noyes Chase (1838–1912), an 1862 graduate of Dartmouth College, was connected with Atlanta University in one capacity or another for thirty-nine years. He was professor of Greek from 1869 to 1888, and a member of the board of trustees for twenty-eight years. He and his first wife, Mary, wrote articles for the *American Missionary.* See his essays "Alabama: Breaking Ground for the New Emerson Institute," 32 (March 1878): 78–79; "Vacation Reports," 34 (January 1880): 9–12; "The Mendi Mission," 34 (November 1880): 359–63; and "Burrell School, Selma Ala.," 47 (1893): 256–59. Consult his alumni file held in the Rauner Special Collections Library at Dartmouth College Library.

21. Henry Ward Beecher (1813–1887) of the Congregational Church was head of the Plymouth Church in Brooklyn.

22. Ware's son was Edward Twitchell Ware (1874–1927), who graduated from Yale University in 1897 and Union Theological Seminary in 1901. He was the third president of Atlanta University and served from 1907 to 1922. Scarborough gave the address in 1908.

23. Lucy Laney (1854–1933) graduated from Lewis High School, studied at Atlanta University, and later became famous as an educator in Augusta.

24. Henry Ossian Flipper (1859–1940) was in 1877 the first black to graduate from the U.S. Military Academy at West Point. At Fort Davis, Texas, in 1881 he was accused of embezzlement and conduct unbecoming an officer. Acquitted of the first charge, he was convicted of the second and dismissed from the army. His 1882 court-martial charge was reversed by the U.S. Army on December 13, 1976. William Jefferson Clinton gave him a presidential pardon in February 1999.

25. Richard T. Greener (1844–1922) was the first African American to graduate with a B.A. from Harvard. Greener was in a position to know about Flipper. He was involved in Johnson Whittaker's case. Whittaker was a black cadet at the U.S. Military Academy at West Point who was found tied up and mutilated there on April 6, 1880. See Michael Mounter, "Richard Theodore Greener: The Idealist, Statesman, Scholar and South Carolinian" (Ph.D. diss., University of South Carolina, 2002).

26. Oliver Otis Howard (1830–1909), soldier, statesman, and educator, graduated from Bowdoin College in 1850 and from the U.S. Military Academy at West Point in 1854. He saw much action in the Civil War and earned a Congressional Medal of Honor in 1893 for bravery at Fair Oaks where he lost his arm. He helped found Howard University and was president from 1869 to 1874.

27. This is John Greenleaf Whittier's anti-slavery poem, "Howard at Atlanta" (1869). The fifth stanza closes with these lines: "And a little boy stood up: 'General / tell 'em we're rising!'"

28. Richard R. Wright, Sr., educator, politician, and editor, later became a banker and businessman of note in Pennsylvania. In 1921 at about age sixty-six, Wright and two of his children opened the Citizens and Southern Bank and Trust Company in Philadelphia, which was one of the few black banks to survive the Great Depression. Scarborough mentions his directorship in correspondence with the Oberlin College Alumni Office. See his Student File, box 805, Oberlin College Archives.

29. The assertion was well-known in the popular sense, but it is not found among John Calhoun's own papers. Crummell overheard two Boston attorneys, David Lee Child and Samuel E. Sewell, in the New York office of the American Antislavery Society's secretary, Elizur Wright, talking about Calhoun, with whom they had recently dined. Crummell said that he heard them reporting Calhoun's words:

> "That if he could find a Negro who knew the Greek syntax, he would then believe that the Negro was a human being and should be treated as a man." Just think of the crude asininity of even a great man! Mr. Calhoun went to Yale, to study the Greek Syntax, and graduated there. His son went to Yale to study the Greek Syntax, and graduated there. His grandson, in recent years, went to Yale, to learn the Greek Syntax, and graduated there. Schools and Colleges were necessary for the Calhouns, and all other white men to learn the Greek syntax. And yet this great man knew that there was not a school, nor a college in which a black boy could learn his A.B.C.'s. He knew that the law in all the Southern States forbade Negro instruction under the severest penalties. How then was the Negro to learn the Greek syntax? How then was he to evidence to Mr. Calhoun his human nature? Why, it is manifest that Mr. Calhoun expected the Greek syntax to grow in *Negro brains* by spontaneous generation!

For information on the two accounts that Crummell gave of this conversation, consult J. R. Oldfield, ed., *Civilization and Black Progress: Selected Writings of Alexander Crummell on the South* (Charlottesville: University Press of Virginia, 1995), 172, 306–07. See Wilson Moses, *Alexander Crummell: A Study of Civilization and Discontent* (New York: Oxford University Press, 1989), 20. For the account given above, consult Alexander Crummell, "The Attitude of the American Mind toward the Negro Intellect (1898)," *American Negro Academy Occasional Papers, 1–22* (New York: Arno Press, 1969), 10–11. See also Anna Julia Cooper's (1858–1964) viewpoint about

Calhoun's alleged comment in her essay, "What Are We Worth? (1892)," in *The Voice of Anna Julia Cooper*, ed. Charles Lemert and Esme Bahn (New York: Rowman and Littlefield, 1998), 175–76.

30. For an account of the scrutiny given to Atlanta University students, see Bacote, *Story of Atlanta University*, 46–53. Michael E. Strieby (1815–1899) graduated in Oberlin College's first class in 1842. He was secretary of the AMA from 1864 to 1896. Joseph Emerson Brown (1821–1894) graduated from Yale Law School in 1846. Pro-slavery and a champion of states rights, he served four terms as Georgia's governor and became one of the state's wealthiest men. He served in the U.S. Senate from 1880 to 1891.

31. The obituary in the *Atlanta University Bulletin*, ser. 2, December 1926, titled "The Passing of Dr. W. S. Scarborough," describes him as the "first advanced student of Atlanta University, . . . the only member of his class, and since the organization of college work was delayed for one year, he transferred to Oberlin where he graduated in 1875, one year earlier than our own first class of 1876 . . . while not technically one of us in the sense of being a graduate, we have always appreciated Dr. Scarborough as one of our distinguished sons."

32. Myron W. Adams (1860–1939) came to Atlanta University in 1889 to teach Greek. After serving as dean of the faculty for twenty-seven years and acting president for four, he was appointed president officially in 1923 and served until 1929. See Scarborough's commencement address, "The Negro Graduate—His Mission, 1908."

33. Scarborough may be reflecting obliquely upon his failure to be appointed to the faculty at Atlanta University during the 1870s.

CHAPTER IV: FOUR YEARS IN OBERLIN COLLEGE

1. Oberlin College, founded in 1833, was the first college to admit women and one of the first to admit African Americans. The standard history is Robert S. Fletcher, *A History of Oberlin College: From Its Foundation through the Civil War*, 2 vols. (Oberlin, 1943).

2. Henry E. Peck (1821–1867), professor of sacred rhetoric at Oberlin, was a staunch abolitionist. He was implicated along with James M. Fitch and Ralph Plumb by the prosecution in the legal battle that resulted from the rescue of John Price, an escaped slave, at Wellington in 1858. He was appointed the first U.S. Minister to Haiti in 1865 and died there two years later. John Mercer Langston did not take part in the rescue. See Roland M. Baumann, *The 1858 Oberlin-Wellington Rescue* (Oberlin: Oberlin College, 2003).

3. Asa Mahan (1799–1889) became the first president of Oberlin College on January 1, 1835. He was a champion of emancipation and coeducation. He left Oberlin in 1850 to found Cleveland University.

4. For information about American diplomatic appointees to Haiti, see James A. Padgett, "Diplomats to Haiti and Their Diplomacy," *Journal of Negro History* 25 (1940): 265–330.

5. Richard Salter Storrs (1821–1900), social reformer and Congregational preacher, graduated from Yale in 1820 and Andover Theological Seminary in 1823. He was pastor of the First Congregational Church in New Haven from 1825 to 1881. See Albert J. Lyman, *Memorial Service in Honor of Richard Salter Storrs, D.D., LL.D.,*

November 19, 1900 (Brooklyn: Eagle Press, 1900). John Hall (1829–1898) came from Ireland in 1867 to preach at the Fifth Avenue Presbyterian Church in New York City. See his *God's Word through Preaching* (1875) and *Christian Home* (1884). Leonard Bacon (1802–1881), with an M.A. from Amherst College in 1842 and D.D. from Union Theological Seminary in 1853, was associate editor of the *Independent* from 1848 to 1861. See Hugh Davis, *Leonard Bacon, New England Reformer and Antislavery Moderate* (Baton Rouge: Louisiana State University Press, 1998).

6. Charles G. Finney (1792–1875), evangelist and mystic, is known as the "father of modern revivalism." He was president of Oberlin from 1851 to 1866. See Keith Hardman, *Charles Grandison Finney, 1792–1875* (Syracuse: Syracuse University Press, 1987).

7. John Mercer Langston, educator, diplomat, orator, and politician, rose from slavery to graduate from Oberlin College in 1849. He became a lawyer in 1855 and moved to Washington, D.C., where he carried out his multifaceted career. See William and Aimee Lee Cheek, *John Mercer Langston and the Fight to Win Black Freedom, 1829–65* (Urbana: University of Illinois Press, 1989).

8. Mifflin Wistar Gibbs (1823–1903), prominent African American social reformer and businessman in California and British Columbia, moved to Oberlin in the 1860s where his wife, Maria Ann Alexander Gibbs (n.d.–1904), had attended college. The couple's daughter, Ida Gibbs (1862–1957), attended the Oberlin public schools and Oberlin College. See biographical entry on Ida Gibbs Hunt by Roland M. Baumann, *African American Women: A Biographical Dictionary*, ed. Dorothy C. Salem (New York: Garland, 1993), 257–59.

9. Matthew Anderson and his wife founded the Berean Manual Training and Industrial School in 1889. For a description of life at Oberlin College, see his book *Presbyterianism: Its Relation to the Negro* (Philadelphia: John McGill White and Company, 1897), 143–54, 162.

10. Mary Church Terrell (1863–1954) majored in classics at Oberlin College and received her bachelor's degree in 1884. In 1891 she married Robert H. Terrell (1857–1925), whom she met in Washington after teaching for a brief time at Wilberforce. See her autobiography, *A Colored Woman in a White World* (Washington, D.C.: Ransdell, 1940).

11. Anna Jones (n.d.–1932).

12. William H. Prescott (1796–1859), renowned historian from Massachusetts, turned from law to the study of Spanish interests in the New World after suffering an eye injury.

13. Thomas Hughes (1822–1896) wrote *Tom Brown at Oxford* (London: Macmillan, 1874). Five volumes of a seven-volume set of De Quincy's works remain at Rembert E. Stokes Library, Wilberforce University. These bear Scarborough's bookplate and notes saying they were purchased in November, 1874, from the Ladies Society Library in Oberlin.

14. Thomas De Quincy (1785–1859) was born in Greenheys, an area near the center of Manchester, England.

15. There is a postcard from Mrs. Scarborough to her brother George sent from Coblentz Hotel on the Rhine, which bears the date August 9, 1911. See photograph (hereafter PG) 396, folder 2, Scarborough Family Papers.

16. Theodore E. Burton (1851–1929) was a Republican representative and later senator from Ohio.

17. Ernest Ingersoll (1852–1946) was the author and illustrator of books and articles on plant and animal life.

18. For information on Shurtleff (1831–1904), see "Giles Waldo Shurtleff," *Oberlin Alumni Magazine* 7 (June 1911): 305–25. For information on Ryder (1842–1918), see John Wesley Hanson, *Biography of William Henry Ryder, D.D.* (Boston: Universalist Publishing House, 1891). For the letters of endorsement from Ryder, dated November 26, 1872, and Shurtleff, dated November 27, 1872, see box 8, Correspondence, Various Persons to WSS, folder 1872–1879, WSS Papers.

19. The Enterprise Academy in Albany, Ohio, was owned and controlled by black educators. It opened in 1864. Thomas Jefferson Furguson (1830–1887), cofounder of the Ohio Colored Teachers Association, was president of the academy from 1863 to 1886. For a photo of the school in 1872, see box 12, Photographs, WSS Papers.

20. Olivia Davidson Washington (1854–1889) grew up in Ohio. She graduated from Hampton Institute in 1878 and married Booker T. Washington in 1886. Scarborough seems to have forgotten Fannie Norton Smith, who was Washington's first wife. Fannie died in 1884.

21. E. C. Berry (1855–n.d.), son of Cornelius Berry, was the owner and proprietor of the Hotel Berry, which in 1899 had forty-six rooms to let and a dining room that could seat seventy-five. For more information including photos of Berry and his hotel, see G. F. Richings, *Evidences of Progress among Colored People* (Philadelphia: George S. Ferguson, 1903), 552–55.

22. James Harris Fairchild (1817–1902) was president of Oberlin College from 1866 to 1889. See Albert Swing, *Life of James Harris Fairchild* (New York: F. H. Revell, 1906). Elijah's mantle is mentioned in 1 Kings 19:19, "Elijah passed by him and cast his mantle upon him," and again in 2 Kings 2:11–13.

23. Charles Henry Churchill (1824–1904) graduated from Dartmouth in 1845. He began teaching at Oberlin in 1858. For Churchill's letter of recommendation dated November 24, 1872, see box 8, Correspondence, Various Letters to WSS, folder 1872–1879, WSS Papers.

24. Adelia Antoinette Field Johnston (1837–1910) was the principal of the Ladies Department at Oberlin for thirty years. She was Oberlin's first female faculty member. See Harriet Keeler, *Life of Adelia A. Field Johnston* (Cleveland: Korner & Wood, 1912). A copy of this book was in Scarborough's library. See "Catalogue of the Private Library of William Sanders Scarborough," box 13, WSS Papers, p. 8.

25. Consult James Monroe Marks, *Memorabilia of the Class of 1875 Oberlin College* (N.p., 1933). See also the section in chapter XXVII concerning the fiftieth reunion of the Oberlin class of 1875. Scarborough preserved his class yearbook, which holds photos of various classmates and teachers. See box 13, Miscellaneous, WSS Papers.

CHAPTER V: SEEKING A PATH

1. Francis James Grimké (1850–1937) was a civil rights activist pastor and author. Daniel W. Culp (fl. 1870) was the editor of *Twentieth Century Negro Literature*.

2. For the original endorsement, see box 8, Correspondence, Various Letters to WSS, folder 1872–1879, WSS Papers.

3. See Scarborough's correspondence to E. M. Cravath and Michael E. Strieby, AMA officials, in 1875–1876 asking for an appointment. In a letter to Cravath dated August 14, 1875, Scarborough says, "I prefer a chair in Atlanta University, but any will suffice." Amistad Research Center, Tulane University.

4. See a letter from E. A. Ware dated August 7, 1876, stating that there are no vacancies at Atlanta University and asking about Scarborough's plans at Oberlin. Box 8, Correspondence, Various Letters to WSS, folder 1872–1879, WSS Papers.

5. For information about the AMA, see James M. McPherson, *The Abolitionist Legacy* (Princeton: Princeton University Press, 1975).

6. The Mendi Mission was founded upon the return of the Amistad Africans to West Africa in 1856. On Scarborough's visit and the Mendi Mission, see Anderson, *Presbyterianism,* 177–82.

7. On the fire, see the *Macon Telegraph and Messenger,* March 27, 1877, and June 3, 1879. *The Helping Hand* 3 (June 1884) featured an illustration of the grounds of the Lewis Normal Institute on its cover. See box 4, Manuscripts, WSS Papers.

8. The name of the other teacher at that time was Mrs. Sarah Cordelia Bierce.

9. Richard H. Cain (1825–1887), editor, politician, and religious leader in South Carolina, was the fourteenth bishop of the A.M.E. Church. John Mifflin Brown (1817–1893), eleventh bishop of the A.M.E. Church, helped organize colleges in South Carolina and Texas including Payne Institute in 1871.

10. Allen University was incorporated in December 1880. The campus was moved from Cokesbury to Columbia, South Carolina. See an 1877 announcement of the Payne Institute at Cokesbury, Abbeville County, listing "W. S. Scarborough, A.B." as principal. Box 3, WSS Papers.

11. Franklin J. Moses, Jr. (1838–1906), was Republican governor of South Carolina from 1872 to 1874 and known for his corruption.

12. Wade Hampton (1818–1902) was a prominent figure in the politics of South Carolina before and after the Civil War. Daniel H. Chamberlain (1835–1907), Republican governor of South Carolina in 1874, was an ex-abolitionist who supported reform. The two men fought for the governorship in a bitterly contested election, and Chamberlain won.

13. Washington Gladden (1836–1918), ordained minister and author from Marietta, Ohio, was a well-known social reformer.

14. Richard T. Greener (1844–1922) attended Oberlin College and Phillips Academy. In 1870 he graduated from Harvard with prizes in oratory. While teaching in South Carolina, he earned a law degree. In 1875 he became the first African American member of the American Philological Association (APA). From 1877 to 1880 he was associated with the law department at Howard University. After several different jobs in New York City, he was appointed in July 1898 as the first consul to serve at Vladivostok. His talent and training never found an appropriate outlet.

15. Scarborough published an article against migration back to Africa about a year later. See "The Exodus—A Suicidal Scheme—The Machinations of Disappointed Office Seekers," *Christian Recorder* 16 (January 3, 1878): 4.

CHAPTER VI: THE PATH FOUND

1. Consult Payne's *Sermons and Addresses, 1853–1891,* ed. Charles Killian (New York: Arno, 1972). Benjamin F. Lee served as president of Wilberforce from 1877 to 1884. It was he who hired Scarborough. For the letter of appointment, see box 8, Correspondence, Various Letters to WSS, folder 1872–1879, WSS Papers.

2. John's brother Samuel T. Mitchell (1851–1901) was the fourth president of Wilberforce University. He served from 1884 to 1900.

3. Alvin Victor Donahey (1873–1946) was governor of Ohio from 1923 to 1929. He served as auditor until 1921.

4. John Mifflin Brown was principal of Union Seminary. Frances Ellen Watkins Harper (1825–1911) taught sewing at Union Seminary from 1850 to 1852. In addition to being a writer, she was an advocate of the Women's Christian Temperance Union and of voting rights for women. See Boyd, *Discarded Legacy.*

5. William Wilberforce (1759–1833) was Britain's leading abolitionist who helped stop the African slave trade.

6. Richard Sutton Rust (1815–1906), a secretary of the Freedman's Aid Society, helped establish Rust College in Holly Springs, Mississippi, in 1866.

7. Consult Frederick McGinnis, *A History and an Interpretation of Wilberforce University* (Wilberforce: N.p., 1941).

8. For this postcard sent to Pine Street in Philadelphia, see box 8, Correspondence, Various Letters to WSS, folder 1872–1879, WSS Papers.

9. The main station was located in Xenia, but there was a stop three and a half miles away at Wilberforce.

10. Myron W. Adams wrote *The History of Atlanta University, 1865–1929* (Atlanta: Atlanta University Press, 1930). He worked closely for thirty years with John Hope (1808–1936), who became the school's next president in 1929.

11. Edward Austin Sheldon (1823–1897) developed the "Oswego Method," which shaped teacher training schools throughout the country. There is a photograph of him among Mrs. Scarborough's papers. See PG 396, folder 1, Scarborough Family Papers.

12. This is Sarah Cordelia Bierce Scarborough, who became Scarborough's wife in 1881.

13. Salmon P. Chase (1808–1873), Republican governor of Ohio from 1856 to 1860, was appointed Chief Justice of the Supreme Court by Lincoln and presided over the trial of Jefferson Davis. Chase gave Wilberforce $10,000 in 1873. Gerrit Smith (1797–1874), reformer and wealthy philanthropist, gave $10,000 to Berea College in Kentucky. He gave $500 to Wilberforce in its early days. For a discussion of Chase's donation, see "Wilberforce University," *People's Advocate,* January 30, 1881.

CHAPTER VII:
WIDENING FIELDS—WORKING, LEARNING, GROWING

1. The Secretary's Notebook (1878–1883) with Scarborough's notes from January 1878 to September 1879, and September 1881 to May 1883 is held at the National Afro-American Museum and Cultural Center, Wilberforce, Ohio.

2. General Warren Keifer (1836–1932) was in uniform from 1861 to 1899. See his letter of endorsement, box 8, Correspondence, Various Letters to WSS, folder 1872–1879, WSS Papers.

3. According to Lucretia Newman Coleman, the author of *Poor Ben* (Nashville: A.M.E. Sunday School Union, 1890), 182, Reverend J.T. Jenifer was the first colored man in the state of Ohio appointed to the office of postmaster. He served at Wilberforce University and was put in place by President Andrew Johnson in 1866. Scarborough was postmaster from August 1879 to August 1880. John A. Clark, secretary of Wilberforce University served until October 1883. At that point, J. P. Maxwell took over. See Maxwell's account in Benjamin W. Arnett and Samuel T. Michell, *Wilberforce Alumnal* (Xenia, Ohio: printed at the Gazette Office, 1885). For a brief biography of Maxwell, see Horace Talbert, *Sons of Allen* (Xenia, Ohio, Aldine Press, 1906), 96–97.

4. Frances N. Peloubet (1831–1920) wrote materials and texts for Sunday schools.

5. Henry Augustus Ward (1834–1906), naturalist, mineralogist, and miner, supplied collections of scientific specimens to more than two hundred schools and public museums in the United States, including the nucleus of the Field Museum in Chicago. In 1862 he founded Ward's Natural Science Establishment and assembled an exemplary exhibit of minerals and fossils at the University of Rochester.

6. Horace Mann (1796–1859), lawyer, politician, educator, and reformer, transformed the Massachusetts school system. After being defeated in his run for governor of Massachusetts in 1852, he became president of Antioch College.

7. On Ward's donation, see McGinnis, *A History and an Interpretation of Wilberforce University,* 125. See also Daniel Payne, *Recollections of Seventy Years* (Nashville: A.M.E. Sunday School Union, 1888), 228–29.

8. This is J. F. W. Ware, who gave $300 for the Art Room. See McGinnis, *A History and an Interpretation of Wilberforce University,* 125. See also Sarah C. B. Scarborough's account in Arnett and Mitchell, *Wilberforce Alumnal,* 35–39.

9. In Greek myth Scylla, who was a sea monster, and Charybdis, who was a tidal whirlpool, terrorized sailors in the straits of Messenia.

10. Reverend John Burns Weston (1821–1912) was a member of the first graduating class at Antioch College. He was also a three-time acting president of Antioch College (1862–1865, 1876–1877, 1880–1881). Edward W. Claypole (1835–1901) was chair of natural science at Antioch College from 1873 to 1881. Nicholas Paine Gilman (1849–1912) was professor of ethics, English literature, and German from 1876 to 1881.

11. Henry W. Bellows (1814–1882) was one of the founders of Antioch College. Edward Everett Hale (1822–1909) was a trustee of Antioch College from 1865 to 1899.

12. Albert E. Winship (1845–1933) wrote a number of works about education.

13. Wendell Phillips (1811–1885) was a noted orator and abolitionist.

CHAPTER VIII: AUTHORSHIP—GREEK BOOK— MARRIAGE

1. For the original letter from New York City dated April 28, 1881, see box 8, Correspondence, Various Letters to WSS, folder 1881–1889, WSS Papers.

2. In the book's preface, Scarborough states that his text was patterned on Jones's *First Lessons in Latin*. It complemented the grammar books of Hadley and Goodwin and it was meant for a "two-term study." Sarah Cordelia Bierce assisted in his work. She completed the Classical Course at the State Normal and Training School at Oswego and was licensed to teach June 28, 1875. This diploma, an honorary master in pedagogy from Wilberforce University, and a certificate of membership in the MLA are held by the National Afro-American Museum and Cultural Center in Wilberforce, gifts of Sarah A. Grant. See Michele Valerie Ronnick, "*First Lessons in Greek* (1881): William Sanders Scarborough's Date with Destiny," *A.M.E. Church Review* 118 (2002): 30–43.

3. The book sold for $1.25 retail and $.90 wholesale. See the advertisement in *People's Advocate* 6, no. 19 (August 20, 1881). Scarborough lists some of the costs. See box 7, Writings, Account Book, 1881–1890, WSS Papers.

1st lot 50 copies (complimentary)

400 '"@$1 per piece $400.00

50 '" @.75 per piece 37.50

July 1st order printed 1,000 copies

100 copies (complimentary)

500 copies@90 ct per piece $810.00

4. Adelphi Academy was founded in 1863. Scarborough's publisher was Alfred Smith Barnes (1817–1888). With partner Charles Davies, they introduced the National Series of standard schoolbooks in 1844. By the 1880s, Barnes's five sons had begun to join in the work. Barnes left money to Tuskegee. See "Booker T. Washington and Warren Logan to the Executors of the Alfred S. Barnes Estate," in *Booker T. Washington Papers,* ed. Louis Harlan (Urbana: University of Illinois Press, 1972), 2:452–53, 487. See also "Barnes, Alfred S.," *National Cyclopedia of American Biography* (New York: James T. White, 1904), 196–97.

5. For more reactions, see "Scarborough's Greek Lessons," *People's Advocate* 6, no. 31 (November 12, 1881), and William J. Simmons, *Men of Mark* (Cleveland: George M. Rewell, 1887), 416.

6. W. Goodell Frost was a professor of Greek at Oberlin College. Later he became the head of Berea College in Kentucky. He was the grandson of William Goodell, the anti-slavery editor. He is quoted in *People's Advocate* 6, no. 31 (November 12, 1881), saying: "I have examined Prof. Scarborough's *First Lessons in Greek* with some care and am much interested in the book. It is clear and accurate, develops the subject naturally and easily, and is handsomely printed. The method of a practical teacher is everywhere seen."

7. For Turner's text, see his front-page article, "Prof. Scarborough's Book," *Christian Recorder,* September 22, 1881.

8. For Greener's text, see his front-page article, "First Lessons in Greek— Prof. W. S. Scarborough," *Christian Recorder,* September 29, 1881. Greener studied for a time as a youth in Oberlin.

9. This quote is from Ralph Waldo Emerson, *Spiritual Laws, First Series* (1841). The text reads: "What has he done? Is the divine question which searches men and transpierces every false reputation. A fop may sit in any chair of the world, nor be dis-

tinguished for his hour from Homer and Washington; but there need never be any doubt concerning the respective ability of human beings. Pretension may sit still, but cannot act. Pretension never feigned an act of real greatness. Pretension never wrote an *Iliad* nor drove back Xerxes nor Christianized the world nor abolished slavery" (chap. 8, sec. 8).

10. The reference to the old man of the sea comes from the tale of Sinbad's Fifth Voyage in the *Arabian Nights.*

11. This is a common phrase of praise in Latin meaning "prosper in your valor" or, simply, "well done." See examples of its usage in Virgil, *Aeneid,* 9.641 and in Livy, *Ab Urbe Condita,* 2.12. Scarborough himself used the phrase in a letter written on Wilberforce University letterhead and dated March 14, 1907. In it he congratulated Alain Locke for winning a Rhodes Scholarship. He wrote in part: "You have done well and we are all proud of you. This splendid achievement will do more toward helping to adjust the race problem than all the bombast and pyrotechnics of our enemies and would-be-leaders combined. Again I congratulate you—Macte Virtute." See Alain Locke Papers, Moorland-Spingarn Research Collection, Howard University, Washington, D.C.

12. John F. Slater (1815–1884), a wealthy industrialist from Norwich, Connecticut, endowed a fund for the education of blacks in 1882. Slater's letter dated June 28, 1882, is included in Simmons, *Men of Mark,* 416–17.

13. Alexander Crummell (1819–1898) studied Greek at Queen's College, Cambridge University, and earned a B.A. in 1853. He is the first man of African descent to learn Greek thoroughly in the United States. Scarborough was the second. Both refuted Calhoun's aspersion.

14. The couple was married in New York City on August 2, 1881. Bishop William Fisher Dickerson (1844–1884) officiated. Dickerson was pastor of Bethel on Sullivan Street and the wedding may have taken place there. Bishop Jabez Pitt Campbell, Bishop James A. Shorter, and Hallie Q. Brown were witnesses. The *Cleveland Gazette,* February 21, 1885, noted that "Prof. Scarborough has been authorized to write the biography of the late Bishop Dickerson; also to collect and edit his addresses, public documents, public correspondence, etc. He will enter upon this work in the spring." Campbell (1815–1891) was made a bishop of the A.M.E. Church in 1864. Shorter (1817–1887) was made a bishop of the A.M.E. Church in 1868. Brown (1845–1949), educator, lecturer, and reformer, was a Wilberforce graduate and taught there from 1893 to 1903.

15. Lucy Chase (1822–1909) and Sarah Chase (1836–1911) came from a wealthy family of Quakers in Worcester, Massachusetts. They went south in 1863 to help blacks on Craney Island near Norfolk, Virginia. For a series of letters the sisters wrote between 1861 and 1870, see Henry Lee Swint, *Dear Ones at Home: Letters from Contraband Camps* (Nashville: Vanderbilt University Press, 1966).

16. This quote comes from the second line of the poem "The Isles of Greece" (1819) by George Gordon, Lord Byron (1788–1824). One acorn bead remains from the necklace, which is in the possession of Sarah A. Grant, Warren, Ohio.

17. A small booklet among Scarborough's papers opens on page 1 with this handwritten note: "For my biography dedicated to my beloved wife, the inspiration of all my ambitions." See box 1, Manuscripts, Bibliography, WSS Papers.

18. Charles Spencer Smith (1852–1923) organized the A.M.E. Sunday School Union, which produced the *Child's Recorder* and *Our Sunday School Review.* In 1900 he became the twenty-eighth bishop of the A.M.E. Church.

19. Fitch died on April 12, 1892. He was not the first member of the class of 1875 to die but was perhaps the first of Scarborough's friends to die. Both John Allen Winters and Dwight Batchley Bradley predeceased him. See the necrology made by Arthur T. Burnell in James Monroe Marks, *Memorabilia of the Class of 1875, Oberlin College* (N.p., 1933), 120–22. A page from the *Author's Review and Scrapbook* dated June 1883 has a short story titled "'Little People' by Aunt Fanny." A note in an unidentified hand says: "Aunt Fanny was Dr. S.—who thus aided his friend Fitch's adventure." See box 9, Scrapbook, WSS Papers.

CHAPTER IX: PHILOLOGY AND POLITICS

1. The diploma notes "Board of Trustees, January 13, 1882 resolved that an honorary degree Doctor of Laws be conferred upon Prof. W.S. Scarborough, M.A.," signed "Alfred R. King, Secretary for Trustees." See box 3, WSS Papers.

2. The APA was founded in 1869. The meeting took place July 11–13.

3. Edward W. Blyden (1832–1912), famed for his work in Liberia as a college professor and diplomat, was the second black member in 1881, and Scarborough was the third in 1882. Blyden and Scarborough were full-fledged professors of Greek and Latin. Greener taught classics as part of his work at the University of South Carolina and for a fairly short period of time.

4. William Edward Armytage Axon (1840–1913) wrote a number of books on the history of Manchester. The two men were friends for decades. See W. E. A. Axon, W. S. Scarborough correspondence, John Rylands University Library of Manchester, England.

5. Catherine Impey (1847–1923), a Quaker from Street, Somerset, England, published *Anti-Caste,* a leaflet "devoted to the concerns of the Coloured Races," from March 1888 to July 1895.

6. Hermann Osthoff (1847–1909), *Das Verbum in der nominal composition im Deutschen Griechischen, Slavischen und Romanischen* (Jena: N.p., 1878).

7. A summary of this paper can be found in *Transactions of the American Philological Association* 15 (1884): vi. See also "Prof. W. S. Scarborough of Wilberforce at the Sixteenth Annual Session of the American Philological Association," *Cleveland Gazette,* February 7, 1885. The papers began at 4:20 p.m. and Scarborough was the first scholar to speak. He was followed by Bernadotte Perrin of Adelbert College and Charles Lanman of Harvard. The session was adjourned at 8:00 p.m.

8. The American and Foreign Anti-Slavery Society was founded under William Lloyd Garrison (1805–1879) and existed from 1833 until 1870. Scarborough joined the Modern Language Association (MLA) in 1884. See Ronnick, "William Sanders Scarborough: The First African American Member of the Modern Language Association."

9. The meeting took place July 8–10.

10. Charles R. Lanman (1850–1941), noted scholar of Sanskrit at Harvard from 1880 to 1926, was secretary of the APA from 1879 to 1884.

11. William Watson Goodwin (1831–1912) was a distinguished Hellenist who was associated with Harvard from 1856 to 1909. He was president of the APA from 1871 to 1872 and from 1884 to 1885. William D. Whitney (1827–1894), noted Sanskritist and linguist, was associated with Yale from 1854 to 1894. Thomas D. Seymour (1848–1907) was a noted expert on Homer. He taught at Western Reserve from 1872 to 1880 and then at Yale from 1880 to 1907. Tracy Peck (1838–1921) was a brilliant teacher, an expert at Latin composition, and had a deep knowledge of Rome. He taught at Cornell from 1871 to 1880 and at Yale from 1880 to 1908. John H. Wright (1852–1908) was known for his promotion of graduate studies and his knowledge of Athens. He taught at Dartmouth from 1878 to 1886. Richard C. Jebb (1841–1905) was professor of Greek at Glasgow from 1875 to 1889 and Regius professor of Greek at Cambridge from 1889 to 1905.

12. Ernest Gottlieb Sihler (1853–1942) was a Lutheran layman and a classical scholar. He was a member of Basil Gildersleeve's first class at Johns Hopkins University and earned the first Ph.D. in philology granted by the institution. He trained in Berlin and Leipzig from 1872 to 1875, and later taught at New York University from 1892 to 1923.

13. Kimball Union Academy in Meriden, New Hampshire, was founded in 1813.

14. William B. Derrick (1843–1913) became a bishop of the A.M.E. Church in 1896.

15. Hiram Hitchcock (1832–1900) established the Fifth Avenue Hotel in 1852 with two partners. One of the most famous hostelries in the United States, it was razed in 1908.

16. Henry Elijah Parker (1821–1896) taught Latin at Dartmouth from 1866 to 1890. He graduated from Dartmouth in 1841 and Union Theological Seminary in 1847. He was a chaplain with the Second New Hampshire Regiment from 1861 to 1865. In 1856 he married Mary Elizabeth Brackett Huntley from Lansingburgh, New York, and their daughter, Alice, was born in Concord, New Hampshire, on March 12, 1865. In 1893 Alice married Albert Tenney, and in the same year Professor Parker came to live with the couple in Boston. Bradford Academy, an old academy in New Hampshire, had close ties with Dartmouth College.

17. Lake Memphremagog is located on the Vermont state line.

18. Scarborough is wrong about the date of Greener's membership; Greener joined in 1875. See *Transactions of the American Philological Association* 16 (1875): 8, 34.

19. William J. Bulkley (1861–1933) earned a Ph.D. in Latin from Syracuse University; Lewis B. Moore (1866–1928) won his Ph.D. from the University of Pennsylvania in 1896 with his dissertation, "The Stage in Sophocles' Plays"; John Wesley Gilbert (ca. 1865–1923), B.A., M.A. Brown University, was the first person of African descent to attend the American School in Athens. He was a professor of Greek at Paine College in Augusta, Georgia, until his death. William Henry Crogman (1841–1931) was a professor of Greek at Clark University from 1880 to 1921 and was president from 1903 to 1910. See Ronnick, "William Henry Crogman," 67–68.

20. Blyden's paper has not been found in APA records.

21. See Ronnick, "John Wesley Gilbert," 113–14. The letter is not among Scarborough's papers at Wilberforce.

22. Harry Clay Smith (1863–1941) owned the *Gazette* for fifty-two years.

23. Benjamin Tucker Tanner (1835–1923), eighteenth bishop of the A.M.E. Church, was the editor of the *Christian Recorder* from 1868 to 1884. In 1884 he helped launch the *A.M.E. Church Review,* which was for many years the premier black literary magazine in the United States.

24. Samuel T. Mitchell was the "principal of the colored schools" in Springfield from 1879 to 1884.

25. The article is "The Greek of the New Testament," *A.M.E. Church Review* 1 (1884): 37–45.

26. These are Frederick Douglass (1817–1895), Blanche K. Bruce (1841–1898), Richard T. Greener, and P. B. S. Pinchback (1837–1921). Pinchback was acting governor of Louisiana from 1872 to 1873. See "The Democratic Return to Power—It's Effect?" *A. M. E. Church Review* 1(1885): 213–50.

27. Joseph B. Foraker, *Notes from a Busy Life,* 2 vols. (Cincinnati: Stewart and Kidd, 1916).

28. Alphonso Taft (1810–1891) moved to Cincinnati in 1841 and served as secretary of war and attorney general from 1876 to 1877.

29. On June 27, 1863, untested African American soldiers successfully defended Milliken's Bend near Vicksburg, Mississippi, but the casualties were very high. At Port Hudson, Louisiana, African American troops proved their worth in May 1863 under General Nathaniel P. Banks. They bravely attacked a Confederate stronghold at great human cost. On April 12, 1864, when Fort Pillow, Tennessee, fell to General Nathan Bedford Forest, his troops buried 300 union soldiers alive, 230 of whom were African American.

30. A copy of the fifteen-page speech, which was given on Tuesday, April 29, was printed as a pamphlet (Xenia, Ohio: Torchlight Job Rooms, 1884). See *The Frederick Douglass Papers,* microfilm edition, box 39, reel 25.

31. John R. Lynch (1847–1939) was elected temporary chairman in 1884 and was the first black to deliver a keynote address before a national political convention. Powell Clayton (1833–1914) was supported by James G. Blaine (1830–1893), a lawyer, journalist, and politician from Maine. Clayton was governor of Arkansas from 1868 to 1871.

32. This is John Sherman (1823–1900), the brother of William Tecumseh Sherman, who was a Republican senator from Ohio from 1861 to 1877.

33. James G. Blaine lost his bid for the presidency to Grover Cleveland because of the "Rum, Romanism and Rebellion" incident with Dr. Samuel D. Burchard (1812–1890). In an address in New York City to a gathering of the Religious Bureau of the Republican National Committee, Burchard declared, "[W]e don't propose to identify ourselves with the party whose antecedents have been 'Rum, Romanism, and Rebellion.'"

34. George A. Hoadly (1826–1902) was governor of Ohio, 1884–86.

35. See Scarborough, "Ohio Black Laws," *Cleveland Gazette,* February 14, 1885.

36. Benjamin W. Arnett (1838–1906) was elected to the House in Ohio in 1886. His home in Wilberforce was known as Tawawa Chimney Corner. He became a bishop of the A.M.E. Church in 1868 and was a powerful force.

37. T. J. Pringle was an attorney in Springfield; James P. Poindexter (1819–1907), black clergyman, abolitionist, and politician, was a prominent figure in Columbus, Ohio; C. M. Nichols was editor of the *Springfield Daily Republican;* Asa Bushnell, governor of Ohio from 1896 to 1900, was a businessman in Springfield; Thomas F. McGrew, secretary of the Springfield Board of Trade, delivered an oration at Springfield's centennial, July 4, 1876; Pastor William H. Warren began his work at the First Orthodox Congregational Church in Springfield in September 1875; and J. K. Mower, president of the Champion Shelf Manufacturing Company, officiated over the dedication of the Civil War Monument in Springfield in May 1870. Details about Goodwin, Zeigler, and Buford are not known.

38. See Lucretia Newman Coleman's account of this meeting in *Poor Ben* (Nashville: A.M.E. Sunday School Union, 1890), 163–64. She quotes Scarborough as saying: "There was a great principle at stake in the battle that has been going on— the principle of equality. The Black Laws have been erased, and that principle is established."

CHAPTER X:
PHILOLOGY AND OTHER LITERARY WORK

1. See David A. Gerber, *Black Ohio and the Color Line, 1860–1915* (Urbana: University of Illinois Press, 1976).

2. The first Morrill Act (1862) sponsored by Justin Morrill of Vermont gave every Union state 30,000 acres of land for every member of its congressional delegation to provide for colleges in agriculture and the mechanical arts. For more, see Lathardus Goggins, *Central State University: The First One Hundred Years, 1887–1987* (Wilberforce, OH: Central State University, 1987), 12–16.

3. These are J.A. Howells (1832–1912), William Dean Howells (1837–1920), R. McMurdy (n.d.), and John O'Neill (1822–1905). A women's dormitory opened in 1890 at Wilberforce, which was named for O'Neill. It was razed in 1975. O'Neill, a lawyer, was elected as a Democrat to the 38th Congress (1863–1865) and was a member of the Senate from 1883 to 1885.

4. Wiley Lane (1852–1885), Phi Beta Kappa graduate of Amherst, 1879, M.A. from Howard University, 1881, was professor of Greek from 1883 to 1885. See "Appoint Prof. W. S. Scarborough," *Cleveland Gazette,* March 14, 1885. See Ronnick, "Wiley Lane," 108–9.

5. This was John W. Cromwell (1846–1927). See this letter dated February 20, 1885, box 8, Correspondence, Various persons to WSS, folder 1881–1889, WSS Papers.

6. Judson Smith (1837–1906), Congregational minister, was a candidate for president of Oberlin College in 1889. See letters of support from Thomas N. Chase from Atlanta University dated March 28, 1885; Judson Smith dated March 14, 1885, saying that he is willing to write to President Patton of Howard; Michael E. Strieby dated March 5, 1885; and M. L. D'Ooge dated March 2, 1885, box 8, Correspondence, Various Persons to WSS, folder 1881–1889, WSS Papers.

7. See Francis Grimké's letter about this dated June 16, 1885, box 8 Correspondence, Various Persons to WSS, folder 1881–1889, WSS Papers. Grimké mentioned in a postscript to his letter: "I have written an article on the subject of the reputation of colored men in colored institutions that I hope to see published in some

one of the papers or magazines." For more on the conflict between the white administration and African American faculty at Howard, see Francis Grimké, "Colored Men as Professors in Colored Institutions," *A.M.E. Church Review* 2 (1885): 142–48.

8. The successful applicant was Carlos A. Kenaston, husband of Lucy Fairchild and son-in-law of J. H. Fairchild. The vote was 11–6 against Scarborough. Kenaston did not distinguish himself in the field of classical studies.

9. Greener had been an instructor at and then dean of Howard University Law School (1877–1880). In June 1885 he was practicing law in Washington, D.C.

10. This is *First Lessons in Latin* by David Young Comstock (1852–n.d.), who taught at Phillips-Andover Academy. A notice of Scarborough's efforts is found in the *Cleveland Gazette,* December 27, 1884. For Scarborough's manuscript of *Questions on Latin Grammar,* see box 10, WSS Papers.

11. A summary of this paper is found in *Transactions of the American Philological Association* 16 (1885): xxxvi–xxxvii.

12. Scarborough wrote an obituary for Ward (1835–1916) published in the *Independent* 86 (September 11, 1916): 386–87. Ward was director of the Wolfe Archaeological Expedition in Babylonia from 1884 to 1885.

13. James Albert Harrison (1848–1911) was a professor and author of many books on literature. He presented a paper titled "Negro-English" at the American Philological Association Meeting in July 1885.

14. The American Dialect Society was founded in 1889.

15. William D. Whitney was the first president of the APA. He was at the forefront of Oriental and linguistic studies. He taught at Yale from 1854 to 1894.

16. Scarborough is listed with Whitney and Richardson in *Transactions of the American Philological Association* 16 (1885): xxx. Leonard W. Richardson (1853–1929), Episcopal clergyman and classicist, taught at New York State Normal College from 1895 to 1929.

17. Friedrich Max Müller (1823–1900) was a renowned philologist of Semitic and Indo-European languages at Oxford University. Whitney and Müller disagreed over the origin of language and Whitney disliked his methods. In "Darwinism and Language," *North American Review* 119 (July 1874): 61–88, Whitney declared Müller "careless of logical sequence and connection preferring to pour himself out, as it were, over his subject in a gush of genial assertion and interesting illustration." For more criticism, see Whitney, *Max Müller and the Science of Language* (New York: D. Appleton and Company, 1892).

18. From 1879 to 1882 Francis Andrew March (1825–1911), professor of English at Lafayette College in Easton, Pennsylvania, directed the volunteer readers of the *Oxford English Dictionary* in the United States. He pioneered the philological approach of teaching English like Greek and Latin and was among the first scholars in the United States to study English scientifically. He was twice president of the APA (1873–1874, 1895–1896). He was president of the MLA from 1891 to 1893.

19. *Murray's Dictionary* is another name for the *Oxford English Dictionary.* Sir James A. H. Murray (1837–1915) was its chief editor.

20. Charles Payson Gurley Scott (1853–1936) earned his doctorate at Lafayette College in 1878 with a dissertation on the laws of Alfred the Great in Anglo-Saxon.

21. The Spelling Reform Association was founded in 1876.

22. A summary of this paper is found in *Transactions of the American Philological Association* 17 (1886): vii. A notice about this is found in the *Cleveland Gazette,* July 17, 1886.

23. Johann Wilhelm Süvern's (1775–1829) book *Essay on the Birds of Aristophanes* was translated into English by William Hamilton and was published by Murray in London in 1835.

24. *The Birds of Aristophanes: A Theory of Interpretation* (Boston: J. H. Cushing, 1886). See a letter from Professor Charles Lanman of Harvard dated February 20, 1887, thanking Scarborough for sending a copy of *Birds* to him. Box 8, Correspondence, Various Persons to WSS, folder 1881–1889, WSS Papers.

25. Aaron Marshall Elliott (1844–1910) founded the MLA and the journal *Modern Language Notes.*

26. Wells College was founded in 1868 by Henry Wells in Aurora, New York. It is the oldest women's liberal arts college in the United States.

27. The American School of Classical Studies was founded by a consortium of colleges and universities in 1882. Scarborough corresponded with John Williams White (1849–1917), professor of Greek at Harvard and president of the Archaeological Institute of America (1897–1903) about the school, which Scarborough hoped to attend. White grew up in Ohio. See a letter from White to Scarborough dated March 8, 1886, Scarborough's draft of a letter to White dated March 8, 1886, and White's response dated March 16, 1886, box 8, Correspondence, Various Persons to WSS, folder 1881–1889, WSS Papers.

28. William J. Simmons (1849–1890), educator and clergyman, published *Men of Mark.*

29. I. Garland Penn (1867–1930), teacher, editor, and author, published *The Afro-American Press* (Springfield, MA: Willey and Co., 1891), for which Scarborough wrote a five-page introduction.

30. Summaries of these papers are found in *Transactions of the American Philological Association* 18 (1887): v–vi, xxxviii. The articles are "The Teaching of the Classical Languages IV, Ancipiti (Caesar's de Bello Gallico)," *Education* 8 (1888): 263–68, and "On Grote's Interpretation of Anelpistoi," *Education* 12 (January 1892): 286–93.

31. The *Anabasis* of Xenophon (ca. 428–ca. 354 B.C.), concerning an expedition of Greek mercenaries under Cyrus (580 B.C.–529 B.C.), the first Achaemenian king of Persia, was a common school text. Scarborough wanted to chart a new course with Andocides (ca. 440–ca. 390 B.C.). Andocides was a member of a distinguished Athenian family. He gave several noteworthy speeches, but their study has never been widespread in the United States. Scarborough had in his personal library W. J. Hickie's edition of *De Mysteriis* by Andocides (London: Macmillan, 1885). See "Private Library of W. S. Scarborough," box 13, p. 19, WSS Papers.

32. See Scarborough, "Xenophon, Andocides—Which?" *Journal of Education* 27 (May 17, 1888): 31, and his "Xenophon, Andocides, Cebes—Which?" *Journal of Education* 10 (September 20, 1888): 191. Cebes's *Tablet,* also know as Cebes's *Pinax,* is a work from Hellenistic times that has been traditionally misidentified with Cebes of Thebes, a pupil of Socrates. The work, an allegorical treatment dealing with ways

of living and the purposes of education, was popular in Europe from the fifteenth to the eighteenth centuries.

33. Peter Humphries Clark (1829–1926), politician and activist, was principal of the Colored High School in Cincinnati and an early proponent of socialism. Scarborough attacked Clark's support of the Democratic Party and its attempt to lure the black vote. See "Democrats Rewarding Peter Clark," *Cleveland Gazette,* March 29, 1884; "Professor Scarborough on Colored Democrats," *Cleveland Gazette,* June 21, 1884; and "Prof. Peter H. Clark Interviewed," *Washington Bee,* March 14, 1885.

CHAPTER XI: IN POLITICS AND MAGAZINES

1. James Boyle (1853–1939) came from England to Ohio in 1870. He was private secretary to Governor William McKinley from 1892 to 1896 and American consul to Liverpool from 1897 to 1905.

2. John A. Beaver (1837–1914), Civil War veteran, served as Republican governor of Pennsylvania from 1887 to 1891; Cyrus G. Luce (1824–1905) was a Republican governor of Michigan from 1887 to 1891; John Sherman was secretary of the treasury under President Hayes; James Peers Foster (1848–n.d.) was a lawyer trained at Columbia University; Charles Foster (1828–1904) was a Republican governor from 1880 to 1884 and later secretary of the treasury under President Harrison; Murat Halstead (1829–1909) joined the *Gazette* in 1853 and later became the majority stock owner; Benjamin Butterworth (1837–1898), Civil War veteran and lawyer, was Republican congressman from 1879 to 1883; William H. West (n.d.) was state attorney general for Ohio from 1866 to 1868 and a justice of the state supreme court from 1872 to 1873; William H. Gibson (1821–1894), commander of the Forty-Ninth Ohio Volunteers, was a well-known orator; and W. H. Smiley has not been identified.

3. Joseph B. Foraker, Civil War veteran and judge, was Republican governor of Ohio from 1886 to 1890 and U.S. senator from 1897 to 1909. Julia Bundy became Mrs. Foraker in 1870.

4. The *Toledo Blade* began in 1835.

5. This is Frederick Douglass, orator, journalist, and reformer. Cedar Hill on the Anacostia River was his home from 1877 to 1895. It was designated on February 12, 1988, as the Frederick Douglass National Historic Site and is open to visitors. Scarborough wrote the introduction to James M. Gregory's biography, *Frederick Douglass, the Orator* (Springfield, MA: Willey and Co, 1893). Later he gave a eulogy for Douglass at a memorial service held at Wilberforce University on March 9, 1895. See Gregory's letter to Scarborough dated March 29, 1893, asking him to write the book's introduction. Box 8, Correspondence, Various Persons to WSS, folder 1881–1889, WSS Papers. See Scarborough's article concerning honorary degrees given to McKinley and Douglass, "McKinley and Douglass," *Cleveland Gazette,* May 25, 1895.

6. Robert Smalls (1839–1915) was a congressman from Beaufort, South Carolina; Isaac S. Mullens's identity is not known; W. H. Johnson, president of Lincoln University, was among the founders of John Wesley African Methodist Episcopal Zion Church in 1849 in Washington, D.C.; P. B. S. Pinchback was a politician and businessman from New Orleans; Ferdinand L. Barnett (fl. 1880), attorney and publisher

in Chicago, was the husband of Ida B. Wells-Barnett (1862–1931); I. C. Wears (1822–1900), a cousin of Richard T. Greener, was a Republican politician from Philadelphia and president of the Statistical Association of the Colored People of Philadelphia; John W. Cromwell, lawyer, editor, and historian, was secretary of the American Negro Academy; James Mathew Townsend (1841–n.d.), principal of colored schools in Evansville, Indiana, was ordained bishop in 1871 and received an honorary D.D. from Wilberforce University in 1883; John R. Lynch, was a lawyer and congressman from Mississippi; Perry Carson (n.d.–1884) was a member of the delegation from the District of Columbia to the Republican National Convention in 1884.

7. No copy of the appeal seems to have survived.

8. Daniel Joseph Ryan (1855–1923).

9. Harry C. Smith was a member of the Ohio General Assembly from 1894 to 1898 and again from 1900 to 1902.

10. Pomeroy is a small town on the Ohio River thirty-eight miles southeast of Marietta. Ripley is in southwest Ohio forty-two miles from Cincinnati. Ripley was a famous stop on the Underground Railroad. It was the home of the fearless Presbyterian abolitionist Reverend John Rankin (1793–1886). For a study of him in Ripley, see Ann Hagedorn, *Beyond the River* (New York: Simon and Schuster, 2002). See letter from "C. Kurtz" of the Buckeye Paving Company, Columbus, Ohio, dated December 23, 1892, Correspondence, Various Persons to WSS, folder 1890–1899, WSS Papers.

11. George W. Cable (1844–1925) was a novelist and supporter of racial harmony. See Cable's correspondence regarding the Mohonk Conference dated March 21, 1890, advising Scarborough, if invited by host Albert K. Smiley (1828–1912), to attend. Box 8, Correspondence, Various Persons to WSS, folder 1890–1890, WSS Papers.

12. *Forum* was begun in New York in March 1886. The magazine was known for handling controversial issues.

13. *Frank Leslie's Weekly* was begun by Henry Carter (1821–1880).

14. Joseph Cook (1838–1901) graduated from Harvard in 1865 and Andover Theological Seminary in 1868. He founded *Our Day,* a review of reform, and ran it for seven years. He took an active part in the World's Parliament of Religions at the Columbian Exposition in Chicago in 1893. He received an LL.D. from Howard University in 1892. John A. Sleicher (1848–n.d.), Republican and journalist, took charge of *Leslie's Weekly* in 1889. From 1890 to 1893 he was editor-in-chief of the New York *Daily Mail & Express.* A piece Scarborough published about this time was "The Political Necessity of a Federal Election on Law," *Our Day* 6 (July 1890): 25–33.

15. This was "The Future of the Negro," *Forum* 7 (1889): 80–89.

16. This was "The Race Problem," *Arena* 2 (October 1890): 560–67. Benjamin Orange Flower (1858–1918), Christian Socialist, progressive, and proto-muckraker, was editor of *Arena* from 1889 to 1896. See Allen J. Matuson, "The Mind of Benjamin Orange Flower," *New England Quarterly* 34 (1961): 492–509. Wade Hampton (1818–1902), Confederate general and twice governor of South Carolina, was U.S. senator from South Carolina from 1879 to 1891. His article was "The Race Problem," *Arena* 2 (1890): 132–38. The volume also contains: Senator John Morgan, "The Race Question," *Arena* 2 (1890): 385–98; C. A. Seiders, "The Race Problem: A

Criticism of Senator Hampton's Paper," *Arena* 2 (1890): 633–35; and Professor N. S. Slater, "The African Element in America," *Arena* 2 (1890): 660–73. John Cabell Breckinridge (1821–1875), Democrat, soldier, and Confederate, was vice president from 1857 to 1861 under James Buchanan. His article was "The Race Question," *Arena* 2 (1890): 39–56.

17. Booker T. Washington was the leading spokesman for his race to white people.

18. The article was "The Future of the American Negro," *Annals of the American Academy of Political and Social Science* 16 (July–November 1900): 145–47.

19. Henry W. Blair (1834–1920), senator from New Hampshire, sponsored the Blair Bill for the support of black education. The bill failed amid much controversy.

20. Charles Read Baskervill (1872–1935), professor of English literature, taught at Vanderbilt from 1898 to 1899, later at the University of Texas, and then at the University of Chicago. It is hard to say with certainty who "Professor Smith" is. Perhaps this is Charles Alphonso Smith (1864–1924), who at this time was a professor of English language and literature at Louisiana State, serving from 1893 to 1902.

21. Selim H. Peabody (1829–1903) taught engineering and physics at the University of Illinois but was a strong advocate of classical education. He served as the school's regent from 1880 to 1891.

22. See correspondence in Scarborough's papers about items "too foul to print." Box 8, Correspondence, Various Persons to WSS, folder 1890–1899, WSS Papers.

23. Scarborough, "The Race Problem."

24. See "A Macon Negro's Piece," *Macon Telegraph,* March 21, 1901.

25. The meeting was held July 10–12 in Amherst, Massachusetts. A summary of the paper can be found in *Transactions of the American Philological Association* 19 (1888): xxxvi–xxxviii. It was published as "The Teaching of the Classical Languages VI: Observations on the Fourth Eclogue of Virgil," *Education* 10 (September 1889): 28–33.

26. See his "Notes on Andocides," *Transactions of the American Philological Association* 20 (1889): v–vi. Notice of his trip, "Twenty-first Annual Meeting," is found in the *Cleveland Gazette,* July 13, 1889.

27. William Watson Goodwin was professor of Greek at Harvard University and the first director of the American School in Athens. Augustus Chapman Merriam (1842–1895) was professor of archaeology and epigraphy at Columbia University.

28. Hampton Institute (now Hampton University) was founded in 1868 by Samuel C. Armstrong (1839–1893).

29. Douglass had resigned in June 1891. On this subject, see Padgett, "Diplomats to Haiti and Their Diplomacy," 265–30.

30. Blaine served as secretary of state under Presidents Garfield and Harrison.

31. John S. Durham (1861–1919), diplomat, lawyer, and journalist, served in Haiti from 1891 to 1893.

32. John Wannamaker (1838–1922), the well-known merchant, was made postmaster general under President Harrison in 1889.

33. Tanner's "paper" was the *Christian Recorder.*

34. Robert C. Ogden (1836–1913), a merchant and philanthropist from New York, was a trustee of both Hampton and Tuskegee.

35. Samuel C. Armstrong was principal of Hampton Institute and founder of the industrial education system.

36. Scarborough's articles in this journal include "Creole Folk-Tale," 25 (1896):186–88;"Folklore and Ethnology,"25 (1896):206;"The Negro and the Trades," 26 (1897): 26–27;"Our New Possessions," 29 (1900): 422–27;"The Negro as a Factor in Business,"30 (1901):455–59;"Henry Ossian Tanner,"31 (1902):661–70;"Alexander Dumas," 32 (1903): 313–17; "Daniel Alexander Payne," 33 (1904): 683–88; and "Alexander Sergeivitch Puskin," 33 (1904): 162–65; 234–36.

37. Printed in *Hampton Negro Conference* 3 (July 1899): 64–68.

38. Asa Bushnell (1834–1904) was the fortieth governor of Ohio (1896–1900). Judson Harmon (1846–1927), lawyer and judge, was Democratic governor of Ohio from 1909 to 1913.

39. See *Our Day* 6 (July 1890): 25–33.

40. See Scarborough, "The Race Problem." The piece called "Lawlessness vs. Lawlessness" appeared several years later in *Arena* 24 (1900): 478–83.

41. A version of Scarborough's paper,"The Negro Question from the Negro Point of View," was published in *Arena* 4 (July 1891): 219–22.

42. For information on this meeting, see Karl V. Nylander, *Orientalist-kongressen i Stockholm-Kristiania* (Upsala: Almquist and Wiksells, 1890).

43. The novel *Mr. Scarborough's Family* was written in 1881 by Anthony Trollope (1815–1882), serialized in 1882, and published in 1883 by Chatto and Windus in London. The novel is a study of avarice. As Mr. Scarborough, the wealthy owner of Tretton Park, is dying, those around him think about inheritance.

44. This is Axon, *The Story of a Noble Life: William Lloyd Garrison* (London: Partridge, 1890). See "Catalogue of Private Library of William Sanders Scarborough," box 13, WSS Papers, p. 89. See Axon's dedication.

45. William Huntington Tibbals was born in Union, New Jersey, in 1848 and died in an automobile accident on December 22, 1911, in Salt Lake City. See his student file in Alumni Records (RG 28), box 941, Oberlin College Archives.

46. See "The Scarborough Case," *Kansas City Times,* May 23, 1891, p. 5;"The Scarborough Incident," *Kansas City Star,* May 22, 1891, p. 4; "Rejected the Black Man—The Western Authors' and Artists' Club Draws the Color Line," *Kansas City Star,* May 22, 1891, p. 6.

47. Francis Landey Patton (1843–1932) was president of Princeton from 1888 to 1902.

48. Scarborough received an LL.D. from Liberia College in 1882.

49. The Society for the Encouragement of Arts, Manufactures and Commerce was begun in London in 1754.

50. Records of the Missouri Classical Association indicate no date of founding nor are there any lists of early membership.

51. The American Society for the Extension of University Teaching, first called the Philadelphia Society for the Extension of University Teaching, was founded by Edmund J. James (1855–1935), who was the first director of the Wharton School of Business at the University of Pennsylvania from 1883 to 1896.

52. Scarborough wrote the introduction to Wesley J. Gaines (1840–1912), *Twenty-Five Years of Freedom* (Atlanta: Franklin, 1890). Henry McNeal Turner had been in Macon when Scarborough was a child.

53. Scarborough seems to have annoyed Bishop Arnett, who had much influence at Wilberforce. See David Levering Lewis's account of this event in *W.E.B. DuBois: A Biography of a Race, 1869–1919* (New York: Holt, 1993), 152–53. Horace Talbert (1853–ca. 1910) was named to Scarborough's professorship in 1892. He was secretary of Wilberforce University from 1896 to 1915. Among his children was a set of twin boys whom he named Homer and Virgil. Talbert was succeeded by DuBois, who came to Wilberforce in 1894. Edward Clark took over when DuBois resigned in 1896.

CHAPTER XII: IN PAYNE SEMINARY AND AT A SOUTHERN UNIVERSITY

1. J.W.H.'s identity is not known.

2. John G. Mitchell was the brother of Samuel T. Mitchell, the first lay president of Wilberforce University. George W. Prioleau (1856–1927) was appointed professor of theology and homiletics in 1889 at Wilberforce. In 1890 he transferred to Payne Seminary. He resigned in 1894 to become a chaplain in the Ninth Cavalry of the U.S. Army. He was succeeded in his position at Wilberforce by George W. Woodson of Drew Seminary. See Tanner's letter to Scarborough dated October 20, 1891, in which he says that he "is talking you up for the *Recorder* editor." Box 8, Correspondence, Various Persons to WSS, folder 1890–1899, WSS Papers.

3. Her salary was a good one. Figures for the year 1903 in the *Sixteenth Annual Report of the Board of Trustees of Wilberforce University* show that she earned the second highest salary ($80 a month). The highest salary was $100 and it went to the superintendent, William A. Joiner.

4. Mrs. Scarborough compiled the material for Payne's books *Recollections* and *History of the African Methodist Episcopal Church,* ed. C. S. Smith (Nashville: A.M.E. Sunday School Union, 1891).

5. The meeting took place July 7–9. The summary of the paper titled "Bellerophon's Letters: *Iliad* VI, 168ff.," appeared in *Transactions of the American Philological Association* 22 (1891): l–liii. See "The American Philological Association—Its Meeting in Princeton," *Princeton Press,* July 11, 1891, p. 2. Scarborough is listed with his paper in the program. No mention of race was made. The manuscript (ten handwritten pages) is archived at Wilberforce University, Manuscripts, WSS Papers. William S. Tyler (1810–1897) was professor of Latin and Greek at Amherst College for fifty-six years.

6. Sir Arthur J. Evans (1851–1941) was a British archaeologist renowned for his discoveries at Knossos in Crete. He was curator of the Ashmolean Museum from 1884 to 1908.

7. These are: Thomas D. Seymour, *Life in the Homeric Age* (New York: Macmillan, 1914); James Baikie (1866–1931), *Sea Kings of Crete* (London: A. and C. Black, 910); Arthur J. Evans, *Scripta Minoa* (Oxford: Clarendon, 1909–1952); Henry Browne (1853–1941), *Handbook of Homeric Study* (London: Longmans, 1905).

8. Seymour, professor of Greek and an expert on Homer, taught at Western Reserve University and later at Yale.

9. Sir William Ridgeway (1853–1926), classical scholar, appointed professor of Greek at University College at Cork in 1883, moved on to a chair at Cambridge in 1892. He had an untiring interest in research and those carrying it out. He was knighted in 1919.

10. Charles Forster Smith (1852–1931) was a professor of Greek with an interest in Thucydides. He taught at the University of Wisconsin from 1894 to 1917. Smith was a student of Basil Gildersleeve at Johns Hopkins and a native Southerner. He taught at Vanderbilt University from 1882 to 1894.

11. For an application of this term meaning "troublesome," see S. B. Turner, "Of Several Principal 'Kickers' of the Late Springfield Ill., Colored Convention," *Cleveland Gazette,* November 14, 1885.

12. The Epworth League was begun in 1890 by the General Conference of the Methodist Church to benefit and uplift young people. Epworth was the birthplace in England of the founder of Methodism, John Wesley.

13. Ira T. Bryant was the first layman to be secretary-treasurer of the A.M.E. Sunday School Union. He was director of publications in Nashville from 1908 to 1936.

14. *Teachers' Quarterly* was one of five publications regularly issued by the Sunday School Union.

15. Reverend William D. Chappelle was the second secretary-treasurer of the A.M.E. Sunday School Union from 1900 to 1908. He succeeded Reverend Charles S. Smith, who served from 1882 to 1900.

16. Ira M. Price (1856–1939) earned a Ph.D. at Leipzig in 1887 and taught religious courses at the University of Chicago from 1892 to 1925. A note in the manuscript reads, "At his death in 1926, Doctor Scarborough had copy ready for [the] printer to [the] close of 1928."

17. An article with a different title by Scarborough, "Republicanism and the Force Bill," was published in *Republican Magazine,* November 1892.

18. See his "Race Legislation for Railways," *Our Day* 9 (July 1892): 478–85.

19. The West Virginia Colored Institute was a land-grant school founded in 1891 in Kanawha County. It is now West Virginia State College. The Peabody Educational Fund was founded by the wealthy philanthropist George Peabody (1795–1869). In 1867 he supported schools in the south for the common people. Control of the Peabody Fund was transferred to the Slater Fund. Both are now under the auspices of the Southern Education Foundation.

20. The American Association of Educators of Colored Youth was founded on March 27, 1890, as the result of a conference of educators of colored youth assembled by the Alumni Association of Howard University. The minutes for the meeting held in 1894 in Baltimore place "W. S. Scarborough of Ohio" under the board of directors. He is listed as giving a paper during the evening session on July 26 titled "Literary Activity of the Colored Race." See a letter from James Monroe Gregory dated October 15, 1891, inviting Scarborough to attend the next session in December ("we have not had the pleasure of you being at a meeting"). Box 8, Correspondence, Various Persons to WSS, folder 1890–1899, WSS Papers. See *Journal of the Proceedings of the American Association of Educators of Colored Youth* (Winston-Salem, NC, 1892).

21. The academy, founded in 1817, is the oldest scientific organization in New York.

22. The event was mentioned in "The Celebration: Professor W. S. Scarborough One of the Speakers," *Cleveland Gazette,* October 1, 1892.

23. Scarborough lists Kentucky State, but in fact the school was the State University at Louisville. The diploma reads, "Procuratores Universitatis Respublicae in Urbe Louisvilliensi Kentuckiensi, June 1892, James A. Garnett, Praeses, Charles F. Sneed, Decanus." See box 2, WSS Papers.

24. The *Cleveland Gazette,* November 13, 1892, gives a summary of Scarborough's article, "Republicanism and the Force Bill."

25. Walter Hines Page (1855–1918), North Carolina–born journalist and diplomat, held a fellowship for two years at Johns Hopkins University to study Latin and Greek under the tutelage of the arch-Southerner Basil Gildersleeve (1831–1924) before turning to his life's work as an editor of the *Forum, Atlantic Monthly,* and *World's Work* (he founded the latter). He was ambassador to Great Britain from 1913 to 1918. His 1902 *Rebuilding of Old Commonwealths* (New York: AMS, 1970), 132–33, provides this anecdote:

> One morning I went to a school for the Negroes and I heard a very black boy trans-
> late a passage from Xenophon. His teacher was also a full-blooded Negro. It hap-
> pened that I went straight from the school to a club where I encountered a group
> of gentlemen discussing the limitations of the African mind. "Teach 'em Greek!"
> said old judge So-and-so. Now a nigger could learn the Greek alphabet by rote, but
> he could never intelligently construe a passage from any Greek writer–impossible!
> I told him what I had just heard. "Read it? understood it? was black? a black man
> teaching him? I beg your pardon, but do you read Greek yourself?" "Sir," said he at
> last, "I do not for a moment doubt your word. I know you think the nigger read
> Greek; but you were deceived. I shouldn't believe it if I saw it with my own eyes
> and heard it with my own ears."

26. The meeting took place July 12–14, 1892. Faculty from the University of Virginia who participated in this meeting were Milton Wylie Humphreys (1844–1928) who was president of the American Philological Association from 1882 to 1883 and had served in the Confederate Army, James Mercer Garnet (1840–1926) who was president of the American Philological Association from 1893 to 1894, William Gardner Hale (1849–1928), Savannah-born classicist who was professor and head of Latin at the University of Chicago from 1892 to 1919, and Robert Somerville Radford (1869–1936), then instructor at the University of Virginia, who had earned a Ph.D. in classics at the Univeristy of Virginia in 1891 and another at Johns Hopkins in 1895. Radford gave two papers, but his name is not listed among the list of atten-dees. Thirty five members were present and James M. Garnett was chairman of the local committee. For these details see *Transactions of the American Philosophical Association* 23 (1892) vii–xiii and xxxix. Scarborough had published in 1887 an article on Hale's book *The Art of Reading Latin: How to Teach It* (Boston: Ginn & Company, 1887). See W. S. Scarborough, "Hale on the Art of Reading Latin," *Education* 8 (1887): 198–202. Scarborough's pamphlet, *The Birds of Aristophanes* (Boston: J. H. Cushing, 1886), is held by the Alderman Library at the University of Virginia catalogued under the rubric "classical pamphlets."

27. The paper, "The Chronological Order of Plato's Dialogues," can be found in *Transactions of the American Philological Association* 23 (1892): vi–viii. A later version of the paper appeared in *Education* 14 (December 1893): 213–18.

28. The challenge of John C. Calhoun (1782–1850), politician from South Carolina, was widely known.

29. Jefferson Davis (1808–1889) was an excellent student of Greek at Transylvania University in Lexington, Kentucky, from 1823 to 1824.

30. This may be her work, "Yellow Chrysanthemums," *Frank Leslie's Weekly* 77 (November 23, 1893), n.p.

31. Bartlett Arkell (1862–1946) was the first president of the Beech-Nut Packing Company and founder of the Canajoharie Library and Art Gallery.

CHAPTER XIII: AT THE WORLD'S CONGRESS AUXILIARY OF THE COLUMBIAN EXPOSITION

1. See Scarborough's article on the Congress, "The Negro Problem," *Frank Leslie's Weekly,* September 28, 1893, p. 206.

2. Joseph-Edmond Roy (1858–1913) sent a letter dated July 13, 1893, asking if Scarborough would come to Chicago. Box 8, Correspondence, Various Persons to WSS, folder 1890–1899, WSS Papers.

3. See Frederic Perry Noble, "Africa at the Columbian Exposition," *Our Day* 9 (November 1892): 773–89. Noble was assistant librarian at the Newberry Library from 1891 to 1893.

4. Robert Needham Cust (1821–1909), an Orientalist with extensive service in India until 1867, published more than fifty volumes on Oriental philology and religious beliefs.

5. These are *A Sketch of the Modern Languages of Africa Rediviva* (London: Trübner, 1883) and *Africa Rediviva, or The Occupation of Africa by Christian Missionaries of Europe and North America* (London: E. Stock, 1891).

6. Archibald H. Sayce (1845–1933) authored and coauthored many volumes on the Near East, among them *The Ancient Empires of the East* (London: MacMillan, 1884).

7. Lewis Grout (1815–1905) wrote *Zulu-Land* (Philadelphia: Presbyterian Publishing, 1864); George M. Ebers (1837–1898) was the author of many works of fiction and history; Yakub Artin Pasha (1842–1919) wrote a book on education, *L'instruction publique en Égypte* (Paris: E. Leroux, 1890); Abigail M. H. Christensen, *Afro-American Folklore* (Boston: J. G. Cupples, 1892); Jeremiah E. Rankin (1828–1904), Congregational clergyman, was president of Howard University from 1889 to 1903.

8. See his "Function and Future of Foreign Languages in Africa," *Methodist Review* 76 (November–December 1894): 890–99.

9. John Thomas Jenifer (1835–1919), A.M.E. bishop and church historiographer, was a close friend of Frederick Douglass. He preached a sermon at his funeral.

10. Mary French-Sheldon (1848–1936), born in Pittsburgh, was a "Victorian lady traveler." She made her first trip to East Africa in 1891.

11. See Richard H. Seager, ed., *Dawn of Religious Pluralism: Voices from the World's Parliament on Religions, 1893* (La Salle, IL: Open Court, 1993). Scarborough

wrote the introduction to Tanner's book, *The Color of Solomon, What?* (Philadelphia: A.M.E. Book Concern, 1895). See Tanner's letter to Scarborough dated March 12, 1895, asking him to write the introduction, box 8, Correspondence, Various Persons to WSS, folder 1890–1899, WSS Papers.

12. The auxiliary conducted 224 congresses. See David J. Bertuca, ed., *The World's Columbian Exposition* (Westport, CT: Greenwood, 1996).

13. The meeting took place July 11–13. The paper, "Hunc Inventum Inveni (Plautus, *Captivi* 442)," can be found in *Transactions of the American Philological Association* 24 (1893): xvi–xix.

14. Paul Laurence Dunbar came from Dayton, Ohio, not far from Wilberforce. Howells was also an Ohioan.

15. Héli Chatelain (1859–1908) was the author of *Folktales from Angola* (Boston: Houghton Mifflin, 1894), and *Kimbundu Grammar* (Ridgewood, NJ: Gregg Press, 1964), whose introduction was written by Robert Needham Cust.

16. French-Sheldon was the author of *Sultan to Sultan: Adventures among the Masai and Other Tribes of East Africa* (Boston: Arena, 1892). Scarborough's copy is owned by the National Afro-American Museum and Cultural Center, Wilberforce, Ohio, a gift of Sarah A. Grant.

CHAPTER XIV: FRIENDS AND HELPERS—DEATHS

1. Hollis Burke Frissell (1851–1917) was principal of Hampton Institute from 1893 to 1918.

2. J. C. Price (1854–1893) helped establish Livingstone College in North Carolina.

3. These are "Bishop Payne as an Educator," *Christian Recorder* 41 (January 25, 1894), front page, and "The Late Daniel A. Payne, D.D., Senior Bishop of the A.M.E. Church," *Independent* 45 (December 28, 1893), 5–6. Scarborough also wrote "The Late Bishop Daniel A. Payne, D.D.," *Frank Leslie's Weekly,* January 11, 1894, p. 23.

4. Wilbur Patterson Thirkhield (1854–1936), bishop of the A.M.E. Church, was the first president of Gammon Theological Seminary from 1883 to 1900 and general secretary of the Epworth League in 1899.

5. This occurred during President Cleveland's second term.

6. John Hanks Alexander (1864–1894) enrolled at Oberlin in 1882. In 1883 he was tendered an appointment to West Point as an alternate from the 14th Congressional District. The efforts of President S. T. Mitchell with the War Department brought him assignment to Wilberforce in January 1894. See Alexander's letter dated January 19, 1894, from Fort Robinson, Nebraska, to Scarborough, box 8, Correspondence, Various Persons to WSS, folder 1881–1889, WSS Papers. See also a brief article on his excellent examinations in 1883 among the "codfish aristocracy": "We Will Not Down," *People's Advocate,* July 7, 1883, p. 2.

7. Morrison R. Waite (1816–1888), Ohio State representative, was Chief Justice of the Supreme Court from 1874 to 1888.

8. Samuel T. Mitchell was president then.

9. See Lieutenant C. D. Rhodes's letter to Scarborough, March 28, 1894, box 8, Correspondence, Various Persons to WSS, folder 1890–1899, WSS Papers.

10. James Biddle (1832–1922) died with the rank of brigadier general and is buried in Arlington Cemetery.

11. These were Henry Flipper, John Alexander, and Charles Young. See Scarborough's articles "The Negro as an Army Officer," *Christian Register,* August 18, 1898, pp. 933–34, and "From Spade to Sword," *Christian Register,* February 23, 1899, pp. 207–08.

12. Young (1864–1922) died in Nigeria on a mission for the State Department in January 1922. See Scarborough, *A Tribute to Colonel Young* (Philadelphia: A.M.E. Book Concern, 1922).

13. Right Reverend Samuel M. Fallows was president of the Illinois Commission on the Half-Century Anniversary of Negro Freedom.

14. John Greenleaf Whittier (1807–1892), the Massachusetts-born Quaker and poet, was a keen abolitionist. See a clipping from August 1917, no source attributed, announcing that Scarborough was one of the speakers expected to make an address, "A Four-Fold Centenary, Niagara Conference to Celebrate Abolition of Slave Trade and Births of Whittier, Longfellow, and Agassiz." Box 1, WSS Papers.

15. The Chautauqua Literary and Scientific Association was founded in 1878. Chapters of this group sprang up across the country.

16. "Professor Atkins" has not been identified. In 1893 the group had met in Atlantic City, New Jersey.

17. The meeting took place July 10–12, 1894. See two notes from Woodmansee in June 1894, box 8, Correspondence, Various Persons to WSS, folder 1890–1899, WSS Papers.

18. See Scarborough, "McKinley and Douglass," for details.

19. A summary of the paper titled "Cena, Deipnon, Prandium, Ariston," can be found in *Transactions of the American Philological Association* 25 (1894): xxiii–xxv.

20. Scarborough means here perhaps his essay, "The Roman Cena," *A.M.E. Church Review* 10 (1894): 348–57, and not the journal *Education.*

21. Mount Greylock in Lanesborough, Massachusetts, is 3,491 feet high.

22. The identity of Miss Bascom is not known.

23. James A. Garfield (1831–1881), twentieth U.S. president, had trained to be a teacher of the classics.

24. Mark Hopkins (1802–1887), the famous educator, was president of Williams College in Massachusetts from 1836 to 1872.

25. Whitney died on June 7, 1894, in New Haven, Connecticut.

26. A special session was held in Philadelphia, December 27–28, 1894, during which a memorial assembly was held on Friday, December 28 at 8:00 p.m. for Whitney. No list of attendees was published by *Transactions of the American Philological Association*. On this session, see *Whitney Memorial Meeting: A Report,* ed. C. R. Lanman (Boston: Ginn and Co., 1897).

27. See Talcott Williams (1849–1928), *Historical Survivals in Morocco* (New York: American Historical Association, 1890), and *Turkey: A World Problem of Today* (Garden City, NY: Doubleday, 1922).

28. Douglass died in Washington, D.C., on February 20, 1895.

29. Based in Albion, Michigan, the bureau was an interdenominational group "established in the interest of young Christians of America." The president at the

time was Reverend Washington Gardner. See the letter of invitation dated January 7, 1893, from E. F. Voorhees, secretary of the Albion International Young People's Lecture Bureau, box 8, Correspondence, Various Persons to WSS, folder 1890–1899, WSS Papers.

30. The meeting took place July 9–11, 1895. A paper, "The Languages of Africa," along with this parenthetical notice, "(no abstract if this paper has been received)," is listed in *Transactions of the American Philological Association* 25 (1895): xi.

31. Samuel Mather (1851–1931), industrialist and philanthropist, was upon his death the richest man in Ohio. His wife dedicated herself to religious, educational, and social reform activities.

32. Samuel Mather, *In Memoriam, Flora Stone Mather, 1852–1909* (Cleveland: Arthur H. Clark, 1910).

33. An act passed on March 19, 1887, by the Ohio legislature established the Combined Normal and Industrial Department [C.N.&I.], which was to be supported with state funds.

34. This may be Joseph P. Shorter (1845–1910), professor of mathematics, who became superintendent of the C. N. & I. Department in 1892 and served until his death.

35. This is William Albert Galloway (1860–1931). Shorter was said to have had disagreements with him.

36. These are "Folklore and Ethnology," *Southern Workman* 25 (October 1896): 206, and "Negro Folk-lore and Dialect," *Arena* 17 (January 1897): 186–92.

37. The meeting took place July 7–9. A summary of Scarborough's paper, "Notes on the Function of Modern Languages in Africa," can be found in *Transactions of the American Philological Association* 27 (1896): xvi–xix.

38. Harold North Fowler (1859–1955), archaeologist and classical philologist, spent most of his career at Western Reserve University from 1893 to 1929. He was the first student of the American School at Athens from 1882 to 1883.

CHAPTER XV: BACK TO THE CLASSICAL PROFESSORSHIP AND A VICE PRESIDENCY

1. See *Journal of the Twentieth Quadrennial Session of the General Conference of the African Methodist Episcopal Church* (Philadelphia: A.M.E. Publishing, 1896).

2. This is John Henry Murphy (1840–1922), editor and publisher of the newspaper *Baltimore Afro-American*.

3. This is likely W.E.B. DuBois (1868–1963), who taught Greek at Wilberforce from 1894 to 1896. An account of his experience at Wilberforce can be found in Lewis, *W.E.B. DuBois,* 151–54.

4. Scarborough takes care to mention throughout his narrative his hotel accommodations and his lack of them as well giving name, date, place, and occasion.

5. Elmer Dover (1873–n.d.), newspaper reporter, editor, and U.S. senator, was secretary to the politician Mark Hanna (1837–1904) from 1897 to 1904.

6. Myron Herrick (1854–1929), Cleveland-based politician and lawyer, was the governor of Ohio from 1904 to 1906.

7. Edward Arkell has not been identified.

8. Campbell L. Maxwell (n.d.) was consul to Santo Domingo under President Harrison and again under President McKinley.

9. William Frank Powell (1848–1920), an African American from New Jersey, was minister to Haiti from 1897 to 1905 under President McKinley. Henry Watson Furness (1868–1955), an African American from Indianapolis, was minister to Haiti from 1905 to 1913 under President Roosevelt. Letters to Roosevelt from Scarborough from 1909 to 1911 about an appointment to an investigatory commission to Liberia and again to Haiti are held by the National Archives, Records Group 59, General Records of the Department of State, Applications and Recommendations for Appointment to Consular and Diplomatic Services, 1910 to 1924.

10. This is perhaps Ralph Waldo Tyler (1859–1921), war correspondent and political appointee under Roosevelt, who was from Columbus, Ohio. It could also be Richard T. Greener.

11. This was "Negro Folk-lore and Dialect," *Arena* (December, 1896) 186–92.

12. See Alfred Moss, *The American Negro Academy* (Baton Rouge: Louisiana State University Press, 1981).

13. This was *The Educated Negro and His Mission: Occasional Paper 8* (Washington, D.C.: The Academy, 1903).

14. John Williams White to Scarborough, March 29, 1898, box 8, Correspondence, Various Persons to WSS, folder 1890–1899, WSS Papers. With Charles Eliot Norton (1827–1908), professor of art history at Harvard, and William Watson Goodwin he founded the Archaeological Institute of America in 1879. He was president of the group from 1897 to 1903. White told Scarborough, "[I]t would be pleasant for Dr. Fowler to have you become a member of the Cleveland Chapter." Fowler is Harold North Fowler.

15. Francis W. Kelsey (1858–1927) worked for thirty-eight years to establish the classics department at the University of Michigan as a center for papyrological research.

16. The meeting took place July 5–7, 1898. Mrs. Scarborough's work on Alphonse Lamartine (1790–1869) was noted in "Golden Opportunity," *Cleveland Gazette,* December 1, 1881. For an excerpt see Paula Bernat Bennett, ed., *Nineteenth-Century American Poets* (Malden, MA: Blackwell, 1998), 481–83, who notes that "Scarborough's translation of Lamartine suggests she was an accomplished poet as well as linguist." Scarborough's literary papers are held by the Western Reserve Historical Society, Cleveland, Ohio.

17. See Scarborough's speech, "The Party of Freedom and the Freedom— A Reciprocal Duty," *Masterpieces of Negro Eloquence,* ed. Alice Dunbar (New York: Bookery, 1914), 219–26.

18. The identity of Mr. B. is not known. It may be Asa Bushnell.

19. Robert Nevin and C. W. Raymond have not been identified. Cushman K. Davis (1838–1900), politician and lawyer, was governor of Minnesota from 1874 to 1876. W. O. Bradley (1847–1914), lawyer, was governor of Kentucky from 1895 to 1899.

20. The meeting took place July 5–7. A summary of the paper can be found in *Transactions of the American Philological Association* 30 (1899): v–vi.

21. The article is "Booker T. Washington and His Work," *Education* 20 (1900): 270.

22. This was Wilberforce's fourth president, Samuel T. Mitchell.

23. The hotel was located on McMillan Street in East Walnut Hills.

24. This is the Republican Harry Clay Smith, who established the *Cleveland Gazette* in 1882.

25. Gibson House, a grand hotel, opened in the 1870s.

26. See Ronnick, "William Sanders Scarborough: The First African American Member of the Modern Language Association," 1781–93.

27. This was in June 1884.

28. Williams Pickens (1881–1954), the NAACP activist, met Scarborough while traveling in the summer of 1900 on a fund-raising campaign for Talladega College. Pickens transferred to Yale in 1902 and graduated from Yale in 1904, the second black to join Yale's chapter of Phi Beta Kappa. In his autobiography, *The Heir of Slaves* (Bloomington: Indiana University Press, 1991), 32–33, he describes the occasion:

> It was Commencement time when we reached Oberlin, and the class of 1875 was celebrating its twenty-fifth anniversary. Professor Scarborough of Wilberforce University, the Negro scholar who is a member of this class, was present at an impromptu parlor entertainment by the five boys of the party, and he so much liked a recitation which I combined from Spartacus to the Gladiators and The Christian Gladiator that when we parted he gave me in the act of handshaking a silver half dollar. I noticed what he did not notice, that the coin bore the date of "1875," the year of his class—and I have it now, black with age and nonuse in my purse.

29. Joshua H. Jones (1856–1932) was Wilberforce's fifth president, serving from 1900 to 1908.

30. James S. Metcalfe (1858–1927) was an editor, publisher, and drama critic in New York.

31. The summer meeting took place July 3–5. The special session took place December 27–29. It was a business meeting held purposively to coincide with the Fourth International Congress of Classical Studies.

32. The first paper, "Iphigenia in Euripides and Racine," can be found in *Transactions of the American Philological Association* 29 (1891): lviii–lx. The second paper, "Iphigenia in Euripides, Racine and Goethe," can be found in the same journal, 32 (1901): xxxvii–xxxix.

33. "One Heroine—Three Poets, Part I," *Education* 19 (December 1898): 213–21, and "One Heroine—Three Poets, Part II," *Education* 20 (January 1899): 285–93.

34. John Wesley Gilbert (ca. 1865–1923) was the first of his race to attend the American School in Athens. This he did in 1890 to 1891 after finishing his M.A. at Brown University. See Ronnick, "John Wesley Gilbert," *Classical Outlook* 78 (2001): 113–14.

35. The society was established in 1883.

36. The article was "The Future of the American Negro," *Annals of the American Academy of Political and Social Science* 16 (July–November 1900): 145–47. See also a letter from the *Annals of the American Academy of Political and Social Science* dated May 27, 1901, asking for a seven-hundred-word review of Washington's *Up from Slavery*. Box 8, Correspondence, Various Persons to WSS, folder 1900–1909, WSS Papers.

37. The meeting took place July 9–11. A summary of the paper, "Brief Notes on Thucydides," can be found in *Transactions of the American Philological Association* 32 (1901): lxxix.

38. John Henry Wright, a member of the first faculty at Ohio State University, was professor of Greek and then a dean at Harvard from 1897 to 1908.

39. See Exodus 1:8 for the phrase "there arose a king in Egypt who knew not Joseph."

40. The Barber Institute was located in Alabama. For information on the cottage and for photos of Margaret M. Barber, her husband, Phineas M. Barber, and the Anderson family, see Anderson, *Presbyterianism,* 44–45, 250–52, and plates facing pp. 48, 128, 131, 240.

41. Mrs. Anderson was Caroline Virginia Still Wiley Anderson (1848–1919). She studied at Oberlin College and Howard University. In August 1880 she married Matthew Anderson, her second husband.

42. This is possibly Charles M. Wiley, the first black postmaster of Columbia, South Carolina. He is buried in Randolph Cemetery.

43. See a related letter by Scarborough, "Color Line Question in London," *New York Times,* July 28, 1902, p. 8, col. 6.

44. This is James Newbury Fitzgerald (1837–1907). He was elected a bishop in 1888. He was co-author of a book of hymns, *Ocean Grove Songs* (n.p.: n.d.).

CHAPTER XVI: FIRST EUROPEAN TRIP

1. The delegates were Bishops Gaines, B. T. Tanner, B. W. Arnett, M. B. Salter, W. B. Derrick, Evans Tyree, and C. S. Smith; Reverends J. E. Edwards, L. H. Evans, P. A. Hubbard, John Hurst, T. H. Jackson, J. Albert Johnson, E. W. Lee, and Reverdy Ransom; and Professors H. T. Kealing and William Scarborough.

2. Samuel Cunard's (1784–1865) luxury liner, *Campania,* was in service from 1839 to 1918. Known for speed, the vessel could carry two thousand passengers.

3. See Scarborough's account of this trip, "From the Thames to the Tiber," *Voice of the Negro* 1 (1904): 466–75.

4. Tanner settled in Paris with his wife and son in 1891.

5. The painting was the *Raising of Lazarus* purchased by the French government for the Luxembourg Gallery, which Scarborough called the "gateway to the Louvre" in his article, "Henry Ossian [*sic*] Tanner," *Southern Workman* 31 (1902): 661–70.

6. This is Jean Joseph Benjamin Constant (1767–1830).

7. Mihaly Munkacsy (1844–1900) was the leading Hungarian artist of the nineteenth century.

8. Scarborough's reference here is unknown.

9. This comes from lines 9–12 of Joseph Addison's (1672–1719) "A Letter from Italy" (1703) to Charles, Lord Halifax.

For wheresoe'er I turn my ravish'd eyes,
Gay gilded scenes and shining prospects rise,

Poetic fields encompass me around,
And still I seem to tread on classic ground.

10. This is the phrase "Hannibal ad portam."

11. The excavations in the Roman Forum at that time were under the super-vision of Rudolf Amedeo Lanciani (1847–1929), who was in charge of all excava-tions within the city of Rome.

12. Mary Sheldon Barnes (1850–1898) was the first female professor at Stanford University. Prior to that she taught at Wellesley and at her father's school, the Oswego State Normal and Training School in upstate New York. There she taught classical languages and history from 1874 to 1876 and from 1882 to 1884.

13. The traditional epitaph is: *Mantua me genuit Calabri rapuere tenet nunc / Parthenope; cecini pascua, rura, duces.*

14. Scarborough's reference here to Holmes is unknown.

15. The citation in the *New York Herald* has not been located.

16. Harry Richardson has not been identified. Scarborough describes the incident and mentions Richardson with no further details on page 348 in his article "English Principle vs. American Prejudice," *Voice of the Negro* (1906): 347–49.

17. The citation in the *London Chronicle* has not been located.

18. Baroness Angela Burdett-Coutts (1823–1906), philanthropist, was one of the richest heiresses in England. Her husband, William Ashmead-Bartlett (1851–1921), assumed her name upon their marriage in 1881. The "secretary" must have been her husband's nephew Ellis Ashmead-Bartlett (1881–1931), for he was liv-ing with them in London in 1901. See a note from her at 1 Stratton Street, London, dated May 4, 1903, box 8, Correspondence, Various Persons to WSS, folder 1900–1909, WSS Papers.

19. John Scott Lidgett (1854–1953), British social worker, was committed to educational and social reforms. He was vice chancellor of the University of London from 1912 to 1932. See a short letter from him dated January 5, 1903, box 8, Correspondence, Various Persons to WSS, folder 1900–1909, WSS Papers.

20. The full program of papers as well as the dinner program and seating arrangement at the Hotel Cecil on September 13, 1921, can be found on microfilm roll 4, Charles Spencer Smith Collection, Bentley Historical Collection, University of Michigan, Ann Arbor (hereafter BHR).

21. Hightower T. Kealing (1860–1918), editor and teacher, was managing editor of the *A.M.E. Church Review* from 1896 to 1912.

22. Details about Mrs. Kendall Clark are not known.

23. The Portman Rooms on Baker Street were used for public lectures in the early twentieth century.

24. For details on the life of Sir Robert Perks, Baronet (1849–1934), see his autobiography, *Sir Robert Williams Perks, Baronet* (London: Epworth Press, 1936). See an undated letter in tatters from him at 11 Kensington Palace Gardens, London, to Scarborough, box 3, Correspondence, WSS Papers.

25. William McKinley (1873–1901) was shot twice by Leon Czolgosz, a twenty-eight-year-old factory worker from Cleveland, at the Pan-American Exhibition in Buffalo on September 6, 1901. McKinley died a few days later. Czolgosz

died in the electric chair on October 29, 1901. Queen Victoria (1819–1901) died January 22, 1901, after a reign of sixty-three years.

26. "Mr. N." is Edward Williams Bryon Nicholson (1849–1912). He was chief librarian from 1881 until his death in 1912. What Scarborough saw was Duke Humfry's Library, the oldest and still the chief reading room in the Bodleian. Scarborough's essay, *The Educated Negro and His Mission* (Washington, DC: American Negro Academy, 1903), is still listed in the library's catalog as part of the collection.

27. St. Mary's Church dates back to the eleventh century. John Wycliffe (ca. 1320–1384), who translated the Bible into English and was later accused of heresy, was once rector. Thomas Cranmer (1489–1556), the archbishop of Canterbury, refused to acknowledge in public at St. Mary's a recantation he had made in private. He was burned at the stake on March 21, 1556.

28. John Wesley (1703–1791) and his brother Charles (1707–1788) were the founders of Methodism. John graduated from Christ Church, Oxford, in 1724 and was a fellow of Lincoln College from 1726 to 1735. Charles, who graduated from Christ Church, Oxford, in 1730, became famous for his hymns.

29. Nicholas Ridley (ca. 1503–1555), a scholar of Greek and Latin, was a spokesman for the Protestants. He and Hugh Latimer (ca. 1491–1555), bishop of Worcester and reformer of the Church of England, were burned at the stake on October 16, 1555.

30. The four colleges open to women at Oxford at that time were: Lady Margaret Hall (1878), Sumerville (1879), St. Hughs (1886), and St. Hildas (1893). Women were not admitted to degrees until 1920.

31. Axon wrote several treatises on vegetarianism. See, for example, his edition of Percy Bysshe Shelley's *Vindication of Natural Diet* (Manchester: J. Heywood, 1884), *Sixty Years of the Vegetarian Society* (Manchester: Vegetarian Society, 1907).

32. This is, perhaps, Sir John James Harwood (1832–1906), who wrote several books about Manchester, England.

33. See Scarborough's narrative, "In and around Edinburgh," *Voice of the Negro* 2 (1905): 548–55.

34. Miss Darling has not been identified. She is perhaps related to the subject of a volume in Scarborough's private library titled *James Darling, A Memorial Sketch* (Edinburgh: A. Eliot, 1891). See "Catalogue of the Private Library of William Sanders Scarborough," box 13, WSS papers, p.4.

35. This is, perhaps, John Ritchie (1882–n.d.), Fellow of the Royal Astronomical Society.

36. James Graham Montrose (1612–1651), Scottish nobleman, fifth Earl of Montrose, was imprisoned from 1640 to 1641 by Archibald Campbell, Eighth Earl of Argyll. On May 21, 1651, he was hanged, drawn, and quartered.

37. John Knox (ca. 1514–1572), Scottish reformer and Protestant preacher, had an open break with Queen Mary in 1561.

38. This may be a reference to the famous series of readers designed by William Holmes McGuffey (1800–1873). McGuffey's *Fifth Eclectic Reader* does not contain any title with the word "Maida," however.

39. William Blackwood III (1836–1912) was editor and manager of *Blackwood's Magazine* at that time.

CHAPTER XVII: MISCELLANEOUS ACTIVITIES

1. The SS *Umbria* was launched in 1884 and saw military service in 1885 and 1900–1901. She was scrapped in 1910.

2. The Afro-American League was begun on January 25, 1890, by Thomas Fortune. The organization was revived as the National Afro-American Council in 1898 and remained active until 1906.

3. A. Kirkland Soga was the first black to be ordained a minister in South Africa. He was the first editor of *Izwi Labantu,* a newspaper from East London financed by Cecil John Rhodes that was published from 1897 to 1909.

4. Scarborough has the wrong title. The pamphlet's title is *Call the Black Man to Conference* (East London, South Africa: n.p., n.d.)

5. The first Pan African Conference, organized by Henry S. Williams (1869–1911), was held in July 1900 in London.

6. Scarborough's reference here is not clear; there was no *Ethiopian Review* at this time.

7. William Copley Winslow (1840–1925), Boston clergyman and archaeologist, founded the American branch of the Egyptian Exploration Fund. In 1885 he became its vice president and in 1889 its honorary secretary.

8. The meeting was a special session held December 27–29. It was sponsored by the Congress of Philological and Archaeological Societies, consisting of the Archaeological Institute of America and the American Philological Association.

9. Horace Bumstead (1841–1919), Congregational minister and educator, was professor of Latin at Atlanta University from 1880 to 1896 and president from 1888 to 1907.

10. The American Folklore Society was founded in 1888. Scarborough noted this meeting among his lectures, but lists December and not July. See box 3, Manuscript, Bibliography, p. 4, WSS Papers.

11. The Boston Literary and Historical Society was organized in 1901 by Francis Grimké and William Trotter, which was a forum for black intellectuals, especially those who opposed Booker T. Washington.

12. See Scarborough, "The Negro and Our New Possessions," *Forum* 31 (May 1901): 341–49.

13. See his essays, "The Negro's Duty to Himself," *Hampton Negro Conference* 4 (July 1900): 51–55, and "The Negro as a Factor in Business," *Southern Workman* 29 (July 1900): 422–27.

14. See Scarborough, "The Negro and Higher Learning," *Forum* 33 (May 1902): 349–55.

15. The meeting was held July 8–10, 1902.

16. Katherine Abbott Sanborn (1839–1917), writer, teacher, and lecturer, was the daughter of Edwin Sanborn (1808–1885), who was a professor of Latin and later of Anglo-Saxon at Dartmouth College from 1837 to 1882.

17. Sihler did mention Scarborough and a list of other American scholars in "Klassiche Studien und Klassischer Unterricht in den Vereinigten Staaten," *Neue Jahrbücher für Pedgogic* 10 (1902): 515.

18. The citation from the *London Daily Chronicle* has not been found.

19. The meeting was held July 13–15, 1886.

20. Hotel Hollenden, once Cleveland's finest hotel, opened on June 7, 1885. George A. Meyers (1859–1930), an African American Republican, owned the hotel barbershop from 1888 to 1930, which was a center for political activity. See the letter of invitation dated March 7, 1904, from R. R. Wright asking Scarborough to come to Baltimore (April 5–7) and speak about the Negro college. Box 8, Correspondence, Various Persons to WSS, folder 1900–1909, WSS Papers.

21. The chapel takes its name from William Paul Quinn (1788–1873), the fourth bishop of the A.M.E. Church.

22. This is Simon Newcomb (1835–1909), celebrated scientist, astronomer, and mathematician.

23. Albert Broadbent (1867–1912) was the secretary of the Manchester Vegetarian Society and the author of several books on the topic. Guido Biagi (1855–1925) was head of the Laurentian and Riccardian libraries at Florence. He startled audiences in St. Louis by forecasting that in the twentieth century people will prefer listening to books rather than reading them.

24. The meeting was held September 16–19, 1904.

25. James Thomas Hefflin (1869–1951), Alabama lawyer, served in the U.S. House of Representatives from 1904 to 1920 and in the Senate from 1920 to 1931. Washington dined with Roosevelt at the White House in October 1901.

26. The Brownsville Affair occurred at Fort Brown, Texas, in 1906 when 167 African American men in the Twenty-Fifth Infantry were accused of a series of shootings. Roosevelt supported the results of an investigation that found the men guilty. After the election of 1906, he had the men dismissed without honor. Foraker's defense of the soldiers enraged Roosevelt.

27. The American Republican League was founded on May 17, 1892, at the University of Michigan by James Francis Burke (1867–1932). Burke later served as U.S. representative for the 31st District of Pennsylvania from 1905 to 1915. The organization still exists.

28. This was Campbell L. Maxwell, who was made consul to Santo Domingo in January 1892. From April 1898 until July 1904 he was consul general. See his letter dated May 21, 1904, box 8, Correspondence, Various Persons to WSS, folder 1900–1909, WSS Papers.

29. Herrick had to negotiate differences among three Republican factions in Ohio represented by Hanna, Cox, and Foraker. He was ambassador to France, 1912–1914; 1921–1929.

30. The meeting was held December 27–29, 1905.

31. In 1905 the editor of the *Southwestern Christian Advocate* was Robert E. Jones.

32. Arnett died of uremic poisoning in October 1906. He was buried in Tarbox Cemetery near Wilberforce. William Oxley Thompson (1855–1933) was the fifth president of Ohio State University serving from 1899 to 1925.

33. Scarborough had participated in the first meeting of the Afro-American Council, December 29–30, 1898, at the Metropolitan Baptist Church on R Street in Washington, D.C. He was part of the seventh session of speakers held at 11:00 a.m. on December 30 titled "The Negro in the Department of Letters."

34. See "Professor W. S. Scarborough Ph.D., Lectures on Greek Language," *Record,* January 11, 1907, which mentions his talks at Mother Bethel A.M.E. Church and at George Washington University.

35. This is Henry Dale, who translated Thucydides, *History of the Peloponnesian War* (London: H. G. Bohn, 1853).

36. The meeting was held January 2–4. A summary of the paper "Notes on Thucydides" can be found in *Transactions of the American Philological Association* 37 (1906): xxx–xxxi.

37. Seymour was president of the Archaeological Institute of America from 1903 to 1907.

38. The identity of "R.W.T." who seems to be "T." is not known.

39. Beacom Gymnasium was erected on Wilberforce's campus in 1919 in honor of Madison W. Beacom (1854–1927), who graduated Oberlin in 1879. It was destroyed by fire in the 1970s.

40. Ray Stannard Baker (1870–1946), journalist and biographer, was the first prominent journalist to focus on race in America. Baker's article "The Tragedy of the Mulatto," *American Magazine* 65 (April 1908): 582–98, has Scarborough's photo with the caption, "Whose Greek text-book has been used at Harvard and other colleges?"

41. See the handwritten note about this essay dated October 31, 1907, from the editorial rooms at 130 Fulton Street, New York City, box 8, Correspondence, Various Persons to WSS, folder 1900–1909, WSS Papers.

42. The meeting was held December 27–30. A summary of the paper can be found in *Transactions of the American Philological Association* 35 (1908): xxii–xxiii.

CHAPTER XVIII:
MADE PRESIDENT OF WILBERFORCE UNIVERSITY

1. Ware was the third president of Atlanta University and served from 1907 to 1919.

2. For the text of this speech, see "Commencement Address: The Negro Graduate—His Mission," Clipping File, William R. and Norma B. Harvey Library, Hampton University. Scarborough's obituary in the *Atlanta University Bulletin,* ser. 2, December 1926, says that Scarborough completed the college preparatory course in 1871 and "since he was the only member of his class the organization of college work was delayed for one year and he transferred to Oberlin where he graduated in 1875, one year before our own first college class of 1876 ... [while] not technically one of us in a sense of being a graduate, we have always appreciated Dr. Scarborough as one of our distinguished sons." Student File, box 508, Oberlin College Archives. See Ware's letter dated June 8, 1908, acknowledging the return of Scarborough's commencement address manuscript, which Ware had edited for publication in the *Atlanta University Bulletin.* Box 8, Correspondence, Various Persons to WSS, folder 1900–1909, WSS Papers.

3. Jane Addams (1860–1935), feminist and social worker, won the Nobel Peace Prize in 1931, which she shared with another of Scarborough's associates, Nicholas Murray Butler, president of Columbia University. In regard to Scarborough and Addams, see the letter from W.E.B. DuBois at Atlanta University to Mary White Ovington (April 16, 1908), in which he says, "[W]e are going to have as I think I have

told you before, Miss Jane Addams here, and I have hopes of . . . Prof. Scarborough of Wilberforce. This is for our conference in May. Do you think you can come?" Mary White Ovington Papers, Walter Reuther Library, Wayne State University, Detroit.

4. This is the last line of a letter from Ware dated June 8, 1908, box 8, Correspondence, Various Persons to WSS, folder 1900–1909, WSS Papers.

5. Morris Brown College, founded in 1885 in honor of Morris Brown (1770–1849), the second bishop of the A.M.E. Church, was the first educational institution in Georgia under sole African American management. The diploma reads in part, "Morrisum Brownum Collegium June 3, 1908 granting an honorary Ph.D. J. S. Flipper Praeses." See box 6, WSS Papers.

6. The identity of L. H. Reynolds is not known.

7. See Ware's letter of congratulations to Scarborough dated August 15, 1908, box 8, Correspondence, Various Persons to WSS, folder 1900–1909, WSS Papers. William Henry Crogman also sent congratulations in a letter dated August 3, 1908. See box 8, Correspondence, Various Persons to WSS, folder 1900–1909, WSS Papers.

8. John Millott Ellis (1831–1894), public servant and professor of Greek and philosophy, was connected with Oberlin College for thirty-seven years.

9. Oscar Taylor Corson (1857–n.d.) was elected state commissioner of common schools in 1891 and in 1894. He was president of the National Education Association in 1900. John Bradley Peaslee (1842–n.d.), well-known Ohio educator, was superintendent of the Cincinnati public schools from 1874 to 1888.

10. The meeting, the first to be held in Canada, was December 28–30, 1908.

11. See "Carnegie to Help Wilberforce," *Afro-American Ledger,* August 14, 1908, and "Scarborough in NYC to Raise Money to Match Carnegie Gift," *New York Times,* July 28, 1909, p. 3, col. 2.

12. See "Noted Colored Orator: Professor Scarborough Chief Speaker at Brooklyn's Lincoln Celebration," *Afro-American Ledger,* February 6, 1909.

13. William Newton Hartshorn (1843–1920) was the editor of *An Era of Progress and Promise, 1863–1910* (Boston: Priscilla, 1910). Scarborough's article, "Wilberforce University, Wilberforce, Ohio," appears on pp. 279–82. A sketch of his life, "William S. Scarborough, A.M., LL.D.," is on p. 491.

14. See a letter about the inaugural parade dated January 8, 1909, box 8, Correspondence, Various Persons to WSS, folder 1900–1909, WSS Papers.

15. The original of this letter is in the Hallie Q. Brown Library, Central State University, Wilberforce, Ohio.

16. Charles W. Dustin left an account. See Dustin, "Paul Laurence Dunbar: A Reminiscent Sketch," *Dayton Journal,* February 14, 1906.

17. This is the first line of Dunbar's poem "A Death Song" (1898): "Lay me down beneaf de willers in de grass."

18. Scarborough's speech can be found in Davis Wasgatt Clark, *Paul Laurence Dunbar—Laurel Decked* (Dayton: Commissioner of the Paul Laurence Dunbar Scholarship Fund, 1906), 13–15.

19. Consult clippings about Dustin and two letters, the first on Dunbar Memorial letterhead dated May 22, 1909, asking Scarborough to join and the second dated May 27, 1909, detailing the type of speech Scarborough should give. Box 8, Correspondence, Various Persons to WSS, folder 1900–1909, WSS Papers.

20. Matthew A. Henson (1866–1955) and Robert Peary discovered the North Pole on April 6, 1909.

21. The Archaeological Institute of America was founded in Boston on May 10, 1879.

22. Mitchell Carroll (1870–1925), professor at George Washington University, was secretary of the Archaeological Institute of America from 1908 to 1918. He was an enthusiastic popularizer and built up the membership substantially. See extant letter from Carroll to Scarborough dated November 12, 1909, box 8, Correspondence, Various Persons to WSS, folder 1900–1909, WSS Papers. This is curious for Carroll addresses Scarborough as "a new member." Scarborough's membership must have lapsed somewhere between 1898 and 1909. Perhaps he failed to pay his initial dues in 1898.

23. The National Geographic Society was founded on January 13, 1888, in the Cosmos Club in Washington, D.C.

24. Charles Frederick Forshaw (1863–n.d.). See certificate of membership in S. Columba's College dated October 26, 1909, and a letter from Reverend J. Sowter on letterhead dated August 16, 1911, box 8, Correspondence, Various Persons to WSS, folder 1900–1909, WSS Papers. At his death Scarborough left several items from Forshaw to William Galloway, his friend and physician. They included: 1) an autograph of William Wilberforce authenticated by Forshaw; 2) the Hull House Medal that Forshaw gave to Scarborough; and 3) five volumes of Forshaw's work, *Yorkshire Notes*. The latter is *Yorkshire Notes and Queries, Being the Antiquarian History of Yorkshire*, 5 vols. (Bradford: H. C. Derwent, 1905–1909). See MS 133–18, Greene County Room, Greene County Library, Xenia, Ohio.

25. The meeting took place December 28–30, 1909.

26. Francis W. Kelsey (1858–1927), classics professor at the University of Michigan, was the immediate past president of the APA at the time and the current president of the Archaeological Institute of America.

27. That meeting was held December 28–30, 1920.

28. Hallie Q. Brown (ca. 1845–1949) taught in various places after earning her B.A. from Wilberforce in 1878. In 1893 she returned as professor of elocution and, with several periods of travel interspersed, worked at Wilberforce as an instructor and as a trustee. Emery Hall still stands on the old Wilberforce campus, almost a ruin.

29. William Tecumseh Vernon, A.M.E. bishop, was registrar of the U.S. Treasury from 1906 to 1911. See "Register Vernon," *Cleveland Journal*, Sept. 8, 1906. Salmon P. Chase was senator from Ohio in 1860. Under Lincoln he served as secretary of the treasury from 1861 to 1864, and then as justice of the Supreme Court.

30. John M. Harlan (1833–1911) was appointed in 1877 by President Hayes as a justice of the U.S. Supreme Court.

31. Charles W. F. Dick (1858–1945) was a Republican politician and served in the U.S. Senate from 1904 to 1911.

32. George A. Gates (1851–1912) was president of Fisk University from 1909 to 1912.

33. Jacob G. Schmidlapp (1849–1919), founder of the Union Savings Bank and Trust of Cincinnati, was president from 1890 to 1907 and CEO from 1907 to 1919. He was a patron of the arts and active in the peace movement.

34. William T. Spear (1833–1913) served from 1855 to 1912; William Z. Davis (1839–1926) served from 1900 to 1912; John Allen Shauck (1841–1918) served from 1894 to 1915; James Latimer Price (1840–1912) served from 1901 to 1912; James Granville Johnson (1857–n.d.) served from 1911 to 1922 and Maurice H. Donahue (1864–1928) served from 1910 to 1919.

35. Isaac R. Sherwood (1835–1912), lawyer, abolitionist, and Civil War veteran, graduated from Antioch College in 1854 and was elected to the U.S. Congress in 1872.

36. John Wesley Hill (1863–1936) wrote *Abraham Lincoln, Man of God* (New York: G. P. Putnam's Sons, 1920).

37. The Xi chapter of Alpha Phi Alpha was founded at Wilberforce on December 14, 1912, by Clarence A. Jones, an alumnus of the Kappa chapter. A delegate of three students had appeared in person on December 14, 1911, at the fourth national convention to secure permission to apply. They were admitted the following year. The chapter was asked at the eleventh convention why it had been inactive during the Student Army Training Corps (SATC) trouble during World War I when black students were being segregated in Ohio. Scarborough gave a brief speech at the sixteenth convention held in Columbus, December 27–31, 1923, as did C. H. Tobias, George Kelley, and Norman McGhee. Scarborough was inducted as an honorary member twice. Two certificates exist, the first dated December 14, 1912, under chapter president C. E. Burch, and the second dated January 31, 1914, under chapter president Charles Spivey. See box 6, WSS Papers. See also the sketch circa 1922 about Scarborough titled "Who's Who in APA?" box 9, WSS Papers. The Xi chapter held its eighth annual "Go to College" night on May 8, 1927, in honor of Scarborough, who had died nine months earlier. See its invitation to Mrs. Scarborough, box 2, Death of WSS, folder 2, WSS Papers.

CHAPTER XIX: SECOND TRIP TO EUROPE

1. On Lord Wearsdale's activities, see "Report of the First Universal Races Congress, University of London, July 26–29, 1911," *African Times and Orient Review,* July 1912, pp. 27–30.

2. Gustav Spiller worked tirelessly to bring about the Congress.

3. First Races Congress, London, July 26–29, 1911, is also known as the Universal Race Congress. Concerning DuBois's activities there, see Lewis, *W.E.B. DuBois,* 439–43.

4. Theophilus Gould Steward (1843–1924), clergyman, author, educator, and soldier, had lifelong connections with Scarborough. Steward served a Macon congregation from 1868 to 1871. He was nearly elected president of Wilberforce University in 1884. In 1907 he became its vice president and served as chaplain and professor of history, French, and logic. Susan Maria Steward (1847–1918) was one of the first African American women to graduate from medical school, the New York Medical College for Women in 1870. When Mrs. Steward died, Scarborough accompanied Mr. Steward as he brought the body of his wife back to New York. Her older sister was Mrs. Sarah S. J. Garnet (1831–1911), who was married to Henry Highland

Garnet (1815–1882), minister and abolitionist. The identity of the "Richard Garnett" mentioned here is not clear.

5. Mrs. Scarborough's son from an earlier marriage, Francis Granger Grant, who was born in April 28, 1866, had died on March 3, 1910, at the age of forty-four. He left a wife, Ida May Williams (1890–1936), and four children, Edna May, William Francis, Harry Irwin, and Louis Howard. He, his wife, and two sons are buried in the Danby Rural Cemetery, sec. 4, row 1, in Danby, New York. See his death certificate, New York State Bureau of Vital Statistics, #10520, which states that "Francis Grant came to his death from a [unreadable] shot in his head, self-inflicted suicide."

6. The SS *Carmania* was once the largest ship in the Cunard fleet. In service from 1905 to 1932, the *Carmania* was the first passenger liner with a steam turbine engine.

7. "Dr. Peres" has not been identified.

8. Albert Bigelow Paine (1861–1937), author and editor, wrote *Mark Twain: A Biography* (New York: Harper and Brothers, 1912), *Mark Twain's Letters* (New York: Harper and Brothers, 1917), and *Mark Twain's Notebook* (New York: Harper and Brothers, 1935). In chapter 133, titled "The Three Fires—Some Benefactions," in the second volume of Bigelow's biography, is a note that "Mark Twain paid 2 colored students through college. One of them educated in a Southern institution became a minister of the gospel. The other graduated from Yale Law School."

9. This is William Thomas Horton (1864–1925). H. Ryder Haggard published *Mahatma and the Hare* (New York: Longmans, Green, 1911) and (New York: Holt and Company, 1911). No such title from Macmillan in 1911 can be located.

10. The battle at Spanish Fort in Mobile Bay, Alabama, in August 1864 was one of the last important battles of the Civil War. Benjamin Butler (1818–1893), staunch Unionist, was a general in the Civil War. His abuses during his occupation of New Orleans from May to December 1862 earned him the names "Beast" and "Monster." He was removed by Lincoln. "Colonel Anderson" has not been identified. Perhaps Scarborough has confused him with the Confederate soldier Colonel Charles D. Anderson of the 21st Alabama Infantry who surrendered Fort Gaines on Dauphin Island at the mouth of Mobile Bay to Union forces on August 8, 1864. See Jack Friend, *West Wind Flood Tide: The Battle of Mobile Bay* (Annapolis: Naval Institute Press, 2004), 252–53.

11. James Duncan (1857–1928) was a labor official who got his start as a granite cutter. He served as the first elected vice president of the American Labor Federation from 1895 to 1928.

12. See Scarborough's account, "The Congress of Races—Dr. Scarborough Talks Interestingly of Some Happenings at the Congress of Races," *Christian Recorder,* September 14, 1941, Clipping File, William R. and Norma B. Harvey Library, Hampton University, Hampton, Virginia.

13. Felix von Luschan (1854–1924) was an anthropologist, ethnologist, biologist, and collector of African art. Giuseppe Sergi (1841–1936), a prominent social scientist with interests in psychology and anthropology, was asked by W.E.B. DuBois to serve on the editorial board of his *Encyclopaedia Africana* in 1909. Frederick W. H. Myers (1843–1901) was a professor of classics at Cambridge. In 1892 he helped found the Society for Psychic Research.

14. Jean Finot (1858–1922), French journalist, maintained the idea that race categories exist only as fictions in our brain. See his *Race Prejudice* (New York: E. P. Dutton, 1906).

15. Francois Denys Legitime was the president of Haiti from December 16, 1888, to October 17, 1889, at which time he was overthrown.

16. Annie Besant (1847–1933), champion of women's rights, turned to theosophy later in life. She died in India.

17. Charles A. Eastman (1858–1939), a Santee Sioux Indian, was the author of a number of books about his life as a Native American.

18. Duse Mohammed (1866–1945) founded the *African Times and Orient Review,* a pan-African newspaper in London, with Samuel Coleridge Taylor. He also edited the Nigerian newspaper the *Comet.* A brief biography of Scarborough appeared in *African Times and Orient Review* 1 (August 1912): 70. He was quoted as part of "Our Symposium and Why," 1 (1912): 16.

19. John Milholland (1860–1925), newspaperman, Republican, and defender of the constitutional rights of African Americans, was one of the forces behind the World's Race Congress in 1911.

20. This is Madeleine Powell Black (n.d.), author of *Civilize the Nations* (New York: Stewart, 1911) and *A Terminal Market System* (New York: Willett, 1912).

21. Frances Evelyn Maynard Greville, Countess of Warwick (1861–1938), society beauty and social reformer, married the fifth Earl of Warwick in 1881. She was quoted in "Symposium," *African Times and Oriental Review* 1 (July 1912): 14.

22. Elizabeth Julia Emery (n.d.–1913), from the wealthy Emery family of Cincinnati, lived abroad in France and England. She also paid for the Emery dormitories at Tuskegee. Her brother, Thomas J. Emery, and his wife carried on their own considerable philanthropies.

23. The identity of Mr. Lydgett is not known.

24. This may be a reference to McGuffey's *Fifth Eclectic Reader,* which contains a poem, "The Soldier of the Rhine," by Caroline Norton, which mentions Bingen.

25. An international conference was held at Algeciras in 1906 to settle a dispute between France and Germany over Morocco.

26. The Ill is 120 miles long. Its tributaries are the Thürfecht and Brühe Rivers. It flows from its source in the Jurna Mountains north-northeast into the Rhine River. A postcard dated August 9, 1911, sent by Mrs. Scarborough from Coblentz survives.

27. John Frederick Oberlin (1740–1826), German-Lutheran clergyman, served his impoverished parish in every way. Oberlin College was named in his honor.

28. The identity of "Mr. R" is not known.

29. See Scarborough's letter of condolence dated January 26, 1914, to Ernest Axon on the death of his father, W. E. A. Axon, W. E. A. Axon–W.S.S. correspondence, John Rylands University Library of Manchester, England.

CHAPTER XX: LABORS FOR WILBERFORCE UNIVERSITY

1. Guy Potter Benton (1865–1927), president of Miami University from 1902 to 1911 and from 1911 to 1919, was later president of the University of Vermont.

See Benton's letter dated June 6, 1910, saying that he may be going to work at Boston University. Box 8, Correspondence, Various Persons to WSS, folder 1910–1919, WSS Papers. General Oliver Otis Howard (1830–1909) had retired to Burlington, Vermont in 1894. The brother mentioned is probably Charles Henry Howard (1838–1909).

2. See his *The Real College* (Cincinnati: Jennings and Graham, 1909).

3. The National Economic League was organized to oppose socialism and class hatred. See a letter from the organization in Boston dated January 1, 1912, asking Scarborough to become a member. Box 8, Correspondence, Various Persons to WSS, folder 1910–1919, WSS Papers.

4. The meeting at Brown was held December 27–29, 1910. The meeting in Pittsburgh was held on the same dates in 1911.

5. Scarborough means the Hotel Schenley, which opened in 1898 in Pittsburgh. It is now owned by the University of Pittsburgh.

6. Wesley J. Gaines (1840–1912), born in slavery in Georgia, was a bishop of the A.M.E. Church from 1888 to 1912. Reverdy Ransom in his *Pilgrimage of Harriet Ransom's Son* (Nashville: A.M.E. Sunday School Union, n.d.), 75, says

> the late Bishop W.J. Gaines of Georgia had drawn down the wrath of the General Conference upon him because it was alleged he had assisted in bringing upon the scene of the General Conference an abandoned wife of the late William Preston of St. Louis, Mo., who was at the same time the most popular favorite for election to the Bishopric; it was alleged that Preston in his youth had abandoned his wife.... The Rev. Levi J. Coppin, who was a protege and favorite of Bishop W.J. Gaines, became the victim of the wrath of many delegates, who not being able to strike Bishop Gaines, took it out upon Dr. Coppin.

Scarborough wrote a three-page introduction to Gaines's *Twenty-Five Years of Freedom* (Atlanta: Franklin Publishing House, 1890).

7. The article is "Wilberforce University, Wilberforce, O.," *Cyclopedia of Education,* ed. Paul Monroe (New York: Macmillan, 1911–1913), 4:773.

8. The cup measures ten inches at the handle. It was made by the Wilcox Silverplate Company and is stamped "462." The inscription reads: "Class '13 to Pres. and Mrs. W. S. Scarborough, Feb. 10, 1912." It is in the collection of the National Afro-American Museum and Cultural Center, Wilberforce, Ohio, a gift of Sarah A. Grant.

9. Among Scarborough's papers is a program in ten parts with speeches and music "rendered by the Caesar Class of Wilberforce University at the home of Prof. W. S. Scarborough" held on February 16, 1907. See box 4, Miscellaneous, WSS Papers.

10. Frances Scarborough was attended by Dr. Steward. Her death was noted in an article by R. G. Bruce, "Mrs. Frances Scarborough Dead," *Chicago Defender,* April 19, 1922. He later described the funeral, "Wilberforce University," *Chicago Defender,* April, 27, 1912. See box 9, Scrapbook, WSS Papers.

11. See Culp, *Twentieth Century Negro Literature,* 414–47. Scarborough uses Negro National Educational Congress (pp. 211, 264) and Negro National Education Conference (p. 228) interchangeably.

12. Judson Harmon was U.S. attorney general from 1895 to 1897.

13. See *Index to the William Howard Taft Papers* (Washington, D.C.: Library of Congress, 1972), 5:1799.

14. It is likely that the presence of Harold North Fowler and Samuel Platner (1863–1921) on the faculty at Western Reserve University in Cleveland influenced Scarborough's decision.

15. The meeting was held December 27–30, 1912. The president of the university was Charles Herbert Stockton (1845–1924), the ninth president, serving from 1910 to 1918. The chair of Latin and Greek was Charles Sidney Smith (1867–1951), who held the position from 1910 to 1934.

16. As late as 1921 smokers were held at AIA meetings. See Stephen L. Dyson, *Ancient Marbles to American Shores* (Philadelphia: University of Pennsylvania Press, 2000), 201.

17. Mrs. Foster was Ann M. Olmsted, the daughter of Judge Jesse Olmsted.

18. Edward Everett Hale, Unitarian clergyman, reformer, and prolific writer, was chaplain of the U.S. Senate from 1903 to 1909.

19. The "National Congress of Colored Educators" has not been identified.

20. For the original letter dated July 28, 1923, see box 6, WSS Papers.

21. Stephen M. Newman (1845–1924), with a B.A. and an M.A. from Bowdoin College, was inaugurated on December 13, 1912, and Scarborough delivered a speech then. Newman served until 1918.

22. Moses Buckingham Salter (1841–1913) studied at Wilberforce from 1870 to 1874 and became a bishop of the A.M.E. Church in 1892. He died in Charleston, S.C. William B. Derrick (1843–1913), elected bishop in 1896, had died in Flushing, N.Y. in April. See "The Chief of the Staff conducts the Funeral of the Late Miss Emery," *The War Cry* (March 1, 1913), box 9, Scrapbook, WSS Papers.

23. See Page, *The Life and Letters of Walter Hines Page,* 3 vols. (New York: Doubleday, Page, 1922).

24. The meeting was held December 29–31, 1913. Scarborough's paper is not listed.

25. The meeting was held December 27–29, 1916.

26. Other honorary members of the International Longfellow Society were Mary Bethune, Jane Addams, and Mahatma Gandhi.

27. John R. Mott (1865–1955), American missionary and educator, had close ties to the YMCA. In 1946 he won a Nobel Peace Prize.

28. The "St. Mark Musical and Literary Union" has not been identified.

29. Scarborough must mean the World Court Congress, whose goal was to establish a "true International Court of Justice." See letter from its chair, John Hays Hammond, about the meeting in Cleveland May 12–15, box 3, Correspondence, Democracy and Citizenship, WSS Papers.

30. The Hotel Statler was a grand hotel of one thousand rooms built in 1912 at Euclid Avenue and East 12th Street in Cleveland by the architectural firms G. B. Post and Sons of New York and Charles Schneider of Cleveland. It is now the Statler Office Tower.

31. See "Prof. L. F. Palmer," *The Sodalian* 8 (October 1913): 9–10.

32. Frank B. Willis (1871–1928), Republican governor of Ohio from 1915 to 1919 and U.S. senator, nominated Harding in 1920.

33. Darius Cobb (1834–1919), painter, poet, and lecturer, and his twin brother, Cyrus (1834–1903), worked together in Boston on historical and religious

paintings. On January 1, 1866, the brothers were married by their father in a double wedding ceremony to the Lillie sisters, lineal descendants of John Alden. The painting hangs today in the Rembert E. Stokes Library at Wilberforce University. Cobb's father, Sylvanus Cobb (1798–1866), was a well-known Universalist clergyman. Cobb's brother Sylvanus Cobb, Jr. (1823–1887), was a prolific writer of fiction. Scarborough seems to have conflated father and son. See Cobb's obituaries: "Darius Cobb, Painter, Dies," *New York Times,* April 24, 1919; "Darius Cobb Is Dead in Newton," *Boston Herald,* April 24, 1919; and "Death of Darius Cobb," *Boston Transcript,* April 24, 1919.

34. The citation in the *Boston Transcript* has not been found.

35. Scarborough must mean the National Association of Colored Women.

36. Fannie Barrier Williams and Reverend Celia Parker Woolley founded the Douglass Center of Chicago in 1905.

37. Zona Gale (1874–1938), Wisconsin-born writer and feminist, won a Pulitzer Prize in 1921 for drama. Scarborough's copy of *Peace in Friendship Village* (New York: Macmillan, 1919) is in the collection of Sarah A. Grant. The chapter Scarborough mentions describes the reaction of a small village when a young black couple purchases a house there. See pp. 205–31.

38. Gilbert Parker (1862–1932), Canadian novelist, was a member of the British Parliament from 1900 to 1918.

39. See Hill, *Abraham Lincoln, Man of God.* See also a letter from Hill dated April 12, 1915, about the meeting of the World Court Congress in May 1915. Box 8, Correspondence, Various Persons to WSS, folder 1910–1919, WSS Papers.

40. Charles C. Moore (1868–1932) headed the exposition in San Francisco, which ran from February to December 1915. He edited *The Legacy of the Exhibition: Interpretation of the Intellectual and Moral Heritage Left to Mankind by the World Celebration in San Francisco in 1915* (San Francisco: J. H. Nash, 1916).

41. See "The President's Trip," *The Sodalian* (1915): 9–10, Rembert E. Stokes Clipping File, Wilberforce University. *The Sodalian* was a student publication established by B. F. Lee, J. P. Shorter, H. A. Knight, and S. T. Mitchell, which operated from 1871 to 1914. Its Latin motto was *scholae non discimus sed vitae.* This is the last line of Epistle 106 by Lucius Annaeas Seneca (ca. 4 B.C.–65 A.D.), which treated the problem of making virtue real and the need to avoid the superfluous in order to live well.

42. Scarborough is perhaps referring to the commotion stirred up by DuBois's article "The New Wilberforce," *Crisis* 4 (August 1914): 191–94, which described the burgeoning C. N. & I. Department with praise and implied that the Old Wilberforce was in trouble. Scarborough sent a letter dated September 18, 1914, to J. E. Spingarn about the trouble. As president he felt he should reply and he wrote: "The writer knew that many of the statements were false and at this point we believe that it was intended to hurt the institution. It is further believed here that that superintendent of the [C. N. & I] school was the real writer of the article. . . . The feeling around here has been very intense and I have been forced to take it." Spingarn Collection, Moorland-Spingarn Research Center, Howard University.

CHAPTER XXI: TRIPS—SOUTH, WEST, AND EAST

1. Mary Bethune (1875–1955), civil rights leader, founded the Daytona Normal and Industrial School, now Bethune Cookman College, in 1904. While in Jacksonville, Scarborough was the guest of A. L. Lewis. Abraham Lincoln Lewis (1865–1947) established the Afro American Life Insurance Company in 1901 and became Jacksonville's first African American millionaire. A civic leader and dedicated member of the Mt. Olive A.M.E. Church, he founded American Beach, a resort for African Americans, on Amelia Island in 1935. See Russ Rymer, *American Beach: A Saga of Race, Wealth and Memory* (New York: HarperCollins, 1998).

2. Edward Waters College, founded in 1866 as Brown Theological Institute by the A.M.E. Church to train clergy in Jacksonville, Florida, is now a small liberal arts college.

3. Henry McNeal Turner died in Windsor, Ontario, on May 8, 1915, and was buried in Atlanta.

4. During the meeting in Cleveland, Scarborough stayed at the Forest Hill Hotel.

5. The Worcester Polytechnic Institute, founded in 1865 by John Boynton and Ichabod Washburn, is still a technical institute. The Bancroft Hotel, a luxury hotel at 50 Franklin Street, designed by Esen, Wein and Johnson of Buffalo, was built in 1912. It is now an apartment building. John Wingate Weeks (1860–1926) was Republican senator from Massachusetts from 1913 to 1919, and secretary of war from 1921 to 1925. Major General Leonard Wood (1860–1927), personal physician to President McKinley and his family, was made chief of staff of the army in 1910. For a letter dated June 14, 1915, thanking Scarborough for coming to the event, see box 8, Correspondence, Various Persons to WSS, folder 1910–1919, WSS Papers.

6. Fayette A. McKenzie (1872–1957) was president of Fisk University from 1915 to 1925.

7. Hastings Harnell Hart (1851–1932), a member of Scarborough's class of 1875, was a reformer with interests in prisons and child welfare. He received two honorary LL.D.s, the first from Oberlin College in 1898 and the second from Wilberforce in 1920. Albert Bushnell Hart (1854–1943), author and distinguished professor of history at Harvard from 1883 to 1926, had a keen interest in slavery and abolition, and influenced W.E.B. DuBois.

8. The Carnegie Fund for Pensions was established in 1905 by Carnegie with a $10 million endowment. Pensioners included Booker T. Washington and William Henry Crogman.

9. Charles Alexander had been an instructor of printing at Wilberforce. Scarborough was one of the original members of the NAACP's general committee, which numbered sixty-five in 1910.

10. John Henry McCracken (1875–1948) was inaugurated as the ninth president of Lafayette College in October 1915. For the eight-page program of the inauguration of McCracken, LL.D. as the ninth president of Lafayette, October 19 and 20, 1915, see box 2, WSS Papers.

11. Ernest Gottlieb Sihler received an honorary Litt.D. from Lafayette College in 1915.

12. The National Arts Club was founded by Charles de Kay, the literary and art critic for the *New York Times,* in 1898.

13. Glendale was a main stop on the Underground Railroad.

14. See a note from Emmett Scott, dated Nov. 16, 1915, informing Scarborough when to arrive for the funeral. Box 8, Correspondence, Various Persons to WSS, folder 1910–1919, WSS Papers. See *Tuskegee Student,* Nov. 17, 1915, which lists Scarborough as an honorary pallbearer, p. 3, Tuskegee University Archives.

15. Robert Russa Moton (1867–1940) was commandant of the male student cadet corps at Hampton from 1891 to 1915. He followed Booker T. Washington as principal of Tuskegee Institute from 1915 to 1935.

16. The Association of American Colleges was founded in 1915, and the Ohio College Association was founded in 1867.

17. Benjamin O. Davis (1877–1970) was professor of military science and tactics at Wilberforce four times: 1905–1909, 1915–1917, 1929–1930, and again in 1937. He rose to brigadier general and retired in 1948 after fifty years of military service.

18. The Religious Education Association was founded in 1903 by William Raney Harper, the first president of the University of Chicago.

19. Philip Melancthon Watters received a D.D. from Wesleyan University. He was inaugurated in 1915.

20. St. Paul's A.M.E. Church was the first church building constructed by and for an African American congregation in St. Louis.

21. "Wilcox" cannot be verified.

22. The president of the College of Wooster in 1916 was John Campbell White. He served from 1915 to 1919.

23. Hamilton Holt (1872–1951), newspaperman and longtime editor of the *Independent,* became the eighth president of Rollins College, Winter Park, Florida, in 1927.

24. See "William Hayes Ward," *Independent,* September 11, 1916, pp. 386–87.

25. The conference took place November 21–24, 1916. Scarborough's lecture was printed as a pamphlet titled *What Should Be the Standard of the University, College, Normal School Teacher Training and Secondary Schools* (Durham, NC: National Training School, 1916).

26. Scarborough hosted African students. See "Wilberforce University and Her African Students," *Xenia Daily Gazette,* October 11, 1915.

27. The first American Jewish Congress convened in Philadelphia's Metropolitan Opera House in December 1918. A letter dated June 8, 1915, acknowledges Scarborough's membership and asks him to come to New York to help launch the movement. It is signed "Judge Gustav Hartman temporary president and Henry Green temporary secretary." See box 8, Correspondence, Various Persons to WSS, folder 1910–1919, WSS Papers.

CHAPTER XXII: WORLD WAR I WORK

1. James M. Cox (1870–1957) was thrice governor of Ohio starting in 1898. He was defeated by Warren G. Harding in a bid for the presidential nomination in 1920.

2. Newton D. Baker (1871–1937), lawyer, Democratic mayor of Cleveland from 1912 to 1916, was secretary of war from 1917 to 1920. Oberlin College con-

ferred an honorary LL.D. on him in 1923. Benjamin O. Davis (1877–1970) was the first African American general officer in the U.S. Army.

    3. Atlee Pomerene (1863–1937), lawyer, was elected Democratic senator from Ohio and served from 1911 to 1923.

    4. See the letter from Emmett J. Scott to Scarborough dated August 16, 1918, in which he says: "Colonel Young's matter is coming along satisfactorily as you have doubtless heard." Charles Young Collection, National Afro-American Museum and Cultural Center, Wilberforce, Ohio. In the same month Scarborough attended a conference at Madame Walker's Villa Lewaro in Irvington on the Hudson. See "Conference at Villa Lewaro," *New York Age,* August 31, 1918, p. 1.

    5. Kelly Miller (1863–1939), public intellectual, studied mathematics, physics, and astronomy at Johns Hopkins before serving as professor of mathematics and sociology at Howard University from 1890 to 1934.

    6. Baker won an LL.D. from Oberlin College in 1923.

    7. Fort Des Moines was established in Iowa in 1903 and actively manned until the 1960s.

    8. John E. Green was a member of the Twenty-Fifth Infantry.

    9. Fred C. Croxton (1871–1960), Cleveland industrial relations expert, was vice-chairman of the Ohio branch of the Council of National Defense during World War I.

    10. See Croxton's letter dated May 17, 1918, box 8, Correspondence, Various Persons to WSS, folder 1910–1919, WSS Papers.

    11. The reference to the "Southern Migration Conference" is not clear.

    12. See Scarborough's pamphlet, *Wilberforce in the War* (Xenia, OH: Eckerle, 1918), and his article "Wilberforce War Work," *Wilberforcian* 1 (March 1919): 3–5.

    13. Alpha Phi Alpha rebuked the Xi chapter at Wilberforce for not taking a stand on this issue.

    14. Emmett Jay Scott (1873–1957) was Booker T. Washington's private secretary from 1897 to 1915. He was secretary-treasurer and business manager of Howard University from 1919 to 1932. During World War I he was special assistant to the secretary of war in charge of Negro affairs.

    15. On this quota, see McGinnis, *A History and an Interpretation of Wilberforce,* 81.

    16. This may be the "L. Palmer" mentioned in chapter XX, note 31.

    17. Camp Funston is now part of Fort Riley, Kansas. The camp was named for the Kansas hero Frederick Funston (1865–1917). Charles C. Ballou (n.d.–1928) was the white commander of the all-black Ninety-Second Division. His appointment was controversial as was his extreme racism. See a letter, polite and perfunctory, from Ballou dated November 11, 1917, from Camp Funston to Scarborough, box 8, Correspondence, Various Persons to WSS, folder 1910–1919, WSS Papers.

    18. The article is found on page 223.

    19. The identity of "Dr. T." is not known.

    20. On the Avery Institute, see McGinnis, *A History and an Interpretation of Wilberforce,* 125.

CHAPTER XXIII: LOCAL AND CLOSING WAR LABORS

1. See Scarborough's letter "On Ohio Black Laws," *Cleveland Gazette*, February 14, 1885.

2. For details, see McGinnis, *A History and an Interpretation of Wilberforce University*, 107–14.

3. N. H. Fairbanks and E. M. Fullerton were members of the Ohio Republican State Advisory Committee. Fairbanks was also chairman of the Ohio State Central Committee and was based in Springfield. Fullerton was vice-chairman of the Republican State Advisory Committee and represented Columbus.

4. William Harrison Hays (1879–1954), born in Sullivan, Indiana, was chairman of the Republican National Committee from 1918 to 1921 and postmaster general from 1921 to 1922.

5. Scarborough quotes here in part his *Report of the President, Secretary and Treasurer of Wilberforce University to the Twenty-Sixth General Conference of the A.M.E. Church* (Wilberforce, OH, 1920), 45.

6. In 1939 a plan for restructuring the board articulated by the Gillespie Bill was passed by the Ohio legislature. It empowered the governor to appoint six board members rather than five of the C. N. & I. department to its board of trustees and reduce the number of members chosen by the university's board of trustees from three to two. On the relationship of church and state at Wilberforce, see McGinnis, *A History and an Interpretation of Wilberforce University*, 103–19.

7. See the letter from George H. Clark, chairman of the Ohio State Advisory Committee, January 15, 1920, to Hon. F. E. Whittemore, which says: "If there is any legislation pending or if any is introduced affecting Wilberforce University, please see that it remains in status quo until we have had opportunity to advise with you concerning the matter. We do not desire any legislation to be enacted covering Wilberforce University at this session." Charles Spencer Smith Collection, BHR.

8. See Scarborough, "Howard's Semi-Centennial," *Independent* 89 (March 19, 1917): 505.

9. John Purroy Mitchell (1874–1918), reform mayor of New York City, with the encouragement of the National Urban League, appointed a black to the New York City board of education.

10. Reverdy Cassius Ransom (1861–1959) graduated from Wilberforce University with a B.D. in 1886 and became the forty-eighth bishop of the A.M.E. Church in 1924. From 1912 to 1924 he was the editor of the *A.M.E. Church Review.*

11. The League to Enforce Peace was begun June 15, 1915, by Hamilton Holt and Theodore Marbury at Independence Hall, Philadelphia, with William Taft as president. Its aim was peace through military and economic sanctions, and it influenced Woodrow Wilson to support the formation of the League of Nations.

12. The Bellevue Stratford operated from 1904 to 1979. After a year under the name of the Fairmount Hotel it reverted to its old name. It is said to be haunted. Hotel Walton, known for its exotic interiors, opened in 1896. It was razed in 1966. The Hotel Hershey, now the Doubletree, stands there today. Both buildings are located on Broad Street in Philadelphia.

13. These activities of Scarborough were briefly noted in the *Oberlin Alumni Magazine,* May 1918. Other activities en route to Camp Funston and Camp Grant to

visit Wilberforce soldiers are noted in "President Scarborough Is Entertained by Former Pupils," *Chicago Defender,* April 20, 1918. For a notice with a photograph titled "He Is Coming to Lexington, Ky." advertising Scarborough's lecture at St. John A.M.E. Church on March 31, see the back pages of "Catalogue of the Private Library of William Sanders Scarborough," box 13, WSS Papers.

14. For a copy of this lecture, see box 4, WSS Papers.

15. See *Wilberforce in the War* (Xenia, OH: Eckerle Printing Co., 1918).

16. This is, perhaps, Henry A. Atkinson (1877–1960) clergyman and association executive.

17. The editor of the *Christian Herald* was George H. Sandison (1850–ca. 1926).

18. Clarence Powers Bill (1875–1966) was professor of Greek and Latin at Western Reserve University, Cleveland, from 1898 to 1946. He was secretary-treasurer of the APA from 1916 to 1925 and president from 1927 to 1928. Scarborough was a lifelong member of the APA. His death was noted in the organization's necrology. See "List of Deceased Members," *Transactions of the American Philological Association* 57 (1926): xiv. Joseph W. Hewitt (1875–1938), who earned a doctorate from Harvard in 1902 and was secretary of the APA from 1925 to 1931, would later send two notes of condolence to Mrs. Scarborough. The first dated November 1, 1926 reads:

My dear Mrs. Scarborough, I am very sorry to hear of the death of your husband. He was one of the most faithful members of the Association. His chief activity came in the years before I myself was active, but I have heard a good deal about him and that couched in the highest terms of praise from my older colleague, Professor Harrington.

Very cordially yours, J. W. Hewitt

Hewitt's colleague was Karl Pomeroy Harrington (1861–1953). The two men taught at Wesleyan in Middletown, Connecticut. The second, dated January 5, 1927, reads:

My dear Mrs. Scarborough. It is not the custom of the Philological Association to pass definite resolution over their deceased members but this year for the first time a list of those who had died in the course of the year was read. Your husband's name was among them and many kind things were said among the members about him.

Very cordially yours, J. W. Hewitt

See box 3, file 2, Correspondence, Death of Scarborough, WSS Papers.

19. Cornelius T. Shaffer (n.d.–1919), Ohio-born graduate of Berea College, was elected bishop of the A.M.E. Church in 1900.

20. Annie Turnbo Pope Malone (1869–1957) was an entrepreneur who sold beauty products for black women. After becoming one of the first African American millionaires in the United States, she turned to philanthropy.

21. Charles F. Thwing (1853–1937), Congregational churchman and educator, was president of Western Reserve University from 1870 to 1921. After 1905 he was a trustee of the Carnegie Foundation and of Adelbert College.

22. See the letter from Demos dated July 3, 1919, box 8, Correspondence, Various Persons to WSS, folder 1910–1919, WSS Papers.

23. The Interchurch World Movement was established in 1918 with the goal of global evangelism and of uniting Christian factions. It was short-lived and ended in 1920.

24. No details have been found about the American Asiatic Association's activities.

25. The Horticultural Society of New York was founded in 1900.

26. For more information on the Betterment Plan, see McGinnis, *A History and an Interpretation of Wilberforce University*, 111–12.

27. This is D. Augustus Straker (1842–1908), who earned a law degree from Howard University in 1871. In 1892 he was elected commissioner of the Wayne County Circuit Court in Detroit. See a letter from him dated March 3, 1905, box 8, Correspondence, Various Persons to WSS, folder 1899–1909, WSS Papers.

CHAPTER XXIV: CLOSE OF FORTY-FIVE YEARS IN THE FIELD OF EDUCATION

1. Scarborough's predecessor was Joshua H. Jones, who had been president from 1900 to 1908. Jones, born in 1856, earned a B.A. from Claflin College in 1885 and a B.D. from Wilberforce in 1887. After his presidency he became president of Wilberforce's board of trustees. His son, Gilbert H. Jones, was dean of the College of Liberal Arts for ten years, and he later served as the school's eighth president from 1924 to 1932. McGinnis in his *History and an Interpretation of Wilberforce University*, 70, mentions Scarborough's "long feud" with Bishop Jones. Scarborough was evidently looking for other work at this time. A letter from Mary Bethune dated July 9, 1920, from Daytona Normal and Industrial Institute states: "My idea is to have you as executive secretary of our school to tour the north and wherever you think it wise, finding people who have money and bringing this work to their attention." See box 3, Correspondence, Democracy and Citizenship, WSS Papers.

2. This is from the 4th Canto, stanza 141, of *Childe Harold* published in April 1818 by George Gordon, Lord Byron (1788–1824). The lines read: "There was their Dacian mother: he their sire / Butchered to make a Roman Holiday."

3. It reads:

My Dear Sirs, In view of the fact that I find it impossible to maintain my dignity and self-respect while serving under Bishop Joshua H. Jones now President of the University Board of Trustees succeeding the late Bishop Shaffer, and in view of the fact that I most positively disapprove of Bishop Jones' son being both Dean and Vice-President of the University with his father as President of the Board, making the entire situation embarrassing and intolerable, I, hereby, offer my resignation as President of Wilberforce University to take effect at the close of the school year; and I beg the immediate acceptance of the same.

Yours respectfully, William Sanders Scarborough

See "Scarborough Out at Wilberforce," *Cleveland Advocate,* June 26, 1920. For his letter of resignation, see box 9, Scrapbook, WSS Papers.

4. McGinnis mentions an earlier donation from Dr. Charles Avery of $10,000. *A History and an Interpretation of Wilberforce University,* 123.

5. Levi Jenkins Coppin (1848–1924) became the thirtieth bishop of the A.M.E. Church in 1900. M. B. Salter (1841–1913) studied at Wilberforce from 1870 to 1874 and became a bishop of the A.M.E. Church in 1892.

6. John A. Gregg (1877–153) was the seventh president of Wilberforce University. He served from 1920 to 1924. He had been president of Edward Waters College in Jacksonville, Florida.

7. This issue of the *Archiviste* is in the archives at the Rembert E. Stokes Library at Wilberforce University.

8. The other delegates in attendance were Bishops C. S. Smith, L. J. Coppin, W. H. Heard, J. H. Jones, W. D. Johnson, and A. J. Carey; Reverends R. R. Wright, Jr., J. B. Bell, C. E. Allen, H. N. Newsome, S. L. Green, G. W. Allen, and J. C. Caldwell; Professors J. R. Hawkins and A. S. Jackson; and Dr. A. T. White.

9. N. H. Fairbanks's brother, Charles Warren Fairbanks (1852–1928), was Republican senator from 1897 to 1905, and vice president under Theodore Roosevelt from 1897 to 1905.

10. Harry L. Davis (1878–1950), three times mayor of Cleveland, served as governor of Ohio from 1921 to 1923 in a sweep of Republican victories.

11. George Busby Christian, Jr., was the son of Harding's friend Colonel George B. Christian and his wife, Lydia Morris Christian. He was born near Marion, Ohio, on March 25, 1873. From 1915 to 1921 he was Harding's private secretary.

12. Harry M. Daugherty (1860–1941), Ohio lobbyist, was U.S. attorney general from 1922 to 1923.

13. Marcus Shoup (1867–1928), lawyer and judge, was from Xenia, Ohio.

14. Leonard Wood (1860–1927) trained as a physician at Harvard and was President McKinley's personal physician. He saw action in San Juan, was governor of Cuba from 1900 to 1902, and then trained soldiers for World War I. From 1921 to 1927 he was the governor general of the Philippines. Hiram Warren Johnson (1866–1945), twice governor of California in 1910 and 1914 and U.S. senator from California from 1917 to 1945, was a progressive and later supported Franklin Roosevelt. Frank O. Lowden (1861–1943) was governor of Illinois from 1916 to 1920. Lowden and Wood lost the Republican nomination to Warren Harding, and Johnson declined offers for nomination for the vice presidency.

CHAPTER XXV: THIRD VISIT TO EUROPE

1. John Russell Hawkins (1862–1939), educated at Hampton Institute and Howard University, was president of Kittrell College, North Carolina, from 1890 to 1896. He was financial secretary of the A.M.E. Church from 1912 to 1939, and was trustee and fiscal agent of Wilberforce University from 1925 to 1939.

2. See "Wilberforce," *Xenia Evening Gazette,* November 6, 1922, which says "Mrs. S. C. B. Scarborough who has been visiting relatives in New York State has

returned for the winter." For a copy of passport photo of Mrs. Scarborough in 1921, see PG 396, folder 1, Scarborough Family Papers.

3. Philip Gibbs (1877–1962). This was the first naval engagement between armed liners. Under the command of Royal Navy Captain Noel Grant (1868–1920), the refitted *Carmania* sank the Hamburg-South American liner *Cap Trafalgar* on September 14, 1914, near Bermuda.

4. Hotel Cecil, built in the 1890s, was an 800-room facility with richly appointed rooms. Westminster Training College was a Wesleyan Methodist establishment located on Horseferry Road near Parliament.

5. The Classical Association was founded in December 1903 by John Percival Postgate (1853–1926), professor of Latin at Liverpool from 1910 to 1920 and emeritus professor 1921 to 1926, and E. A. Sonnenschein (1851–1929), professor of Greek and Latin at the University of Birmingham. The group's goal was the defense and promotion of the classics as a discipline, but its focus was pronouncedly scholarly. On Scarborough's presence at the meeting, see the articles "Classics in England and America," "Classics and Industry," and "Elegaic Style, Close of Classical Association Conference," Clipping File, National Afro-American Museum and Cultural Center, Wilberforce, Ohio.

6. The University Arms located on Regent Street has operated for over 160 years. It is a De Vere Hotel today.

7. The "Oresteia film" was one of the earliest attempts to film a Greek tragedy. The 1500-foot film was shot on the New Theatre Stage by the Gaumont Company. For notices in the local papers, see Clipping File, Rare Book Department, Cambridge University Library.

8. John Harrower (1857–n.d.) wrote several books on the history of Aberdeen University as well as on Shakespeare. He published a translation of Sophocles' *Antigone*.

9. Walter Leaf (1852–1927) was a banker and a Homeric scholar.

10. Coolidge delivered a talk, "The Classics for America," at the University of Pennsylvania during the second annual meeting of the American Classical League. The speech was published as pamphlet (Princeton: American Classical League, 1923).

11. Desire Joseph Mercier (1851–1926), Belgian Catholic churchman, was ordained cardinal in 1907, and Nicholas Murray Butler, president of Columbia University, laid the cornerstone. See "Cardinal Mercier Issues Invitation to Scarborough," and "Butler to Lay Cornerstone of Louvain Library," Clipping File, National Afro-American Museum and Cultural Center, Wilberforce, Ohio.

12. Quentin Roosevelt (1897–1918), the youngest son of Theodore Roosevelt, was shot down by German flyers on July 14, 1918, near Chemery, France. He was twenty years old.

13. The full program of papers as well as the dinner program and seating arrangement at the Hotel Cecil on September 13, 1921, can be found on microfilm roll 4, Charles Spencer Smith Collection, BHR. Other delegates to the Fifth Ecumenical Methodist Conference, September 6–16, 1921, were Bishops C. S. Smith, L. J. Coppin, J. S. Flipper, W. H. Heard, W. D. Chappelle, J. H. Jones, W. W. Beckett, W. D. Johnson, A. J. Carey, and W. A. Fountain; Reverends R. R. Wright, Jr., J. B. Bell, C. E. Allen, H. N. Newsome, S. L. Green, G. W. Allen, and J. C. Caldwell; Professors

J. R. Hawkins, and A. S. Jackson; and Drs. A. T. White and J. H. Hale. See Scarborough's Certificate of Delegate's Election dated June 24, 1921, and signed by Benjamin F. Lee in Chicago on behalf of the bishops of the A.M.E Church, box 7, Miscellaneous, Ecumenical Methodist Conference 1901, 1921, WSS Papers.

14. Reverend S. P. Rose, D.D., of Montreal gave the opening sermon at 6:30 p.m. on Tuesday, September 6, at Wesley Chapel, City Road, London. For the source of the quote consult 2 Corinthians 5:17: "Old things are done away and all things have become new," and Revelations 21:5: "Behold, I make all things new."

15. The Japanese bishop was Kogor Usaki, D.D., who gave an address at 2:45 p.m. during the second session on Wednesday, September 7. Microfilm roll 4, Charles Spencer Smith Collection, BHR.

16. A. S. Jackson, president of Paul Quinn College, represented the Central Texas Conference for the A.M.E. Church. John Russell Hawkins (1862–1935), a leading member of the A.M.E. Church, was a trustee of Wilberforce from 1925 to 1935. Jackson and Hawkins are not listed among the speakers in the general session, but these A.M.E. Church men are: W. H. Heard, first session at 9:45 on Wednesday, September 7; G. W. Allen, third session at 7:00 p.m. on Friday, September 9; J. H. Jones, second session at 2:45 p.m. on Wednesday, September 14; L. J. Coppin, second session at 2:45 p.m. on Wednesday, September 14; and R. R. Wright, second session at 2:45 p.m. on Thursday, September 15. Microfilm roll 4, Charles Spencer Smith Collection, BHR.

17. "Dr. Burkilt" and the "Sherwoods" have not been identified.

18. Perks was one of three men to give an address at the devotional session during the first session on Friday, September 9, 1921. Microfilm roll 4, Charles Spencer Smith Collection, BHR. A photo of the delegates upon their return from Europe can be found on the front page of the *New York Amsterdam News,* October 5, 1921. Scarborough is erroneously listed as "J. C. Scarborough, Wilberforce."

19. Edward Price Bell (1869–1943), Indiana-born newspaperman, was a Nobel Prize nominee. He stopped writing for the *Chicago Daily News* in 1932.

20. See William Sanders Scarborough, *A Tribute to Colonel Young* (Philadelphia: A.M.E. Book Concern, 1922).

21. The SS *Adriatic* was a luxury liner operated by Cunard's rival, the White Star Line, which was at that time under the ownership of J. P. Morgan.

CHAPTER XXVI: A NEW FIELD OF LABOR

1. Scarborough does not explain the significance of this.

2. The identity of "C" is not known.

3. Scarborough's letter of appointment to Farm Management and Farm Economics dated November 29, 1921, gives his monthly salary as $250, effective November 1, 1921. See box 3, Democracy and Citizenship, Correspondence, WSS Papers.

4. See Titlow's letter dated December 19, 1922, saying that "we have rendered a very great service to 100s of colored farmers," box 8, Correspondence, Various Persons to WSS, folder 1922–1923, WSS Papers.

5. In Washington Scarborough's home address was 942 I Street, NW, and his office address was Office Building C, between 6th and 7th Streets SW. See his Student File, box 508, Oberlin College Archives.

6. Consult Shakespeare's (1564–1616) *Hamlet* (1603), act IV, scene 5: "There's such divinity doth hedge a king that treason can but peep to what it would."

7. Emanuel Celler (1888–1981), a Democrat from Brooklyn, was U.S. representative from 1923 to 1973. Israel Moore Foster (1873–1950) of Athens, Ohio, served as a U.S. representative from 1919 to 1925.

8. Albert Baird Cummins (1850–1926), Republican from Des Moines, was governor of Iowa from 1902 to 1908 and U.S. senator from 1908 to 1926.

9. This reference to the "National Legislative Chairman of the Federation of Colored Women's Clubs" has not been identified.

10. James John Davis (1873–1947), a Republican from Pennsylvania, was secretary of the Department of Labor from 1921 to 1930.

11. The dedication of the Lincoln Memorial took place on May 30, 1922. The crowd numbered more than 50,000 and was segregated by race. Dr. Robert Moton was among the speakers that day. The Douglass Memorial Home was established by Helen Pitts Douglass and the National Association of Colored Women's Clubs. The *Souvenir Program Dedicatory Exercises of the Frederick Douglass Memorial Home, Cedar Hill, Anacostia, D.C., Saturday, August Twelfth, Nineteen Twenty-Two* (Buffalo: Union and Times Press, 1922), lists Scarborough as a contributor. His name is inscribed on one of three commemorative tablets erected. These bear the names of donors of at least twenty-five dollars and are arranged by state.

12. See "Wm. S. Scarborough Speaks at YMCA Sunday November 11," a newspaper article dated March 10, 1923, without attribution in Joseph D. Lewis Clipping File, Central State University, Wilberforce, Ohio.

13. The identity of Judge Allen Barker or Parker is not clear. Scarborough must mean the Fourth Assembly on the League of Nations held in September 1923. See the *League of Nations Official Journal,* special supplement, n. 13 (September 24, 1923): 75–87.

14. Colonel Charles Young's remains were brought back from Lagos at the request of his wife. A memorial service was held for him in the Memorial Amphitheater at Arlington Cemetery. See the *Washington Evening Star,* June 1, 1923.

15. The Willard Hotel, located close to the White House on 14th St. and Pennsylvania Avenue, was named for its owner Henry Willard, who bought the existing property in 1850.

16. Nicholas Longworth (1869–1931), Ohio congressman, served terms from 1903 to 1913 and 1915 to 1931. He was elected Speaker of the House in 1925 and in 1927.

CHAPTER XXVII: RETIREMENT FROM PUBLIC LIFE

1. Harding died at the Palace Hotel in San Francisco on April 2, 1923, of apoplexy. The Harding Memorial Association was established on October 11, 1923. There were over a million contributors from all over the world. The ground was bro-

ken on April 26, 1926, and the cornerstone of white Georgia marble was laid on May 30, 1926 in Marion, Ohio.

2. Campbell Bascom Slemp (1866–1944) served in the House of Representatives from 1907 to 1923 and was President Harding's secretary. He was succeeded by James Everett Sanders (1882–1950), who was secretary to President Coolidge and was Republican Party chairman.

3. This is Henry Churchill King (1858–1934). No record of this event has been found in the Oberlin Archives.

4. Oberlin's *Alumni Magazine,* December 1925, notes that Scarborough received an invitation to the annual dinner at the Hotel Astor held on November 4, 1925, in honor of the imperial "Highnesses Prince and Princess Asaka." Student File, box 508, Oberlin College Archives.

5. Henry Goddard Leach (1880–1970) was editor of the *Forum* from 1923 to 1940.

6. See "Dr. Scarborough Is Honored Guest of New Yorkers," *New York Amsterdam News,* December 19, 1924, and "Dr. W. S. Scarborough Praised in New York," *Indianapolis Freedman,* January 3, 1925.

7. Franz Boas (1852–1942), German-born intellectual and ethnologist, became the first professor of anthropology at Columbia University in 1899.

8. Richard B. Harrison (1864–1935), the Canadian-born actor, was a friend and business associate of Paul Laurence Dunbar.

9. An invitation came from London after Scarborough's death to become a member of the Society for the Promotion of Hellenic Studies founded in 1880. See box 6, WSS Papers.

10. Whitelaw Reid (1837–1912), American journalist and diplomat, became the managing editor of the *New York Herald* in 1868. Coates Kinney (1826–1904) was once known as the poet laureate of Ohio. He studied at Antioch College and owned as well as edited the *Xenia Torchlight,* a.k.a. *Xenia Gazette.* His poem, "Rain on the Roof," which he wrote in 1849, made him famous. Henry Mitchell McCracken (1840–1918) grew up in Kenton, Ohio, and taught classics at Xenia High School. He received a Doctor of Divinity from Wittenburg College in 1878. From 1891 to 1910 he was chancellor of the University of the City of New York (New York University).

11. This movie also known as *The Clansman* was one of the biggest moneymakers of its day. It was based on the work of Thomas Dixon (1865–1946).

12. A. Victor Donahey, Democrat, was the first governor of Ohio to serve three consecutive terms from 1923 to 1929.

13. John Raphael Rogers (1856–1934) taught school until his patent for stereotype matrices in 1888 launched his career as a businessman.

14. On Scarborough's YMCA talk, see "'International Leader Needed,' Says W. S. Scarborough," *New York Amsterdam News,* December 2, 1925, Student File, box 508, Oberlin College Archives. A few months before this, Scarborough spoke at the St. James Presbyterian Church in New York City. See his "Speaker at Meeting on University Day," July 18, 1925, Student File, box 508, Oberlin College Archives.

15. An article, "A New Publication," in Scarborough's Student File, box 508, Oberlin College Archives, quotes a letter to L. C. Gray, Division of Economics in Washington, D.C. (July 2, 1925), from E. G. Silher, New York University:

Dear Sir: I am sincerely interested to hear that Dr. W. S. Scarborough of Washington is to publish some of his classical papers in a volume. The small number of classical scholars which I have taught who were students of colored birth were without exception earnest and industrious pupils, one of them Countee Cullen, excelling in advanced Latin prose, as well as in reasoning about incidental problems. I have always held that we should welcome the advancement of a race so long condemned to slavery for others an advance concretely proven as possible by such worthy representatives as Dr. Scarborough, felicitating them in the spirit of Abraham Lincoln.

E. G. Sihler, Professor Emeritus of the Latin Language and Literature 1892 to 1923, N.Y. University, now head of the American Academy in Rome, Italy.

An Oberlin College Alumni Report sent from his home, Tretton Place, on September 1, 1925, says that Scarborough's "Studies in Philology," 150 pages, is forthcoming in the "fall of 1926, now in press." Student File, box 508, Oberlin College Archives. The book was never published.

16. See also several letters exchanged between Lanman and Scarborough during September 1922 in the Papers of Charles Rockwell Lanman (HUG 4510.55), Harvard University Archives.

17. These are "The Negro Farmer's Progress in Virginia," *Current History* 21 (January 1925): 565–69; "The Negro Farmer in the South," *Current History* 25 (December 1926): 384–87; and "Optimism in Negro Farm Life," *Opportunity* 4 (February 1926): 65–66.

18. This is "Tenancy and Ownership among Negro Farmers in Southampton County, Virginia, Bulletin 1401" (Washington, D.C.: U.S. Department of Agriculture, 1926). A footnote to the text says: "The field work in gathering the materials for this bulletin was performed mainly by W. S. Scarborough. The study was prepared under the direction of L. C. Gray, and the bulletin for the most part has been written by him because of the resignation of Doctor Scarborough."

19. This quote comes from Herodotus, *History of the Persian Wars,* 4.150. It is the reply of Grinnus, a descendant of the founder of island community of Thera, to oracular advice given to him at Delphi that he should found a city in Libya. The Thereans had no idea where Libya was, but several years later after a period of drought, they took up the quest. See John Morley (1838–1923), *Life of Gladstone* (London: Macmillan, 1903), vol. 2, p. 497. "Catalogue of the Private Library of William Sanders Scarborough," Box 13, WSS Papers.

20. Arthur Quiller Couch (1863–1944), *The Art of Reading* (New York: Putnam, 1920).

21. Simply translated, the phrase means "the soul is a hospital." A short title and author catalog of Scarborough's private library arranged by subject survives. See box 13, WSS Papers.

22. Scarborough is a philhellene here, and uses the Greek verb, *eureka,* which means literally "I have found [it]."

23. This foundation was set up in 1905 endowed with $15 million to encourage and uphold the profession of teaching.

24. This is probably Robert A. Franks (n.d.), who was treasurer and trustee of the Carnegie Corporation from 1910 to 1935. For this letter dated June 6, 1925, and bearing an indecipherable signature, see box 3, WSS Papers.

25. Scarborough is right about the omission. The section in question reads:

S.T. Mitchell was succeeded in the presidency by the Rev. J. H. Jones, under whom the institution made rapid growth, reaching an enrollment of 595 pupils and 33 officers and teachers. In June 1906, the university celebrated its Fiftieth Anniversary or Golden Jubilee, which proved to be an occasion of great interest and profit. Aside from renewed inspiration and impetus given the work, it was the occasion of liberal offerings on the part of interested friends and sympathizers throughout the Convention, nearly $5,000 being raised during the Jubilee Celebration. This, too, was the occasion for the dedication of Galloway Hall, a large stone and brick building erected by the State of Ohio at a cost of over $60,000, and the Carnegie Library, generously donated by Mr. Andrew Carnegie at a cost of about $18,350.

At the last meeting of the Board of Trustees (1922) the secretary's report showed that the university has assets, including Endowment and Trust Funds, to the amount of $238,262.21.

For the scholastic year ending June 19, 1922, there had been an enrollment of 281 in the college department. In December, 1922, a disastrous fire completely destroyed the interior of Shorter Hall. This was not only a great loss to the university, but practically removed one of the ancient landmarks. Steps were immediately taken to erect a new and more commodious Shorter Hall. Plans were drawn and a contract was let calling for expenditure of $271,671. The building is absolutely fireproof, modern in every particular and the very last word in construction and appointments. There are 26 classrooms, dormitory accommodations for 444 students, administrative offices, a dining room that seats 800 at one time, and an auditorium with a seating capacity of 2,000. Rev. J. A. Gregg is the president.

26. The two couples had known each other for many years. The Scarboroughs were upset by Smith's death, and there is no trace of ill will in their expressions of grief. The note Mrs. Scarborough sent Mrs. Smith read in part: "You must know, however, that with the passing of your husband, we feel the loss of a friend of many years standing—the last one, too, of the group that for years gathered at our home. The changes have been many. The last time I saw him, he said 'Well, I am the last of the Old Guard, and may never come again' and he did not. He felt keenly the loss of his old associates here and the ruthless changes that have taken place." Scarborough himself sent a telegram from Washington, D.C., which read: "Death of Bishop Smith shocks us. Mrs. Scarborough and myself sorrow with you and send you and your family our deepest sympathy." Microfilm roll 6, Charles Spencer Smith Collection, BHR.

27. Joseph Gomez (1890–1979), teacher and civil rights activist, was born an out-of-wedlock child in Antigua. He came to the United States in 1918. In 1948 he became a bishop in the A.M.E. Church. See the account by Annetta Louise Gomez-Jefferson, *In Darkness with God: The Life of Joseph Gomez* (Kent: Kent State University Press, 1998), 36. Joseph Gomez has kind words for the Scarboroughs:

Although Scarborough had spoken in New York on many occasions Joseph had not met him before. He had his first opportunity at Chapel that fall [1911]. Listening to his address, Joseph understood why so many people praised his brilliance. After his speech to the assembly he introduced his wife, Sara [sic] C. Bierce, a white woman, who had come to Wilberforce as a professor of natural science in 1877, taught French from 1884 to 1887, and was currently the principal of the Normal Department. Joseph came to admire Scarborough for his mild manner, dignity, scholarly demeanor, and impracticability—he was the prototype of the "absent-minded professor." Joseph was also fond of Sara [sic], who had dedicated her life to the education of Negroes.

28. These are lines 33–36, stanza 9, of the poem "Battle-Field" (1837) by William Cullen Bryant (1794–1878).

29. Etsu Sugimoto (1873–n.d.), *A Daughter of the Samurai* (Garden City, NY: Doubleday, 1925).

CHAPTER XXVIII: LOOKING BACKWARD AND FORWARD

1. Scarborough may be referring to Montesquieu's *Spirit of the Laws* (1758). See chapter 9, "Of the Severity of Punishments in Different Governments": "It is mediocrity alone and a mixture of prosperous and adverse fortune that inspires us with lenity and pity."

2. The citation in the *Boston Transcript* has not been found.

3. See Scarborough's "Journalism and Colored Journalists," *People's Advocate,* November 12, 1881, and "Journalists," *People's Advocate,* February 4, 1882.

4. This is Frederick Douglass, "The Color Line," *North American Review* 132 (June 1881): 567–78.

5. This is a polysyllabic word of 170 letters describing an impossible conglomeration of different foods made up by Aristophanes, and used in his play *Ekklesiazousae,* 1169–75.

6. In Greek mythology Briareos was one of the three children of Ouranos (Sky) and Ge (Earth). The children were known as the Hecatonchires, and each had one hundred arms and fifty heads.

7. These letters have not been located.

8. Greener spoke at commencement in 1917 and there was awarded an honorary LL.D. See "Commencement at Wilberforce to Open Next Sunday," *Xenia Evening Gazette,* June 11, 1917, which says "Greener to Speak June 21st at Galloway Hall," and "Wilberforce Commencement," *Xenia Evening Gazette,* June 21, 1917, which gives details of his honorary degree. The Greek Aristides, considered by some an upright and just aristocrat and by others cunning and pro-democratic, was ostracized in 482 B.C. Before his ostracism he helped his fellow Athenians defeat the Persians at Marathon in 490 B.C. and after his recall, he helped his countrymen in the battle of Salamis in 480 B.C. Once wealthy, he died a poor man.

9. Greener himself knew well the pitfalls of diplomatic life. His work in Russia ended with his recall from service. The charges made against him that were used to bring about his recall were never proven.

10. Booker T. Washington made his "Atlanta Compromise Speech" on September 18, 1895.

11. Abram Grant (1848–1911), founder of Payne Theological Seminary and trustee of Wilberforce University, was elected a bishop of the A.M.E. Church in 1888.

12. Scarborough used a Shakespearean allusion years before to title his essay "As You Like It," *Cleveland Gazette,* October 1, 1892.

13. George H. Pendleton (1825–1889), Democratic representative from 1857 to 1865, senator from 1879 to 1885, and minister to Germany from 1885 to 1889, married Mary Alicia Lloyd Key (1823–1886), the daughter of Francis Scott Key (1779–1843), on June 2, 1846.

14. Scarborough's physician was William A. Galloway. Galloway Hall, which was completed in 1906, was named for him. He was president of the board of trustees of the C. N. & I. Department. All but the clock tower of Galloway Hall was destroyed on April 3, 1973, by a tornado.

15. Theodore Roosevelt first used the phrase "a square deal for every man" in a brief speech he made at the Grand Canyon on May 6, 1903.

16. This is an anonymous poem. The entire poem reads:

Spin cheerfully, not tearfully,
Though wearily you plod;
The shuttles of His purpose move
To carry out His own design.

Seek not too soon to disapprove
His work, nor yet assign
Dark motives, when, with silent dread,
You view each somber fold;
For, lo! Within each darker thread
There twines a thread of gold.
Spin cheerfully, not tearfully,
He knows the way you plod;
Spin carefully, Spin prayerfully,
But leave the thread to God.

17. See Job 13:15, "Though he slay me, yet will I trust in him, but I will maintain mine own ways before him."

CHAPTER XXIX:
THE END [MRS. SCARBOROUGH'S RECORD OF PROFESSOR SCARBOROUGH'S LAST DAYS]

1. Notes in the manuscript state that Mrs. Scarborough and Bernice Sanders, a close family friend, are responsible for this chapter. Bernice Sanders was the daughter of J. W. Sanders, pastor of the Bethel A.M.E. Church in Baltimore. She graduated from the classical course with the highest honors in 1915. See "Miss Bernice Sanders, A.B.," *A.M.E. Church Review* 32 (1915): 102. She taught physics at Wilberforce in 1916. Consult McGinnis, *A History and an Interpretation of Wilberforce University,* 153. About Mrs. Scarborough Reverdy Ransom recalled: "Mrs. S. C. Bierce whom Professor Scarborough married was one of the most cultured and scholarly members of the faculty. Their married life extended over a period of more than forty years in a

companionship of mind and spirit which was idyllic. In her attitude toward colored people, she never either condescended or descended even remotely. Once in her presence all thought or feeling of race vanished in the sweet winsomeness of her personality." See his autobiography, *The Pilgrimage of Harriet Ransom's Son* (Nashville: Sunday School Union, n.d.), 30. After her husband's death she sold Tretton Place to Wilberforce University and moved to Cleveland in 1929. She lived with one of her grandsons, William Francis Grant, at 7802 Linwood Street until her death there on July 1, 1933. Her death certificate, Register # 5020, lists the principal cause of death as cardiac decompensation that began on June 15 and senility as a contributing factor. For details concerning her retirement, see *Xenia Evening Gazette,* August 12, 1929.

2. Dean Woodson was professor of systematic theology and New Testament Greek.

3. This is very likely T. B. Caldwell from the Tennessee Conference.

4. W. A. Anderson was a classmate of Reverdy Ransom, who later became a successful businessman. William A. Galloway wrote an obituary about Scarborough. See "Dr. Galloway's Tribute," *Cleveland Gazette,* September 25, 1926. Scarborough left Galloway a number of interesting items concerning William Wilberforce "in loving remembrance of the care and cheer which you gave me as my physician for some thirty-six years." See MS 133–18, Greene County Room, Greene County Library, Xenia, Ohio. Other obituaries of the day include: "Scarborough, a Race Exhibit," *New York News,* September 18, 1926; "Dr. W. S. Scarborough Passes Out," *Xenia Gazette,* September 18, 1926; "Noted Scholar and Educator Dies Suddenly," *Philadelphia Tribune,* September 18, 1926; "A Tribute to the Late Dr. W. S. Scarborough," *New York Amsterdam News,* September 15, 1926; "Noted Dean Is Dead," *Chicago Whip,* September 18, 1926; "William Sanders Scarborough," *Southern Workman,* November 1926; "Dr. William Scarborough," *New York Times,* September 12, 1926; and "Negro Educator Dead," *Cleveland Plain Dealer,* September 10, 1926.

5. This is Albert M. Howe (1867–1947), pastor of the Third Baptist Church in Xenia from 1909 to 1931. See his obituary, "Rev. A. M. Howe," *Xenia Evening Gazette,* May 29, 1947.

6. Mrs. Scarborough planned to issue a book of these but did not. Instead the final chapter of this manuscript contains a number of them. They include letters of condolence from: Myron Adams, Atlanta University; S. G. Atkins, Winston Salem College; E. M. Baker, Japan Society; James Bertram for the Carnegie Foundation; Hope B. Billups, Association of Trade and Commerce; Bishop J. N. Bishop; Bishop W. S. Brooks; Arthur T. Burnell, OC '75; George B. Christian; Davis Wasgatt Clark; Governor Myers Y. Cooper; Mrs. Levi Coppin; J. E. Davis; Mrs. W. B. Derrick; A. Victor Donahey; J. Stanley Durkee; Bishop A. L. Gaines; William A. Galloway; Dennis Goodsell, OC '75; L. C. Gray, Bureau of Agriculture Economics; Bishop John Gregg; Hastings H. Hart; John R. Hawkins, A.M.E. Church; Joseph W. Hewitt for the APA; Hamilton Holt, Rollins College; Bishop John Hurst; Mary Kenney, OC '75; Elizabeth Graham Kimmel, OC '75; Henry C. King, Oberlin College; J.H.R. Lee, Florida A&M University; James Monroe Marks, OC '75; Mary Bethune McLeod, Bethune Cookman College; R. R. Moton, Tuskegee Institute; J. C. Napier; Mary White Ovington; John F. Peck, OC '75; George A. Plympton, Ginn and Company, Boston; Ira T. Price; Reverdy Ransom; J. R. Rogers, OC '75; Everett Sanders, secretary to

President Coolidge; William H. Taft; Senator Frank B. Willis; Stanley Wood, OC '75; R. R. Wright, Sr.; and Nathan Young, Lincoln University. The student Greek letter societies, Chi Lambda, Kappa Alpha Psi, Alpha Kappa Alpha, and Delta Sigma Theta, also sent letters.

7. This is "Dead My Lords," a poem by James Whitcomb Riley (1849–1916). Lines 5–8 have been omitted from the version in the text. They are:

> Curb your praises now as then;
> Dead, my lords and gentlemen,—
> What he wrought found its reward
> In the tolerance of the Lord.

ARCHIVAL MATERIALS: A SELECTED SOURCE LIST

Charles Spencer Smith Collection, Bentley Historical Library, University of Michigan, Ann Arbor. Abbreviated in the notes as [BHR]

Genealogical and Historical Room, Washington Memorial Library, Macon, Georgia. Abbreviated in the notes as [GHR]

Scarborough Clipping File, Schomburg Center for Research in Black Culture, New York Public Library, New York City

Scarborough Collection and Clipping File, National Afro-American Museum and Culture Center, Wilberforce, Ohio

W. E. A. Axon-W. S. Scarborough Correspondence, John Rylands University Library of Manchester, England

William Sanders Scarborough Papers, Rembert E. Stokes Library, Wilberforce University, Wilberforce, Ohio. Abbreviated in the notes as [WSS]

William Sanders Scarborough and Sarah Cordelia Bierce Scarborough Papers, Western Reserve Historical Society, Cleveland, Ohio

William S. Scarborough, MIC 179, Ohio Historical Society, Columbus

W. S. Scarborough. Student File, Oberlin College Archives, Oberlin, Ohio

INDEX